Six upon the World

Toward an American Culture for an Industrial Age

Paul F. Douglass

SIX
UPON THE WORLD

*Toward an American Culture
for an Industrial Age*

LITTLE, BROWN AND COMPANY · BOSTON

The author wishes to thank the following for permission to quote from copyrighted material:

Columbia University Press for quotations from MODERN SCIENCE AND MODERN MAN by James Bryant Conant.

Doubleday & Company, Inc. for quotations from ADVENTURES OF A WHITE–COLLAR MAN, by Alfred P. Sloan Jr. and Boyden Sparkes. Copyright 1940, 1941 by Alfred P. Sloan Jr. and Boyden Sparkes, reprinted by permission of Doubleday & Company, Inc.; and for quotations from THE TURNING WHEEL by Arthur Pound. Copyright 1934 by Doubleday & Company, Inc.

Harvard University Press for quotations from EDUCATION IN A DIVIDED WORLD by James Bryant Conant.

International Publishers for quotations from William Z. Foster's PAGES FROM A WORKER'S LIFE, THE TWILIGHT OF CAPITALISM, AMERICAN TRADE UNION–ISM, THE NEW EUROPE.

Charles Scribner's Sons for selections reprinted from WHAT AMERICA MEANS TO ME AND OTHER POEMS AND PRAYERS by Francis Cardinal Spellman, used by permission of the publishers; from PRAYERS AND POEMS by Francis Cardinal Spellman, used by permission of the publishers; from ACTION THIS DAY by Francis Cardinal Spellman, used by permission of the publishers.

Yale University Press for a quotation from SCIENCE AND COMMON SENSE by James Bryant Conant.

TO DUNCAN AND MARJORIE PHILLIPS

whose encouragement of the arts with a
vision of tomorrow has leavened life in the
Capital of the Nation and in America

*Art stands for the creative and
the many-minded in universal man
and for the communicative and
social instincts. We must demand
from it only the artist's sincerity.
Art must be the flowering of an
industrial age, the fruit of its more
abundant leisure, the challenge of
its mechanization.*

Duncan Phillips

8338

Contents

Illustrations

Six upon the World

Toward an American Culture for an Industrial Age

Men Make History

THIS BOOK TELLS THE STORY OF SIX CONTEMPORARY Americans who have acted ably upon their convictions to shape the kind of world they want to live in. From the examination of their experience it appears that beneath the upheaval in this century there moves a deep-seated positive activity. Out of a period of tensions and inventions the outlines of a unified and coherent American culture begin to take shape. *Six upon the World* as a title, therefore, refers to a half-dozen leaders whose careers have matured in the America of two World Wars, a decade of economic woe, and a present period of positive resistance to Soviet imperialism.

Each of these six men stands as an influential person within the framework of some one institutional pattern: commerce, revolutionary socialism, industry, trade-unionism, Christianity, or science. Through his life experiences, each man from his own point of view has become aware of issues which have commanded his concern and made heavy demands upon his energies. By a method which is partly clinical and partly a case approach, the six narrative chapters describe how these men have been led, step by step, from living in their own uncomplicated back yards as American boys into the complexities of concern for achieving the societal pattern best designed to further the welfare of men. The studies do not attempt to present complete biographies nor do they intend to describe fully the institutions with which the men are identified. They give details sufficient only to bring into correct focus the idea for which each man stands; to present the concrete background against which each idea has developed.

The characteristics which distinguish the twentieth century decades to which these six men have given a directional leadership may be summed up in three words: *power, proximity,* and *production.* An abundance of inanimate energy has released American men and women from drudgery. A series of inventions providing

[3]

swift transportation and instantaneous communication has established the fact of geographic — if not spiritual — nearness. The miracle of mass production has created a surplus above man's minimum needs. At the center of the age supporting these conditions stands a new and potent trinity: the scientist in his laboratory, the engineer in his drafting room, and the industrialist in his factory.

The twentieth century has brought to American man enjoyable decades — but decades qualified by uncertainty. The pleasant experiences of trying new inventions, using leisure, and producing surplus have come in a period of increasing anxiety. These biographies, which examine cross sections of American experience, show how a great promise for the good of man has evolved, and suggest some of the perils which threaten its full realization. The thesis of this book is that *American man has within his grasp the elements which can be forged into a significant culture.*

Reference Calendar: Men and Events

Men	Year	Events
Alfred P. Sloan, Jr., born	1875	Wisconsin offers $10,000 bounty for successful steam carriage
	1876	Telephone patented by Bell
William Foster, born	1881	American Federation of Labor organized
	1887	Internal combustion engine invented
Francis J. Spellman, born	1889	
Paul G. Hoffman, born	1891	
Foster, age 10, goes to work	1892	Duryea demonstrates automobile
James B. Conant born	1893	
Sloan goes to work for Hyatt Roller Bearing Company	1895	Motion picture projected on screen
	1896	Discovery of radio activity
Foster joins Socialist Party	1900	
	1903	First powered flight of heavier than air machine
	1905	Einstein's equation. $E = mc^2$ - matter might be converted to energy
	1906	First electron amplified 3-element vacuum tube
Walter Reuther born	1907	
	1908	Ford begins production of Model T
Foster joins I.W.W.	1909	
Hoffman starts as Studebaker salesman	1911	
Foster becomes national secretary of Syndicalist League of North America	1912	

Men	Year	Events
Conant starts as Harvard instructor	1914	World War I
Spellman ordained to priesthood	1916	
Hoffman and Conant join army	1917	United States enters World War I
		Lenin seizes power in Russia for Soviets
Foster leads steel strike	1919	
	1920	Scheduled radio broadcasting begins
Foster sees Lenin to Moscow	1921	
Sloan becomes president of General Motors Corporation	1923	
Reuther goes to work as apprentice tool and die maker	1924	
Foster runs as Communist candidate for United States President		
	1927	First nonstop flight, New York to Paris
Foster runs as Communist candidate for United States President	1928	
	1929	Stock market crash
Foster runs as Communist candidate for United States President	1932	
Reuther, unemployed, begins world odyssey		
Conant elected Harvard president	1933	"Bank holiday"
Sloan establishes Foundation	1935	CIO organizes as industrial union; Automobile, Aircraft, and Agricultural Implement Workers organized
Hoffman elected president of the Studebaker Corporation		
Spellman becomes Archbishop of New York	1939	Hitler begins war on Poland — World War II
Conant begins secret committee-work to develop atom bomb	1940	
	1941	Pearl Harbor — United States joins World War II
Hoffman becomes president of Committee on Economic Development	1942	

Men	Year	Events
	1945	First atom bomb exploded; television equipment commercially marketed
Reuther elected president of United Auto Workers	1946	
Spellman raised to Cardinal		
Hoffman appointed ECA administrator	1948	
	1949	Shannon and Weaver state mathematical theory of communication; age of automobility
Foster indicted on charges of conspiracy to overthrow government	1950	United Nations act to hold aggression in Korea
Hoffman becomes president of Ford Foundation	1952	First hydrogen bomb exploded
Reuther elected president CIO		
Conant named High Commissioner for Germany	1953	Malenkov succeeds Stalin
Hoffman becomes Studebaker Board chairman		
Sloan begins General Motors billion dollar expansion	1954	Atom-powered submarine launched

I

Paul G. Hoffman

Chairman of the Board, The Studebaker Corporation

The Public Office
of the Private Citizen

PAUL G. HOFFMAN

"Free men want freedom, opportunity, and abundant productive employment with rising standards of living in a peaceful world."

PAUL G. HOFFMAN SAYS:

FREE MEN WANT to make a good living and to live good lives. They want an opportunity to grow and develop socially, intellectually, and spiritually. Above all they want to be treated as individuals endowed with certain "unalienable rights" by their Creator. ⋖§*Here in America men do have the opportunity to make a good living — the best living that can be made anywhere on earth. With less than 7 per cent of the world's population, we have more than one third of the world's wealth. This is the result of a unique economic system which might well be called "mutual capitalism." Almost everyone in America has had a share in developing it. It is capitalism not for the capitalists but capitalism for everybody.* ⋖§*It is difficult to select the one element in our economic system which has contributed the most to its amazing success. Fundamentally perhaps it is because it puts stress on individualism and for this reason squares with the basic concept of a free society. There have been rich rewards for those individuals who were willing to work hard and to think hard; there have been mild penalties for inaction.* ⋖§*Our system puts emphasis on competition because competition makes for equality of opportunity and also promotes hard thinking for both manager and worker. Another feature of the system is the great diffusion in decision making. Under Communism or Socialism decision making is in the hands of a tight little monopoly. In America millions make the decisions which "make the wheels go round." Our system also high-lights voluntaryism. Firms in the same line of business work together to enlarge their market and then engage in tough competition for shares in this enlarged market.* ⋖§*The facts that our system has extraordinary capacity to create wealth and further that this wealth has been on the whole equitably distributed open up opportunities for Americans to live good lives.*

[11]

For the first time in history advanced education is being made available to all. Hours of work have been shortened, too, thus assuring more leisure for study, growth, and development. We have come close to realizing the age-old dream of man of so organizing a society that every individual born into it will have the opportunity to realize his capacities to the full.

୫୫ ହ୨ଡ଼

The Public Office
of the Private Citizen

IN 1907 PAUL HOFFMAN'S FATHER BOUGHT A SECOND-
hand 1905 open-model Pope Toledo for fifteen hundred dollars and
drove it home. Around the dinner table in the Chicago suburb of
Western Springs the family planned an adventure: to motor sixty
miles to Sycamore to visit relatives and show them the vehicle. One
Saturday morning the Hoffmans rolled off toward their destination.
Packed in the car, with Father and Mother Hoffman, Grandpa,
Auntie, Paul, and a big hamper of lunch, was the emergency equipment — sixteen extra spark plugs, a supply of inner tubes, two extra
casings, and enough tools to equip a small garage.

Trials began soon after the family left the limits of Western
Springs. During the first four miles Father Hoffman changed spark
plugs five times. When he fumbled the shift from third to second
on Fox River Hill, the car began to roll back. With a scream Auntie
tossed the lunch basket to safety and followed it by a flying leap.
Father Hoffman, co-operating with gravity, let the "Mile-a-Minute
Bullet" ease back into a sandbank. The vehicle had no sooner
stopped rolling than eighteen-year-old Paul was out cutting brush
to hurl under the wheels to provide traction so that the motor car
could pull itself out of the hole. He had been studying all winter
what to do in motoring emergencies. Brush supplied the answer for
soft sand. Armed with that knowledge, Paul had moved quickly
to "do something" about the family predicament. As the tires dug in,
the Hoffman family proceeded on toward Sycamore — but not far.
Presently the car sank into a mud bog. By this time it was dark.
Grandpa climbed out to light the rock-carbide lamps, which flick-
ered and went out. The wheels spun. The "Mile-a-Minute Bullet"
slid inch by inch not toward Sycamore but into the ditch. Father,
Grandpa, and Paul co-operated in the "recovery program" while

[13]

clay packed on their feet and nervous Mother and Auntie made arrangements to spend the night in a farmhouse by the highway. As the evening wore on, Father, Grandpa, and Paul, still at work in the ditch, held a caucus. They had, they said, covered forty-five miles and had endured enough.

When the long night broke with the dawn, the vehicle was on firm ground again. The three men collected their womenfolks and started homeward toward Chicago. Presently the engine stopped cold. Grandpa, getting out to crank, gashed his forehead on the sharp tip of the radiator. As blood came, Mother and Auntie began to cry at the same time that Father discovered that the valve at the bottom of the crankcase had broken loose when the car slid into the ditch. Upon examination the men agreed, to the dismay of the women, that the bearings had burned out. . . .

But the story is already too long. When the "Mile-a-Minute Bullet" began to roll down the hill into West Chicago, Auntie spied a streetcar. Taking Mother with her, she forsook Father, Grandpa, and Paul, and boarded "safe transportation" home. The men, now by themselves, bumped over fifty thank-you-ma'ams in the next fourteen miles, both encouraged and consoled by Grandpa's vivid vocabulary.

In the years between that family trip and the introduction of the Studebaker post-World-War-II motor cars, Paul Hoffman was a personal participant in a revolution in ways of living made possible by power supplied by the internal combustion engine.

The Sycamore-bound adventure in itself is not significant. Anyone with memories back to 1907 motoring survived similar ordeals. The significance of the story is that Paul Hoffman exhibited a reaction which has characterized his whole life. When the "Bullet" sank helplessly back into the sand bank, it was Paul Hoffman who proposed: "Let's do something about it." Because he knew what to do under the circumstances, he did it. Paul Hoffman built the formula which he so spontaneously expressed, on that day of the family excursion, into a pillar of his philosophy of life: *"Let's do something about it."* Men must act to solve their problems.

✿   ✿   ✿

Despite exasperating motoring experiences in these early days, Paul Hoffman liked automobiles. From the time he was twenty he sold Studebaker motor cars — sold them successfully. The importance of Paul Hoffman to twentieth-century America, however, resulted from his activities in citizen jobs beyond the operations necessary to earn his living and support his growing family. He had a habit of acting upon private conviction with contagious public sincerity. By his performance as a private citizen he helped to rekindle faith in America as a businessman's way of free life.

Paul Hoffman fell really in love with automobiles at age eighteen — the same freshman year that he fell out with college education at the University of Chicago. What he especially liked about motor cars was the excitement of selling them, in the days when the merchandising of automobiles was becoming less of a gamble and more of a business. He learned the economics of the market the hard way — by peddling vehicles to buyers, rather than through academic reading in Harper Library about theories of exchange.

By layman's arithmetic Paul decided that Los Angeles promised more potential automobile buyers than any other city in the world — at least for him. To sell that market, he moved to the West Coast at the age of twenty. Giving up his job as a repair-shop foreman in the Holladay Sales Company service headquarters in Chicago, he opened shop in California to sell Studebakers "on the hoof." That is a trade way of saying that in the morning he would start out from the showroom with a car, demonstrate it to prospect after prospect until he sold it, and then return to headquarters on foot for another vehicle. He always felt, he said, that the way to celebrate a sale was to make another one. As a result, his record always stood at the top of the salesman list. He learned to love competition by practicing it. In the process he wedded himself for life to Studebaker as a product, and to California as a climate.

At twenty-four on December 18, 1915 he married Dorothy Brown. The families of both Hoffman and his wife reached back to colonial days. Paul's father, an inventor, was proud of his forebears, who fought for American independence. He made his son a present of a life membership in the Sons of the American Revolution. Dorothy still owns lands in New Hampshire granted to her family by King James in 1638. If she were more interested in descendants than ascendants, she could join the Daughters of the American Revolution through both the paternal and maternal lines of her family.

Two years after his marriage, the young salesman of twenty-six advanced to the position of regional Studebaker manager and was just getting established in Los Angeles business life when World War I broke out. In 1917 he entered the army as a private. After an eighteen-month tour of duty, he returned as a first lieutenant in the field artillery. As an officer candidate he was an indifferent soldier with a reputation for being a good mathematician. This reputation was enchanced by an incident which helped him win his commission. Three groups of officer candidates were engaged in artillery target practice. Paul was directing the fire of the group which shot last. After a careful calculation, based more on the errors of his predecessors than on range and terrain, he ordered: "Right, two! Down, one! Fire!" He had meant to say, "Right, two! Up, one!" Before he could correct his mistake the sergeant had yanked the lanyard. The gun fired; shrapnel shell demolished the target. Hoffman was commissioned.

When the war was over, Hoffman, still in uniform, called on Albert Russel Erskine, Studebaker president. He wanted to distribute Studebaker cars in Los Angeles. Erskine countered with an offer: he invited the twenty-eight-year-old soldier to accept a job as manager of the New York retail branch at a salary of fifty thousand dollars a year. Hoffman declined. He wanted something more than a job; he wanted a business of his own. Paul's refusal of the position in Manhattan touched off a stormy argument that ended when Erskine agreed to sell him Studebaker's Los Angeles retail branch. When he left the West Coast six years later to move to South Bend, Indiana, as Studebaker sales vice-president, his own firm was doing an annual wholesale business of seven million dollars a year. Paul had safely invested a million dollars of savings.

The move to South Bend came as a natural result of selective service. As few other distributors, Paul Hoffman knew how to sell Studebaker automobiles. At thirty-three he began his new work as vice-president in charge of sales under the same Mr. Erskine who had offered him fifty thousand a year to retail automobiles in Manhattan six years before. From the time he arrived at the factory, there was little doubt about who did the bossing at Studebaker headquarters. In the trade it was said that all three models were named after Erskine as the "President," the "Commander," and the "Dictator."

In his enthusiasm for growth, Erskine in his one-man show expanded Studebaker too fast. In 1928 he acquired Pierce Arrow. In 1930 he assumed that the back of the depression had broken and that the time was right to introduce a new car known as the "Rockne." Contrary to Erskine's optimism, the depression worsened. On March 18, 1933, the company went into receivership. Even receivership, however, failed to quench Paul Hoffman's zest for selling Studebakers. Within hours he convinced the Federal judge who had ordered the receivership that the company should have a hundred thousand dollars for advertising. Newspapers which a few hours before had carried the heartbreaking news of the company's troubles now proclaimed in headlines: STUDEBAKER CARRIES ON.

Knowing from his own Los Angeles experience how essential it was to keep the dealer organization intact, Hoffman declared that Studebaker was the "friendliest factory in the world." He proceeded to prove it by taking a personal interest in the problems of hundreds of dealers. Two years later, in March 1935, Studebaker emerged from the receivership with Harold Vance as chairman of the board and Paul Hoffman as president. Vance and Hoffman became in fact as much of a management partnership as the Studebaker brothers had been before them.

As president, Hoffman was one of the few automobile executives to rise through sales to a top manufacturing position. People believed in Paul Hoffman; dealers commented on his "stark sincerity."

When the Hoffmans moved East they brought California architecture to South Bend, and an agreement that they would return to California within five years. (They underestimated their stay by two decades.) In Indiana they built a new home around a roofed-over Mexican patio banked with palms. Rooms opened off surrounding balconies. South Benders, speaking of the new arrivals, remarked that the Hoffman house was a bedlam of seven children, other people's children, and dogs. Still, Paul and Dorothy kept their home in Pasadena, year by year expecting to return.

Vance and Hoffman knew how to pull together. Team play, new Wall Street money, good engineering, good management, and World War II combined to bring prosperity to the corporation and distinction to Paul Hoffman as an executive and as a citizen.

In 1938, Vance and Hoffman made a bold decision to enter the low-priced motor car field. They staked the company's resources on a new and different model that was destined to become the famous Studebaker "Champion." Quickly it won public acceptance and lifted Studebaker to first place among independent car manufacturers. The "Champion" was a good car. It was priced right. It held up under hard service. So proud were Studebaker employees of their company's entrance into the low-priced field that trade-unions made a levy on their members to raise funds for a half-page advertisement in South Bend newspapers to tell about the new policy. Employee interest was a testimony to the soundness of Studebaker's labor relations.

At about the time that the "Champion" entered the market, the United States was moving into the preliminary stages of World War II. The global crisis brought huge orders to South Bend. The company made its first war sale of military trucks to the United States Government. By 1941 Studebaker was producing airplane engines on government order to the tune of a third of a billion dollars. It was manufacturing the "Weasel," which went where no other vehicle could venture. By the end of the war Studebaker had produced almost sixty-four thousand Wright cyclone engines for Flying Fortress bombers, and it had produced them at one of the lowest unit costs. It had manufactured almost two hundred thousand heavy-duty trucks — which took punishment by weather and terrain from the Persian Gulf to the Arctic Ocean. Hoffman was not modest in the least about these wartime achievements. "What assets equipped Studebaker to perform these production and engineering miracles and to deliver every order on schedule?" he asked, and answered his own question: "Management, brains, engineering genius, and craftsmanship."

The tasks of wartime, however, did not force Hoffman to forget his dealers. He knew that for the moment there was plenty — too much — war business. He also knew that the company, sooner than it might expect, would again be in the competitive business of "selling" automobiles. Immediately after Pearl Harbor, Hoffman set up a service to advise his dealers on wartime operations. He was determined to keep his dealer organization together. He knew that sometime Studebaker would have to depend upon its dealers and its peacetime products. The company would again have to compete in the market. Paul understood that kind of business. Looking toward V-Day, he eliminated the distributor from the Studebaker system in 1944 in a program to ensure the dealer a larger profit margin. The idea was a part of his basic philosophy of increasing business incentive: he wanted his dealers to make more money than their rivals.

He was equally determined to supply them with a product which would set the pace for competition. Studebaker girded for battle to fight for its place in the postwar automobile market. The company proceeded to spend twelve million dollars in preparing to produce new models as soon as the government lifted regulations and permitted the manufacture of motor vehicles for civilian use. By 1946, Studebaker was leading all other independent manufacturers in the combined production of motor cars and trucks.

Studebaker's performance was a demonstration of postwar planning of the kind which Vance and Hoffman had been preaching. If they had wanted to follow a different course, Vance and Hoffman would have gone on selling their models to the automobile-starved market without retooling at least until 1948; but instead of coasting, the company introduced new models which changed the entire trend of automotive design.

The more Paul Hoffman thought about the Studebaker organization, the more the company seemed to him like a chapter of the American epic. It bore a proud tradition. Back in 1852 Henry and Clem Studebaker had opened a wagon-building and blacksmith establishment in South Bend with two forges and sixty-eight dollars in working capital. For a century Studebaker had stood before the public as an honest and enterprising household name. It had shifted from wagon production in the blacksmith shop to mass manufacture of automobiles on the assembly line as a part of the twentieth-century application of power to human affairs. In 1870, Studebaker workers received an average of sixteen dollars and fifty-six cents (in

1947 dollars) for a sixty-four hour week. Between 1870 and 1908, Studebaker continued to make wagons and carriages largely by handicraft methods. The Wages crawled up to twenty-eight dollars and fifty-three cents (in 1947 dollars) for a sixty-four hour week. In 1908, Studebaker employees were earning better than sixty dollars a week for a forty-hour week. The working week had shortened by a third, while the average wage had doubled. So had output per man doubled. Horsepower per worker had multiplied four times.

What mechanization meant to employees and customers Hoffman illustrated by the story of a Studebaker gas-tank cap. Three men using a forty-five-thousand-dollar machine in the Studebaker plant, he said, in 1947 were making 180 tank caps an hour. For that work, they received an hourly base-pay rate of $1.49 an hour. The labor on each tank cap thus cost 2½ cents. . . . It would take a skilled tinsmith at least 8 hours to do this same job. If this tinsmith were paid 2½ cents for each cap he hammered out, his pay would amount to $\frac{3}{10}$ of a cent an hour. To earn one dollar, he would have to work 41 days at the exacting task. If, on the other hand, he were paid $1.49 an hour, the cost of the tank cap to Studebaker would be $11.92, for labor alone. Building the car on this basis — if it could be so built — would cost more than $50,000. "Of course," said Hoffman, "we wouldn't sell any cars, so there wouldn't be any work or any wages for workers."

This dynamic American system of productivity, of which Studebaker was just one example, seemed to Hoffman to explain why the United States had won economic leadership in the world. "We are able to build automobiles and sell them at low prices," he said, "not only because many men thought hard, invented, innovated, and worked together well, but also because men were willing to risk many millions of dollars for investment in machines and in horsepower. It is the powerful incentives, the rich rewards, and the mild penalties that have been responsible for activating both people and dollars. This is the fact we must not overlook."

Dynamic productivity under the American system seemed, the more Paul Hoffman looked at it, to offer a method to redeem the world from poverty. Far from being distressed at evidences of what Howard Mumford Jones called "a century of increasing hor-

ror," Hoffman began to inventory the evidences of progress, and
the new opportunities for men to grow and to develop as individuals. In 1900, he began to enumerate, the material benefits of the
American economic system were largely limited to those born on
the right side of the tracks. By mid-century there was almost no
"other side of the tracks." Nine out of every ten Americans rated
themselves as belonging to the middle class. In fifty years, the United
States had become the richest, most productive nation on earth. The
reasons for this economic and social progress Hoffman found in a
series of events. Production had steadily increased in efficiency.
Machines were progressively relieving men of drudgery. The national income had multiplied almost four times. The number of high-
school graduates had increased thirteen times; the number of college
graduates six times. America had passed from a smug disregard for
social conditions to a lively awareness of responsibilities for the
welfare of the other man. A new hopeful concern for brotherhood
and equality of opportunity was everywhere in evidence, without
regard to race, creed, color, or sex. The people of the United States
were determined to make their government one of laws and not of
men.

When he compared this American achievement with the performance of the rest of the world, he was further strengthened in
his opinion that American enterprise held a magic key. In 1900,
for example, the United States had possessed 6 per cent of the
world's population and 15 per cent of the world's tangible wealth.
By 1940, with 7 per cent of the world's population, America held
fully half of the world's tangible wealth. Since the turn of the
twentieth century one great invention after another — the automobile, the radio, the airplane, television, the utilization of atomic
energy — had given a start to new industries now grown into giants.

Paul Hoffman was clear about the causes of this widespread
economic blessing. "We perfected," he said, "the techniques of mass
production, streamlined our distribution, and modernized our merchandising. We have seen the income of the average American
family doubled." In fact, Paul Hoffman saw America about to make
"an age-old dream of man come true."

"Within the next twenty-five years," he predicted, "we can practically abolish poverty. We can come close to creating conditions

which will give every man, woman, and child in America not only
equality of opportunity but certainty of opportunity for growth and
development — intellectually, socially, and spiritually."

During the years of the twentieth century Paul Hoffman had developed these deep convictions about the American way. As the
prosperity of Studebaker grew in the 1940's, he emerged as an important industrial personality. He became a director of the Federal
Reserve Bank of Chicago, of the New York Life Insurance Company, of United Air Lines, of the *Encyclopedia Britannica,* of the
Chicago Corporation, and of the Automobile Manufacturers Association. He became a patron of educational and charitable work.
In education, he became a trustee of the University of Chicago, of
Kenyon College, of the Tax Foundation, of the Public Administration Clearinghouse, and a member of the visiting committee of the
Department of Government of Harvard University. In philanthropy
he headed the seven-million-dollar campaign for United China Relief. In politics he advanced to membership on the Business and
Advisory Council of the Department of Commerce and on President Truman's Committee on Foreign Aid.

These honors, of course, belong to men of industrial corporate
prestige. Paul Hoffman deserved them: his evolution as a citizen
had gone hand-in-hand with his development as a businessman.

As far back as 1921 he had discovered some of the public duties
which fall to the office of the private citizen. It had, at that time,
become apparent that Los Angeles needed new and better highways. It was equally apparent to Hoffman that unless some relief
to congestion came soon, the sale of Studebaker automobiles would
be handicapped. Therefore he organized a Major Highways Committee. The association at once employed America's leading highways planners to study the problem. The result was a three-hun-
dred-million-dollar street-and-highway plan for metropolitan Los
Angeles. It was adopted as the official program. This far-sighted
project took the strait jacket off the California city and let it grow.
Before he left the West Coast for South Bend, in 1925, Hoffman
had seen the first hundred million dollars of public funds appropriated to initiate the plan.

This Los Angeles traffic program was the first of a series of steps through which Hoffman became involved in operations which made it clearer and clearer to him that *industrial problems are also social and political problems. The private citizen, in Hoffman's philosophy, holds a most important public office in providing ways and means for their solution.*

Thus it was that Hoffman, who as a boy in 1909 had rescued the family automobile by providing traction, twenty-six years later became one of the leaders of the auto industry in its 1935 campaign for highway safety. When the appearance in the *Reader's Digest* of the article ". . . and Sudden Death" crystallized national public opinion on the horrors of highway accidents, Hoffman had already planned how to "do something about it." He wrote an answer to the *Reader's Digest* article in the *Saturday Evening Post,* and prepared a book for Harper on *Seven Roads to Safety.*

Paul declared war on highway accidents with a program to reduce the numbers of these tragedies of "sudden death." He proposed to the automobile industry an "enlightened selfishness." "We looked over the situation," he recalls, "and found that there already existed the enforcement, engineering, and educational techniques necessary sharply to reduce highway accidents, but they had to be applied in a balanced program by cities and states. Evidence, facts, experience, inescapable conclusions, have been accumulated on highway safety. Something can be done about highway safety — *that something must be done;* that something is being done, as America is ready to pay the price. People have been shocked. They want to know what to do about the highway menace."

He came up with a program which joined industry and government in a partnership of engineering, education, personnel, politics, and public relations. This seven-point attack on the evil required (1) motor vehicle *legislation,* (2) *administration* of motor vehicle laws, (3) *enforcement* of traffic regulations, (4) *engineering,* (5) *education,* (6) *training* of technical personnel, and (7) *research.*

The outcome of Hoffman's determination was the establishment of the Automotive Safety Foundation, supported by the entire automobile trade and allied industries. Paul Hoffman became its first chairman. The achievement of this foundation can only be appreciated when one realizes that, at the time of its organization, the industry as a whole took the position that manufacturers had no responsibility for the uses to which motor vehicles might be put by purchasers. The pattern of attack which he established became important in his later direction of the Committee on Economic Development.

Five years later, despite the demands on his time and energy made by Studebaker resurgence and the successful introduction of the "Champion," he turned his attention to a very serious human and economic problem: unemployment. Despite the best efforts of government and industry, ten million Americans were still without work. "People were beginning to doubt," said Hoffman, "that the problem could be mastered by a free economy. My own deep conviction was that the problem could be solved provided an objective, nonpolitical approach could be made." Others who shared Hoffman's views were President Robert Hutchins and Vice-president William Benton of the University of Chicago. He had often talked with them about the problem. Hoffman, Hutchins, and Benton agreed that the first step in thinking through the difficulties should be the forming of seminars, discussions, and conferences where mixed groups of businessmen and academicians could meet jointly to exchange views and information.

The arrival of World War II, with resulting full employment, and the preoccupation of industrialists with successful production of war goods caused lack of interest in the idea of such discussions, and the seminars never got under way. In those preliminary meetings, however, a seed had been sown in Paul Hoffman's mind that was to flower in days of acute stress. In the next few years, he underwent a metamorphosis — from intense industrial leader to maturing citizen.

Once industry had "tooled up" and war production was pouring from the assembly lines, various little groups of industrialists began to think about what was going to happen when the war was over. In wartime, employment had jumped from forty-six to fifty-five million. What lay ahead? Would peace bring unemployment? Certain labor leaders asserted that mass unemployment even greater than that of the 1930's could be avoided in the postwar period only by extensive government planning and interference with the normal economy of the nation.

"The danger of a period of mass unemployment for those workers who were turning out war goods was very real," says Hoffman. "It could be averted by a quick conversion to peacetime production and by an expansion of the capacity to produce peacetime goods." Demand was building up. Money — purchasing power — was piling up as savings in the hands of a fully employed nation, producing war goods by overtime work. The danger that postwar conversion would be too late and too little existed as a possibility: too late if wartime savings were used up during a long transition period of unemployment; too little if capacity were not expanded, since the prewar production level was not high enough to maintain an employment rate of fifty-five million. On the other hand, it was clear that the pent-up demand and savings gave assurance to industry that it could soundly plan for an expansion above the 1942 level. Business had everything to gain by quick conversion.

In Washington the war had created a three-party pattern of cooperation: industry, labor, and government. In the Potomac atmosphere it was habitual for discussions as to the type of organization needed to cope with a postwar problem to come up with a tripartite design. Hoffman now took a position which approached heresy in the capital. He proposed a program *for industry operated solely by industry in the interest of industry.* He felt it to be the clear responsibility of business to make its own plan, to assume full responsibility for the effectiveness of the plan, and to avoid any attempt to shift any part of that responsibility to the shoulders of labor or of government. These other groups could be informed and their cooperation could be invited. Any organization that counted on Paul Hoffman for leadership, however, needed to take a clear industrial stand and to bear full responsibility. Hoffman won the battle over this basic policy. He says that the struggle to hold the Committee for Economic Development as a pure industry program unentangled with government and labor representatives was the decisive moment in the movement. From the time that the policy victory was achieved, industry had a program — and Paul Hoffman was its leader.

*   *   *

During the summer of 1942 Jesse Jones, Owen Young, Ralph Flanders, Paul Hoffman, and other industrialists sat as an informal group to select a chairman for industry's *own* postwar planning program. At the very moment when Owen D. Young was telling the group that he could not take over the leadership of the movement, Paul Hoffman was called from the conference room to answer a long-distance telephone call. When he returned, the group had placed the mantle on his shoulders. Paul Hoffman was tagged as the chairman of what was to become known as the Committee for Economic Development.

As noted earlier, Hoffman had already been doing a lot of thinking and planning at Studebaker about the very postwar problems which now concerned the industrialists as a group. He had been thinking from Studebaker out. Now he was cast in a role where he had to think about economic issues on the national and international level and presently from an ideological position as well.

From the beginning Hoffman insisted that the CED policy-thinking should be firmly based on economic and social science. "I think it is very important," he said, "that we as a group think of ourselves not as 'right,' 'left,' 'conservative,' or 'radical,' but as responsible. What we are trying to do is to get at the facts about the way this economy functions, to face the facts, and then go down the roads indicated."

Now, within a few brief months, Paul Hoffman became one of the foremost industrial spokesmen for the American way of life. Working tirelessly, writing and delivering speeches by the score, taking a short six or seven hours of sleep, and playing poker and bridge with his competitive zeal less often, Hoffman brought to the leadership of CED the same conscientious administration which he had already demonstrated in the reorganization of Studebaker. In CED he found a vehicle for his leadership; American industrial leaders found in him the warm heart and mental energy it needed. By June 1946 the CED had organized three thousand local units, recruited seventy-five thousand volunteer members, and built up a powerful research and policy operation which provided a leavening interaction between theoretical economists and hard-headed industrial leaders who had payrolls to meet. Hoffman saw and talked with streams of people. He had the habits of a Puritan and the stamina of an athlete, seldom taking a drink and never smoking. He put people immediately at their ease and put them to work. Everywhere he declared that *"the primary responsibility of a businessman is to operate his business profitably."* But, he added, to operate profitably in the postwar period there was need for immediate and bold planning.

From the pulpit of the CED Paul Hoffman preached the gospel of American enterprise with evangelical fervor. "The best way I can serve Studebaker, my family, and myself," he testified, "is to help fortify capitalism against all attacks, to help keep it strong and dynamic." As the quarterback on the CED team, Hoffman was depending upon tens of thousands of individual enterprises as a natural reservoir of jobs, in the transition from war to civilian economy. He wanted the postwar environment to be favorable to the expansion of such enterprises. Everywhere he devoted himself tirelessly to the encouragement and stimulation of individual businessmen to plan for themselves and to look forward. He wanted to help his neighbors face up to their problems on the CED two-way street, which ran back and forth from the advisory board to the local committees, through twelve regions and one hundred and fifty districts. Paul Hoffman was depending on the *local* man.

"There has been a lot of pretty confused talk going around for a good many years about the 'common man,'" he observed. "In a democracy — with its basis of equality and opportunity — it has always seemed to me that we are all common men, but that almost all of us have some uncommon talents. The success of democracy is just about decided by how fully we manage to get uncommon talents into play." The exhortation to the American businessman to get busy and to make money and to keep America's postwar economy humming was Hoffman's Point 1, Point 4, and all the other points in his economic compass.

As Paul Hoffman and his fellow businessmen preached their sermons from the economic pulpit, they were supplied with chapter, verse, and text from that other steadily developing arm of the CED — economic research. As chairman of CED Hoffman proceeded to join scientific method to economic research for a very practical purpose. He wanted to broaden the base of entrepreneural action. He wanted to stimulate industry to a forward look, to rich rewards resulting from industrial activity. He wanted to encourage the common man to uncommon performance. As he listened to Theodore Yntema, the CED's director of research, to Sumner Slichter of Harvard, to Robert Calkins of the Rockefeller Foundation, to Jacob Viner of Princeton, to others kicking ideas back and forth with businessmen on the Research and Policy Committee, Hoffman discovered at first hand that theoretical knowledge is important. As a Chicago freshman a third of a century before, he had doubted this conclusion so much that he had left the campus to sell automobiles. "It took me quite a while," he confesses, "to find out that sound research is quite different from information to support one's cherished prejudices. It demands that you face *all* the facts before you draw *any* conclusions."

The pattern of research which CED developed will go down in American history as significant. It proceeded in four steps. Step 1 dealt exclusively with *analysis*. This analysis was focused on the problem of business fluctuations, on the study of the strategic factors in business cycles. Step 2 dealt with *fact-gathering*. Here too the inquiry was directed toward learning about the impact of influences on the business cycle and their relative effect in helping or hindering economic progress. Step 3 dealt with the *sifting of facts*, the microscopic scrutiny of data by businessmen and economists to join theory with practice in getting down to fundamental strategic elements. Step 4 dealt with the *interpretation of the facts*. At this point policy formulation began. It looked toward recommendations to shoot at the central target goals: high productive employment and greater cyclical stability.

Under Paul Hoffman's inspiration the CED research machine became a continuous top-side educational seminar. Staff teamwork developed to a high level of perfection. Counseled by the best available experts and social scientists, practical, hard-headed businessmen assumed responsibility of CED policy statements on long-range and transitional policies. The whole purpose of CED research was "to guide men to act more sensibly." The Research and Policy Committee, composed of businessmen selected by the CED Board of Trustees, directed the entire research program. This committee was alone responsible for statements on national policy. These statements were worked out through months of careful study and frequent meetings between members of the Research Advisory Board and the research staff. In all political and economic history, no pattern of citizen action had ever been developed to compare with this research operation designed to help men to act "more sensibly."

Quite naturally, the CED research took its point of departure from the assumption of competition. This assumption was stated in the form of a creed:

We believe in competition because
  It requires many independent centers of decision and innovation.
  It rewards efficiency and penalizes inefficiency.
  It keeps the doors of opportunity open.
  It limits economic power.
  It moderates strife between power groups.
  It obviates the necessity for direct control by the state.

Here was a statement that Paul Hoffman's whole career could subscribe to. He was learning to like professors!

Hoffman understood from his assumption of competition why America's economy had blessed the American people with material bounty. *But why had this dynamically productive system been unstable?* Until that question was answered, capitalism was not safe in tomorrow's world. During the preceding century no less than twenty-six business depressions had occurred, culminating in the "boom" of the 1920's and the "bust" of the 1930's. Within this cycle of instability the specter of unemployment haunted human beings with fear. CED thinking was determined to provide jobs for free men. Hoffman recognized that the average man is going to judge his economic system pretty much by the yardstick of abundant employment. As an industrialist, he knew that useful jobs stem only from the output of goods and services. Hoffman crystallized his thinking in this classic paragraph:

Free men want freedom and abundant, productive employment with rising standards of living in a peaceful world. But free men want employment not as a single goal but as one among other desired goals. They want employment of their own choosing: well-paid, productive, worthwhile, and satisfying. They want the opportunity to grow and develop materially, intellectually, socially, and spiritually. They want political freedom and the opportunity to govern themselves through chosen representatives and the attendant individual liberties of pen and property — freedom of speech, freedom of press, freedom of working, and freedom of peaceful assembly. They want to live in a progressive economy that affords an abundance of things for their material welfare and under a government that promises these goals for all people and for their children. They want to live in a world of peace at home and abroad. *Free men want freedom and abundant productive employment with rising standards of living in a peaceful world.*

To achieve the goals listed in this clearly stated program, Hoffman accepted as CED's number-one task the development of an economic plan which would stabilize effective demand and cut the peak-to-valley distance in the business cycle from 50 per cent to 15 per cent. He was clear that there was nothing "inevitable" about economic cycles. Booms and busts resulted from the behavior of men. "If men act more sensibly in the future than they have in the past," he predicted, "fluctuations in the business cycle can be moderated. If we fail to check a climactic boom or if we have a disastrous depression, it will not be because of an act of God or because of a convulsion of nature. It will be because of the acts of men — American men, American leaders — you and other men like you. Looking backwards we can see that all past depressions were caused by things men did, things which they could have refrained from doing, and things which they failed to do which they could have done."

As the CED staff studied the subject of business cycles, it became clearer that the economic welfare of the people as well as the stability of the free economy depend upon the creation of conditions which encourage the raising of real wages. No other way exists. And the primary responsibility for achieving such conditions rests upon business and industry. The government has the duty of providing an economic climate in which free enterprise can work and expand effectively. It would be idle to say that government should step aside and leave all economic problems and their solution to the nation's businessmen. The government has obligations it must carry out in order that business will have full and proper opportunity to meet its responsibilities. Both can benefit by counseling soundly with each other. But it is important to get the horse hitched correctly to the wagon. *Government is the instrument of economics; the economy is not the instrument of government. Freedom depends upon keeping this distinction clear.*

It was the government's role, Hoffman felt, to direct fiscal policies in peacetime so as to contribute to this goal of the raising of real wages. One of the important devices necessary for achievement of proper public fiscal policy, the CED proposed, should be a "stabilizing budget." The stabilizing-budget mechanism was to supersede the "managed compensatory budget policy." It would contribute to rather than impair the health and growth of the economy.

This stabilizing budget would achieve at least four purposes, CED felt. It would help to make the economy more stable by acting to restrain the demand for goods and services when inflation prevails and to stimulate demand when depression exists. It would foster economy in government. It would provide for the reduction of the Federal debt. It would eliminate frequent change in tax rates which unsettle business and personal planning. To provide a program to encourage personal prosperity in a free economy CED proposed to take the Federal budget permanently out of politics by means of the "stabilizing policy." To establish such a budget, CED proposed to set rates to balance the budget and provide a surplus for debt retirement at an agreed high level of employment and national income. Having set these rates, government, CED held, ought to leave them alone unless some major change in national policy or the conditions of national life occurred. All that was necessary in fixing the stabilizing budget mechanism, Hoffman's advisers pointed out, was to calculate three fundamental economic factors:

1. The level of employment.
2. The national income.
3. The price level.

Social scientists would need to define "high" employment, calculate at what price level and at what figure of national income the country would experience high employment, adjust tax rates to balance the budget and provide a surplus of the desired size at the high employment level, and then leave the apparatus alone. Public fiscal policy would no longer depend upon "impossibly accurate economic forecasts or impossible rapid congressional action."

No matter from what angle CED studied the economy, one fact came sharply to focus: the command of the common man over economic goods and services will determine the economic pattern of the social order. Hoffman held that *the system which best raises real wages will win out.*" The experience of the first half of the twentieth century demonstrated the capacity of the American system to provide for workers to live well. An hour worked in 1950, for example, bought more than three times as much in goods and services as an hour worked in 1900. The increase in real wages — what money-wages buy — amounted to 2½ per cent per man hour each year, while at the same time the quality of the goods improved, the variety broadened, and the average hours of work decreased a third. The magic key which made this increase in real wages possible, over and over, the CED staff assured Hoffman, was "production per man-hour."

The increase of output per man-hour resulted, as the CED staff saw it, from a revolutionary change in methods of production; a 37 per cent increase of capital required for each worker in a period of half a century; a steady improvement in the labor force in health, training, and experience; a steadily growing corps of skilled and semiskilled personnel, and the foresight and planning of business management. The record of the first half of the century was as clear as it was remarkable. The important question remained: to what extent could the general level of wages be raised in the future? Hoffman predicted that real wages would go right on climbing to the year 2000 just as they had been doing since the end of the nineteenth century and as a result of the same causes.

To encourage more output, the CED proposed ten "particularly promising" ways of increasing production to raise real wages. Do these things, advised CED:

1. Stabilize the growth of industry and avoid serious business recessions.
2. Reduce seasonal unemployment.

3. Improve the quality of business births and reduce the infant mortality among business concerns.
4. Reform the tax system to make risk taking more attractive.
5. Stimulate more rapid replacement of equipment.
6. Increase the imports of the United States relative to its exports.
7. Provide more employment opportunities for older people.
8. Improve the incentives for efficiency among the rank and file of employees.
9. Develop regular methods of drawing upon the knowledge and training of the labor force.
10. Abolish make-work rules and featherbedding.

In his evolution from salesman-on-the-hoof to industrial statesman Paul Hoffman had discovered, to his concern, the close relationship which exists between *political freedom* — speech, assembly, voting — and *economic freedom:* the right to choose one's own job, to buy what one wants, to make a profit, or to go broke. Precisely at this point Paul Hoffman became a political philosopher. "What the government does," he advised "is important. What the government refrains from doing is almost equally important in the economic field. *The most vital function of government is to establish conditions under which private enterprise can operate most effectively through the market process of voluntary exchange. The economic environment must permit enterprise to flourish. Economic freedom is the condition precedent to political freedom."*

As he looked at history from the perspective of his reading, Hoffman realized anew both how precious and how scarce freedom has been in the experience of mankind.

"Few people have enjoyed it," he said. "Of the approximately forty-five billion people who have lived on the earth since Christ, less than 3 per cent have lived since the Industrial Revolution and in countries where the state serves the people. For twenty centuries 97 per cent of the people have lived under a theory that the people are servants of the state." It was in the Industrial Revolution that Hoffman found the one identifiable root for the flowering of freedom. It was the Industrial Revolution, as he read the record, which rocked feudalism from its throne and gave peasants a choice between near-starvation on the farms and a prospect of relative security in the city.

Hoffman was not "just talking"; he was practicing what he preached. His strenuous efforts on behalf of American industry, during World War II and the adjustment period into postwar economy, were matched by his efforts to lead Studebaker forward. No company was better prepared to enter the new era than his own. Studebaker had America's first completely new postwar passenger car ready to run off the assembly line. As Studebaker president, Hoffman helped his own company to achieve high prestige and corporate success. At the same time, through the Committee for Economic Development, he helped American industry to realize high productive output and to enjoy a general economic prosperity.

The prophets of doom who had predicted when the atom bomb fell on Hiroshima that eight million Americans would be unemployed by Christmas stood open-jawed before the ever-climbing employment charts as the nation swung into peacetime production. They had not reckoned on the zeal, ability, and accomplishment of the one-time Illinois boy and his associates who had been cutting brush to put under the wheels of America's industrial giants.

This miracle of America's recovery was emphasized by the trials of other nations. Stalwart Britons embraced socialism. The nations of the Western European continent floundered in confusion as they attempted to replace their economies — geared to the exigencies of war at home, bombed cities, and weakened resources — with systems of productivity promising rehabilitation, goods, and employment.

It was becoming evident that the situation in Europe was so serious that, unless America came quickly to the assistance of its nations, those nations might be swept into the swelling empire of the Soviets. In World War II one enemy had been defeated by arms, and now in the postwar era a new one threatened the peace of the world. The United States chose to fight this new adversary with its economic might.

As the instrument of American policy, Congress set up a European Recovery Program under the direction of the Economic Co-operation Administration. On April 9, 1948, Paul Hoffman was sworn in to be its administrator. He agreed to serve for one year. Upon the recommendation of Senator Arthur Vandenberg, and despite the fact that Paul was not a "New Dealer," President Truman agreed to appoint the stanch Republican to "a job without precedent." Washington reached Hoffman by telephone with the offer when he was en route from Japan. (He had intentionally gone to the Far East so that he would be out of sight and therefore out of consideration when the appointment of the ECA administrator came up.) Now as Europe writhed in its postwar agonies, the private citizen who had been the apostle of America's transition to postwar productivity became the public citizen of this nation to be charged with the responsibility of doing a like job among the other free nations of the world.

On his way back from taking the oath of office, the new administrator stopped at a corner drugstore, bought a dollar-ninety-eight globe, and proceeded to Room W–900 in the Statler Hotel. There he began to build up an organization of three thousand specialists and technicians to administer the billions of dollars appropriated by Congress. He first telephoned M. T. Moore, Studebaker's general counsel, and persuaded him to come to Washington as his top assistant. From Massachusetts Institute of Technology he brought Richard Bissell as his economist and righthand man. Next he lured Wayne Chatfield Taylor, who knew the "cowpaths" of Washington intimately, from his farm in Virginia. Then Hoffman set to work on the most important personnel task of all: wooing Averell Harriman from his post as Secretary of Commerce to take on the assignment as United States Special Representative. Harriman so ably performed this work that he earned the title of "roving ambassador for ECA."

On the success of the calculated risk of the recovery program which Hoffman now directed the State Department at the time rested its chief hope for world peace. Cabell Philipps described the new job well when he wrote in the *New York Times* that Hoffman had become the "chief technician in a prodigious global experiment to determine whether American dollars and initiative could be so applied to the broken economy and tottering morale of Western

Europe that it could stand up against the onslaught of world communism."

The scope of the project was huge; so was the effort of the administrator. At the ECA headquarters in a functional new building across Lafayette Park from the White House, Hoffman's procession of callers and conferences became endless. Twenty or thirty overseas cables from mission chiefs or from Averell Harriman were tapped out as a matter of daily routine. The trans-Atlantic telephone buzzed incessantly. Hoffman's calendar bristled with scheduled speeches, budget hearings on Capitol Hill, and appointments to meet all kinds of vested-interest groups who kept coming and coming to ask the whys and wherefores about potato flour, typewriters, Southern hardwoods, tung oil, trade balances in Morocco, or what-have-you.

While Hoffman in Washington wove the fabric of interagency relationships, Ambassador Harriman roved Europe making agreements to organize the Continent for economic co-operation. Together Hoffman and Harriman co-ordinated the most complicated economic operation in the history of American foreign policy. Whether they were faced with the dollar gap, the necessity for a European Payments Union, the silver currency block, Sir Stafford Cripps himself, or "Buy American" campaigns, Hoffman and Harriman never once let Europe or America forget that the two continents were partners in a "shared opportunity," that international trade lives on a two-way street, and that Europe must competitively produce, and sell to the United States, enough of the things America wants for the Continent to pay for the things it must have from America. Hoffman and Harriman insisted that the United States had both to "help Europe" and "let Europe help."

To the shaping of the Economic Recovery Program Hoffman brought fresh theories and experience from the CED. He gave to the political purpose of the State Department's economic program a philosophical position. It was "his" position. He explained his idea clearly to the House of Representatives Committee on Appropriations by saying: "I would like to say finally that it is our hope that, as the Europeans learn more about America and its economy — which I consider of course on the record the world's best economic system — that the drift toward extreme socialism will be reversed, not because we will say 'you have to'; but because they will conclude that if they are to enjoy the things that America enjoys they will have to take a look at this American system."

Hoffman proposed to encourage the rest of the world to engage in business enterprise, to raise real wages, and to bless mankind on a global scale with economy bounty. Impatiently he exhorted the Council of the Organization for European Economic Co-operation to speed up the development of competitive large-scale and low-cost production in European industry. While he organized and administered the government program, Hoffman preached an old-fashioned gospel. He personalized his idea, made it vivid. He pounded away at the problem — and always found in the American system the medicine necessary to cure Europe's illness.

The Russians, he said, had perfected a low-cost, low-risk method of world conquest. The recovery program which he administered was America's low-cost answer to the question of how to stop the Russians in their new technique of global imperialism. The European Recovery Program, he asserted, was waging a fight in Europe "with Europeans bearing the brunt of it." The fight was directed against "hunger, desperation, chaos, and poverty." It was "a cold war being waged against the conditions in which Communism breeds."

While Studebaker's Hoffman found nothing insurmountable in the new task, the slowness with which objectives came within range of achievement supplied ample frustration. For emphasis Hoffman oversimplified problems of world trade. In Europe or America or China, he said, it was "the simple exchanging of goods for goods." To his record made in selling Studebakers in Los Angeles Hoffman now added the achievement of selling statistics — to himself and to his staff, at least, if not to Europe. What Western Europe needed, he insisted, was *economic integration.* That was the theme of Hoffman's recurring lecture tours to the Continent. What Western Europe must achieve for its own salvation, for the good of the United States, and for the good of the whole world, was just this effective integration of Europeans into a single mass market of two hundred and seventy million people enjoying a possible income of two hundred and fifty million dollars in a climate of freedom and democracy. Europe needed to cultivate the economic climate of personal prosperity by encouraging economic bigness. Gone then, said Hoffman, would be the primitive pattern of bilateral barter, the chokeweeds of high tariffs, and the exchange controls that clogged the flow of goods. One single mass market on the Continent would overcome the old inertias, the old vested interests, the old jealousies. Such a mass market, made alert by competition, would exert the continuing "discipline" on costs and prices necessary to redeem Europe from its "vicious cycle of economic nationalism." To the Old World, Hoffman brought the same determined and constructive enthusiasm which had helped lift Studebaker out of receivership fifteen years before. The *New York Times* observed that the continental countries might "find it easier to follow his advice than to resist his salesmanship."

Paul Hoffman was frank enough to admit that what he hoped Europe would accomplish in twenty-five months might under less compelling circumstances easily require twenty-five years. Whatever the time schedule, however, Hoffman was sure that the treatment for Europe's sickness was mass production for mass markets in a progressively free and integrated continental economy. What Europe required, he repeated, was not more rehabilitation; the whole continent had to start moving in a new direction. "What it needs," he said at the time, "cannot be set in the frame of an old picture or traced on an old design. It cannot be brought about by old ways of doing business or through old concepts of how a nation's interests are best served. New patterns of European trade and exchange must be found and better use must be made of Europe's resources if the potentialities of that continent are to be realized."

When Europe failed to respond promptly to these exhortations, Hoffman, toward the end of 1949, set a short-range goal of ninety days for Europe to prove by "actions rather than by words" that at long last it was determined to reverse its trend toward economic nationalism. End the dual price system he bluntly told the Continental leaders. Produce a "meaningful list" of goods to be excluded from quota restrictions. Establish some means to facilitate the convertibility of currencies. Open a clearinghouse so that the English pound, the French franc, or any other national currency can be accepted anywhere in Europe, and thereby make buying and selling in every country easy. Over and over again he repeated his position. "Some people," he observed, "say that I asked for a United States of Europe. That is an oversimplification, hence inaccurate; though to be candid, I could think of nothing better for Europe. Actually, I ask for European integration. What I mean is an ultimate creation of a free mass market of two hundred seventy million Europeans to encourage mass production of newer and better consumer goods. I also ask for real competition. In short, I ask for the sort of incentives and conditions that would result inevitably in better living standards for all the population. They are the sort of incentives and conditions we take for granted in the United States though they are strange and unusual in Europe. However, I feel nothing less is required if Western Europe is to remain free and if we are to avoid becoming a garrison state."

In fact, Hoffman felt that the hour had come for decision. "There are moments in history," he said, "when even the most difficult of tasks can be accomplished. It is my view that this is such a moment in the history of Western Europe. A combination of threats from the East and economic aid from the West gives hope that the many and varied problems attendant upon integration will be resolved." Always ahead in the focus of his efforts Paul Hoffman saw "peace — the kind of a peace under which free men can live." If only the efforts of the European Recovery Program could succeed, he felt America would get "history's greatest bargain." The free world would recover the initiative in international affairs. In its second half, the twentieth century could resume its forward march. Faith in man as an individual would survive. Men could live in decency and dignity. Free institutions and free inquiry could flourish.

To the American Society of International Laws in the spring of 1950 Hoffman proposed that the United States must accept new responsibilities or let the fate of the free world be decided by communist Russia. "The day is past," he concluded, "when American security can be preserved by American action in America alone." If Europe did not unite and integrate, if business and markets on the Continent did not both become "big," then thoughtful men should consider the alternatives to integration. Markets would cumulatively narrow. High-cost industries would continue under political protection. Restrictive controls would mushroom. Trade would shrink into primitive patterns of barter. Such an alternative offered no pretty picture.

At precisely this point Paul Hoffman made another discovery. In Europe, as resistance to his preaching stiffened and the lines against Communist propaganda tightened, Paul Hoffman learned that outcomes in this kind of world are being decided in the minds and hearts of men. He became aware that *ideas must fight ideas at arm's length* and by the use of very polished psychological weapons. Through the Economic Co-operation Administration (ECA) Hoffman had learned and perfected a faith; now he was compelled to devise ways and means to "propagate" that faith. In Kipling's words, Hoffman found it necessary to "walk up and down in the hearts of men." He had to convert Europe to his gospel of freedom. To do so he must use every available device on a Continental terrain where Communist information experts already outnumbered Americans fifty to one.

An American businessman's axiom became painfully appropriate to Hoffman: "It isn't enough to have a good product, the product must be advertised." Hoffman was sure that ECA was a good product. It required promotion. Hoffman's "sales position" was being threatened by the mass communication of the Soviet theses. Free world ideas were jammed by the powerful beams of Soviet broadcasting stations. Hoffman knew that the results of the contest on Continental terrain depended upon effective communication.

Not only did Hoffman now realize that his program depended on psychological victory as a condition precedent to economic progress; he discovered that there were no conventional public information programs adequate for the task. He held staff meetings to discuss that problem. He stepped up ECA information budgets. He recruited top talent from American newspapers, magazines, radio networks, and movie concerns. Mobile carnivals began to tour Western European countries carrying their own tents, their own motion pictures, and their own puppet shows. ECA traveling circuses released a half-million balloons in the "still free air of Europe" to proclaim that "Europe Builds." They were brightly colored, hydrogen-filled balloons about a foot in diameter. Each carried a postal card with a return address. It was signed by the person who sent the balloon up and carried a greeting of friendship and good will from one European to another. These balloons floated hundreds of miles until they dropped silently into East Germany, into Poland, into Hungary, into Austria, into Czechoslovakia, and into Lithuania.

In Italy wandering Hoffman minstrels strummed their guitars to sing *Amore in Punto di Morte* — "Love at the Point of Death." This ballad was the love story of the beautiful but jilted Mariella Giordano, who threw herself into the Tiber, overcome by unrequited love. Rescued by her repentant lover, only to catch pneumonia, she was finally saved by prompt applications of ECA penicillin!

It became increasingly clearer to Hoffman, as he approved all kinds of mass communication experiments, that there was need for huge new governmental expenditures and for a nongovernmental agency to "supply, organize, train, and direct a hard core of oral missionaries" to carry the doctrine of the free world into every village, neighborhood, shop, farm community, union hall, or other group and to undertake a sustained propaganda offensive to destroy the credibility of the Communist allegations.

In the discharge of his administrative duties Paul Hoffman was compelled to circle the globe. He was with Syngman Rhee in Seoul, with Madame Chiang Kai-shek in Nanking, with Sir Stafford Cripps in London, with congressmen "on the Hill" in Washington. Everywhere he insisted on the "economic purposes" of his program. "I can think of nothing more tragic," he declared before the House Foreign Affairs Committee, than "to take funds that I think should be used for recovery and to use those funds to build armaments. The business of ECA is peace, not war, and if we ever confuse those objectives, in my opinion, we will lose the greatest advantage we have."

Despite his official position, Hoffman reserved the right to speak out for himself. He was a public officer *and* a private citizen. He never let the two merge or interfere with each other, although the combination sometimes caused embarrassment to the State Department. He talked to political leaders in European countries as frankly as he did to congressmen on the Hill. Sir Oliver Frank, the British Ambassador in Washington, observed that had anyone else said the things that Paul Hoffman expressed, American foreign policy would have congealed a solid front of resistance. It was not so much what Paul Hoffman said as his way of saying it. Just as the public believed Hoffman when he was helping pull Studebaker out of receivership, now nobody on the Continent doubted his sincerity or the fairness and good intentions of his comment.

As he plugged away at his economic recovery program, Hoffman became more concerned with the kind of people who represented America abroad. He had his personnel officer tell the agency staff that every contact with peoples of other countries represents a "symbol of America." "The kind of democracy we stand for will be interpreted by how we act," he said. "We can give the impression of arrogance, pleasure-seeking, and insensitivity; or we can give an impression of sincerity, humility and friendliness."

As Hoffman's concern over the personal and human quotient in the struggle for ideas deepened, he gave more attention to youth. Wayne Chatfield Taylor, who stood close at his side, noticed particularly Hoffman's great desire to inspire and to motivate young men and women. In the presence of the younger generation he found a warmth and idealism which in turn encouraged him.

In the fall of 1950 Hoffman was recovering from an emergency operation. While he was lying on his back for thirty days, he had "time to think." He began to ask himself why, after victory, the United States had not found peace. He gave his answer to newspaper editors in Washington. He said: *"The reason why military victory has not been followed by real peace is because we never have been willing to wage the peace with the same dedication, the same sense of sacrifice, the same resourcefulness which we have always accepted as essential to the winning of a war. We have felt that peace would come automatically. By now we should have learned that peace does not come of itself. It has to be earned to be deserved."* And Paul Hoffman, as a private citizen in a public office, had done his best to earn it.

He had agreed to serve one year as administrator of the program. His term had already extended nearly two and a half years. He saw that the output of European industry had increased 40 per cent over the last prewar year of 1938. Agricultural production was up 15 per cent. When ECA had begun its work, both indices were 25 per cent below 1938. In view of this trend Hoffman felt he was entitled to turn his thoughts to Paul Hoffman, private citizen, and to go on with his own affairs.

Since his public contributions had been made possible through the strengths and experience drawn from the wellsprings of his life as a salesman and industrialist, he decided his primary interest was business. And while he was reluctant to devote again all his energy, as he had in the days of Studebaker's revival, to business administration, he hoped to return to Studebaker in a nonoperating capacity that would enable him to realize three goals: (1) leisure in which to think; (2) work which would permit him to return to his beloved California and get acquainted with his family; (3) freedom to undertake from time to time special missions that challenged his imagination and ability. With these goals ahead and in this frame of mind, on September 21, 1950, he handed the Economic Co-operation Administration over to other competent hands. Upon the announcement, Senator Arthur H. Vandenberg sat down and wrote Paul Hoffman this letter:

> I read of your ECA resignation with regret. But I am bound to say that you have performed so magnificently in your difficult assignment — successfully carrying ECA through all of its major crises — you are entitled to consult your own desires and wishes. I simply want to tell you that you have justified every confidence I ever placed in you and that I shall always be exceptionally proud of having had a key part not only in drafting you for this public service but also in loyally upholding your hands . . .
>
> I am sure your public career is not ended. You have given the American people the kind of service they desire and demand and I am sure you will face other calls to duty to which you will respond with continuing patriotism and success.

There was only one fault with Paul Hoffman's plan for his future as he cleared his Washington desk. Someone might come up with a "temporary" mission that was more challenging and interesting than a return to the business world. . . . Someone did. He stepped out of public service from administering the hugest economic effort any nation in history had ever made to become president of the Ford Foundation. In this position he experienced the magnitude of a private philanthropy which exceeded in bigness anything America had previously known.

The Ford Foundation had been established in 1936 with Edsel B. Ford as its first president. The purpose of the foundation was to receive and administer funds for scientific, educational, and charitable purposes, *all for the public welfare.* Receiving Ford gifts over a period of seven years and substantial funds as a result of the successive deaths of Edsel Ford and his father, Henry Ford, the Ford Foundation came into possession of more than nine tenths of the nonvoting stock of the Ford Motor Company. The voting stock remained almost wholly in the hands of Mrs. Clara Ford, the widow of Henry Ford, and Mrs. Edsel Ford, her daughter-in-law, with legal provisions which will eventually vest the legal control of the company in the three sons and one daughter of Mrs. Edsel Ford. Through the mechanism of the foundation the Ford Motor Company exists as the biggest family-held corporation in the world.

While Paul Hoffman was busy organizing the European Recovery Program in 1948, the trustees of the Ford Foundation, anticipating final settlement of Federal estate matters and the receipt of funds to enable them to undertake an expanded program, set in motion a planning study. They wanted expert recommendations to guide them in the formulation of a policy and program for the foundation. As chairman of the board of trustees of the foundation, Henry Ford, II, made the advisory report public in October 1950. When Paul Hoffman resigned as administrator of the Economic Co-operation Administration, the policy of the Ford Foundation had therefore been established. Seeking to define the meaning of the words "human welfare," the keystone words in the foundation's charter, the policy report said that "today's most critical problems are those which are social rather than physical in character — those which arise in man's relation to man rather than in his relation to nature. Here, it was concluded, is the realm where the greatest problems exist, where the least progress is being made, and where the gravest threat to democracy and human welfare lies. The

Committee believes that these problems may be attacked and human welfare furthered by programs in the establishment of peace, the strengthening of democracy, the strengthening of the economy, the improvement of education, and the better understanding of man."

As basic to human welfare the policy report outlined four ideas:

Human Dignity — the conviction that society must accord all men equal rights and equal opportunities to develop their capabilities and must in addition encourage individuality and inventive and creative talent.

Personal Freedom and Rights — the rights of each person to enjoy the largest measure of liberty consistent with the equal claims of other persons under a rule of law so that all may share equally in its benefits and opportunities.

Political Freedom and Rights — freedom of worship, freedom of speech, and freedom of association; self-government; justice; and the right and opportunity of every citizen to play a real and effective part in his government.

Social Responsibility and the Duty of Service — the exercise of political, economic, and social power at all levels and in all forms by those who possess it with a full sense of social responsibility, recognizing that every person is under moral obligation to use his capabilities to contribute positively to the welfare of society.

In substance, the policy of the Ford Foundation as transmitted to Paul Hoffman to administer was Jeffersonian liberalism extended and restated in the terminology and frame of reference of late twentieth-century crisis in industrial and political circumstances. The policy of the foundation fitted perfectly with the natural history of Paul Hoffman as salesman, industrialist, citizen, economist, government administrator, and private citizen. The times, the man, and the money seemed to have met. Hoffman's purposes in life as defined by his experiences were now equipped with Ford family funds. Hoffman stood in a position of historic leadership — a catalyst for the impact of social and political ideas upon industrial civilization engaged in global struggle.

On the day in October 1950 when Henry Ford II issued the *Report of the Study for the Ford Foundation on Policy and Program,*

Paul G. Hoffman, "consultant" of the Economic Co-operation Administration, was speaking to a crowd in Germany at the Berlin Trade Fair. In concluding his remarks he observed: "We must, above all, prove by our deeds and accomplishments that the free way of life is the only way of life under which men can live in decency and dignity and peace."

At sixty, Paul Hoffman began his new work for Ford with his characteristic energy, the spirit of "Let's do something about it" — once again in the "public office of the private citizen." After a quarter of a century's absence, he now moved back to Pasadena. Mrs. Hoffman — who had been promised when the family moved to South Bend in 1925 that they would return to California within five years — was overjoyed. Their home at 1500 El Mirador Drive was waiting for them. Now with Paul's permission Dorothy sold the home in South Bend and devoted the proceeds to the repair and improvement of the Pasadena residence. Paul's generous provision for motor transportation for the household was his answer to the question as to whether the American automobile market was going to be able to absorb American production. In Pasadena there was a personal car each for father, mother, and daughter, a family car, a station wagon, and a truck!

During the twenty-five years absence of Paul and Dorothy from the home where they had begun life, the Hoffman children had grown up and mostly married. Hallock, the oldest son, married a Danish girl and was a worker with the Friends' Service Committee. Peter was in India with Rurmidi Davi, a leader in cultural activities. Donald had married a Scotch-Irish girl and was employed as assistant to the president of Encyclopedia Britannica Films Corporation. Robert had married an American girl and was associated with an engineering firm in Pasadena. Lathrop married a second-generation French-Irish girl and became a Studebaker dealer. All five brothers had served in the air corps or army in World War II. Kiriki, one of the Hoffman daughters, was in New York seeking fame as an artist. Barbara, the other daughter, was the only one of seven children to move into the Pasadena residence.

In Pasadena the Hoffmans found again the real satisfaction of living which they expected. To Pasadena Paul moved his offices as president of the Ford Foundation and his very distinguished staff. Organizing the staff, developing the program of the Ford Foundation, and putting the principles of the Ford policy report into action, Paul Hoffman felt, were some of the greatest accomplishments of his career. He attracted to the top leadership men of a type not often found in foundation work. He established policies of functional and decentralized operations.

He set out at once to build a working organization. First of all he proposed to bring the services of leading citizens to the guidance of the foundation's projects. He set up procedures for analyzing tens of thousands of requests received for support of projects. He blocked out a basic pattern of action. One part of this pattern consisted in the creation of a series of subsidiary corporations for independent service to special fields supported by grants from the parent foundation. Such subsidiary organizations included the Fund for Adult Education; the Fund for the Advancement of Education; the East European Fund; Intercultural Publications, Inc.; Resources for the Future, Inc.; and the Fund for the Republic.

To carry forward pilot activities that promised contributions to world peace Hoffman experimented with assisting free nations in their struggle to achieve stability and a better standard of living. The foundation concentrated its early program largely in India, Pakistan, and the Near East — the areas of the newly emergent nations. In these regions Ford proceeded along three interrelated lines: first to help these new nations make fuller and wiser use of their human and natural resources; second to enable their nationals to develop the knowledge and understanding necessary to this end through study and training in other lands; and third to increase the number of competent Americans who have sympathetic insight into the culture, history, institutions, aspirations, and current problems of the peoples and governments of these regions. In many ways this phase of the foundation's program was a private continuation of the Economic Co-operation Administration directed toward Asia.

In India the foundation undertook development projects to help villagers master improved methods in agriculture, public health, and social education. It set up programs to train industrial workers and supervisory personnel, placing emphasis on improving mechanical skills. In Latin America the foundation undertook an evaluation of the technical assistance programs. It promoted exchange-of-person projects through grants to such organizations as the Institute of International Education, the National Association of Foreign Student Advisors, and the Y.M.C.A.'s Committee on Friendly Relations. It supported programs of 4-H Clubs to bring young farmers from forty different countries to the United States to work on American farms and to send young American farmers abroad on similar visits. To increase the number of Americans trained for service in government, education, and business dealing with foreign areas both at home and abroad, the foundation established a Foreign Study and Research Fellowship program. One of the purposes of this operation was to define the requirements for training Americans for service in foreign affairs. It set up still another operation to help find permanent solutions to the problems of more than ten million refugees in Western Europe. Through the East European Fund, Inc., it experimented with programs by which refugees from the Soviet Union, recently arrived in the United States, could best be oriented to American life.

To advance understanding among peoples of the world and to further mutual appreciation of differing cultural and intellectual backgrounds, the foundation established a subsidiary known as Intercultural Publications, Inc. The group immediately began the publication of a quarterly magazine known as *Perspectives USA*, published in English, French, German, and Italian. It granted support to the International Press Institute to study ways and means to increase and improve the flow of news into and out of the United States. It sought opportunities to contribute in practical ways to the strengthening of the United Nations. It made a substantial grant to Harvard University to conduct, in association with the Fiscal Division of the United Nations, a co-operative project in research and training relating to tax laws and administration in underdeveloped areas.

Recognizing the importance of the wise use of resources, the foundation, under Hoffman's leadership, appointed a Resources Program Development Committee to find out how Ford might contribute something worthwhile to the development of private, state, and Federal programs that would insure the resources required for the nation's growth, welfare, and security. This committee in turn organized Resources for the Future, Inc., and arranged a national citizens' conference on the development and conservation of resources as a forum where government, private agencies, and individuals could discuss the problem. It made grants to Harvard University, the University of Chicago, and Massachusetts Institute of Technology to conduct research programs in economic development, political stability, and United States foreign policy. It made grants to the National Bureau of Economic Research especially to study the growth of government economic activities in Western Europe and the United States. It gave help to the Population Reference Bureau to gather and correlate facts on population changes and trends.

The foundation's largest appropriation went to support activities to improve education. It recognized education as basic to self-government and the welfare of a free people. Through the Fund for the Advancement of Education, Ford proposed to clarify educational philosophy and the functions of the various parts of the educational system and to improve the preparation of teachers at all levels. It sought to better opportunities for education in the armed services and to develop ways and means of financial support for private educational institutions. Through the Fund for Adult Education, the foundation concerned itself with opportunities and facilities for the voluntary continuance of education after formal schooling is over. Particularly it attempted to encourage "the ability to think independently and clearly about fundamental human values and common human needs" and "habits of critical thought rather than passive acceptance of ready-made opinions." The objective was to create a fuller comprehension of responsible citizenship to strengthen free society. The chief emphasis of the work was directed to the areas of international, political, and economic understanding, and to the humanities, with emphasis on ways and means to stimulate discussion.

To develop programs and materials both for mass distribution and discussion groups the foundation made large grants. It gave assistance to the National Citizens' Committee for Educational Television, set aside appropriations to aid the construction of educational television stations, and assisted in the development of program material. At the same time it supported a variety of "face-to-face" discussion programs, reinvigorated the Adult Education Association of the United States, and aided this organization to form a Council of National Organizations through which associations concerned with adult educational activities could collaborate more closely. In "test cities" it set up projects to determine the best methods for co-ordinating adult education activities through various types of local councils and full-time professional workers.

Through its TV-Radio Workshop the foundation developed a network program entitled "The People Act," brought the sessions of "Assembly VI" of the United Nations General Assembly in Paris to the American people by weekly film, and telecast a program of literary, musical, artistic, historical, and scientific material to advance television standards. The program was known as "Omnibus." Hoffman felt this program demonstrated that quality in a program and audience acceptance are not mutually contradictory goals in the operation of commercial television.

In the area of human behavior, the foundation proposed to increase man's knowledge about himself and bring that knowledge to bear upon critical social problems. The scope of its activity included the study of such subjects as political behavior, communication, values and belief, individual development and adjustment, and the processes of social change. It sought to increase the number of highly qualified people in the behavioral sciences and established a Center for Advanced Study in the Behavioral Sciences. To lay a solid base for its further work the Ford Foundation inaugurated a series of systematic inventories of the state of knowledge in six major fields: organization and management, political behavior, child development, social structure, economic development and cultural change, and communications. It undertook a series of projects directed toward applying scientific knowledge of human behavior to practical affairs. It made a grant to the University of Chicago to carry on research in law and the behavioral science, to Harvard University to support work in the field of juvenile delinquency, and to the Massachusetts Institute of Technology to support a research program in international communications at its Center for International Studies. In this last program anthropologists, sociologists, psychologists, historians, economists, lawyers, political scientists, and natural scientists concentrated initially on such studies as determining what information and ideas reach various kinds of people in foreign countries; by what channels information and ideas are conveyed; the effect of psychological, institutional, political, economic, and philosophical factors on the ways in which people interpret and react to information and ideas.

Hoffman's leadership as a private citizen acting in the public interest developed a bold and unorthodox pattern of action for dealing with an industrial civilization that has grown to global proportions and that depends for its stability on the quality of leadership exercised by large numbers of highly qualified and technically equipped individuals. His platform was committed to the improvement of human life, and to the invigoration of free men so that they can handle their own affairs. The blocking-out of this experimental pattern — the formulation of policies, and the recruitment of an outstanding leadership in the various areas — represents an achievement which Hoffman quite correctly describes as the most significant in his whole life. No other individual till then had administered such ample resources devoted to a concern for the fundamental issues of human welfare and world peace. No one could have undertaken this task with more vision and sincerity, or executed it with more sustained hard work. Hoffman made sure first that the foundation established sound policies; then he placed the administration of those policies in the hands of the persons best qualified to carry them out. As a salesman for the foundation's purposes he was thus able to persuade outstanding men to undertake outstanding tasks.

When Hoffman undertook the presidency of the Ford Foundation the trustees set no time limit on his tenure. It was clearly understood that he would be free to undertake work as a private citizen. As the 1952 national election approached he determined to put his personal effort into the growing campaign to secure the nomination and election of Dwight D. Eisenhower as President of the United States. Consequently in mid-March, 1952, Hoffman took a four-month leave of absence from the Ford Foundation to work for Eisenhower for President.

His decision was rooted neither in partisan politics nor in political ambition. He sought Eisenhower's election because he believed, as he says, that the great general in the White House could bring the world further along the road to peace than could any other man. His belief was founded on three convictions. First, Eisenhower could do more than any other individual to cement the relationships among the free nations of the world and lead the campaign for peace. Second, he was the one man in the world most feared and respected by Soviet leaders, hence he was best qualified to lead the free nations into genuine negotiations for peace with the Soviets. Third, he was a man of such outstanding good will that he could do more than any other American to appeal to other men of good will in our country and restore a feeling of trust, confidence, and comradeship to the nation so beset with distrust, suspicion, and hate.

Hoffman's pre-campaign resolve to stay out of public life was reinforced after the election when, following a meeting with President-elect Eisenhower, the latter's press secretary stated that "Mr. Hoffman was not seeking and could not accept, because of unusual circumstances, any position at this time in the incoming administration. Of course, Mr. Hoffman will be available for consultation and advice as well as for temporary emergency assignment should the President-elect want to call on him." Appreciation for the great contribution made by Mr. Hoffman to Republican victory was expressed in a statement by President-elect Eisenhower, who regretted exceedingly that Hoffman did not feel that he could accept a government position at this time. "It is gratifying to know," said Eisenhower, "that his qualities of character and ability will be available to me and to members of my administration."

Back in his pleasant office at the headquarters of Ford Foundation, Californian Hoffman plunged with renewed vigor into what had become to him personally the most excitingly urgent of all the areas which Ford was exploring. Hoffman was concerned with the preservation and extension of civil liberties. He was deeply concerned by what he considered to be "the chipping-away of the rights guaranteed under our Bill of Rights." He felt that activities to preserve those rights could best be handled by an independent organization. With his associates Hoffman had urged the trustees of the Foundation to give financial aid to a new and independent organization to be known as the Fund for the Republic. In principle the trustees approved the creation of this new agency but insisted that before funds were appropriated they should know the men who would be responsible for administering the program. Hoffman began to devote much of his time to recruiting a group of men with a deep interest in the maintenance of the free way of life. He wanted men with the courage to fight for their convictions; men who were ready to give the time necessary to the cause. In a matter of months he was successful in selecting a board of the kind he wanted.

The Fund for the Republic came into being to support activities directed toward the elimination of restrictions on freedom of thought, inquiry, and expression in the United States. It proposed to develop policies and procedures best adapted to protect these rights. To develop a sound and realistic program, the new board felt it necessary to undertake two studies. It directed the first study to determine as accurately as possible the extent and nature of the internal Communist menace and its effect on the American community and its institutions. It hoped to offer recommendations consistent with the American way of life for dealing effectively with this menace. In Hoffman's mind the menace was very real. The second study had as its aim a re-identification of the deep sources of strength of free society to fill the pressing need for a clear statement in contemporary terms of the legacy of American liberty.

While the shape and form of the Fund for the Republic had been developing, the emphasis of the entire Ford Foundation operation had shifted from planning to administration. With this shift came a growing feeling on the part of the Ford trustees that headquarters should be moved from Pasadena to New York. When confronted with the possibility of moving from California to Manhattan, Hoffman recalled the goals he had set for Paul Hoffman, private citizen, when he left Washington in 1950. He decided to remain in Pasadena and to make the Fund for the Republic his principal extracurricular activity. He resigned as president of the Ford Foundation, was elected chairman of the Fund for the Republic, and returned to industry as chairman of the board of The Studebaker Corporation. "If my main interest is business, certainly the business in which I am most interested is Studebaker," he said, as he returned, March 1, 1953, to the company where he had spent all but fifty months of his active career.

In his new freedom Hoffman entertained a strong belief that he could make the best use of his talents by sticking to the pattern of living which he defined for himself in 1950: a nonoperating business career giving him time to think, to live with his family, and to take on special assignments and extracurricular activities that challenged his imagination and interest. He found his return to active participation in business as satisfying as he had anticipated. "There's no discipline quite like having to come face to face with a profit and loss statement," he said. He expressed the personal policy of his public life in these words: "I want to be a good private citizen."

Paul Hoffman was practicing that private citizenship as he stood before the 1953 graduating class at Occidental College to tell its members that "Freedom Is for the Brave." He said:

> You have just spent four years in an atmosphere where ideas like freedom and bravery are important. We older people haven't had that advantage. We have been out in a world where making a living, getting ahead, and "being regular" have seemed more important to many of us. We have the right to look to you to keep your vision of freedom — to be brave — to act the way your conscience tells you to act. What matters most is that you act as you know you ought, even at the risk of unpleasant consequences. That is the discipline of freedom. That is the essence of bravery. If you speak freely, write freely, worship freely, and assemble for discussions with anyone who you think can teach you something worthwhile, you will have us older people doing the same thing before too long. And if enough of us show something of the courage of our forefathers, these United States will remain the "land of the free and the home of the brave."

II

William Z. Foster

*Chairman of the National Committee, Communist Party
of the United States*

Revolution to Socialism

WILLIAM Z. FOSTER

*"We are living in a great historical period, that of the replace-
ment of capitalism by socialism."*

WILLIAM Z. FOSTER SAYS:

WE ARE LIVING in a great historical period, that of the replacement of capitalism by socialism. The motive power behind the vast international socialist movement is the imperative demand of the workers for greater freedom and well-being. The transition from capitalism to socialism involves a fundamental reorganization of the nation's economy, from one based on the private ownership of industry for private profit to one of collective ownership for social use. It brings about a basic political shift from the tyrannical rule of a small group of monopolists to the democratic regime of the broad working class and its allies which leads to the abolition of class society. Therefore it is a revolution. World socialism will liberate man from his age-long slavery and open up before him a perspective of freedom, development, and happiness that he now hardly dreams of. ⸙Capitalism has at its base a fundamental contradiction: it carries on production socially while the means of production are owned individually. This incompatibility brings about the collision between the workers and capitalists over wages, working conditions, various other issues, and eventually the control of society. Out of this basic contradiction between the social mode of production and the private mode of expropriation flows a whole series of other destructive contradictions. Among these are the antagonism between the unplanned production and limited markets of capitalism, between competing groups of capitalists in industry, finance, and trade, between the capitalist states and the peoples in the colonial and semicolonial countries, and between rival capitalist powers striving to capture markets, raw materials, and strategic positions. Capitalism is a prey to its own general crisis brought about by a sharpening of all the internal and external contradictions inherent in its system. Consequently this is a period of great wars and

[57]

proletarian revolutions as society is transformed from a capitalist to a socialist basis. ⌘*The movement for socialism is the great international peace movement. It is the inveterate foe of militarism and war.* ⌘*In the United States the Communist Party works for a people's government representing a broad coalition made up of the political and economic organizations of the workers, the Negro, small farmers, intellectuals, and other democratic strata who constitute the great bulk of the American people.* ⌘*My life in the Communist movement has been a happy one. It has given me the opportunity to do the thing closest to my heart and mind — to fight for progressive socialism. If I were starting out my life all over again, I would take the same course I have done.*

Revolution to Socialism

As a revolutionary socialist for more than half a century, William Z. Foster has found encouragement over the years in the question which Thoreau, as legend has it, directed to Emerson. Thoreau had gone to jail for refusal to pay his poll tax. He did not want any dollar of his to buy "a man or a musket to shoot one with." For such civil disobedience he was seized and locked up for a night by the village constable. "Henry," said Emerson as he visited his friend in the cell, "why are you there?" Thoreau replied: "Tell me, Ralph, why you are not here." According to Foster, a man who stands on principle may well expect punishment at the hands of a reactionary society intent upon maintaining its orthodoxy by police methods. Imprisonment to him is just an incidental occupational hazard of the reformer's life. As a matter of fact at the moment that he was relating the legend, Foster himself was under indictment for seeking to overthrow the government of the United States by force and violence, a "trumped-up charge fabricated by warmongering Wall Street capitalists," as he views it.

Upon the death of Joseph Vissarionovich Stalin, Foster as chairman of the National Committee of the Communist Party of the United States cabled a note of condolence to the Central Committee of the Communist Party of the Soviet Union. "Joseph Stalin," the message read in part, "was the best-loved man on earth. We will redouble our efforts to unite the American people, Negro and white, to stop the Wall Street atomaniacs from plunging humanity into a sea of blood, to stop their fascist-like plans to rule the world. Joseph Stalin will live forever in the new world arising in the radiant tomorrow of a socialist life for all."

Now, with Georgi M. Malenkov at the helm, Foster saw the world ripe for "a rapid march forward into communism." Malenkov indeed had enjoyed a "superb Marxist-Leninist training" under Stalin, "the greatest of all tutors." Such a preparation, Foster felt, should make the Soviet successor "a giant compared to the petty politicians currently heading the capitalist states of the world." Malenkov, as the new chairman of the Council of Ministers of the Union of Soviet Socialist Republics, possessed, Foster pointed out, some advantages which Stalin had not enjoyed when he rose to power. Behind Malenkov stood a "solidly united and greatly expanded Party, a powerful and flourishing national economy, and many potent foreign allies." Under the leadership of the great Communist Party of the Soviet Union with Malenkov as its leader — predicted Foster — "all the organized war-mad powers of capitalism cannot halt the historic advance of the peoples. If capitalism dares to try to do this, arms in hand, it will surely bring about its own destruction."

For more than a third of a century Foster had devoted his mature life to the application of the principles of Marx-Leninism to "specific American conditions." To him, the central political process of the times expresses itself in the "growing collapse of capitalism and the rallying to Communist leadership during the past generation of about eight hundred million people on their way to the building of socialism." Life had given to Foster the "opportunity" to play his role in the militant movement of "a great historical period, that of the replacement of capitalism by socialism."

As preparation for his part in the movement his early life had been an effectual training. From the evening when he first learned of socialism from a soapbox orator on a Philadelphia street corner in 1900, he was to pursue a single consistent and unswerving purpose: to bring to America the benefits which he believes flow from the ownership of the economic means of production by the political state, for administration in the interests of those who toil; and to look forward to the withering-away of the state itself, when, he holds, socialism arrives at its mature stage in communism.

William Z. Foster was born on February 25, 1881, in Taunton, Massachusetts. Both the birthplace and the birth year are important. In itself, the mill town which lies at the head of navigation on the Taunton River flowing south to Mount Hope Bay is just another industrial city. Communists, however, now remind themselves that it was in Taunton, *Old* England, that "bloody Judge

Jeffreys" hanged some 320 people and banished 800 more in the year 1685. It was over the village green in Taunton, *New* England, that the flag of the American Revolution was first hoisted in 1776. Someday, comrades think, the Taunton Green will be renamed for the Irish boy born there beside the stove factory. So much for the place.

The birth year of 1881 stands likewise as a date of significant coincidence; Foster was born in the same year that the American Federation of Labor was nationally organized in Pittsburgh. In this Pennsylvania city thirty-eight years later, Foster was to lead the bitter steel strike — directed, as he says, against the "shocking conditions," such as "the twelve-hour day, the seven-day week, company unionism, boss tyranny, and company domination in the steel towns."

The middle name deserves comment because of a long and erroneous legend that the name of Zebulon was given to him by his devout Christian mother to identify him with the tenth son of Jacob. As a matter of fact his parents christened him William *Edward*. Twenty-eight years later while he was militantly engaged in a class struggle which he remembers as "a free speech fight," in Spokane in 1909, he gave himself the middle initial "Z.," the last letter of the alphabet, to identify the "correct" William Foster's mail at the General Delivery window. The "Z." stuck.

His parents came from peasant stock and laboring classes of the Old World. By political preference James Foster, the father, was a Fenian. He was born in County Carlow, Ireland. To promote the overthrow of British rule he enlisted in the British Army, there to agitate among the Irish soldiers. In the regiment, he reasoned, he would occupy a strategic place from which to plan a revolt, by means of which the Irish squadrons would seize Ireland and set the island free. When the idea collapsed, James Foster fled to Boston. He arrived as a political refugee in 1868 and continued to make the achievement of Irish independence the chief interest of his life. His modest home became a rallying center for Irish patriots and militant Irish nationalists, as well as a sort of "kitchen club room" open to ball players, pugilists, horse-race fans, and dogfight promoters. Powerfully built and physically active, "Jim," as the Taunton Irish called the father, was himself a rough-and-tumble scrapper of local renown. He washed carriages in a Taunton livery stable. Like many other Irish immigrants, he took citizenship, joined the Democratic Party, and became active among the sporting elements of the community. He died at sixty.

William Foster's mother, Elizabeth McLaughlin, came from English and Scottish blood in Carlisle, England. A weaver by trade, she had labored in English textile mills, knew the sternness of factory work. She was slender of build, frail in health, yet bore twenty-three children; only six survived. She died at fifty-three, a devout Roman Catholic entertaining high hopes of her son's usefulness to the Church. (Moving in the same direction as young Bill, the son of a Caucasian artisan by the name of Dzugashvili, two years older than Foster, had entered the theological seminary at Tiflis in Transcaucasia, only to leave the Catholic faith under the influence of Marxism, and later to assume the name Joseph Stalin.)

A few months before the blizzard of 1888 the Foster family moved to Philadelphia to settle in the cheap-rent slum area of the old "West End" at Seventeenth and "Kater" Streets. William was seven. The home was near livery stables, a wood yard, a carpet-cleaning works, a battery of whorehouses, and a line of ramshackle dwellings which fringed the alley with outside privies. Gas and kerosene still lighted the cobbled streets over which moved horse-and-cable cars, carriages, and bicycles. In the City of Brotherly Love, James Foster opened his house as a refuge to the "Molly Maguires" who were fleeing from what he termed the "persecution" of the "coal barons" in the anthracite regions of Pennsylvania.

Had Elizabeth McLaughlin Foster, the mother, and Father Joseph O'Connor, pastor of St. Theresa's Parish, had their way, William would have become a priest. For his part Father O'Connor proposed to send the boy to a Jesuit college. Bill's education, however, took a very different direction. "Circumstances" educated William Foster, until he took hold of himself to acquire as sound an education as any man can obtain in hobo jungles, industrial conflicts, global travel, public libraries, omnivorous reading, and constant discussion.

Bill Foster's "kindergarten" schooling began in the neighborhood gangs of Philadelphia. Poor but big families supplied the membership for these roving bands which, when mobilized to full power, sometimes reached the formidable strength of five hundred. The virile aggregations of roving boys named themselves after animals, rivers, streets, districts, and parks. There were "Lions," "Parksparrows," "Reedies," and "Schuylkill Rangers." Whatever youthful social cohesion existed in the neighborhoods came from these organizations, which gave the lads a role to play in life. Experience in the gangs constituted a good part of a boy's fundamental education. Foster belonged to the "Bulldogs," a gang which controlled a sovereign territory running from Sixteenth to Seventeenth Streets and from South to Fitzwater. The Bulldogs, like the other bands which wandered the Philadelphia streets, constantly waged "war." Any boy away from his "corners" could expect to "shell out" — that is, to be robbed of his skates, cap, swimming tights, or pocket knife. Battles of rival gangs were pitched with fists, sticks, stones, and knives. The Bulldogs, operating in an especially tough neighborhood, boasted that no gang had ever licked them. The members were mostly Irish Catholics with a few Protestant boys sprinkled in. Structurally the Bulldogs fell into three age groups — the young boys, the youths, and the grown men up to forty. Leadership usually fell to the best scrapper. The parents of gang members, like the Fosters themselves, were mostly hard-working, honest immigrant laborers — poor teamsters, longshoremen, construction gang men — with a sprinkling of those who, as Foster says, never worked but preferred to "live by their wits."

The slum atmosphere of Kater Street bred indolence, thuggery, crime, disease, drunkenness, and general social disintegration. The younger boys smoked, drank, shot crap, indulged in petty thievery and sex perversion, broke street gas lamps for sport, pilfered hucksters, and stoned "horseless carriages." To a man they hated Jews. The Irish boys tore along South Street upsetting and stealing displayed goods, breaking shop windows, and punching the heads of Jewish peddlers "just for fun." The gang members expressed their feelings toward Negroes in even more violent ways. "Blacks" were quarantined at Lombard Street one square north and at Broad Street two squares east. The bounds were strictly enforced; no "nigger" crossed over into Bulldog territory. Many of the boys played truant from school and grew to manhood unable to read or write. Their contingents filled the pool halls. They patronized the whorehouses both as pimps and customers. Some of the older Bulldogs stood ready to "roll" a drunk, commit a burglary, or perpetrate a stick-up. On election day they sold their votes as a matter of course, became repeaters at the polls, and helped the Republican bosses faithfully to "produce" the slum vote. The social club of these older gang members was a gambling hideout and Sunday speak-easy. Here bums, crooks, pimps, gamblers, race-track touts, political henchmen, and idle laborers assembled. The gang and club system in Philadelphia was an "efficient school." Its "educational" program produced a steady stream of recruits for reform schools, penitentiaries, and the Philadelphia Republican Party. This "sick" neighborhood of a rich American city was the boyhood environment of the leader of American communism.

Bill Foster's formal education took place between the ages of seven and ten as an interlude between life in the gang and a hobo existence which comprised the next dozen years of his life. During his four years of formal study in the Philadelphia public schools, no noticeable impressions were made on his life. Driven by economic necessity and by the custom of the neighborhood, he went to work. At seven he began to sell newspapers — the *Philadelphia Evening Star, News, Item,* and *Call.* At ten, he "finished" school and was on his own.

Foster took his first full-time job in 1891. He apprenticed himself to a master German sculptor and steel die-sinker, who made souvenir medals for conventions; his wage was one dollar and fifty cents a week. In this employment he traveled. He accompanied his boss to meetings in New York, Boston, and Washington. On these trips he learned a good deal about how public assembly operates. "Old Kretchman," as the sculptor was known, liked the boy. He taught him all his arts — clay modeling, plaster-of-Paris work, wood carving, stonecutting, drawing, painting, electroplating, diesinking, and engraving. On his part Foster enjoyed the trips but not the business. "The idea of selling anything," he said, "went a hundred per cent against my grain."

Feeling no life call in the world of art, he quit his apprenticeship after three years to become an "industrial worker." When he was thirteen Bill began a three-year tour of duty with the American Type Founders Company. Later he shifted to become a fireman at the Harrison White Lead Works in Philadelphia. Here he took special notice of the pulverizing room. Laborers in the plant often remarked that if a man working in this "death house" saved his money diligently he could "buy himself a coffin by the time the lead poisoning finished him." At any rate Foster got an introduction to the industrial problem of occupational diseases. The knowledge served him well in his subsequent career.

Before he entered his teens, Bill learned about strikes. The collective action of workingmen to achieve economic objectives impressed upon him as a boy the power of industrial workers. He observed that bitter strikes placed the workers' incomes, jobs, savings, unions, homes, and lives in jeopardy. He knew that a strike was a serious matter for a worker. At eleven he experienced his father's Irish indignation when the Philadelphia National Guard regiments went to Pittsburgh to put down the Homestead strike called by the steel workers. With his father he watched labor troubles in the anthracite districts of Pennsylvania.

As a working boy he took an alert interest in the unrest among laboring people. He was living through the heyday of the Knights of Labor and the foundation struggles of the American Federation of Labor. Some of the fiercest industrial struggles in American history were taking place as he grew up, through a whole decade of extreme working-class militancy ignited by the movement for an eight-hour day. In 1890 Congress passed the Sherman Anti-Trust Act in an attempt to check the growth of monopoly. In May 1894 Eugene Debs led the Chicago Pullman strike. In the Rocky Mountain states William D. Haywood headed a series of strikes among metal miners. Foster records that he was profoundly stirred by all these events. "My sense of solidarity with the workers," he said, "was actively aroused." In 1896 Bryan campaigned on a general background of discontent among workers, farmers, and the urban middle classes. On Easter Sunday, 1894, Coxey's Army marched from Massillon, Ohio; its leaders were arrested in Washington on May Day for walking on the White House lawn. On his way to work Foster would linger around the recruiting office for Coxey's Army at Thirteenth and Filbert Streets in Philadelphia to read progress bulletins from all over the country on the movements of the various detachments of this army of the unemployed.

Foster's "baptism" in strike violence came when he was fourteen. He was "ripe" to appreciate the experience when the motormen and conductors of the Philadelphia Traction Company walked out. Bill took the day off from work to watch the uniformed streetcar men parade on Market Street, each man carrying a new broom. The head of the parade had just passed Fifteenth Street when suddenly out of the City Hall courtyard a cavalry of mounted police galloped into the strikers' ranks, laying on them with night sticks. The unexpected assault dispersed the paraders in confusion. Foster — who by this time had joined the action — found himself jammed in a hall doorway by the side of a uniformed motorman. As he remembers, an unmounted policeman made a swing with his club at the motorman and then turned to give Foster a "belt in the jaw with his fist."

During the controversy the Bulldog gang decided to take advantage of the opportunity to exhibit its skill. On the car tracks the gang erected a barricade using lumber, boxes, ashes, and stones. As the trolley car came along the boys observed four policemen, revolvers in hand, riding the front and rear platforms to guard the "scab" motorman and conductor. When the motorman attempted to rush the barricade at top speed, he derailed the car.

The Philadelphia traction strike provided Foster's first practical lesson in the harsh realities of labor conflict. It was, as he said, his "introduction to class struggle." He understood it as a method and promptly learned how to use the strike as a weapon. Years later he summarized his experience by saying that "since 1894, when I began active participation in the class struggle, I have been in numerous battles of the workers against their capitalist oppressors, including scores of strikes in many industries — by the American Federation of Labor, the Industrial Workers of the World, the Railway Brotherhoods, the Trade Union Unity League, the Congress of Industrial Organizations, and various independent unions. I have also participated in many free speech fights, unemployment movements, election campaigns, and political demonstrations." He knew the psychology and tactics of collective action firsthand.

It was at this time, in his teens, that Foster took his first long step toward what he calls a "rational working-class view of life and politics." He liquidated the religious beliefs which his mother and Father O'Connor had tried to teach him in their common ambition to prepare him for the Roman Catholic priesthood. Long before he had come into contact with any socialistic writings, he read a series of books the total effect of which was to root religion out of his life. Among the more important of these works, in the order in which Foster read them, were Paine's *Age of Reason,* Lecky's *History of European Morals,* Draper's *Conflict between Science and Religion,* Gibbon's *Decline and Fall of the Roman Empire,* Darwin's *Origin of Species* and *Descent of Man,* and Spencer's *Data of Sociology.* "When I got finished reading or, rather, devouring these books which were written in the days when capitalism was more honest intellectually than it is now," Foster said later, "there was very little if any religion left in me. All I needed for a complete materialistic outlook on life were the works of Marx and Engels which I was to read some years later."

Foster's break with religion had a material effect on the course of his whole life. His reading had led him beyond the control of the Roman Catholic Church. While Father O'Connor was sadly disappointed, the priest little realized how complete the rupture actually was.

With materialistic theories of socialism and militant action substituted for Christian faith, Foster now tried his hand at a procession of industrial jobs. Beginning at the age of seventeen, he worked successively as a laborer in a fertilizer factory, as a steam fitter, as a fireman, as an engineer, and as a skilled fertilizer mixer. At the plant of the American Reduction Company in West Reading, Pennsylvania, he saw "garbage, mixed with rotting swill and decaying cats," festering in the sun, "covered with flies and maggots as a sickening mess." At the dead animal disposal plant, he saw laborers skin dead animals, hack them to pieces, and boil the mass down into tankage. Then the whole concoction would be mixed with guano, potash, other chemicals, and according to Foster, clay — *especially* clay. He remembers that he was nauseated by the cooking odor of putrefied flesh. Often the butcher's helpers contracted such diseases as glanders from the dead animals. Foster took mental note of the "industrial setting." He noted likewise that the machines in the plants where he worked were unprotected. Often workers were mangled and crippled. Clouds of dust thrown out from grinding mills, mixers, conveyers, baggers, and chutes irritated lungs and made tuberculosis among the workmen common. Foster likes to tell his comrades how, thirty years later, physicians X-raying him at the Kremlin hospital in Moscow found traces of healed-over tuberculosis scars on his lungs.

In the open air of a warm summer evening in 1900 — he was nineteen at the time — Foster stopped to listen to a soapbox orator at the corner of Broad and South Streets, Philadelphia. The occasion, he says, was "the most important day of my life." For the first time he "met up with Marxism." The preaching of the Marxist orator convinced Foster "immediately and completely" that capitalists are both "useless and harmful to society," that the "workers are the useful producers," that they are "potentially strong enough to take over society," and that once in power they would be "quite capable of managing the economic and political system infinitely better than the capitalists were doing." It was at this time that Foster took his place in the ranks of the "international movement of socialism."

"Many times since then in the fight for socialism," he said, fifty years later, "I have had a shifting conception of political strategy and tactics. Nevertheless the heart of my new viewpoint was as sound as oak and it has persisted with me. My whole experience has gone to justify the correctness of the basic decision I then took to work and fight for socialism." Before he was old enough to vote, Foster had been converted to the left wing of Marxian socialism.

Although he was too young to cast his ballot in the November election of 1900, Foster did the best he could to support the Socialist ticket. He took his first political step by piloting a fellow workman from the fertilizer plant — six miles, on foot — to the polls to vote for Eugene V. Debs. When he quit the plant at the end of the year, Foster himself had joined the Socialist Party. At once he pulled up stakes in Pennsylvania and by winter was working his way to Cuba. Soon he was back in Florida. In rapid succession he observed chain gangs and prison camps, rode the rods on a Seaboard Air Line freight train to Turkey Creek, got a job in a lumber camp to earn a "road stake" to beat his way North, "blew" in the morning on the next freight to a sawmill, took a job felling trees at a dollar a day, jumped a "rattler" to Jacksonville, and then, at the age of twenty, worked in New York as a motorman on the Third Avenue line. His pay, he says, was twenty-two cents an hour for a ten-hour day and a seven-day week. In Manhattan Foster was promptly fired for supporting the demands of union motormen for air brakes and seats in vestibules. Thus unemployed, he "beat his way" southwest to Echo, Texas, worked as a "flunkey" in a railroad yard, and rose to the position of second cook.

Then he decided to go to sea. Between 1901 and 1904, Bill Foster sailed in old square-rigged ships once and a half times around the world. Twice he doubled Cape Horn and once rounded the Cape of Good Hope. Counting considerable stays on the coasts of Africa, Australia, and South America, he covered fifty thousand miles in three years and ended up as an able seaman qualified to perform any sailor's work from making a ratline on a spinning jenny to "stepping a mast." During these years at sea, Foster came to know the world at first hand.

While he was thus getting acquainted with the globe, he also had time to read. He read everything he could get his hands on. Wherever he sailed, he took an armful of books. While other seamen played cards day and night in games that went on for weeks, one watch coming below to take the gaming places left vacant by the watch going on deck, Foster studied. He also joined in discussion, for to him sailing provided a "seminar" of "experience-wise" participants. On the old square-riggers Foster learned the sea chanteys, work songs sung by sailors as they pulled ropes and chains. For the rest of his life he could entertain by singing them.

From the time he returned from the sea in 1904, Foster took "peeks" here and there at various patterns of American life. At twenty-three he was again "riding" the rods. In the next twelve years he "beat" his way over thirty-five thousand miles on American railroads. Besides many shorter trips, his hoboing included seven runs from coast-to-coast and two run-offs from Chicago to the Pacific. These transcontinental trips took him over the main lines of the Pennsylvania, Baltimore & Ohio, and the Erie in the East; and the Milwaukee, Great Northern, Northern Pacific, Chicago & Northwestern, Burlington, Southern Pacific, Union Pacific, Rock Island, Oregon Short Line, Denver & Rio Grande, and the Canadian Pacific in the West. To his understanding of ocean transportation he thus added a firsthand experience with rails. For the most part his extensive hoboing was not motivated by the casual worker's desire to find employment and see the country; mostly Foster traveled on "business" to promote revolutionary purposes of socialism for such organizations as the Industrial Workers of the World, the Syndicalist League of North America, and the International Trade Union Educational League. As a result of constant "field experience," Foster perfected his organizing techniques. If industry was going to be big, so big also, he felt, should be the mobilized activities of the workingman.

When Foster gave up the sea, he had staked out for himself an Oregon homestead of a hundred and sixty acres with a timber claim of equal size. After three summers of this homesteading life he proved up his claim. The experience, however, equipped him with a considerable knowledge of the woodsman's craft and a deep and abiding love of the mountains. The venture, as he says, was "the first and last time in my life that I ever attempted to gather together property of any kind: money, houses, or land."

From homesteading, Foster moved to sheepherding on the Deschutes River in Oregon. In the valley, he says, he learned "to hate sheep and love dogs." He soon became disgusted with ranching and hired out to a railroad gang grading the north bank of the Columbia River from Spokane to Portland. The knowledge of this terrain later served him well. From this job he moved on as an I.W.W. "wobblie" to Coeur d'Alene, Idaho, to organize workers in the silver and lead mines.

In the fall of 1909 Foster traveled from Seattle to Spokane to report a so-called "free speech" battle for a Seattle Socialist newspaper. Next, while serving a two-month jail sentence for his part in a labor disturbance, he joined the Industrial Workers of the World as an active member. This revolutionary union had been organized in Chicago four years before. Delegates from forty-three labor organizations, acting under the leadership of Eugene Debs, Daniel DeLeon, William Dudley Haywood, and Vincent St. John, had set it in motion. As a movement the I.W.W. aimed to unite all skilled and unskilled workers in a single body for the purpose of overthrowing capitalism and rebuilding society on a socialist basis. Its methods were direct — agitation, propaganda, the boycott, and the strike.

By the age of twenty-eight Foster was exploring the theory, plans, and practices of militant trade-unionism, which aimed by general strike and direct action to establish control over production through the collective force of organized workers.

By this time Foster had educated himself in the economic foundations of society to a degree sufficient for his subsequent political career. He had learned economic geography by travel, studied sociology as a hobo. He had taken his introduction to rail-and-water transportation by stepping the mast and riding the rods. He had learned public speaking through agitation, and group methods by means of organizing work. He had mastered crafts by working at them. He had become acquainted with books in the public library, in the secondhand stores, on board ship, and from the reading of socialist literature. He had become an omnivorous reader. His fingers itched for books. His mind was restless to encounter ideas. Foster's was a practical education — but make no mistake about it, his kind of preparation was as thorough and complete as it was informal.

At the age of sixty-eight, looking back on his labor experience, Foster once commented that he "was an efficient worker but always a rebellious one. I was a natural for the revolutionary movement." At heart he was concerned with people and ideas and the direct methods by which people are persuaded to act upon those ideas. He was presently to find a pattern of thought and action which accepted a thoroughgoing revolutionary doctrine.

While resting in the Spokane jail he came to see clearly, he says, that the emancipation of the workingman could best be achieved through militant trade-union action culminating in a general strike. In this opinion he was influenced by what he believed to be the spectacular success of the General Confederation of Labor in France. So much did he believe in the idea that he decided to cross the Atlantic to study at first hand how the French Syndicalists were conducting a whole series of local and national general work stoppages. Early in 1910 he left New York for Paris with one hundred dollars in his pocket. During his six-month stay in France he not only studied the French labor movement; he learned to read, speak, and write the French language.

From France, Foster went on to Germany for another six months. In the Reich he continued his education; he learned to read, speak, and write the German language. His experience among the Germans further strengthened his syndicalist conviction about the necessity for a revolutionary labor action program. It broadened his proletarian horizons and acquaintances. In the Reich he attended the funeral of the Social Democratic leader Paul Singer. The ceremony was said by some to have been the biggest funeral in German history. Foster was shocked to count in one section "ninety-six per cent of the Socialists in attendance wearing top hats!" He remarked that he was astonished to see a workers' organization "aping this master class custom." Before he left Germany, Foster met the Socialist writer Karl Kautsky and violently disagreed with him on theoretical lines.

Just as Foster was picking up a reading knowledge of the Italian and Spanish languages preparatory to spending a half-year each in Italy and Spain, he received a cable from the I.W.W. general secretary in Chicago directing him to represent the organization at the meeting of the international trade-union secretariat to convene in Budapest, Hungary, in August 1911. Strapped for funds, Foster set out on foot, walking en route a hundred and fifty miles from Nuremberg to Dresden to attend first the National Congress of the German trade-unions. Upon his arrival in Budapest, Foster challenged the seat claimed by the vice-president of the American Federation of Labor. He demanded it for the I.W.W. Ruled out of order, Foster appealed from the decision of the chair to the house. This characteristic action threw the conference into a debate on the issue. The discussion consumed the rest of the day. When the ballot came, Foster received two votes — both from French Syndicalists. That night, penniless, he was arrested for sleeping in a moving van on the outskirts of the city and narrowly escaped a half-year jail sentence. At this point in his journey he received a cable from the I.W.W., ordering him to return to the United States to attend the sixth I.W.W. convention, to be held in Chicago in September. Never handicapped in his travels by lack of money, Foster headed back to the stockyards city. When he arrived, he found himself out of step ideologically with the Industrial Workers of the World and momentarily inclined toward Syndicalism, with its strategy of revolutionary action for overthrowing existing institutions to make way for the new system. He had high appreciation for the function of productive labor, and a belief in production for "use" rather than for "profit." He took the occasion of the Chicago meeting to break away from what he described as the "dying I.W.W. movement."

From Chicago he traveled to Indianapolis to join a tent show. In the back of a circus wagon, rattling along dusty roads or sitting in an empty tent on long hot afternoons, Foster studied Syndicalism and wrote tracts about the subject. In consultation with Earl G. Ford, a fellow trouper, he scribbled out his systematic pamphlet *Syndicalism.* (This leaflet later played a role in the 1919 steel strike when employers, to picture the strike as a revolutionary attempt to overthrow the government, according to Foster, published and distributed, free, huge quantities of Foster's booklet. In this way the tract achieved a circulation which Foster had not even dared to hope it could attain.) With Ford, Foster now founded the Syndicalist League of North America. Thereupon he quit the tent show work and "piled" back to Chicago to put his principles into operation. He took the initiative in launching a militant program, keyed to direct action. Foster agreed with Ford that Foster should become the national secretary of the movement.

While the Syndicalist League of North America lived only two years, it encouraged the idea of direct action among revolutionary workers. Upon the collapse of the Syndicalist movement, Foster in January 1915 set up a new labor organization — the International Trade Union Educational League. He chose Chicago as its headquarters city and selected himself as secretary. Promptly he set out on a seven-thousand-mile agitation tour, through the West. Despite his strenuous efforts, however, he failed to organize this program on a national scale.

For ten years Foster had worked in various capacities as a railroader. He liked railroads and railway men. There was something about the sense of power of control over long trains that appealed to him; something about the awareness that he occupied a strategic position in industry that gave him satisfaction; something in the opportunity to meet new people daily and to view new scenes that impressed him; something in the realization of the fact that he was a member of a strong labor union that gave him a sense of independence. While working as a brakeman on the Chicago & Northwestern, he narrowly escaped gangrene as a result of an injury received when a hostler started a locomotive while he was lying beneath it. While he was a car inspector in the Chicago switching district, his eyes gave out. For a period of three years he was unable to read. Although Foster remembered that many a car inspector had ruined his eyes by giving the moving cars the swift "once over," he admitted that his own sight was impaired not only by "the long hours" on the railroading job, but more particularly by the close clerical work that had been required by his duties as national secretary of the Syndicalist League of North America. By writing letters and reading correspondence, he had devoted every available waking moment to the promotion of this cause.

With the advent of World War I Foster was to find his real opportunity to advance the welfare of workers — by using the strike as a bargaining weapon in two key industries: in steel, the heart of munitions supply, and in meat-packing, where the slogan was being proclaimed that FOOD WILL WIN THE WAR.

When the United States entered the conflict, Foster entertained some definite ideas about the meaning of American participation to revolutionary Socialists like himself. "Communists and other left-wingers," he explained, "do not support wars just because the capitalist clique controlling the government at the given time sees fit to plunge the country into war to further its class interests." To him, World War I was obviously an imperialist war — a struggle carried on for the division of the world among the "great imperialist powers." The workers had no interest in it, he said, except to bring combat to a conclusion as quickly as possible and upon the most advanced democratic terms that could be found. His position on the war directed the course of his actions. He felt no patriotic urge to support the American course, which he judged to be contrary to the democratic interests of workers and to their economic welfare. Strikes which presently occurred in the meat-packing and steel industry owed much to Foster's inspiration and organizing experience.

By coincidence, when the United States declared war on Germany Foster had just refused "unanimous" renomination by thirteen locals to serve a second year as business agent of the Railway Carmen, a craft union which he had joined in 1914. He went back to the ranks as a car inspector on the Soo Line in Chicago. His mind, however, was turning over possible programs of direct action. "While I inspected freight cars," he says, "I puzzled over what I might do to get some real organization work started. I was working twelve hours a day, seven days a week, and consequently unable even to attend the meetings of the Chicago Federation of Labor to which I was a delegate."

A clear course of procedure occurred to him as he was walking to work on July 11, 1917. He remembers the date well. The idea suddenly popped into his head that he should start by organizing the workers in the great Chicago packing houses. From that moment, the natural history of the strikes, as he tells the story, ran like this.

Foster proposed the scheme to the Chicago District Council of Railway Carmen. This group was dominated by the militant left-wingers from Foster's former organization, the International Trade-Union Educational League. The council quickly endorsed his proposal. Did not the refrigerator car business give Foster's craft a real interest in packing-house "welfare"? Two days later Foster and a committee attended a meeting of the "half-dead" Local 87, Butcher Workmen. Here they forced a reluctant endorsement. Two days afterward, on July 15, the Railway Carmen and the Butcher Workmen joined in a resolution requesting the Chicago Federation of Labor to call a joint organizing campaign meeting of all trades in the local packing industry. The Federation unanimously approved the resolution. Within five days from the time Foster germinated the idea, trade-unions were organizing the workers employed by the great packing companies.

On July 23 Foster tied together a dozen local unions with jurisdiction over packing-house workers into a Stockyard Labor Council. These unions included butcher workmen, railway carmen, machinists, electricians, coopers, carpenters, office workers, steam fitters, engineers, and firemen. Foster, of course, was elected secretary of the committee. He proceeded promptly to build an industrial labor federation by associating the craft unions in the council under one executive board with one set of business agents. He infused the movement with the spirit of industrial trade-unionism, which he believed to be the best weapon of direct workingman's power.

At its first meeting, the Stockyards Labor Council decided to mobilize the unskilled masses. That meant mostly the foreign-born and the Negroes. This program brought Foster face to face with the race issue within his own group. A quarter of the Chicago packing-house workers were Negroes. The skilled crafts barred them from union membership, although the Butcher Workmen admitted colored members. To complicate the situation Negro middle-class elements, embittered by the policy of discrimination of the American Federation of Labor, were openly hostile to the whole organizing movement. Foster experimented with a solution by having the big mass Butcher Workmen local unions take in the Negroes. The Negro leaders, however, protested. They held that placing Negro leaders in white Unions would make them a helpless minority. Therefore Negroes demanded separate unions. Foster agreed, only to find the cry of "Jim Crow" spreading along State Street with devastating effect. He tried another approach. Could he not form mass unions in both Negro and White districts and hold them open alike to Negroes and Whites? The idea was right. Foster promptly built up the largest Negro trade-union membership ever organized in any American city. He likes to say that one of the major Communist achievements has been the "tireless and unending struggle against the shameful discrimination and persecution to which the Negro people are subjected" and that "this concern is a part of the relentless fight of the communists for the liberation of colonial and other oppressed peoples all over the world."

By midsummer, Foster found his movement short of both organizers and money; the American Federation of Labor supplied neither. The Butcher Workmen eyed Foster's movement as a rival. Undaunted by lack of such tools as money and experienced lieutenants, Foster proceeded. Upon the recommendation of the Chicago Federation of Labor and the Railway Carmen's district council, the general president of the Brotherhood of Railway Carmen of America reluctantly appointed Foster an organizer for a trial period of ninety days. He felt that in three months the movement would wear itself out. The appointment ended Foster's ten-year career as a railroad worker. During a decade he had worked on eight railway systems in all corners of America, on jobs including fireman, brakeman, car repairer, airbrake man, car inspector, freight handler, railroad construction teamster, shop laborer, and camp cook.

Under Foster's militant hand the movement to organize the packing houses gained momentum; it produced its own funds and its own organizers. At first Foster concentrated his organizing work in the five great Chicago plants of the biggest packers, which he labeled the "huge beef trust." His progress was discouraging. At the end of six weeks of intensive work he had organized only five hundred workers. Half of his trial term of ninety days had expired. He had to work faster! He saw that the huge packing industry could never be organized by such a "one-by-one" method of recruiting. He must invent a way to start the workers moving into the unions *en masse.* Toward this end he now proposed to his small steering committee a detailed plan whereby his cadre of five hundred members, after good preparation and with the organized assistance of other industry militants, could be used to strike a great mass of sixty thousand workers. Before he had time to try the plan, however, local organizations outside Chicago, stimulated by reports from Foster, began to shape up strikes in various Western packing centers.

Foster immediately shifted his strategy. He called a national conference of packing-house workers to prepare demands to be made upon the major companies. Butcher Workmen leaders reluctantly went along. Quick to seize opportunities for publicity, Foster issued a story to the newspapers over the protest of the Butchers. He stated that the move for a conference would probably culminate in a big packing-house strike. The press, as Foster expected, headlined: STRIKE LOOMS AT YARDS. The publicity catapulted workers into union membership. "Decrepit Local 87, Butcher Workmen," according to Foster, "took in fourteen hundred members at its first meeting after the press announcement of the impending strike." "Our strategy had succeeded," he recorded, "better than we had anticipated. . . . We were over the top in the organization of the great national packing industry, which for years had been considered in trade-union circles to be an utterly hopeless task." Meanwhile, a dozen co-operating packing-house unions joined together nationally in a loose committee of which Bill Foster again was named secretary.

By this time the meat packers began to suspect that some experienced operator was at work more militant than conventional American Federation of Labor tacticians. They countered Foster's operations with a discharge campaign. Libby, McNeil & Libby brought the issue to a climax by firing some fifty of its Chicago employees. Here Foster saw his chance. He was clear that a national strike of packing-house workers must come. He was equally sure that the government could not stand a strike in wartime when foodstuffs were so scarce. He therefore demanded a national union strike vote on the Libby, McNeil & Libby discharge action. As he expected, the vote returned an overwhelming sentiment to support a strike. Foster now drove hard and fast to mature the work stoppage.

At this point, American Federation of Labor national leaders stepped in and proposed government mediation. This intervention upset Foster's whole strategy. He was leading a "left-wing" operation, but the actual control of the international unions involved remained in the hands of "reactionary" American Federation of Labor officials who were now acting to head off his program.

Foster stood in a difficult position. In fact, he lacked an organized group of militants to link him up with the rank-and-file workers in the other packing centers. Upon a demand from President Woodrow Wilson and Samuel Gompers, the president of the American Federation of Labor, he therefore reluctantly accepted government mediation. He had no alternative. By December Foster's committee agreed with Federal mediators on a proposal which provided for the right to organize, to set up shop committees, to present grievances, to attend union conventions, to increase wages 10 per cent, to establish the principle of seniority in employment, to rule out discrimination because of creed, color, or nationality, to abolish arbitrary discharge, and to establish proper dressing-, lunch-, and washrooms.

Early in 1918 the national packing-house arbitration proceedings came on before Federal Judge Altschuler for arbitration decision. There was plenty of legal talent acting for both sides. For three and a half weeks Foster paraded witnesses on the stand. They included workers, economists, labor leaders, and even Samuel Gompers himself. From the forum of the courtroom he gave publicity to the "horrible working and living conditions of the packing-house workers and the fabulous profits being made by the packers." On March 30, 1918, Judge Altschuler handed down an award providing for a 25 per cent wage increase, a basic eight-hour day with ten hours' pay, extra pay for overtime, equal pay for men and women doing the same class of work, a guarantee of five days' work a week in slack seasons, and time off with pay for lunch periods in eight-hour shifts. The judge made the award retroactive. One hundred twenty-five thousand workers of the five big packers received six million dollars in back pay, or an average of forty dollars a worker. Packing-house laborers greeted the award as a great victory. They streamed into unions all over the country, building solid plant organizations.

Foster now turned to the job of mopping up. He made hundreds of small packers sign the Altschuler award. He carried the organization campaign into subsidiary businesses such as retail butcher shops, independent soap, flue, fertilizer, canning, and cooperage works, and into other industries. Workers were swept along by contagious enthusiasm. In one situation, indeed, on one hour's notice, Foster was able to cause a strike among three thousand stock handlers in the Union Stockyards and Transit Company, when the president refused to sign the award. Instantly the movement of all cattle, sheep, and hogs stopped at this center. The Department of Justice now threatened to jail Foster for obstructing the war. Gradually large packing houses, cut off from supplies of animals, had come to a standstill. The menace of a great packing-house strike loomed. . . . Then the Union Stockyards and Transit Company signed on the dotted line.

Foster had achieved his objective. Within a year after the idea popped into his head, the packing-house industry was organized throughout the country. More than two hundred thousand workers had come into the dozen federated unions. They included unskilled as well as skilled workers, immigrants and native-born alike, and fully twenty-five thousand new Negro members.

The meat-packing victory had been won in a struggle in the first mass production industry ever to be organized by trade-unions. It was accomplished by militant policies and by the application of the industrial union principle. To Foster and his militants of the old International Trade Union Educational League, the victory was a "glowing justification" of their policy of working inside the old trade-unions. It showed what could be done "on our theory of organizing the unorganized millions by militantly taking advantage of the war situation."

From the food industry Foster now turned to steel. Its product was basic to the munitions supply. "After considerable thought," Foster observed, he decided "to make a try at steel." Within a week after the Altschuler award was announced, Foster introduced a resolution signed by the Railway Carmen into the meeting of the Chicago Federation of Labor. It called upon the American Federation of Labor to proceed with a joint campaign to be supported by all unions having jurisdiction over workers in the steel industry. It was to take the form of a broad industrial movement. Foster wanted it to include the coal and iron miners who dug the ore, the lake transport workers who moved it to smelting plants, and all the operators throughout the industry up to the men engaged in the end crafts making finished products in the prefabricating divisions of the steel industry. Such a federated movement, like the one he had built in the packing industry, Foster said, "was the most practical approach to be made to the necessary industrial form." The Chicago Federation of Labor unanimously adopted the resolution, and "the great steel campaign was on." Foster's union of course was involved, because there were thousands of steel carbuilders in the great steel plants in Pennsylvania.

The resolution as adopted, however, again ran counter to the war-time policy of "social peace" established by the leaders of the American Federation of Labor. Contesting such a policy, Foster in June 1918 went as a delegate from the Chicago Federation of Labor to the American Federation of Labor convention in St. Paul to get action on his resolution. When the resolution, as he expected, was sidetracked because of the "social peace in wartime" policy, Foster engineered a call for a meeting in a designated corner of the convention hall. The session was to convene during the lunch hour. Foster was on the spot ahead of time. Some delegates on their way to eat in the restaurants and others out of curiosity stopped by to see what was going on. "In the absence of Samuel Gompers," whom he had announced as the convener of the meeting, Foster rapped the meeting to order. Organizer Tom Flynn, according to plan, jumped on the table and began to deliver a speech about the need for organization. Foster, knowing that time was short to accomplish his immediate purpose, interrupted Flynn, proposed that he take the names of all present, and that he call a meeting to be

convened the next night with Samuel Gompers as presiding officer. Then Foster adjourned the "lunch-recess steel-organizers' committee" and promptly extended the invitation to Gompers to be
present and preside next evening. When Gompers refused point-
blank, Foster pulled out of his pocket a list of the officials of the
Federation who had attended the lunch recess meeting — the very
same men who had paused out of curiosity on their way to lunch.
Gompers was alarmed and impressed. By this trick, Foster reports,
"Gompers was roped in for the meeting." Now his task was to lasso
the other necessary leaders into attendance. To tie these leaders
into the "movement," Foster asked Gompers to make the announcement of the proposed steel meeting before the convention. Gompers
gruffly refused, saying to Foster, "No! You do it." Foster was quite
willing. In the afternoon he took the platform and advised the convention that at the request of Mr. Gompers he was authorized to
invite all concerned to a steel conference at which Gompers would
be present. The great steel strike was in motion and Bill Foster was
its engineer!

Foster's use of the name of Gompers in the invitation had the
expected effect. Its prestige attracted a good attendance at the meeting. As Foster summarizes the outcome: "My little strategy of net-
ting Gompers by using the names of my curiosity-seekers had succeeded. Utilizing Gompers' name drew other officials into the
program. By such a device I literally tricked the A. F. of L. leaders
into this vital organization campaign. After this maneuver I felt as
though I had been swimming in a sewer."

Two months later a group of labor leaders representing international unions met in Chicago at the New Morrison Hotel as a "steel
conference." They proceeded to set up a "National Committee for
Organizing Iron and Steel Workers." Samuel Gompers assumed the
chairmanship. Of course Foster was elected secretary. For Foster this
assignment was an unpaid job, just as his secretaryship of the
Stockyards Labor Council had been before. He drew his wages from
the Brotherhood of Railway Carmen of America. This new secretary's position, nevertheless, was all that Foster needed to "get
things moving." With no contributions from the American Federation of Labor, with two thousand four hundred dollars contributed
by the unions represented at the Chicago conference, a half-dozen

organizers, and his experience in the meat-packing industry, Foster began the spadework for the steel strike. The strike came as scheduled on September 22, 1919. In response to a strike call, three hundred and sixty-five thousand steel workers quit work in fifty cities in ten states. Never before had the steel industry seen a strike approaching the magnitude or power of this one. The fury of the strike is a matter of record in American history.

On the eve of the strike Gompers quit the national committee. President Wilson asked the postponement of the walkout. Support of President Wilson's position came from a majority of the union presidents who made up the national committee. Only the blacksmiths and mine, mill, and smeltermen supported the strike plan. What was Foster to do? He went ahead on his own; he alone remained to lead the strike. He wired and telephoned his field organizers. He felt that at least 95 per cent of them were "honest" and wanted to see the steel workers organized. He asked them to express the opinion of their local steel councils. From the field the organizers responded with a flood of telegrams overwhelmingly urging Foster to proceed with the strike. He was willing. The strike moved on according to timetable.

From the day that Foster had first had the idea about organizing the packing-house industry, twenty-two months and nineteen days had expired! He was demonstrating the quick power of direct trade-union action. In fact, Foster now could "sell the strike" movement almost anywhere. He also spoke to a trade-unionist rally in Madison Square Garden in New York following his forcible ejection from the city limits of Johnstown, Pennsylvania. In the course of this talk Foster threw back his head, stretched out his arms, and asked dramatically: "What are you going to do about it?" The audience responded. It contributed one hundred and sixty-five thousand dollars in cash, and three hundred and fifteen thousand dollars in pledges. The basins used as collection plates were filled; Foster asked for derby hats to receive the further gifts.

Everywhere now Foster had focused public attention on the "shocking conditions" existing in the steel industry. In religious circles the Interchurch World Movement set the Protestant conscience to work through a report describing conditions in the steel industry. The report raised the plight of labor to the level of national moral concern. In fact, some industry leaders held the opinion that the Interchurch World Movement report on the steel strike had actually been "written by radicals maintaining close liaison with Foster" whose business was described as "making the labor movement move." Bill Foster agreed. "This splendid solidarity and rapid modification of trade-union tactics and institutions to meet an emergency," he said, "is probably without a parallel in American labor annals." He felt the struggle advanced the labor movement in America in the direction of industrial unionism. The *Nation* referred to the "process of making over the American labor movement in the image designed by Foster and his followers." Sylvia Kapland, a liberal writer, observed that "Mr. Foster's challenge is more formidable because the idea of change has been hurled at labor by the Russian Revolution and the postwar upheaval and all that underlie them."

Before the steel strike, Foster notes, the evils of the industry had included a "twelve-hour day, seven-day week, company unionism, boss tyranny, and company domination in the steel towns." By the time the strike was over, the industry had abolished the twelve-hour day and the seven-day week and had laid the groundwork for the unionization of the steel industry by proving that the industry could be organized "in spite of all employer terrorism."

The meat-packing and steel campaigns, plus the subsequent minor activity campaigns for amalgamation, demonstrated the effectiveness of a militant policy, and had an impact upon the whole trade-union movement in America. "The reactionary Gompers bureaucrats even trembled for their lucrative positions," Foster observed. The strike also gave new strength to radicalism, which Foster defined as meaning "revolutionary as distinct from an evolutionary change in our modern social and industrial system. The basic fulcrum of that change lies in the ownership and operation of industry by the workers themselves. Radicalism brings about such revolutionary change by other means than those of the orderly processes of government by majority action."

The Interchurch report mentioned above actually came about this way. While Foster was organizing and directing the steel strike, conditions in the industry were also being studied by a Commis-

sion of Inquiry of the Interchurch World Movement, headed by
Bishop Francis J. McConnell of the Methodist Episcopal Church
and the Reverend Daniel A. Poling of the United Evangelical
Church. The Presbyterian, Baptist, Disciples of Christ, and Con-
gregational denominations were also represented on the commission
with the United Brethren and Protestant Episcopal Church having
advisory representation. The inquiry into conditions in the steel industry by this major segment of the Protestant Churches was undertaken by the authority of the Executive Committee of the Interchurch World Movement upon the recommendation of the Reverend
Fred B. Fisher, director of the movement's Industrial Relations Department. (Fisher was subsequently elected a bishop of the Methodist Episcopal Church, an office which he later resigned to become
pastor of the Central Methodist Church in Detroit. The Reverend
Daniel L. Marsh, who was to become president of Boston University, at the time of the inquiry was Superintendent of the Methodist
Episcopal Union of Pittsburgh and pastor of the Smithfield Street
Church.)

Perhaps no previous united activity had ever involved the major
Protestant denominations so deeply in industrial controversy. The
commission approached its research with competence and thoroughness. The field investigation began the second week in October
1919, about three weeks after the strike was called on September 22.
It continued intensively to February 1, 1920, almost a month after
the strike ended on January 8. At the end of November and early
December, the commission had made an informal approach looking
toward mediation. During the first three months in 1920 the commission, from its own records and the information supplied by its
experienced investigator, formulated its *Report on the Steel Strike.*
The report was unanimously adopted by the Executive Committee
of the Report. On July 27, 1920, the committee transmitted the report to President Woodrow Wilson, and the next day gave the text to
the press.

The Interchurch World Movement followed the *Report* by the
publication of other documents prepared by its investigation in a
volume called *Public Opinion and the Steel Strike of 1919.* In publishing this second volume, Bishop McConnell observed:

To all of those who have thought of the Interchurch *Report* as radical, we would like to say that every condition in the steel industry which the *Report* criticized is remediable — and remediable without the inauguration of anything even resembling social revolution. There is no improvement which we suggest which the leaders of the steel industry cannot themselves put into effect.

A few examples from the second volume will indicate some of the issues which it raised.

Investigator Robert Littell, formerly with the American Mission to the Allied Maritime Transport Council (London), reported "widespread systems of espionage as an integral part of the anti-union policy of great industrial corporations" and asked these pointed questions. "Must our social organization, our civilization, be shot through with spies?" What of an espionage system which reaches out "into social entities as far removed from manufacture as is the church"? "Can we live without spies?"

Investigator M. K. Wisehart, journalist who had served as a European correspondent for *Leslie's*, reported on the role of the Pittsburgh newspaper in the steel strike. Wisehart analyzed four hundred issues of the seven English-language newspapers in Pittsburgh as published between September 22 and late November, 1919. Among other conclusions, Wisehart reported that the newspapers "prominently displayed the sermons, addresses, and statements of both Protestant and Catholic clergymen when their utterances were in accord with the policy of the United States Steel Corporation and especially when they alleged that the strike was of Bolshevik origin."

Investigator George Soule, who had authored the War Department Report on the Industrial Service Section of Ordinance Department, reported on Civil Rights in western Pennsylvania. He concerned himself especially with evidence related to the reduction of the freedom of assembly.

Investigator David J. Saposs, a research assistant to Professor John R. Commons at the University of Wisconsin, found that the bulk of the strikers were of the "new immigration" and especially Slavs. These newer people in the area began to sense the economic benefits which a heavily industrialized society could provide if workingmen engaged in "united action under the leadership of labor organizations."

In dealing with the "Pulpit and the Strike" the second Interchurch report made a detailed analysis. "No individual or institution can possess the spirit of Christ and not be concerned with the conditions under which people live and work," said Bishop McConnell. The organized activities of the churches were now evidenced by the work of the Commission of Inquiry of the Interchurch World Movement. "The conclusion is inescapable," the commission reported to President Woodrow Wilson, "that a real cause of the persistence of the twelve-hour day and the seven-day week is the defenselessness of the unorganized immigrant worker." The first report raised a question, "Is the nation helpless before conditions in a basic industry which promises a future crisis? Can our democratic society be moved to do industrial justice without the pressure of crisis itself?"

While the steel strike was at its height, the Commission of Inquiry had taken steps to mediate the strike — "with the innocence of teasing childhood," as a pamphlet published by the United States Steel Corporation described this effort. On November 27, 1919, John Fitzpatrick, chairman of the National Committee for Organizing Iron and Steel Workers, had proposed a plan for settlement to the Commission on Inquiry. The commission promptly met and decided to formulate a plan of its own to mediate in behalf of all the steel workers. The Commission of Inquiry then proposed that it would become responsible for a settlement in the steel industry and that, in case the Steel Corporation accepted the plan, the strike leaders should step out of the situation after ordering the men back to work.

As secretary of the National Committee for Organizing Iron and Steel Workers, Foster with John Fitzpatrick on December 2, 1919, had asked the Commission of Inquiry of the Interchurch World Movement to use its good offices to bring about an adjustment of the controversy. Foster felt the Interchurch World Movement was a "neutral interest sufficiently interested" to exert an influence to bring about "a reasonable and fair conclusion of the strike."

Bishop McConnell, Dr. Poling, and Dr. John McDowell, of the Presbyterian Church, on December 5, 1919, called upon Judge Elbert H. Gary — who described the goals of the strike as "the closed shop, Soviets, and the forcible distribution of property."

Immediately after his conference with Judge Gary, who declined to arbitrate, Bishop McConnell dictated a memorandum on the meeting. Gary "repeatedly avowed his belief," wrote the Bishop, "that the only outcome of a victory for unionism would be Sovietism in the United States and forcible distribution of property." McConnell further noted that Judge Gary was unwilling to say anything that might be reported to Foster. Gary inferred that McConnell and Poling had been directed a good deal by "red radicals." At the interview, Gary said that "nobody represented by Foster and Fitzpatrick would be allowed to go back into the mills." In further discussion, Gary observed that one "must remember that Mr. Foster was a very slick one." The conference terminated when Judge Gary advised McConnell, Poling, and McDowell that "there is absolutely no issue" to be discussed.

While the strike was in its early stages, another church group had shown interest. The Committee of the Pittsburgh Federal Council of Churches had directed a letter to Foster to obtain statements of his position in writing, and on October 8, 1919, Foster had replied to the Reverend Daniel L. Marsh.

To Marsh's question as to whether Foster had written a book entitled *Syndicalism* and advocated a theory of social organization which would substitute for the present political and social order one constructed on an industrial rather than a territorial basis and one in which the entire social control would be exercised by workers as such, Foster replied that his plan was to "improve conditions as I find them and to not waste my time speculating about ideal systems of government."

To the question as to whether he advocated and believed in undertaking to secure these ends by methods of violence in which the workers were to proceed by violent seizure of property, Foster replied that he believed the best way for workers to secure their ends was "to proceed in a way that will retain for themselves the support of public opinion." Except in extreme circumstances, therefore, Foster ruled out "all sorts of violence." He went on to say that he did not believe in and advocate sabotage in the sense of deliberately crippling machinery and destroying property as a means of winning benefits for the workers.

To the question as to whether he advocated the taking of property without compensation to the present owners, Foster answered "No," he did not if the property had been honestly acquired. He qualified this statement by saying that he felt that many owners of large fortunes had no better title to them "than the Southern planters had to their black slaves."

In reply to his stand on "fundamental virtues," Foster replied that he had "nothing but respect" for them, but that he had "nothing but contempt" for that "conception of duty which holds that for an American to be true to himself and his country he must take work in the steel mills and become a strike-breaker."

To the question as to whether Foster's publication on *Syndicalism* had been circulated by the committee for organizing the steel industry or by Foster, Foster replied that it had been out of print for a number of years, that he had not circulated it in the present strike campaign, and that he believed the steel corporation had "sent it out in thousands."

In concluding his reply to Marsh, Foster wrote:

> The present strike is one of the most important moves for liberty ever undertaken by workingmen in this country. It is aimed to secure fundamental justice from one of the most heartless and unscrupulous aggregations of predatory wealth upon the face of the globe. The strike is being conducted upon one hundred per cent trade-union principles and for trade-union ends. That is all there is to it. The effort being made to distort it from these principles and ends is merely part of the general campaign of the United States Steel Corporation to defeat the legitimate hopes and aspirations of its downtrodden workers.

A month later John Fitzpatrick wrote to Bishop McConnell and Poling that the National Committee for Organizing Iron and Steel Workers welcomed the interest of the Interchurch Movement's Commission of Inquiry in its efforts to obtain "information, the fullest and most reliable possible, on which Christians can base some understanding of this strike and current industrial unrest." Said

Fitzpatrick: "It may well be that your great organization will materially further honest use in industrial conflicts of the principles taught by the Carpenter of Nazareth."

As a result of these activities, the Protestant churches became publicly and permanently involved in the whole problem of industrial relations. For the rest of his ministry, Bishop McConnell continued to be referred to in conservative circles as a "Red," a "radical," and an advocate of the "social gospel." But the Protestants were not alone in their concern about the pattern of human relationship in the economic order. Speaking at a public meeting at Johnstown, Pennsylvania, during the strike, Father John Ryan, of the Catholic University of America, had declared that Judge Gary's rejection of a meeting with representatives of employees was a rejection not of radicalism but of the first step to a sound system of co-operative economic life. He went on to say that collective bargaining was only the beginning, and that the future of the world was a choice between Socialism, Guild Socialism, and Co-operative Production, in which wage earners would be advanced to the standing of owners.

This discussion is sufficient to indicate why Foster attributed to organized religion usefulness in advancing the interests of workers. As the years went by his respect for the influence of the church in economic life deepened. He saw in its activities a gigantic potential apparatus for the achievement of economic reform.

While Foster was radically organizing the meat-packing and steel industries, in the period of 1917 to 1920, political radicalism in Russia had overthrown the Kerensky government in an October revolution. The Bolshevists had seized power and organized the ideas of the Bolshevist faction of Socialist action into a Communist state. This seizure of power in Russia had its effect upon labor and liberal thinking in America; even as the establishment of a Socialist state in Russia had caused grave concern among conservative groups.

With the organization of the Communist Party in the United States in 1919, revolutionary elements rallied from the Socialist Party, the Socialist Labor Party, the I.W.W., and the Syndicalist League of North America. Eighteen months after it was organized, Foster himself, at the age of forty, joined the Communist Party and became a member of its Political Committee. He had arrived at what he calls "his political destination." For the remainder of his life he found within the party, as he says, the satisfaction at last of being at home among compatriots who shared a matured conception of economics and politics and knew how to use the state as a vehicle of revolution to establish a genuine socialist society. "Becoming a Communist," he says, "meant for me to put the logical capstone upon my whole previous life experience. Since joining the Communist Party it has been a never-ending effort on my part, with such diligence and self-criticism as I can command, to master the revolutionary principles of Marx, Engels, Lenin, and Stalin, and to apply them effectively in the American class struggle." From this position he never deviated. Thirty years later he said that "if I were starting out my life all over again, I would take the same course I have done. One thing I would surely do, despite the press of practical work, would be better to organize my time so as to enable me to indulge more than I have in reading of the science and history I love so much. This is one thing that the youth in the labor and Communist movement should most resolutely strive to accomplish — to combine the theoretical with the practical, to find time for lots of solid reading, notwithstanding the most urgent demands of the day-to-day struggle." To this point Foster had given himself an education tailor-fashioned for the purposes of revolutionary leadership. In the process, he had served as an industrial worker for twenty-three years.

In 1919 Lenin referred to the organization of the Communist International as the "general staff of the world revolution." Foster soon became a partner in the general staff work. With the steel strike over, he sailed the Atlantic — destination Russia. From New York he went by way of London, Liban, Riga, and Reval to Leningrad. In 1921, while attending the Communist International, he first saw Lenin at the Czar's Palace in Moscow. The sight, he says, "was one of the most inspiring moments of my life. There indeed was the great leader of the world's oppressed millions in every corner of the earth. I regarded him so intently as he went about the Congress that his whole makeup and characteristics literally burned themselves into my memory."

Lenin's influence moved Foster farther to the left, "exercising," as Foster says, "a most profound effect upon my ideology and my life work. After more than twenty years of intellectual groping about, I was at last, thanks to Lenin, getting my feet on firm revolutionary ground."

Foster thus became a full-fledged part of the world Communist movement. He attended world congresses, sat in executive meetings of the Comintern, and served in executive sessions of the Red International of Labor Unions. In these congresses and plenums he met, as he says, "the best Marxians in the world, militant revolutionary fighters who, for the past generation, have been in the heart of every great strike movement and revolutionary struggle from London to Shanghai and from Toronto to Buenos Aires." These international meetings, he pointed out, constituted the most interesting and instructive experiences of his political life.

In various congresses and central committee meetings of the Communist Party in the Soviet Union he also watched the triumph of Stalin over Trotsky and Zinoviev. He knew what intra-party struggle meant. He had feverishly read the writings of Lenin, mastered the literature of the party, and found it "spiritually satisfying" — its revolutionary doctrine as well as its atheism. When in the summer of 1935 he saw the vast Soviet Arctic development — on a trip from Moscow to Murmansk *via* the new Stalin Baltic–White Sea Canal — he held in his hand the first watermelon ever grown north of the Arctic Circle. He rejoiced in the fact that there were no churches in the new Socialist city of Murmansk, and he felt a sense of pride that the great canal, built by prison labor under the direction of the O.G.P.U., had offered "opportunity to regenerate the prisoners."

Foster was now ready to run as the Communist Party candidate for President of the United States. He entered the national elections of 1924, 1928, and 1932. In these campaigns he spoke to what he estimates to have been five hundred thousand people in three hundred meetings, gave radio speeches, "inspired" newspaper stories, and organized demonstrations and parades. He traveled sixty thousand miles by train, auto, bus, airplane, steamboat, wagon, and on foot. He covered every important city in every state in the Union. In 1924 he got thirty-six thousand votes, in 1928 fifty thousand votes, and in 1932 one hundred thousand.

On the threshold of the campaign of 1932 Foster was serving sentence in the New York County Penitentiary. His imprisonment was penalty for his part in a demonstration, championed by the Communist Party and led by him, to call attention to the "real starvation conditions prevailing among millions of jobless workers." Foster was leading the fight for "the elementary justice of unemployment relief and insurance." The demonstrations in New York — held on March 6, 1930, at Union Square — were tied in with action on a national scale. More than a hundred thousand workers, he estimates, participated in the Manhattan demonstration.

Later, as he lived "inside" the largest local prison system in the world, which sprawls along Welfare, Riker's and Hart's islands in the East River, Foster declared that his experience every day confirmed the ideas his Communist soul entertained about the capitalist world.

After serving six months of his sentence Foster was paroled. He got out in plenty of time to hurry to Dearborn, Michigan, to report for duty on March 7, 1932, in order to help mobilize a demonstration against the Ford Motor Company. In prison Foster had arranged a tour for himself to agitate generally among the unemployed. He stopped off at Ford, where he was billed as the principal speaker at a mass meeting which had historic labor significance. Several thousand workers turned out to hear his remarks. According to the plan, unemployed workers were to march to the gates of the Ford plant, present their demands for work and relief, and then, as he says, to have dispersed. As the procession of unemployed workers entered Dearborn and approached the plant, however, city police and Ford's private "Bennett Service" opened fire with tear gas, rifles, and machine guns. Four workers were killed and fifty wounded. The *Detroit Free Press* charged that Foster as the main speaker at the mobilization meeting was personally responsible for the killings. The editor proposed that Foster should be arrested along with other Detroit Communist leaders and tried for murder.

Foster left Dearborn on the night train for Milwaukee. When he opened his morning newspaper in the Wisconsin city, he read about the "massacre" of the workers by the police the evening before. At once he boarded a train for New York. He was still on parole under a three-year penitentiary sentence for participating in that Union

Square unemployment demonstration back in 1930 and required to make semimonthly parole reports *in person*. Foster arrived back in Manhattan the day a parole report was due. When he stepped into the parole office, police surrounded him. Inasmuch as the parole commission was in session, Foster expected to receive immediate orders to go back to the New York County Penitentiary as a parole violator and to face felony charges. For their own reasons, the Dearborn police decided not to press the charges against Foster. Nevertheless the New York authorities faced a difficult situation: a parolee was running up and down the country organizing the unemployed. The parole commissioner ordered Foster to serve the rest of his term within the bounds of New York City. If he should leave the city under any pretext, he would immediately be returned to prison to serve the balance of his term.

Events determined a different outcome after the Communist Party nominated William Z. Foster as its candidate for President of the United States of America in the 1932 election. The nomination placed New York officials in another plight. They could not, they had decided, permit Foster to travel around the country agitating among the workers. On the other hand, did they now dare to hold a candidate for President in New York, and make of him a martyr? Caught on the horns of this dilemma, the commissioner lifted the city-limits ban on Foster's activities but threatened him with the continuing discipline of return to prison upon the slightest provocation.

At once Foster was off on the rails, to campaign until his heart gave out during a speech in Moline, Illinois.

Despite his half-year of rest in the penitentiary, Foster has confessed that he was "tired out" when the 1932 presidential campaign began. He had worked vigorously at agitation and politics. He had spent five strenuous months of duty in promoting a coal strike. He had applied himself without stint to the completion of his book *Towards Soviet America*. The heart attack in Moline on September 8, 1932, put him in bed for five months. During the next nineteen months he lay — so he remembers — in bed with an ailment diagnosed as *angina pectoris*. For three years he was unable to make a ten-minute speech. Despite the seriousness of this illness he did, however, have strength enough to play a role in the San Francisco general strike. As soon as he was able to travel, he went to California to recuperate. His condition required "total freedom from all political excitement." Upon arrival on the West Coast, Foster found Harry Bridges leading a coastwide strike of longshoremen. Although Foster's influence in San Francisco was not suspected, because of the condition of his health, William Green as president of the American Federation of Labor recognized certain symptoms. "Foster," he declared, "is the man behind the strike."

While Foster was traveling about the country Communist organizers under his direction were active in various operations designed to take fullest advantage of the depression. One of the most sensational of these activities, to give but one example, was the so-called "National Bonus March" of World War I veterans to Washington in July 1932. Asserting that veterans had been betrayed by the American Legion and "kicked around by the Hoover administration," a group of Party leaders, acting through the Workers Ex-Servicemen's League, took occasion at a hearing of the House Ways and Means Committee in April 1932 to propose a "National Bonus March" on the capital. Within three months groups of veterans began to move into the District of Columbia from various sections of the country. They occupied empty buildings and set up a shack camp on the Anacostia flats. Foster estimated that the number of veterans reached twenty-five thousand. The marchers shouted slogans such as WE FOUGHT FOR DEMOCRACY — WHAT DID WE GET? and HEROES IN 1917 — BUMS IN 1932. The central demand made was for payment of adjusted service pay. When government officials were unable to induce the men to leave the city, President Hoover ordered General Douglas MacArthur with "bayonets and tear gas," as the Communists say, to drive the veterans from the camp and burn it down. (Dwight Eisenhower at the time was MacArthur's aide.) There followed what Foster calls the "Battle of Washington."

The "Bonus March" was one of a series of hunger marches and demonstrations highly organized by the most experienced Communists. On December 6, 1932, three thousand hunger marchers converged on Washington. On the plaza before the United States Capitol, their band played *The Internationale*. In other sections of the country Communist-inspired "unemployed councils" demanded "unemployment insurance" and further immediate relief benefits.

Foster's part in the so-called "Ford massacre," as one phase of the mobilization of the unemployed, was a part of a determined Communist plan to organize the motor car industry and Ford in particular. Foster's strategy required winning in Detroit. "Nowhere in the world," he said, "were workers exploited more systematically and heartlessly. The automobile kings ruled autocratically over their industrial empire with a million unorganized wage slaves."

When the American Federation of Labor expelled the Auto, Aircraft, and Vehicle Workers of America, with twenty-three thousand members, in 1918, the AAVW had turned to Foster's Trade Union Educational League for affiliation. And within the Ford Motor Company, Foster found a devoted collaborator known to Communists as "Brother Bill McKie." "Bill McKie," said Foster, "is a veritable symbol of the indomitable fighting spirit of the working class and of its determination eventually to emancipate itself. He is worlds apart from the Reuthers, Mazeys, and the like — trimmers, turncoats, and opportunists. Bill McKie is of the fine fighting stuff that Communists are made of."

For the next dozen years, however, the operations of the Communist Party in the United States were guided to a large extent by Earl Browder, general secretary of the party, partly because of the condition of Foster's health and partly because of his greater concern with Communist activities at the international level. Foster's later return to active leadership of the Communist Party in the United States came about as a result of a bitter factional struggle. The lines were drawn on theoretical grounds: orthodox Marx-Leninism versus so-called "American Exceptionalism." Browder held to the strategy of Exceptionalism. His ejection from the party, and the triumph of Foster's revolutionary policies, led to a series of actions by the United States Government beginning in 1948, directed to the liquidation of a Communist conspiracy to overthrow the Government of the United States by force and violence. It is therefore necessary briefly to describe Browder's position as well as Foster's in the intra-party struggle.

Comrade Browder, the grandson of an itinerant Kansas Methodist circuit rider, had studied economics and Marxism as a draft evader committed to Leavenworth Penitentiary during World War I. In 1933 he received a full pardon from President Franklin D. Roosevelt. Browder succeeded Foster as the Communist presidential candidate in the national elections of 1936 and 1940. On charges of passport irregularities he was sentenced in 1940 to the Atlanta Penitentiary for four years. When he had served fourteen months of this term, President Roosevelt commuted his sentence. (It is of passing interest to note that the American Legion and the Daughters of the American Revolution, in Yonkers, New York, in 1944, had selected Earl Browder's son Felix, born in Moscow, as the young man most outstanding in scholarship and especially in American history.)

In late November and early December of 1943, Winston Churchill, Joseph Stalin, and Franklin Roosevelt met at the midpoint of World War II in Teheran, the Iranian capital city at the foot of the Elburz Mountains. For the Communists, the outcomes of the conference were epochal. Up to this point the Soviets had felt that Russia was bearing the whole brunt of the Nazi attack. Stalin wanted the United States and Great Britain to open up a second front, in France. At Teheran the chiefs of state agreed to this second front. From the Atlanta penitentiary Browder wired the Communist National Committee in New York: "They have crossed the Rubicon!" The Comintern proceeded to implement the decisions on all Communist-action fronts. Major objectives set at Teheran, as Browder saw them, included the development of an all-out coalition warfare conducted by the Big Three for complete democratic world organization of peoples to maintain international peace and order, and implied the evolution of basic economic programs to meet the gigantic needs for postwar reconstruction.

As the ranking American Communist, Browder took the obligations under the Teheran decisions with desperate seriousness. On December 12, 1943, his sentence to Atlanta having been commuted by President Roosevelt, he delivered a speech at Bridgeport, Connecticut, in which he explained the significance of the Teheran conference. He related the decisions to the political situation in the United States. The text of his Bridgeport address, published in a Communist magazine in January 1944, showed Earl Browder discussing for the first time the necessity for changing the course of the Communist Party U.S.A. The substance of Browder's thesis was that at Teheran capitalism and socialism had begun to find the means leading to peaceful coexistence and collaboration in the framework of one and the same world. "The Teheran Declaration," said Browder, "is the only hope for the continuance of civilization in our time. That is why I can accept and support and believe in the Declaration of Teheran and make it the starting point for all my thinking about the problems of our country and the world."

Taking his point of departure from the decisions arrived at Teheran, Browder drew political conclusions about the problems of the world and about the internal situation in the United States. He saw postwar Western Europe developing on a bourgeois-democratic basis, conditioned by "complete democratic self-determination for each nation." "Old formulas and old prejudices," he said, "are going to be of no use whatever to us as guides to find our way in this world. We are going to draw together all men and all groups with intelligence enough to see the overwhelming importance of this issue, to understand that upon its correct solution depends the fate of our country, and the fate of civilization throughout the world. We shall have to be prepared to break with anyone that refuses to support and fight for the realization of the Teheran agreement and the Anglo-Soviet-American coalition. We must be prepared to give the hand of co-operation and fellowship to everyone who fights for the realization of this coalition."

"Never did even Henry Luce portray the American century as vividly as did Earl Browder," Foster observed. "His idyll of international unity presupposed an idyllic national unity within capitalistic countries. This did not exist."

The ideological differences between Foster and Browder had been widening for a decade. As early as 1934, Browder had proposed at the Eighth Party Convention in Cleveland that "Communism is twentieth-century Americanism." He had, according to Foster, become saturated with the "all-class concept of American democracy," and increasingly denied the class contrasts of "bourgeois democracy." With the outbreak of World War II, Browder had welcomed many signs of a "better world." In President Roosevelt's executive order No. 8802, for instance — prohibiting discrimination in the employment of workers in defense industries or government because of race, creed, color, or national origin — Browder saw a new respect for persons. Browder found the war moving the nation toward socialism. Because maximum war production requires central planning, he felt that prices in a war economy lose their former significance as a register of market relationships and become merely a convenience of bookkeeping and accounting. In fact, Browder had played a part in national policy. In the fall of 1942, Assistant Secretary of State Sumner Welles had called him to Washington to assist in the United States program to unify the forces of Nationalist and Communist China, to effect a policy of turning "all guns against the Japanese." Quite naturally Browder appreciated the necessity for Chinese unity. In the winter of 1945, he was to point out that the policies of Communist China were closer to those of the United States than were those of Chiang Kai-shek. "The economic policies of the Communist-led area are much more closely related to the American 'free enterprise' system than those of Chiang," Browder said. "The Chinese Communists trust America." "In fact," said Foster, in commenting on this position, "Browder even tried to create the false impression that the State Department was backing the Chinese Communists against Chiang."

Foster was quick to recognize heresy in Browder's stated position on Teheran in 1943. He felt the time had come to face the import of his leadership. Browder, Foster said, had fallen a victim to capitalist propaganda. He had degenerated into an agent of American imperialism. Browderism, he judged, was much like social democracy; in its own way, it undertook to cripple the fighting capacity of the working class in the interest of employers.

Immediately after Browder's December 1943 Bridgeport speech, Foster began his battle within the party against Browder. He commenced by submitting a long letter to the members of the National Committee of the Communist Party U.S.A. on January 20, 1944. Foster's position, as expressed in the communication, was rejected at an enlarged meeting of the Political Bureau held on February 8. About forty of the leading party members attended the meeting. Foster addressed this extraordinary session of the national committee in opposition to the Browder line. His remarks provoked violent criticism from the other comrades present, most of whom opposed Foster's arguments and supported Browder's "new course." After a day-long discussion, all the members except Foster himself and a lieutenant from eastern Pennsylvania voted to back the Browder position. Thus overwhelmingly rebuffed, Foster decided to concentrate entirely on a new effort to influence the members of the national committee. For the next eighteen months he waged a one-man ideological battle within the top circles of the party. By means of sharp and continual criticism, by policy proposals, letters, and articles directed toward the elimination of "Browder's opportunistic errors," Foster battled to return the party to a "sound line of policy." In the meantime, the national committee opened up a discussion of Browder's position among the rank and file, in regional congresses, and in the party press. Everywhere, Browder's position was unanimously endorsed.

By late spring Browder had consolidated strength enough to move — at the Congress of the Communist Party U.S.A. on May 20, 1944 — that "the Communist Party be dissolved." He so moved, he said, because he felt that by renouncing "the aim of partisan advantage and the party form of organization, Communists could best help to win the war and secure a durable peace." The congress adopted the Browder resolution. Immediately, the Congress of the Communist Party U.S.A. proclaimed itself to be the Constituent Congress of the Communist Political Association of the United States, and adopted a programmatic introduction to the association's statutes. Thus the Communist Political Association came into being as a non-party organization based on a working-class constituency, to carry forward the "traditions of Washington, Jefferson, Paine, Jackson, and Lincoln, under the changed conditions of modern industrial society." The association pledged itself to "uphold the Declaration of Independence, the United States Constitution, the Bill of Rights, and the achievement of American democracy against all the enemies of popular liberties." It further declared that it looked to the "family of free nations, led by the great coalition of democratic capitalist and socialist states, to inaugurate an era of world peace, expanding production, and economic well-being, and to achieve the liberation and equality of all peoples regardless of race, creed, or color." It looked forward, indeed, "to a future in which America would solve the problems arising out of the contradiction between the social character of production and its private ownership in a form and manner consistent with American tradition and character."

The Constituent Congress of the Communist Political Association adopted a slogan expressive of its objective: NATIONAL UNITY FOR VICTORY, SECURITY, AND A DURABLE PEACE.

Before adjourning, the congress unanimously elected Browder president of the Communist Political Association, and addressed a message to Comrade Stalin and the Red Army which concluded with these words: "All patriotic Americans are determined to strengthen still further the concerted action of the United Nations and its leading coalition of our country, the Soviet Union and England, on which our assurance of victory rests. They are determined to continue and deepen this coalition in the peace to come and to extend the friendship among all our peoples which will cement the alliance of our two powerful nations as the mainstay of victory, national freedom, and an enduring peace." The Communist Political Association thereupon plunged into the 1944 election campaign in support of Franklin D. Roosevelt.

In New York, on September 25, 1944, Browder compounded heresy, in Foster's opinion, when he said: "We must give not only our lives, but we must be ready also to sacrifice our prejudices, our ideologies, and our special interests. We American Communists have applied this rule first of all to ourselves."

By methods which he had developed over the years, Foster now set to work to reconstitute the Communist Party in the United States as a political, class-conscious force. He explicitly stated five counts of heresy in Browder's statement, and outlined five steps that needed to be taken immediately to combat that heresy. These counts deserve brief mention. Foster declared:

1. That the Browder line was a rejection of Marxian economic doctrines, accepting as it did bourgeois theories of the liquidation of the capitalist cyclical and general crisis and rejecting Marx's theory of surplus value and of the exploitation of the workers.

2. That the Browder line rejected the Marxian principle of class struggle.

3. That the Browder line rejected the Marxian concept of the progressive and revolutionary initiative of the working class, and with it the vanguard role of the Communist Party.

4. That the Browder line rejected the Marxist-Leninist perspective of socialism.

5. That the Browder line rejected the Leninist theory of imperialism as the final stage of capitalism.

Foster then stated the ideological counts against Browder and embarked on a struggle against revisionism by launching a campaign to preach the orthodox gospel. He proposed to re-establish the Communist Party, to "renew" and strengthen the party leadership, to re-establish "democratic centralism," and to eliminate a "corroding faction in which Browder was "the key figure and chief moving force." Foster charged Browder with promoting a "system of right-wing bourgeois liberalism," a "liberalism so conservative that on many questions it puts us far to the right of Roosevelt, of the liberal press, and of the main sections of the labor movement." Browder's position, he concluded, was "a complete abandonment of the basic principles of Marxism-Leninism."

While this Foster–Browder factional struggle was raging, Jacques Duclos, secretary of the Communist Party of France, published an article in the April 1944 *Cahiers du Communisme* in which he said that "nothing justifies the dissolution of the American Communist Party." That position taken by Duclos and the French Communist leaders helped to turn the tide of factionalism. Foster intensified his struggle against Browder during the next year. In June 1945 the national committee suspended Browder as general secretary, appointed a provisional secretariat headed by Foster to succeed him, and called an emergency convention to meet in New York at the end of July. This special convention re-established the Communist Party U.S.A., adopted a new constitution, reinvigorated orthodoxy, affirmed the principles of scientific socialism and Marxism-Leninism, and elected Foster as Party chairman.

When the national committee met in February 1946, Comrade Robert Thompson presented a report on "The Path of a Renegade." Browder was forthwith unanimously expelled from the party, together with his wife, his brother, and his "financial angel." Foster says he offered to give Browder some minor party work but he refused. For a time Browder engaged in factional correspondence within the party and continued publication of a sheet called *Distributor's Guide*.

Foster was now the dominant factor in the party. Browder's opportunism and policy of revisionism, he said, had been costly: the party had lost fifteen thousand members. When the Communist Party dissolved into the Communist Political Association, 12 per cent of its number had dropped out. By January 1946 the party registration had fallen to under fifty-three thousand. Before the party was dissolved by the Browder plan in 1944, according to Foster, the membership, including fifteen thousand serving in the armed forces, had risen to a peak of eighty thousand. This was, as he figured it, only five thousand members more than had been reported at the 1938 convention. Moreover, the turnover among members was high. In 1944 Foster estimated that thirty-three thousand members had been enrolled in less than a year, that 14 per cent were Negroes, 46 per cent women, and a quarter were professional and white collar workers. Had it not been for Browder, Foster held, the Communist Party would have emerged from the war with a hundred and fifty thousand solidly organized workers, instead of with hardly a third that number. Events, to Foster, later confirmed the correctness of the party's stand against "Browder's revisionism," for Browder had painted a picture of America, as Foster saw it, in the postwar period living in friendly co-operation with the Soviet Union, systematically improving the living standards and democracy of the American workers, and building the industries and freedoms of the less developed areas all over the world.

After the extermination of revisionism and the re-establishment of the Communist Party U.S.A., Foster left the country on a European tour in the late summer of 1945. American Communists, meanwhile, caught up in domestic legal prosecution and Congressional investigation, began to move vigorously to support Mao Tse-tung in China, revolution in Southeast Asia, revolution in Africa, and to attack "American imperialism" in general. Foster declared that Communist control of China was "of decisive world importance." All during the 1940's a major objective of Soviet policy had been the establishment of a Communist regime in China. To Foster, Mao was not only a living witness of the Communist class-conscious leadership; he was the political leader of the key country in Communism's liquidation of colonialism with the self-determination of peoples and the extension of socialism around the globe. Best of all, Mao was orthodox. There never was any doubt in Foster's mind about Mao's being a reliable, thoroughgoing Communist leading the masses of Asia to "economic freedom." Mao's leadership in China, to Foster, was a long step toward Communism's master plan to extend Soviet culture into the unstable areas of Asia *and* Africa, dominated by "Western imperialism." For a quarter of a century, Communists had faced the fact that three fifths of the human race live in the "grip of colonial oppression." Asia and Africa were, therefore, the first areas of importance in Communism's battle for the world. By sheer biological arithmetic and the procreative force of the Asiatic masses the fact was clear to Moscow that the force which dominates China will control Asia and in time the whole vast continent of Eurasia. During all of Foster's active life in the party, this Asian objective operating through China had remained unchanged. "The issue of the struggle," declared a speaker at the Seventh World Congress of the Comintern, "depends in the last analysis upon the fact that Russia, the Indias, and China, etc., represent a preponderant majority of the world's population." The Orient became a primary front in the "war against the entire capitalistic world," as Lenin had declared it.

The Communist "front," however, was already moving from China into Southeast Asia. Foster was backing the Asian movement through the organization of a Committee for a Democratic Far Eastern Policy with offices located at 80 East 11th Street, New York. It was directed by Maud Russell. The magazine *Far East Spotlight* promptly appeared as the monthly Communist-line report on United States policy and internal events in China, Japan, Korea, the Philippines, Southeast Asia, and India. The committee pressed a national campaign for friendship, trade, and recognition of the People's Republic of China, circulated scrolls for signatures and fund-raising, pushed the sale and distribution of Mao Tse-tung's writing and the circulation of the *Far East Spotlight*. The public-relations program effectively influenced American opinion at the time.

While Communists were concerned about Asia, a group of American liberals directed attention to the "Dark Continent" through an organization called "The Council on African Affairs." It put out a monthly bulletin called *New Africa*. In explaining the African movement, Mrs. Paul Robeson said that "We Americans do not live uptown, downtown, or on the East or West Side. We live in the world. If we people of the United States are to live in the world in peace we must plan to live with these neighbors. The people of Africa like those of Asia do not want their land staked out for foreign military bases, drained by foreign investment projects, or dug up for raw materials for foreigners to take away and use for themselves in other lands. They want to plan for outside help if and when and how they need and want it. They want to live in peace and friendly co-operation with all the other peoples of the world — AS EQUALS!"

Alphaeus Hulton, secretary of the Council on African Affairs, joining the Negro's struggle for full equality and democracy in America with the African campaign, pointed out that "The African people are on the side of democracy and world peace. They, together with the Vietnamese, Malayans, and other colonial peoples, are in the front line of battle. They struggle in actual physical combat with the imperialists. The colonial peoples' resistance is at the very core of the present world struggle. Without Africa's bases, resources, and manpower at their disposal, the schemes of Americans and Western European Imperialists are doomed."

Later Foster took a look closer home. In March 1948 he made a trip to Puerto Rico, talked with Communist leaders, visited the island's distressing slum known as El Fanguito in San Juan, addressed a huge meeting of Puerto Rican workers and progressives on the island, and in April, as National Chairman of the Communist Party U.S.A., directed an open letter to President Truman on Puerto Rico which he simultaneously published in a pamphlet entitled *The Crime of El Fanguito.*

He told the President that he, Foster, as an American citizen conscious of "our nation's heavy responsibility to this oppressed people," burned with shame that such outrageous conditions exist in Puerto Rico "and are caused by us." Puerto Rico, as a colony of the United States, he said, "is the inevitable result of the ruthless exploitation of Puerto Rico by the American sugar trust aided by reactionary Washington politicians." In his public letter to the President of the United States Foster said:

> You are largely responsible for the continuance, if not the origin, of such slums as El Fanguito. . . . But I am well aware, Mr. President, that neither you nor the reactionary Congress

will do voluntarily any of these things. To get them done will be the task of the Puerto Rican people and the growing labor and progressive movement in the United States. The Communist Party will continue to give its full support to this liberation struggle.

You and your big capitalist friends, Mr. President, are extremely alarmed at the rapid growth of the new democracy and socialism in many parts of the world. This is not surprising, for your capitalist system, which bred two world wars, fascism, and the world's most terrible economic crisis, all within one generation, is obsolete and is passing off the world's historical stage. Now to put across your imperialist program, you are trying to organize a third world war. Your desperation is to be measured by the fact that under the Truman-Marshall Plan, you are not only promoting civil war in various lands and openly bringing pressure to dictate other countries' elections, you are militarizing our own country and turning it over to the mercy of the worst jingoist and reactionaries. Capitalism's imperialist wars of exploitation have laid the world in ruins and have forced a billion people into a deepening starvation. All that dying world capitalism has to offer humanity is El Fanguito, the "mud-hole," on an ever-widening scale. And El Fanguito, the symbol of misery and oppression, the world's masses will never accept, nor can they be forced to do so, even with all of Wall Street's money and hypocrisy and bayonets. The tragic significance of Puerto Rico is that it plainly shows American imperialism for what it is, in all its brutal tyranny and exploitation. It is a warning to the democratic world what Wall Street domination would signify. Now is the time, before it is too late, when the people must speak out and utterly smash the imperialists of Wall Street who would extend a Puerto Rico-like slavery all over the world.

Two years after the publication of this letter, Oscar Collazo and Griselio Torresola, Puerto Ricans, on November 1, 1950, were to storm Blair House on Pennsylvania Avenue in Washington in an attempt to assassinate President Harry S. Truman in the temporary White House. Torresola was killed, Collazo wounded, and a White House policeman was slain in the encounter. Promptly from Communist headquarters in New York Foster issued this statement: "As is well known, the Communist Party condemns and rejects assassination and all acts of violence and terror." Foster then made his position clear. "American imperialists," he said, "in their drive to subjugate the earth, realize that the world democratic forces are the main obstacles to their expansion. Hence they are striving to defeat the Soviet Union, the national liberation movements of Asia, the new democracies of Europe, and the Communist parties and trade-unions of the world. Allied internationally with big capitalists and landlords, the Vatican, avowed fascists, and the right-wing Social Democrats, they are driving the world toward fascism and war."

Meanwhile the report of Foster's Continental tour which had taken him to England, France, Switzerland, Italy, Trieste, Yugoslavia, Bulgaria, Czechoslovakia, and Poland, in the order named, was having a wide reading in the volume entitled *The New Europe*. It was issued in a first edition of a hundred thousand copies. The substance of this report was that the countries of Europe were heavy sufferers in the war and that the nations under Soviet influence had recovered most rapidly. Poland, he said, lost six million of its people and Yugoslavia one million, seven hundred thousand in war dead. Hitler had butchered six million Jews, three million of them in Poland. Soviet Russia's losses exceeded those of Poland and Yugoslavia. He was shocked by the war damage, by the ruined cities and industries, and by the industrial and agricultural havoc which had been wrought. He reported dangerously low living standards of the masses all over Europe and felt that the deeply reduced living standards plus the slow rate of industrial and agricultural recovery, the widespread currency inflation, and the black-marketeering, left most of the countries of Europe "exposed to economic and political crisis." "Because the United States grew fabulously rich on the war," Foster said, "our plain duty to our war partners, which is in our interest as well as theirs, is to apply liberally our tremendous industrial and agricultural production to help stricken Europe get back on its feet again." The policy of the United States toward Europe he described as "one of cynical imperialism." His analysis of the economic situation in Europe preceded that issued by the State Department in support of the Marshall Plan. And so did his proposal for American aid.

Looking at Europe as a Communist, Foster found all over the Continent new economic reorganization based on a growing mass realization that "production must be carried on for the benefit of society as a whole and not to swell the profits of a handful of parasitic capitalists who perform no useful role in industry." He held that full employment and planned improvement in the living and cultural standards of the masses must come about through the nationalization of banks, insurance companies, and other financial institutions, through the nationalization of key industries, and through agrarian reform achieved by "putting an end to the great landed estates, long a source of economic stagnation and political reaction."

Foster next reviewed the press and general publishing organizations that the Communist Parties had built up. In France he found fourteen dailies with circulation totaling one million, five hundred thousand — including the famous *l'Humanité* — and seventy-six weeklies with two-million circulation. In Italy he found fourteen Communist dailies including *l'Unità*. In Czechoslovakia the Party had the *Rude Právo,* four other dailies, eighteen political weeklies, and innumerable journals and bulletins for women, youth, children, peasants, and intellectuals. He found that the Communist Party Publishing House in Czechoslovakia had grown in two years in size larger than any "capitalist publishing outfit in all Europe." He saw "imposing and swiftly expanding presses" developed likewise under Red Army encouragement in Yugoslavia, Bulgaria, Rumania, Hungary, Albania.

Everywhere, Foster said, he discovered "the most brilliant and effective body of statesmen in Continental Europe" at the head of Communist Parties, *occupying at the same time important government posts.* "The European peoples," he concluded, "have been able to make a rational appraisal of the Communists." Their decision promoted the "vast growth of the Communist parties and of Communist governmental responsibility."

He reviewed the successes of the Communists and the left-wing Social Democrats in winning the co-operation of great Catholic masses in democratic efforts to break the coalition between religion and the Church-in-politics in their political struggles. "Europe," he concluded, "will not return to 'free enterprise.' To restore 'free enterprise' with all its reactionary influctions, as the United States is trying to do, would be to throw Europe into economic and political chaos. The answer to Europe's critical needs is not American money, bayonets, and puppet government. . . ."

How right Foster was in his estimate of Communist strength on the Continent presently appeared from the movement for a dollar-supported European Recovery Program, that administered by Paul Hoffman.

Foster was back in the United States when Secretary of State George Marshall, at Harvard University on June 5, 1947, defined the policy of the United States as "directed not against any country or doctrine but against hunger, poverty, desperation, and chaos." But Foster, as well as his Communists, from the outset openly opposed Marshall's economic recovery program. He stated forcefully that ECA would not facilitate the bringing about of European recovery, nor would it further the cause of peace and freedom. In Europe and America Communists developed immediate psychological and action programs designed to impair the success of any co-operative effort to achieve economic recovery in Europe.

The Soviet press had declared Secretary Marshall's proposal to be "an addition to the Truman Doctrine." On October 5, 1947, the central committees of nine European Communist Parties — those of the Soviet Union, Yugoslavia, Bulgaria, Rumania, Hungary, Poland, France, Czechoslovakia, and Italy — issued an official communiqué announcing the establishment of an Information Center, made up of representatives of their central committees, to exchange experience and co-ordinate activity on the basis of mutual agreement. The new information bureau, called the Cominform, first was at Belgrade, Yugoslavia. The Cominform forthwith issued a manifesto declaring the wartime unity of the Allies sundered because of divergent aims of the former partners. Two camps, said the Cominform, had emerged: "the camp of imperialism and antidemocratic forces" led by the United States, and an "anti-imperialistic democratic camp" led by the Soviet Union. The Cominform called the "Truman-Marshall Plan" a "European branch of the general world plan of political expansion being realized by the United States of America in all parts of the world."

So, believing their policy of a "divided world" now clearly affirmed, the Communists began aggressively to undermine the European Recovery Program. Foster declared that the "USSR will lend every effort to doom the Marshall Plan to failure." He described the United States policy as "pouring money down a rathole." He reiterated the well-defined position of the Soviet axis. "The Marshall Plan," he said, "is the master scheme of American imperialism for expansion and war." In his opinion, its purpose was to recruit allies among the countries of Western Europe for an anti-Soviet war. Its essence was the attempt of big corporations, "who rule both the Republican and Democratic Parties," to establish their own control over Europe, as a part of their larger scheme to dominate the entire world. "It is a war plan. Any degree of economic recovery that may take place because of its expenditures is entirely secondary to its basic war aims."

Thus, beginning in 1948, Foster collided head-on with America's action program to influence the destiny of Europe. Paul Hoffman and William Foster were now on opposite sides. Upon Hoffman's appointment as administrator of the Economic Co-operation Administration, Foster declared that the Studebaker president was "Wall Street's agent." As an answer to Hoffman's program, Foster said that the formation of the *Cominform* was the Continent's defense against the reconstruction of a "reactionary Europe." "Democratic America," he continued, "was placed by big business in the disgraceful position of being the main organizer of European reaction." Fascist-minded monopolists were determined to scatter the forces of democracy, and to defeat the growth of European socialism. Foster inventoried the anti-Communist axis: Wall Street imperialists, British imperialists, capitalist monopolists and big landlords all over Europe, the Vatican and its powerful Catholic parties in various countries, the fascist organizations and demobilized reactionary military officers in many lands, and the right-wing socialdemocrat parties and governments, particularly in Great Britain, France, Italy, and Germany. In fact the anti-Communist axis, as he blocked it out, included everybody who was not actively pro-Soviet. "The Wall Street offensive," said Foster, "must be beaten back to enable the United States to resume its forward march."

*   *   *

By late 1948, the climate of opinion in the United States had begun to change. The public became more aware of the world crisis and therefore less tolerant of Communist activity. As the 1948 national elections approached, Foster linked the struggle for peace with the mass movements designed to recognize the most pressing economic and democratic demands of the people. His theory was that the aggressive conspiracies "against the democratic peoples abroad" must be shown to be interconnected with the aggression against the people's democratic forces at home. The Communist strategy was opposition to "efforts of the trusts to militarize America" and to extend "armed bases and beachheads everywhere in the globe." "America's growing strength must be stopped if the American people are to receive butter and bread instead of guns and atom bombs," said Eugene Dennis, general secretary of the Communist Party U.S.A. A bridle had to be put on the "most rampant advocates of an American century of Wall Street imperialist expansion and catastrophe."

While the Communists were supporting Henry Wallace for President, the Department of Justice moved against the twelve members of the "American Politbureau." It indicted Foster and eleven other party leaders on charges of conspiracy to organize the Communist Party in 1945 to teach and advocate the overthrow and destruction of the Government of the United States by force and violence. The decisive point in the determination of the revolutionary intent of the Communist Party for purpose of criminal action by the United States was located in the year that Foster superseded Browder as the leader.

The Fourteenth National Convention of the Communist Party U.S.A. met during the summer of 1948 and approved a militant working-class plan for a "Communist M-day" devoted to "peace, democracy and social progress." Eugene Dennis, in an address delivered at Madison Square Garden in New York on September 23, 1948, on the occasion of the twenty-ninth anniversary of the founding of the American Communist Party, proposed that two days be set aside for "mobilization for democracy and peace" to correspond with the opening of the trial of the twelve members of the National Committee of the Communist Party U.S.A. on October 15.

In the meantime, Foster with Dennis had stated the American Communist position in the event of another war. They said:

> We Communists join with millions of other patriotic Americans in opposing those who seek a new world war. We strive for peace and friendship between the U.S.A., and the U.S.S.R., the new democracies, the colonials, and all other peoples. We do not regard a new world holocaust as inevitable. We hold the peaceful co-existence of two different social systems wholly possible. We believe the efforts of the peoples to achieve peace can check the war-makers and create new opportunities to achieve peace. The peace camp is infinitely stronger than the war camp.

An atmosphere, Foster felt, was rapidly being created in "our nation" that to work for peace and American-Soviet amity was considered equivalent to treason. The trial of the Communist leaders, the current witch-hunts, and other attacks on civil liberties were indicative, he said, of today's political climate. If, despite the efforts of the peace forces of America and the world, "Wall Street" should succeed in plunging the world into war, Communists would oppose it as an unjust, aggressive, imperialist war, as an undemocratic and an anti-Socialist war, destructive of the deepest interests of the American people and all humanity. Even as Lincoln while a Congressman opposed the unjust, annexationist Mexican War and demanded its termination, "so would we Communists," said Dennis, "co-operate with all democratic forces to defeat the predatory war aims of American imperialism and bring such a war to a speedy conclusion on the basis of a democratic peace."

> American security and American peace lie in world security and world peace — not in any Wall-Street-*Ueber-Alles* policy decked out in the trappings of the American century. For our part we will work with all those who seek peace, democracy, and social progress. The American people, assuming their historic responsibility, must reject the war policies of the Wall Street-Churchill cartelists and their bipartisan puppets and return our nation to the peace policies of Franklin D. Roosevelt, the "Grand Design" and cornerstone of which is firm American-Soviet friendship.

When the trial of the United States against Foster and the eleven other defendants opened in the United States courthouse on Foley Square in New York before Judge Harold R. Medina, Foster, one of the twelve defendants, was absent. He had been examined by four physicians selected by the court, and found too ill to endure a long and strenuous trial. For this reason his case was severed to await the improvement of his health and the strengthening of his heart action. It was allegedly the same heart which had given out in Moline, Illinois, sixteen years before. In Washington officials intimated that Foster might later be tried on a lesser charge. Communists familiar with Foster's condition said the government was afraid to put him on the stand because he might drop dead in the courtroom and thus become a martyr in Soviet history.

On October 15, 1949, Judge Medina, at the end of one of the longest criminal trials on record, found the eleven remaining defendants guilty of criminal conspiracy. Taking as their theme that "THE NEW CRIME IS THINKING," the Communists produced a stream of material related to the case. Eugene Dennis summed up the trial in a sixty-four-page booklet entitled *In Defense of Your Freedom.* Judge Norval K. Harris of Indiana, as co-chairman of the National Non-Partisan Committee to Defend the Rights of the Twelve Communist Leaders, with offices in Suite A, 23 West 26th Street, New York, produced a sixty-four-page brochure on *Due Process in a Political Trial.* Pamphlets for five cents, fifteen cents, and a quarter began to flood Communist book outlets. Elizabeth Gurley Flynn estimated that the trial cost the Communist Party two hundred and fifty thousand dollars for the defense of its leaders. The verdict, she said, was "just another affront to peace and to the United Nations Charter."

When, on August 12, 1950, Judge Thomas W. Swan, of the United States Court of Appeals, at the request of the government, issued an order directing the eleven Communist leaders to show cause why their appeal bonds should not be revoked leading to their immediate jailing, Foster, still suffering from his heart ailment, issued this statement: "Attorney General J. Howard McGrath has demanded that eleven Communist leaders be taken into 'protective custody' while their case is being appealed to the Supreme Court. Wall Street's government would nullify the rights to bail on the ground that these eleven men, if not jailed, 'forthwith' will make statements dangerous to the public welfare and national security of the United States. There is no precedent in American history for this sinister act. But there are plenty of precedents in the history of Hitler's terror rule."

The trial from which Foster was absent because of ill health cost the United States a million dollars. The testimony exceeded five million words and covered over twenty-one thousand, one hundred and fifty-seven pages.

While the defense was being bitterly conducted at the trial on Foley Square, Foster, approaching seventy and insisting that he was too ill to endure the courtroom strain as a result of the strange recurrence of his chronic heart ailment, had leisure to write as he rested in his modest three-room apartment in the Bronx. He took the opportunity of illness and its consequent exemption from prosecution to write articles, pamphlets, and books which exceeded in systematic sequence anything which he had previously done.

In July 1949 he issued a pamphlet entitled *In Defense of the Communist Party and Its Indicated Leaders.* "The Communist Party is American," he asserted.

We Communists love our vast and beautiful country. We cherish our great people with their splendid achievements in industry, in science, and in democracy. We revere, too, our flag, which has been gloriously carried through two revolutions and through the recent anti-Hitler war. We take second place to nobody in our devotion to the United States. The foundation principles of all Communist policy is to make ours a free, happier, and more prosperous nation. Whoever does not understand this high patriotic motive as the basis of our policy knows precisely nothing about the Communist Party in this country or anywhere else. We are flesh and blood of the American people and we reject with scorn the charges of reactionaries that we are "agents of a foreign power."

Pointing out that the Communist Party is a "working class and people's movement," that it is a "democratic movement," that it is "a peace-loving movement," and that it is "international," Foster said that it is also "revolutionary" because it proposes fundamental changes in America's basic economic system and in its "ruling classes." The establishment of socialism, he held, will complete, the cycle of revolution which the "United States and other countries are inevitably passing through in their advance from lower to higher stages of society. With the power of the capitalists finally eliminated and with socialism definitely established, the road will then be wide open for the peaceful evolution of society to its highest stage, communism. It is political chicanery to assert that they constitute a program of the forceful overthrow of the United States Government."

Foster followed this article with a systematic volume on *The Twilight of World Capitalism*. He dedicated the book to his great-grandson "Joseph Manley Kolko, who will live in a Communist United States." The volume was historical, autobiographical, and theoretical. It showed how the capitalistic world during Foster's life was being transformed by socialism. *The Twilight of Capitalism* expressed the orthodox position that the continuous growth of the socialist world was being furthered by the contradictions inherent in capitalism, such as: the deepening of the cyclical economic crisis, the intensification of the class struggle between the workers and the employees, the extension of the conflict between the capitalist empires and the colonial peoples, and the broadening wars among the capitalist empires themselves. "It will be a great day," he predicted, "when mankind can finally write 'The End' to the capitalist system."

> In the present world situation the United States can live up to its democratic traditions and be an influence for world peace and progress only if our people smash the power of the ruling capitalists, take control themselves and enter into genuinely fraternal relations with other peoples, particularly the U.S.S.R. The American people, with the workers in the lead, we may be confident, will not fail in the end to cleanse our nation and the world of the Wall Street warmongers and atom bomb firebrands.

Still confined to his Bronx apartment by his heart condition, Foster next published a long article in *Political Affairs* on "The Domination of the Capitalist World by the United States." "The United States," he said, "during the post-World War II years has succeeded in achieving a high degree of domination or hegemony over the capitalist world. This country has now reached a position where, arrogantly infringing upon the national independence of many other capitalist countries, it is able largely to dictate to them regarding major domestic and foreign policies. This is a situation unique in the history of world capitalism."

Foster then plunged into a theoretical discussion related to the events of the 1950's. Under the circumstances, he saw the task of the Communists in America "in the period of sharpening national and international struggle" to make the people understand the war-like, imperialist character of American policy, to protect the living standards of the workers, to defend the democratic rights of the Negro people and the toilers generally, and to crush the rising wave of fascism in the United States.

Foster welcomed the year 1951 with a huge *Outline Political History of the Americas.* Called by the International Publishers "a monumental work on the entire Western Hemisphere from the earliest times to the present day," the history presented with elaborate documentation an exhaustive Marxist analysis of the economic and political development of the Western Hemisphere from the earliest Indian settlements. "A general history of the Western Hemisphere as a whole," said Foster, "has become very much needed because of the growing attempt of the United States imperialism to reduce the entire hemisphere to the status of an armed, dominated, and thoroughly controlled Yankee hinterland." Once again Foster saw the developing general crisis, the decay of world capitalism, and the birth and growth of world socialism among three hundred million people who make up the many nations of North, Central, and South America.

No area for Marxian analysis could be more fertile for a Communist practitioner than the field of the Americas. "Under socialism," he concluded, "the exploitation of man by man is abolished and the toiling masses are at last free. It is a society without classes of robbers and robbed. The great historical process which has gone on in the Americas for more than four and a half centuries since Columbus landed in the West Indies does not lead to the fascist, Yankee-dominated world of Wall Street, but to the new free world of socialism."

Dipping his pen to complete the last paragraph of his volume, after almost seven decades of class struggle, Foster inscribed his valedictory with these words:

We are living in a great historical period, that of the replacement of capitalism by socialism. The advent of world socialism, now standing historically at our doors, will liberate man from his age-long slavery and open up before him a perspective of freedom, development, and happiness that he now hardly dares dream of. Before very long the capitalist system, with all its organized greed and violence, will only be a dark memory to man as he travels into a future that will realize the very best of which our species is capable.

In his Bronx apartment Foster completed still another huge manuscript recording the *History of the Communist Party in the United States,* and undertook to write still another major work on the Negro in the United States. Meanwhile, the government had struck still another blow at the party. On April 20, 1953, the Subversive Activities Control Board ordered the Communist Party U.S.A. to register with the Department of Justice as a Communist-action organization "nurtured by the Soviet Union" that seeks to overthrow the Government of the United States and to establish a dictatorship of the proletariat. The party was directed to file annually a list of officers and members and give a financial accounting. With Elizabeth Gurley Flynn and Pettis Perry, Foster at once declared that Communist Party members would not register and "rejected with contempt" the ruling that Communists are "foreign agents," as "slander." The National Committee appealed the ruling. In doing so Foster pointed out that "the foreign agent slander is nothing new in American life. It was hurled at Thomas Jefferson. It was employed against American Catholics when Al Smith ran for President. Today it is the weapon of McCarthyism and McCarranism, not only against the Communist Party but also against organized labor, the Negro people, and all other democratic forces in our country. It is the stock in trade of the pro-fascist forces that would destroy American democratic processes." "Of course the Communist Party is revolutionary," Foster admitted frankly. "When society takes a long step forward involving fundamental changes in its basic economic system and in its ruling classes, this is revolution." Hence socialism, which changes the productive system and abolishes capitalistic class rule, is revolutionary. "But let us not consider the word revolution as something foreign to us or frightening," he explained. "Advancing humanity has passed through a whole series of revolutions: from primitive tribal communism to slavery; from slavery to feudalism; from feudalism to capitalism. It is now beginning to pass from capitalism to socialism. Historically, this series of revolutions constitutes an upward spiral of progress."

The Communist Party, Foster argued, is internationally alert. "Communists have long understood what the American people are just now learning, namely, that all nations live in one world and that the various peoples must and can, in conformity with their deepest national interests, live in harmony and co-operation together." Most of all, continued Foster, the Communist movement is peace-loving. "Communists are the most level-headed and determined opponents of imperialist war. They are the most consistent in striving for the most peaceful line of social development possible under the given conditions. Yet they do not want peace at any price. If, in order to protect their liberties or to secure their just demands, they must fight, they will do so, and resolutely."

The global crusade for peace, said Foster, expresses the conviction of the Communists in all countries. Beginning with the establishment of the People's Republic of China, the outlook for peace improved. In the United States, the cultivation of opinion to favor the recognition of Mao's China joined with activities designed to support civil rights. The objective of the program, thus it seemed to Foster, was to maintain democratic freedoms at home and avoid disastrous war abroad. "The United States must be prevented from engulfing the rest of the world in a suicidal struggle from which the Soviet Union would emerge as the world leader." "World War I," he pointed out, "cost the capitalist system the one-sixth of the earth represented by Russia. World War II resulted in the expansion of the socialist world from the Elbe to the Pacific to include a third of the world's population. World War III will bring the end of the capitalist world." The "fantastic weapons" of the United States, based on "the picnic theory of a war against the Soviets" would not be sufficient for victory, he warned; in the long run he believed the superior ideological strength of socialism would more than make up for the illusory statistical advantage now apparently on the side of capitalism. According to Foster's figures, cited as from an Industrial College of the Armed Forces survey, World War III would cost the

United States four trillion dollars and would push the national debt up to over two trillion dollars. Each successive war since the Civil War, he said, had cost the United States ten times the expense of the previous conflict.

Immediately upon the outbreak of hostilities in Korea, Foster for the American Communists described Truman's purpose as "to conquer the peoples of Asia, to rob them of their natural resources, and to multiply the big business profits from a subjugated world." "Hands off Korea!" shouted the Party from its New York headquarters. "Demand the immediate withdrawal of the United States." "End the shipment of arms to the puppet Rhee government." "Not a cent, not a gun, not a plane for Wall Street's puppet regimes in Korea, Formosa, and Vietnam!" "Demand seating of the People's Republic of China in the United Nations and its recognition by the United States."

Upon the conclusion of a cease-fire agreement for Korea in the summer of 1953, Foster, joined by Elizabeth Gurley Flynn and Pettis Perry, issued a six-page statement for the national committee of the Communist Party of the United States, pointing out that the real credit for the armistice belonged to the North Korean and the Chinese armies which had fought to a standstill "the strongest armed forces that the capitalist world could bring against them." Even a full-scale war, wrote Foster, had not sufficed "to crush the North Koreans and to cow the Chinese." To Foster, Korea stood as a "bold warning to the world that the days are forever past when imperialists can trample roughshod upon the lives and liberties of colonial and semicolonial peoples."

As Foster settles back in an easy chair in his book-lined Bronx apartment, he gives the appearance of a retired university professor of philosophy, or a church deacon who has been especially interested in youth work. His love of books is quickly evident from the organization of his library as a workshop. With a pile of sharpened pencils, he writes and writes. Early in his career he determined to devote the first two hours of each day to his writing. He has followed this routine for more than half a century. As a result his literary production of books, pamphlets, and memorandums has been prolific. As an old railroad man, Foster has a conscientious regard for time. He organizes his time and operates on timetable schedule. He is always punctual — rarely early, never late. In writing his huge volume on the history of the Negro, he promised his publisher to deliver the copy on a schedule of a chapter a week. For fifty weeks he kept the schedule by delivering his manuscript on the same day at the same time. In carrying on his research work he has assistants bring him books from public libraries and from various specialized libraries. He meticulously extracts his notes and checks his material for accuracy of fact and citation. Although he may give an interpretation to facts which is completely different from capitalistic orientation, he is objective in insisting on being in possession of the facts. Mencken once said that Foster wrote with a literary style which distinguished him from all other labor authors. Although he has a wide vocabulary, he struggles against the use of what he calls "dictionary words."

While Foster is thus careful in written work, his public speech has always been extemporaneous. He scribbles his notes on an envelope, card, or scrap of paper, in an orderly outline; he delivers his ideas with simple clarity whether he is speaking from a soapbox, from the platform of Madison Square Garden, or from the lecture rostrum.

In personal habits Foster would pass for an old-fashioned Methodist. He neither smokes nor drinks. In 1912 he married Esther Abramovitch, a woman born in Lithuania; their relations have been congenial throughout the years. At every available opportunity Foster reads. In moments of complete relaxation he reads the classics and science — especially volumes dealing with new scientific developments. Close associates describe him as a "thoroughly disciplined" and "very modest" person. In visiting with him one finds he is quick to grasp ideas, direct, and courteous. To noncommunists he will often comment: "Your approach to many questions is so different from mine." He does not like to have his personal role discussed. "The movement," he says, "is the decisive matter." How differently he thinks can perhaps be seen from a comment on the execution of Julius and Ethel Rosenberg at the end of June 1953 on charges of transmitting atomic secrets to the Soviets. "The Rosenbergs," he said, "are truly heroic figures of our times. It was a shameful scandal the way the Government put to them the dreadful alternative of either act as stool pigeons or die. They rose to that situation, however, with unsurpassed courage. The America of today does not appreciate these brave people, of whom it should be very proud — but it will in all due season."

Since the outbreak of the Korean War in the summer of 1950, Foster has been particularly concerned with avoiding a world war by the application of Marx-Leninist principles to events. "We say," he explains, "that war is not inevitable. Our purpose is to prevent war. Communist leadership may already have stopped World War III. The age of atomaniac diplomacy was ushered in by the bomb dropped on Japan for the purpose of terrorizing the world. When atom-bomb diplomacy broke down, the United States had to shift back quickly to conventional warfare practices. For five major reasons we say that the United States policy is based on war. As the greatest monopoly power the United States must strive to dominate the whole world; war is a means to that end. Capitalism is already falling to pieces. Indeed the world is being held together at this moment by the dollar-dole and the rescue mission of 'American know-how.' The capitalists know that the United States cannot keep its industries in full production without armament production. Hence comes the armament race, the only outcome of which in the capitalist frame of reference is war. For the great productive period of American industry only large-scale preparation for war is responsible. The fantastic figures have no basis in reality. The huge output is leading to a smash-up. America is living in a fool's paradise. Our line is that capitalism has entered a general crisis. The capitalistic system is *kaput*. I say advisedly that the bosses who run America are damn fools. If the United States fights, it will be left by its allies to fight alone. A course leading to such isolation is insane. Under these conditions the workers must take over an exhausted and worn-out capitalism and reorganize society with new and vigorous socialism. Czechoslovakia is an example of what can happen."

On Foster's table in his apartment stands a beautiful Czechoslovakian vase. "What happened in Czechoslovakia," he says, "is this. The balance of parties in the parliament was very close. The American ambassador was so concerned with the comments of the Communist paper *Rude Právo* that he sent memorandums thirty-five times to the editors demanding retraction of misstatements. In fact, the American ambassador felt that the time had come for an American-engineered *coup d'état*. The opportunity came with the resignation of seventeen cabinet ministers. A cabinet reorganization excluding the Communists was to follow. The workers, however, had a different idea. They met in their factories, accepted the cabinet resignation, and assumed responsibility for operating the government. The only known casualty in the transition was one student who suffered a black eye. The establishment of a Communist government in Czechoslovakia was thus a perfectly legal and necessary activity."

As he worked on his manuscript for his book on *The Negro People in American History*, Foster had a clear frame of reference. "Our line," he says, "is that the Negro is an American but that he is a special kind of an American. Lenin was clear about the problem. Within the borders of the United States and under the jurisdiction of a single central government there exist not one but two nations. The first is a dominant white nation with its Anglo-Saxon heritage. The other is a subject black one of African origin. Under the pressure of the domination of the white nation, the black people have developed all the objective attributes of nationhood. Within America the Negro nation must have self-determination to be exercised by it whenever and however it sees fit to use this right. This does not necessarily mean setting up a Negro republic in the South. It does mean that the Negro can exercise his right to nationhood or not as he chooses. The important fact is that as a nation the Negro has the right to determine his own life. Surely there should be a breakup of the plantation system and a redistribution of land to the Negro farmer."

While Foster was somewhat restricted in his activities because of his indictment and the condition of his health, American Communists were severely handicapped in theirs by the government's program to hunt party members and fellow-travelers out of positions of responsibility. Leading members on the policy level were in jail or in hiding. It became increasingly difficult to obtain manuscripts for Communist journals, and somewhat hazardous to circulate them. The circulation of the *Daily Worker*, which in 1949 had been in New York City sixteen thousand, by the end of 1952 dropped to seven thousand. The circulation of the *Worker* Sunday edition in the same period had fallen in New York State from forty-four thousand copies to under sixteen thousand. Comrades abandoned their newspaper routes. By the spring of 1953 the Negro membership in the party had declined to its lowest point since 1937. In four years, Puerto Rican membership in New York City fell 400 per cent. Because of ineffective youth work, three out of five members in New York were between the ages of 35 and 48. In community organization between 75 and 90 per cent of the active workers were women. Work among the farmers had almost come to a stop. Comrades in New York resisted reassignment from community groups to midtown industrial sections where party policy felt them more needed.

Under these circumstances the party had to develop a new strategy. For fifteen years, party members had been trained to organize and lead "left-led" Communist fronts and mass demonstrations. Now the reliable veteran corps of active Communists was reoriented to perform its decisive work inside "right-led" organizations. The new line meant a shift of large numbers of comrades to heavy industry and to functional clubs of housewives, writers, painters, doctors, lawyers, and teachers. The objective of Communist strategy was to make every factory a "stronghold for peace." Workers in every shop were to play a determined role in the "fight to save humanity from imperialist slaughter." This approach demanded the training of new cadres in basic industries. The main base of Communist operations returned to "the shop," where it originally had been carried on.

To strengthen their own ranks the Communists set up some goals for themselves. Every member was to pay his dues, accept assignment to a particular club, to buy and read the *Daily Worker* and the Sunday *Worker* and to stand ready to organize route clubs for the systematic delivery of the papers to subscribers.

As party chairman, Foster felt that the greatest Communist weakness in the United States was the lack of "systematic theoretical work." The mastery of the "line" of Marx-Leninism, to Foster, was a condition for the success of Communist activity at any level. He was not worried about being driven underground. "Why should

I be?" he said. "In Brazil the Communist Party is outlawed yet from its underground it rises as the strongest political influence in the country. It is only by systematic theoretical training that Communists can have a clear policy. We do not fear difficulty."

While Foster can begin a discussion at any point, sooner or later he brings it down to "fundamentals." "We say," Foster explains, "that the economics and politics of the capitalistic system are crazy. In desperation a bewildered man will do all kinds of illogical and insane things. . . . Think," says Foster, "of the gains which the worker has achieved in my lifetime — strong labor unions, a homeland of socialism in the Soviet Union, a third of the world Communist, and capitalism in global disintegration. From my experience I know that these gains have been made because of the application of the doctrines of scientific socialism as stated by Marx and Lenin. I am proud to have been a part of these developments. Every man to be effective must have a policy for his life. A man must have principles and stick to them. He must recognize fundamentals. In living up to the principles of Marx-Leninism, the Communist Party of the United States will one day lead the American working class and the nation, even as it is now the best representative of their interests. All the powers of arrogant capitalist reaction cannot balk the C.P.U.S.A. from fulfilling its historic role."

III

Alfred P. Sloan, Jr.
Chairman of the Board, General Motors Corporation

Technological Outreach to Abundance

ALFRED P. SLOAN, JR.

"The direction is always up — more things for more people in more places — a better standard of living everywhere."

ALFRED P. SLOAN, JR., SAYS:

IN OUR CONTEMPORARY SOCIETY of advanced technology the objective of industry is to produce more things for more people in more places at lower prices with better quality. Thanks to the resourcefulness of the scientist, the inventor, and the engineer, an ascending standard of living results from the continued advance in technology and in efficient work. No other way exists to increase the real income of people and to provide the economic well-being of mankind. The catalytic agents which make continued progress possible are basic knowledge, hard work, and the expectation of profits judged with an equitable concern for all the groups which combine their resources in the productive process. ⋙By the nature of its operation modern industry is big and complex. The technological outreach to abundance negates the premises of an outgrown economic system based on limited markets, restricted rate of growth, little product diversification, and resistance to technological improvement. It affirms the conditions which support basic and applied scientific research, encourage engineering ingenuity, utilize managerial brains, and direct capital investment wisely. ⋙A great industrial organization requires the best of many excellent minds. Hence modern industry concerns itself with the education of promising youth and collaborates closely with colleges, universities, and technological schools. As a continuous stream of competent, aggressive young men flows into industry, a policy which provides for a wide distribution of responsibility develops the talents of men in the stimulating environment of competition. ⋙In its obligation to exact from each dollar its maximum return, management carries on an unending search for facts on which to base business decisions. It must analyze these facts with an open mind, without prejudice, and without the censorship of the dead hand of the past.

From business decisions thus deliberately arrived at come sound policies, reliable products, profitable activity, public confidence, and national wealth. Customers benefit from lower prices. Labor benefits from higher wages. Investors benefit from fair and steady dividends. Management benefits by the identification of its own interests with the prosperity of the corporation. ◆§In its thinking a great *corporation must respect the economic formula that production is equal to consumption plus active savings. It must exercise economic statesmanship and encourage a steady and increasing flow of spending, for the purchase of the products of industry depends upon steady and widespread consumption. The fundamental task before our country is so to manage its economic affairs as to demonstrate the basic truth that economic accomplishment and human happiness exist to the extent that men are permitted to exercise their initiative, their imagination, and their leadership in the atmosphere of a free society. In an industrialized democracy there is no place for economic illiteracy or political apathy.* ◆§Mass production takes place in a *modern society where the distances between minds have widened in complex and bewildering ways. To provide for understanding among its managers, its workers, its shareholders, its dealers, its customers, and its general public, the modern corporation must provide information through all media of communication. By the free flow of facts about its operations and its products, the modern corporation maintains faith in the integrity of its purposes and the quality of its output. In industry conducted according to this pattern lies a wonderful future and a promise for America beyond the dreams of any man now alive.*

◆§ §◆

Technological Outreach
to Abundance

ONE TWILIGHT IN 1895 A YOUNG MAN JUST GRADUATED
from Massachusetts Institute of Technology entered the offices of
Bennett, Sloan & Company at 100 Hudson Street, Manhattan. The
proprietor arose from his desk and accompanied the thin six-foot
salesman to the loft. The two walked between coffee roasters, blend-
ing machines, and belt conveyors. In a corner the coffee dealer
paused for a conference. "Well," he said to his visitor, "do you think
I can save any money by using roller bearings in my business?"

The young man opened an envelope which he carried under his
arm and produced carefully prepared statistical estimates to support
his answer to the question. He proceeded to demonstrate exactly
how many dollars and cents the coffee concern could save by in-
stalling the product of the Hyatt Roller Bearing Company. With his
pencil he underlined how such savings would justify the business
decision. In his discussion, the engineer pointed out how much
money is lost through friction.

That evening Alfred P. Sloan, Jr., completed his first sale; he
took an order from his father for a hundred and fifty dollars' worth
of roller bearings. While the permanence of his job pretty much depended upon completing that sale, the method by which Alfred
took the order exhibited a standard procedure which was to
characterize his whole distinguished career. He relied on facts
for guidance in determining the profitability of a business decision.

To this point in his career, Sloan had enjoyed the happy life of a
representative American family. The eldest of five children — four
brothers and a sister — he was born in New Haven as a Connecticut
Yankee. When he was ten, his family moved to Brooklyn. There he

lived in a brownstone front house identified, among all the others like it in the row on Garfield Place, by the number 240 on the door. His mother was the daughter of a Methodist Episcopal clergyman, his father the son of a private schoolmaster. Mr. Sloan, Sr., maintained his family in easy circumstances and generally employed a servant to do the cooking.

At the age of eleven Alfred entered the Brooklyn Polytechnic Institute to study mechanics and engineering. Upon graduation he proceeded to Massachusetts Institute of Technology. In Boston he devoted himself to his studies with such determination that he described himself as a "grind." He completed his course a year ahead of his class. Equipped with the degree of bachelor of science in electricity and labeled an M.I.T. man, he traveled to New York "to seek a position," as hunting a job was called in those days. Being shy by nature and conscientious in every duty, he was pained to experience the rebuff of the labor market. Day after day he beat his way from employer to employer only to be told over and over that "no openings" existed.

Sloan knew that the times had been hard. Economic reports of the depression of 1893 were still vivid in his mind. As a student in Boston he had followed the news accounts of Coxey's Army, as it marched out of the West on Washington. He was familiar with the preachings of William Jennings Bryan on the need for cheap money to stimulate business. Now he was learning from office door to office door, firsthand, the difficulty of finding a job even when paternal influence is brought to bear at management level through such an influential person as the president of the American Sugar Refining Company. When at last he found a job, it was not in electrical engineering but as a draftsman employed by Hyatt Roller Bearing Company, founded by John Wesley Hyatt, who was the inventor of celluloid and the roller bearing.

Hyatt was one of the many practical inventors of the age who, though practically illiterate in science, carried on experiments in sheds, attics, and blacksmith shops until by patient manipulation and sudden hunches they produced a gadget which sometimes made them rich. These "practical mechanics" played by ear. Often they created remarkable devices without necessarily understanding the principles behind their operation.

Employed at Hyatt, Sloan exerted himself under the urge of a very special incentive: he was impatient to get married. He doubted that his salary of fifty dollars a month would satisfactorily support a new household. With one eye upon his love and the other on industrial advancement, he studied the Hyatt operations as they were conducted in an overgrown barn. As he figured out the situation, the business seemed so inefficiently managed that he felt he would be compelled to look elsewhere for a career. At the factory every pay day precipitated a new crisis. To protect his future and to hasten the time when he could marry, Sloan decided to launch an enterprise of his own. He quit Hyatt to set up a partnership with a lieutenant from the Naval Academy, to manufacture and install "mechanical iceboxes" in apartment houses and hotels. Quite properly, the new concern was named the Hygienic Refrigerator Company.

In New York the partners sold two units and then took a contract in Boston to provide refrigerating equipment and apparatus to circulate ice water for a hotel near the Copley Plaza. Since this transaction gave Sloan a new hope for prosperity, he married in the summer of 1898 Miss Irene Jackson of Roxbury, Massachusetts, a friend of his student days. While the marriage was a permanent success Hygienic was not. The refrigerating machinery, producing "too much cold," wore itself out quickly. Sloan and his partner were faced with the expense of replacing the units they had installed. At this point the lieutenant died and the firm liquidated its interests.

Looking for a job again, Sloan returned to the Hyatt Roller Bearing Company at a salary of one hundred and seventy-five dollars a month. While he had been promoting the Hygienic Refrigerator Company, Sloan's father had bought an interest in Hyatt to save it from bankruptcy. During Alfred's absence, the Hyatt plant had been moved to Harrison, New Jersey. Back at his old job Sloan promptly found opportunity to shoulder new responsibility. Working beside a Norwegian-born bookkeeper, Peter Steenstrup, Sloan put in nine or ten hours a day, six days a week. The two ambitious young men made the business their whole life. They took no recreation, pursued no hobbies, enjoyed no leisure, and felt the need for no relaxation. Together they were soon actually running the business. Steenstrup assumed the title of sales manager; Sloan classified himself as general manager. At the end of the first six months of the operation, under the informal management of "Sloan and Steen-strup," Hyatt earned a profit of twelve thousand dollars. Despite this good showing, the company was constantly short of working capital. One reason for this situation was that the managers kept investing earnings in the growth of the concern. Being thus too successful in relation to its resources, Hyatt continued to face weekly pay-day crises.

While the company was struggling with its problems, Hyatt stood on the threshold of the new age of the motor car. Unexpectedly, one morning in 1899, the postman delivered a letter at the plant written by a man named Elwood Haynes and postmarked Kokomo, Indiana. The Hoosier inquired about the use of roller bearings in the manufacture of horseless carriages. Sales Manager Steenstrup took the next train West and came back with an order. This experience set Sloan to thinking: perhaps the horseless carriage, classified at the moment both as an impractical toy and a dangerous nuisance, might create a new market for anti-friction bearings. . . . The question in his mind was soon answered by the trend in events.

An enthusiasm for manufacturing automobiles began to spread, as Sloan remembers, "like wildfire" or "like a gold rush." To establish technical facts to guide him in producing bearings for the new market, Sloan decided to conduct a kind of Yankee research. He bought a vehicle, proposed to take it to pieces, to conduct experiments with the parts, to design and engineer the kind of article the new industry demanded, and to come out with plans to promote the use of roller bearings in the infant industry. To obtain his "guinea pig" car, Sloan attended the 1903 New York automobile show. Going down the exhibits he passed quickly by the "one-lunged Cadillac" and the Oldsmobile, to discover a fancy vehicle named the "Conrad." It was manufactured in Buffalo by the Conrad Motor Carriage Company. As displayed, the machine was a handsome maroon affair. The exhibitor called the color "automobile red." The car was equipped with patent-leather mudguards, red leather seats, artillery wheels, chain drive, and an entrance door in the back. Sloan liked the Conrad's style; he bought it by barter. For the list price of twelve hundred and fifty dollars free-on-board in Buffalo, he exchanged a supply of Hyatt roller bearings.

When Sloan pulled off the "bonnet," as the hood in those days was called, he discovered to his concern that the "Conrad" lacked an engine. Sloan's only reason for buying the vehicle had been to possess an engine to dismantle and study! Sensing Sloan's disappointment, the salesman began to stroke the red paint tenderly. "The truth is, Mr. Sloan," he said, "we really haven't built the engine yet, but the design is right. Mechanical engineers and automobile experts in this country and in Europe have pronounced it correct." Days later Conrad delivered the engine to the Hyatt factory. The sight of it provoked Alfred to profanity.

"The thing taught me to swear!" he said. "For all my technical education I could not make it run." When other machinists in the shop failed to start it, Sloan wired the Conrad Motor Carriage Company. On the next day Mr. Conrad's son arrived from Buffalo. He was a sporty young man, handsomely dressed with a silk handkerchief in his breast pocket. Young Conrad examined the engine, took the handkerchief from his pocket, stuffed it into the carburetor, and cranked. The engine fired, shook, and began to run. Conrad bowed, left his silk handkerchief with Sloan, and caught the afternoon train back to Buffalo.

Steenstrup parked the vehicle for safekeeping in the back yard of his apartment. There the smoking and belching engine outraged the neighbors. They reported Steenstrup to the police. He was promptly summoned to court on charges of maintaining a nuisance. In a phrase characteristic of desperate motorists of the day, Steenstrup declared that he "would sell the damned thing for a dollar!" In fact he did promptly sell it for that nominal sum. Soon angered by the Conrad's performance, the new purchaser drew it to a Newark meadow and actually blew it up with dynamite.

It was from Cadillac, not from Conrad, that Sloan learned his first lesson about supplying roller bearings to the new industry. "Mr. Sloan," said Henry M. Leland, Cadillac's general manager, "Cadillacs are made to run, not just to sell." Presently Sloan discovered the full import of Leland's comment. He was sitting with Leland in the Cadillac plant in Detroit. On Leland's desk he noticed some Hyatt roller bearings. In his hand Leland held a very disconcerting micrometer. He had been measuring the bearings to establish variances from agreed tolerances. "Your Mr. Steenstrup," Leland began, "told me that these bearings would be accurate, one exactly like another, to within one thousandth of an inch. But look here!" He tapped a fingernail against a guilty bearing. "There is nothing like uniformity." Henry Leland insisted on precision. He continued: "You must grind your bearings, Mr. Sloan. Even though you manufacture thousands of them, the first and the last must be precisely alike."

Sloan was quick to see the point. Unless Hyatt met Leland's standards, Cadillac's business was out. In the shop Sloan and Leland discussed the importance of precision in providing for the interchangeability of parts. The visit oriented Sloan to a new concept in manufacturing. "From that conversation," he says of the incident, "a genuine conception of what mass production should mean grew within me. I was an engineer and a manufacturer. I considered myself conscientious. But after I had said good-by to Mr. Leland I began to see things differently. I was determined to be as fanatical as he in obtaining precision in our work. That conversation established an entirely different standard for Hyatt Roller Bearings!"

Shortly after this visit Leland provided a vivid public demonstration of what he meant by precision manufacture to guarantee the *interchangeability of parts.* In London officials of the Royal Automobile Club drove three Cadillacs from dockside, disassembled them, and jumbled the parts in a pile. Then Cadillac mechanics with wrenches, screwdrivers, hammers, and pliers quickly assembled three Cadillac automobiles and sent them speeding on a five-hundred-mile track test. All cars finished with a perfect score!

Sloan's mind was now becoming increasingly clear about the fundamental principle which lay at the heart of the motor-car age. He saw that a firm, to be successful in the manufacture of automobiles, must produce large quantities of parts, each one just like the other with only a predetermined allowance for inaccuracy. Precise craftsmanship was a condition of industrial leadership. "This conception," said Sloan, "lies at the heart of the American predominance in the methods of mass production. It is a definitely American approach." Sloan understood this system and his company prospered as he built his manufacturing program to meet the demands of the automobile industry.

Sloan's close associate, Peter Steenstrup, felt that the situation was too favorable to last. As he saw it, people just could not continue to buy automobiles at the rate they had been purchasing them!

One day in 1909, Sloan and Steenstrup were eating strawberry shortcake in a Newark café. The Norwegian opened up an earnest business conversation. He had come to the conclusion, he said, that the vehicle market had reached the saturation point. He suggested that he would like to get out of the frantic business before the bubble collapsed. He proposed to sell his share in Hyatt to Sloan, and to move to Oregon to raise apples. Somehow he had the feeling that a fruit orchard would provide a substantial, safe, and steady business with a future. He had a hunch that he would be earning a living long after Hyatt had gone bankrupt for want of a market for its bearings.

When Steenstrup left Harrison for the Pacific Coast, Hyatt lost its sales manager. Sloan felt himself quite unfitted to do the promotion work in the way in which Pete had performed it. For one reason, he did not drink liquor. For another, the camaraderie which made three o'clock in the morning quite as enjoyable to Salesman Pete Steenstrup as three o'clock in the afternoon was alien to Sloan's nature. Sloan, having no choice but to step into promotion and sales, knew that if he was to carry forward a successful program, he had to develop a way of selling which was natural to his way of operating and to his character. He ruled out the "good fellow" approach and decided to merchandise roller bearings purely because they were a good product priced right and because they performed to the advantage of the purchaser. Sloan proceeded to build the Hyatt sales appeal solidly on the foundation of scientific fact. Whatever success other companies might have enjoyed in selling their products by the whisky-and-soda and night club technique did not belong to Alfred P. Sloan, Jr., proprietor of Hyatt Roller Bearing Company. He talked facts — hard, bloodless, scientific, business facts on which men could base business decisions concerning possible profits. He introduced a new quality into salesmanship. To provide data for this new kind of merchandising, he required an organization in Detroit which could perform reliable research. From the young General Motors Company, Sloan purchased a site for Hyatt on which to construct an engineering "staff" laboratory. Research was by now an integral part of Sloan's concept of the industrial age.

Roller bearings, however, were just one of the many parts of an automobile. Other suppliers like Hyatt were springing up to meet the demand for parts to be assembled into cars. New inventions kept appearing; factories opened to produce them. Four examples will illustrate what was happening.

Ben Briscoe was a tinsmith who mended pots and pans or made things to order out of sheet metal for a Detroit hardware store. Presently his specialty had grown into an industry employing twelve hundred men and producing kerosene oil cans, washtubs, pails, and garbage drums. One day two men by the name of R. E. Olds and John D. Maxwell came into Briscoe's factory with a collection of brass tubes which at first glance looked like a small calliope. "These pipes," said Maxwell, "cool water that circulates around the head of a gasoline engine." In a short time Briscoe was producing radiators for motor cars! "In addition," Maxwell continued, "we need a lot more stuff such as seats, tanks, and fenders." Briscoe took a hundred thousand dollars' worth of orders and within a decade had developed as one of the important figures in the automobile industry.

One of the customers of Briscoe's galvanizing plant was the Buick & Sherwood Manufacturing Company, a Detroit firm which manufactured bathroom fixtures. In keeping with the spirit of the decade Buick and Sherwood sold out its plumbing supply business to engage in the manufacture of gasoline marine motors adapted for farm use. When David Buick found himself unable to meet his accounts payable, he went to Briscoe. "Ben," he said, "I can't pay you. I've been making an automobile engine on the side. It has cost me more than I expected. It operates on a new principle." Buick proceeded to show his creditor a "valve-in-the-head" engine. Sensitive to the possibilities in the invention, Briscoe advanced Buick a thousand dollars and departed for a four months' trip to Europe. Before he left Detroit, however, he arranged for Buick to associate himself with the Flint Wagon Works. From this relationship the Buick Motor Car Company emerged.

The story of the growth of the Fisher body business was still another epic of the times. The senior Fisher operated a shop in Norwalk, Ohio, where he shoed horses, repaired carriages, and performed whatever wood or metal work needed to be done in town. His sons, born over a period of twenty-four years so that the eldest had left home before the youngest was born, learned to handle tools as soon as they could toddle. At seventeen the first son, Fred, apprenticed to his father and then left home for wider experience. In big cities he attended night school. To strengthen his mathematics he enrolled in a correspondence course. He accepted employment only in shops which had a reputation for superior craftsmanship, for he had no intention of associating with people who made what he broadly classified as "trash." While one after another of the Fisher boys grew up to be superb craftsmen, Fred located in Detroit. Soon he became the chief designer of the Wilson Body Company. In a few months he advanced to the office of general manager. His brother Charles, a skilled blacksmith, followed him to the Michigan plant. One by one the brothers congregated together until seven of them were operating as partners with the now familiar trademark "Body by Fisher."

Or to take still another example: An Ohio farm boy by the name of Charles F. Kettering was graduated from Ohio State University, Columbus, at the age of twenty-eight. He began work as an installation man for the Star Telephone Company in Ashland, Ohio. "Ket" had the habit of dreaming ahead. As accounting controls took on a new importance with the growth of business in size and complexity, Kettering foresaw a vast market for cash registers. Presently he headed the invention department of the National Cash Register Company. In this position he developed and patented many new ideas. In 1911 he organized the Dayton Engineering Laboratories Company, known as "Delco," to conduct research and develop products. Among other ideas Kettering was working on a hunch that automobile drivers soon would rebel against the inconvenience and hazards of cranking an engine. As he said, the starting of an engine by hand required the strength of Ajax, the cunning of Ulysses, and the speed of Hermes. Ulysses had to adjust the spark and throttle just right; Ajax had to turn the engine over, often many times. Hermes had to dart back and forth like a flash to advance the spark and regulate the gas before the engine went dead again. In the ordeal of starting their cars, drivers gashed their heads, broke their wrists, and sometimes were run over by vehicles which, left in gear, charged ahead when the engine fired. When one of Kettering's close friends was killed in a cranking accident, he decided that the time had come to put an end to the hazard. He decided to produce a reliable electric self-starter. In his developmental work, however, he experienced a series of obstacles which he came to recognize as a pattern of old mind-sets which choked new ideas to early death. Chief among these obstacles was what he labeled for the rest of his life "the closed mind." People began to tell Kettering why an electric self-starter was an impossible invention. Battery manufacturers branded his idea as absurd because they had never built a battery strong enough to turn a motor over. Electric motor manufacturers swore that no unit could be produced in small size with strength enough to crank the engine. Automobile manufacturers re- used to install starters as standard equipment because they were ure that the energy requirements of the motor would soon exhaust the battery. "Everybody," said Kettering, "accepted his frame of reference derived from the past as the final verdict on the future."

A fatal accident finally broke the dead hand of the past and opened up a market for Kettering's new product. An elderly friend of Henry M. Leland was driving a Cadillac over Belle Island bridge in Detroit when the motor stalled. Neglecting to throw the machine out of gear, the driver climbed out and began to crank. As the motor started, the car charged forward and crushed the man. So great was Leland's grief that he asked Kettering to supply Cadillac with electric self-starters. In 1911 Cadillac installed Delco electric self-starters, Delco lighting, and Delco ignition as standard equipment. From that moment Kettering became the high priest of a cult of research which tackled "it-can't-be-done" problems and did them. Like Hyatt and Fisher, Delco became an important supplier to the motor car industry.

While he watched the development of these wings of automobile manufacturing, Sloan was learning a basic lesson in production economics from Henry Ford, the hard way. The principle was this: In an industry where precision craftsmanship makes possible the standardization and interchangeability of parts, mass production makes possible the manufacture of more and better goods at lower prices. In other words, volume production justifies the use of machines and methods which under more limited conditions would be impossible. Mass production, Sloan discovered from Ford, makes possible a more profitable relationship between variable and fixed expenses, enables a manufacturer to reduce costs, to lower his selling price, and to improve his quality. Ford organized this principle at the assembly line. To increase volume still further to lower price, Ford standardized. "The customer can have a car of any color he likes so long as it is black," Ford ruled. Ford statistics soon showed how his theory worked in practice. In 1909 Henry sold 98,664 cars at 950 dollars each. By 1917 he was manufacturing 785,432 cars and selling them at 360 dollars. Volume production, higher quality, lower prices, higher wages — this seemed to Sloan to be the pattern of the new industrial society: more and better things for more people in more places.

Sloan first realized the full significance of the pattern when Harold Wills of the Ford Motor Company suggested to him that the increased production of Ford automobiles, which created a greater demand for Hyatt roller bearings, ought to be reflected in Sloan's quotation of a lower price. Sloan at once felt the pinch: the "suggestion" of Wills was actually a threat. It was the iron hand in a silk glove. During the previous year Ford had taken 65 per cent of Hyatt's annual production. Now Sloan realized that unless he reduced the price of bearings to Ford, he faced the possibility of losing the entire Ford outlet. But how was he to cut production costs to enable him to sell bearings at a lower price? He knew that he should not reduce wages. Savings had to come in economies achieved through better management, better methods, better engineering, and better machines. Presently, Sloan came back to Wills with what he had felt was an impossible answer. He offered Hyatt bearings at a lower price.

It was at this point in his career that Sloan caught the spirit of success in the era of the "new industry." The formula for growth, he clearly saw, demanded a constant improvement in engineering and manufacturing methods, and a constant lowering of price or improvement in quality — or both — to reach an ever-enlarging market. To succeed in the new age a concern needed research, engineering, design, and accounting control.

These were great days for Sloan. Everywhere the automobile business was booming. Demand was a feverish fact. Production could not keep pace with the clamor for motor cars. The demand was so overwhelming that fifteen hundred distinct species of automobiles came on the market. "In world history," Sloan commented, "there is no record to compare with the production effort in motor car development. Humanity never wanted any machine as much as it desired this one." With the expansion of the automobile industry, Hyatt sales soared. People clamored for cars — more cars. Up, up went the demand. The pressure on production became terrific.

Despite his own phenomenal success Sloan nevertheless was worried. His fear was not like that which had consumed Pete Steenstrup — that the industry was reaching a saturation point. What worried Sloan personally was the fact that Hyatt's entire production flowed to two gigantic customers — Ford and General Motors. Suppose one or the other or both should decide to manufacture their own bearings? Then Hyatt would find itself with a plant far bigger than it could use, and it would have no other outlets for its production. Under such a circumstance what would happen to Hyatt? This was the possibility which preyed on Sloan's enjoyment of his evident prosperity. He had put his whole life energy and personal savings into Hyatt's development. Everything he owned was in bricks, machinery, and materials. As Sloan studied into the situation which worried him, he recognized that other suppliers stood in the same precarious position. He began to wonder whether some form of integration might not be worked out, according to which products might be co-ordinated within an omnibus corporation rather than through market competition.

While the specter was haunting Sloan's life and he was worrying about the precarious position of the independent supplier, William C. Durant invited him to lunch. As Sloan prepared to go to the meeting that noon, he was hoping against hope that Durant would make him an offer to buy Hyatt. He walked out of the plant toward the restaurant, remembering that during the previous three years, four fifths of Hyatt's great plant of three quarters of a million square feet of floor space had been constructed. He thought with pride of Hyatt's own fire department with its three-thousand-gallon water reservoir. Yet in his mind he felt that Hyatt faced a hazard far more serious than fire. The means for eliminating the hazard of the independent supplier, Sloan began to see, lay in the organization and integration of industry.

In his mind Sloan reviewed his situation. To enable him to lower prices, he had introduced into his operations all the methods he could devise. More than nine out of ten of his men were employed on piece work; the more they produced, the more they earned. His accountants had instituted effective cost controls. His chemists and metallurgists were applying their science to the improvement of quality, the maintenance of precision standards, and the simplification of operations. Every manufacturing step, from the arrival of the raw material to the production of anti-frictional bearings, was checked by technical tests. His three merchandising divisions were promoting the sale of bearings for coal-mine cars and shaftings, tractors, and motor cars. On his payroll he had four thousand men and he was planning to add more, and yet Sloan was pursued by that haunting fear that somehow Hyatt's position was not secure; the company did not stand in close enough corporate relationship to its manufacturing outlets. . . . Such were the thoughts which sped through his mind as he went to the luncheon.

The moment he shook hands with Durant, he knew that he was in the presence of an operator who possessed imagination and courage — perhaps often too much of both qualities. Durant possessed two well-known strengths: he believed in the future of the automobile industry and he knew how to manipulate corporate and market finances to make things happen. When for example as a result of his deals he was forced out of General Motors, he set to work to organize a new company known as the Chevrolet Motor Company to produce a low-priced car designed by a French racing driver. Upon the organization of this concern, Durant placed Chevrolet stock on the market, saw to it that the price of the shares began to climb, and at the proper time offered General Motors stockholders the opportunity to exchange one share of General Motors stock for five shares of Chevrolet. The exchange meant certain profit to General Motors shareholders. Within four years after he set this operation in motion, Durant was back in office as president of General Motors.

As Sloan sat down to lunch with Durant, he saw that Durant was operating as the spokesman for the Durant-Kaufman syndicate, whose object was to form an omnibus corporation to be known as United Motors. Under the protecting wings of this organization, Durant proposed to combine a group of firms such as Hyatt, Delco, New Departure, Remy Electric, and Jaxon Steel. Durant came quickly to the point in the luncheon conversation. He wanted to buy Hyatt Roller Bearing Company. What was the price? Sloan knew that Durant was not a man to quibble about dollars when he had an object in mind. He felt that the selling price of a company should be determined by its profit potentiality. After discussion which continued for many days, Durant and Sloan agreed on a sum of thirteen million, five hundred thousand dollars.

With the sale of Hyatt to United Motors, Alfred P. Sloan, Jr., began a new stage of his life. He had accepted half-payment for his share in Hyatt by a transfer of United Motors stock; he became president. So intent was Sloan on making the new operation a success that he increased his stock holdings as fast as he could. Presently he found himself in the possession of a great deal of stock and a very little cash. Sloan, however, was no longer worried. He had glimpsed the future lying ahead in the motor car industry; he never for a moment lost that vision. For the rest of his life he remained unconcerned about stock market prices. Speculations held no attraction for him. He believed in the future of America and the technological outreach of industry. To him business provided the opportunity for the exercise of management talent; the true value of an enterprise lay in its operations, not in the stock market quotations.

In United Motors Durant and Sloan worked closely side by side, Sloan as president and Durant as chairman of the board. In the back of his mind Sloan suspected that Durant was at work on a scheme to join United Motors with General Motors, so that General Motors would include the various producers whose items were essential to the manufacture of a *complete* automobile. In due time the merger was completed, United Motors was liquidated, and on November 7, 1918, Sloan became a director of General Motors. Six weeks later he advanced to the office of vice-president.

Despite their close association and mutual esteem, Sloan and Durant had very different habits of working. Their fundamental difference lay in the way they arrived at decisions. Durant came quickly to conclusions, often before he had made a comprehensive analysis of all the facts. He operated with uncanny flashes of insight, acted on hunches, often achieved brilliant performances, and often made costly errors. Sloan was convinced that General Motors had become too big to operate as a "one-man show." He thought that Durant operated a good deal of the time like a dictator. "Dictatorship," said Sloan, "is the most effective way of administration provided the dictator knows the complete answers to all the questions. But he never does and he never will. That is why dictatorship eventually fails."

By this time it was clear to Sloan that if General Motors was going to capitalize on its historic opportunity, the industry would have to be guided by an organization of intellects. Then and there he set it down as an operating principle that a "great industrial organization requires the best of many excellent minds." If Sloan was going to stay with General Motors, he proposed to find a way to discover and to capitalize on the resources of superior ability.

While Sloan was trying to think through what kind of administrative organization would produce the best results for a big and dynamic corporation, Durant came forward with a proposal for extending operations into a field beyond the manufacture of motor cars. One day two boys came to Detroit to urge Durant to rescue their father from a venture which threatened to ruin him. Their father, they said, was trying to manufacture and sell small household electric refrigerators. Sloan knew something about this field; he had manufactured mechanical cooling equipment soon after he was graduated from M.I.T. Now he found Durant overwhelmed with an uncontrollable enthusiasm. "Next to the automobile," predicted Durant, "this is the greatest thing that could be put on the market." He proceeded to conduct a prize contest to name the new product. The winning name was "Frigidaire."

In the summer of 1919 General Motors stockholders authorized the corporation to increase its stock to provide capital for physical expansion. General Motors proceeded to absorb into its organization along with a controlling interest in Fisher Body, such companies as International Arms and Fuse Company, T. W. Warner & Company, gear makers, Pontiac Body Company, and Dayton-Wright Airplane Company.

In many ways the year 1919 may be considered as the beginning of the automobile age. It marked the passing of the linen duster, visored cap, and goggles. It ushered in the greatest car-and-highway building age the world ever experienced. In this year Oregon enacted the first state gasoline tax, providing an ear-marked source of revenue for construction of highways. By 1919 in fact all the states had highway departments and the Federal government stepped forward as a partner of the states in highway construction. The automobile was referred to less as a "pleasure car" and more as a necessary vehicle of transportation.

Sloan had become a member of the General Motors executive committee in 1918. Now, as he looked back over his twenty years in the motor car business, he noted that capital invested in the industry had grown three hundredfold and the number of cars manufactured had increased five hundredfold. By 1919 the industry was producing one million, nine hundred thousand cars annually. The investment in the industry was moving up toward two billion dollars. The motor car industry, including body, parts, accessory companies, was employing nearly four hundred thousand persons. It was paying wages in the amount of six hundred million dollars and manufacturing an annual product with a value over one billion, seven hundred million dollars. More than seven and a half million cars and trucks were traveling the highways.

Leaders attempted to explain why the motor vehicle was winning a public as no other product manufactured in history had done. William S. Knudsen explained the phenomenon by saying that "people want to go from A to B sitting down." Charles F. Kettering later explained the demand for the automobile by saying that "no-

body is where he wants to be and nothing is where he can use it."
A farm wife simplified the situation to a United States Department
of Agriculture investigator who inquired why the family owned a
car before it installed a bathtub. In surprise the woman replied,
"Why, you can't go to town in a bathtub." Thomas A. Edison believed that the value of the automobile was not that it made it
easier and quicker and cheaper to go places but rather that it motivated millions of people to "go." "The auto," he said, "set their gray
matter to work. It has done more to make America a nation of
thinkers than any other invention or agency. It has revealed to
people how petty and meaningless their lives were becoming. The
automobile has made the American people restless. Restlessness is
discontent. And discontent is the first necessity of progress. The
automobile has raised the thinking capacity of society."

The year 1919 was important further because in that year Alfred
P. Sloan, Jr., was debating in his mind whether he should make
General Motors a life career. By the end of the year 1919 General
Motors Corporation had earned a net of sixty million dollars before
dividends. Despite this substantial growth and the obvious prospects of the Corporation, Sloan was disturbed by the administrative
habits of Durant. Although he personally respected Durant, Sloan's
own thinking proceeded from wholly different premises than those
of his chief. Sloan felt that Durant tried "to carry everything in his
own head." He urged his colleague to arrange for an outside audit
of the corporation's accounts. One day Durant suggested that Sloan
go ahead with the plan if he knew anybody who could do the job.
Sloan knew then, as he had always known, that Durant was open to
suggestion; but for some reason the policies and administrative
practices of the corporation seemed to lack the clear-cut focus which
Sloan's nature found so necessary. With the green light from Durant
he proceeded to establish the outside audit. It was another step
in Sloan's pattern of management based on facts. To Sloan "accounting," as the system of fact-control of an industry, became a primary
tool of management.

Sloan's belief that decisions should be arrived at through the unprejudiced analysis of facts was frustrated when Durant made what
Sloan felt a most dangerous decision. As the inflated world price

structure began to fall after World War I in the adjustment to peace-time level, Durant, with a confidence in automobiles and General Motors which exceeded good judgment, announced a policy that General Motors would guarantee prices as a gesture toward holding the economy stable. Sloan looked upon this bold decision as leading General Motors to certain ruin. So concerned was he over the outlook that he asked for a leave of absence for a month to go to London to *think*. He was weighing a personal problem: Should he resign from General Motors? Almost everything that Sloan possessed was invested in General Motors. To its development he had given good years of his active life. The collapse of the corporation as a result of Durant's policy he felt would bring certain ruin to him. He wanted time to think through a "personal policy." From the perspective of the British Isles, his proper course seemed clear: he would get out of General Motors.

When he arrived back in New York to hand in his resignation, he found that Durant was away on vacation. Thus, unable to present his resignation to his boss, Sloan carried on from day to day until Durant might return.

In his analysis of the position of the business Sloan saw that General Motors should be in a most favorable position. The shortage of cars during the war years had opened up a huge, active market. There seemed to be no reason why General Motors prosperity should not continue. Sloan likened the situation to the position of a big oceangoing ship. It was sailing along at full speed. The sun was shining. As far as the sailors could see there was not a single cloud in the sky to indicate an approaching storm.

Yet in September 1920, almost overnight, as Sloan tells the story, values began to fall. The liquidation of inflated wartime prices to peacetime levels struck in earnest. Scheduled orders were canceled. Inventories continued to roll on unchecked. "Before it was realized what was happening," said Sloan, "this great ship of ours was in the midst of a terrific storm." General Motors soon found itself in serious difficulties with bank loans in October 1920 aggregating eighty-two million dollars. As a general part of the liquidation the bottom dropped out of General Motors stock on the New York exchange.

The financial plight in which General Motors found itself was serious. To tide the corporation over its difficulty help from the outside needed to be forthcoming — promptly and in sufficient amount. It was at this point in the crisis that the du Pont family stepped forward and arranged to assume Durant's personal obligations. The financing required such huge sums that the du Ponts with their resources and experience in surmounting difficult industrial problems represented perhaps the only group which could come to the rescue. The plight of the corporation gave a new turn to Sloan's career. Instead of leaving General Motors, as he had intended to do when he returned from his "meditation" trip to England, he stayed on. It was Durant himself who resigned. One result of Durant's withdrawal was that two million, five hundred thousand shares of General Motors stock passed from him to the du Pont family.

Under the changed circumstances, Sloan sat down promptly in conference with Pierre S. du Pont to plead with him to succeed Durant as General Motors president. One position which du Pont did not want, however, was an operating job. He preferred to remain as chairman of the board. He enjoyed his life in Wilmington. He had no desire to spend more time than necessary in Detroit. Sloan's argument was nevertheless persuasive. Sloan talked hard facts; du Pont understood them and surrendered his personal preference for the welfare of the corporation.

Difficult problems immediately faced the new management. How for example could the unwieldy and incoherent aggregation of industrial operations which had been pulled together in the corporation be co-ordinated and unified into a clear-cut pattern? General Motors needed to weed out certain units, strengthen others. It had to move decisively to eliminate unprofitable operations which did not fit into the pattern. It needed enormous quantities of managerial skill. It needed to face facts, to formulate policies, and to develop operational plans which utilized to the fullest extent the group judgment of the most capable and experienced personnel that could be found. More and more Sloan emphasized the importance of approaching problems with an open mind. Because du Pont continued to reside in Delaware and because he disliked to travel, he shifted more and more responsibility to Sloan.

Sloan enjoyed his enlarged responsibility. He began to build castles in the air, to imagine how he would operate General Motors if he were president. As he looked at the corporation's prospects he still found the future promising; he never altered his faith in tomorrow. For a quarter of a century his reason for optimism remained the same. "Thanks to the resourcefulness of scientists, inventors, and engineers," he said, "a continually advancing technology offers an additional opportunity for the production of new and useful things as well as enabling today's things to be produced at lower costs and hence sold at lower prices." More things for more people in more places at lower prices became a creed of General Motors management.

At the time Sloan frankly pointed out to the stockholders that the financial misfortunes which the corporation had experienced did not come from factors involved in the manufacture and sale of General Motors products, but rather from loose and uncontrolled methods which were being permanently corrected.

The painful experience in the deflationary period had taught Sloan two lessons. The first was that the automobile is no longer a pleasure vehicle but a necessary and primary instrument of transportation. The second was that the manufacture and sale of automobiles as a commercial necessity must follow the same careful economic and resourceful methods as those found necessary in other basic industries.

A good many industrial leaders did not share Sloan's optimistic appraisal of America's future. They argued that the collapse of inflation-bred prosperity brought on by World War I and an accompanying prosperity and extravagance had brought a permanent end to the zooming demand for "pleasure cars." Sloan, however, believed without qualification that a new epoch had arrived. He rejected the idea that an old era had ended in an industrial blind alley. With the automobile's coming-of-age, Sloan was convinced that the industry must stop the careless and extravagant production and sales method which had characterized its adolescent "playboy" days. And he kept talking hard industrial facts.

What Sloan was doing in 1921 was to lead the way to the adoption of a fundamental manufacturing policy for General Motors. Substantially the policy determined that the corporation should establish a complete line of motor cars ranging from the lowest to the highest price that would justify quantity production. The corporation would endeavor at all times to develop the best value in each price class which large volume, effective manufacturing methods, aggressive engineering, and efficient means of distribution — all supported by large resources — could make possible. Clear and progressive policies began to give General Motors an industrial coherence which it much needed.

Sloan's leadership did not long go unrecognized. In May 1923 his opportunity to head General Motors arrived. He succeeded Pierre du Pont as president. For years he had been training himself for this opportunity when it should come his way. His concept of the enterprise was clearly focused: a richly efficient mass-production industry founded on the teamwork of scientists, engineers, and manufacturers. There never was a doubt in Sloan's mind about General Motors' continued growth. His concern was to organize a pattern of management adequate for the age of industrial bigness. The pattern which Sloan established proved equal to the need. Sloan had long been debating in his own mind whether General Motors should be organized on a centralized or a decentralized pattern. As he studied the merits of the two possible patterns in his habitually fact-centered and open-minded method, he became convinced that *decentralization was analogous to the freeman's way of life.* Centralization, to his way of thinking, smacked of regimentation and dictatorship. To him the decentralized pattern seemed to be most practical for the kind of growth he expected General Motors presently to experience. In addition there was a practical reason for such a pattern. Firms were being taken under the General Motors wing, firms which had strong managements and profitable industrial histories. They had established organizations and often highly competent personnel. The compelling argument for decentralization in Sloan's mind lay not so much from these practical considerations as from his profound conviction that decentralization most nearly corresponded to what he believed should be the model of free society in general — *the wide distribution of respon-*

sibility. Concerning the correctness of Sloan's decision there has never been a question: the pattern for General Motors worked. The General Motors decentralized pattern combined ability to produce on a large scale with the flexibility of smaller-scale enterprise.

To formalize this decentralized scheme of industrial administration, Sloan sat down with his pencil and worked out an organizational chart. The keystone of his pattern was the division of the organization into as many units as could possibly be operated by placing responsibility in a chief executive who would exercise as much initiative and receive as much financial return as he would if he were operating his own enterprise. In brief, Sloan's theory followed this sequence: Set up each General Motors operation as an integral unit, complete as to itself. Place in charge of each such unit an executive solely responsible for the whole operation. Choose for the job the most capable man who can be found. Cultivate to a maximum the virtues of ambition and responsibility.

Sloan insisted as a theory and constantly demonstrated in practice that the means of executive development lay in the provision of opportunity for men to exercise their talents simultaneously in their own interests and in the interests of the business. The location of responsibility was the productive approach which developed ability, resourcefulness, and leadership as no other method can do. In his search for men of quality Sloan took a vigorous stand against what he called "mediocracy." He considered it his obligation to provide the organizational conditions under which an "uncommon man" could become an unusual success. For to Sloan an industrial organization was *people,* and the way they are organized to work together. Different groups of people and their activities must be coordinated into an efficient organization. C. E. Wilson, who joined Remy Electric in 1919 as chief engineer and sales manager of its automotive activities, who grew into the office of president of the corporation under Sloan's guidance, stated six basic principles which in the day-to-day operations of the business promote teamwork. The principles were these:

1. Put the right people in the right place.
2. Train everyone for the job to be done.
3. Make the organization a co-ordinated team.
4. Supply the right tools and the right conditions.

5. Give security with opportunity, incentive, recognition.
6. Look ahead, plan ahead, for more and better things.

According to Sloan, General Motors should co-ordinate the units of the corporation so that each fully supports and strengthens every other. Thus the pieces are welded together, through common interest in the joint enterprise. Within an efficient organization, said Sloan, there must be a minimum amount of friction and nonproductive or unnecessary work. The proper control of the whole enterprise must be achieved in such a way as to encourage the initiative of the individual employee.

While industrial organization resided in the human structure, attitudes, skill, and competence, Sloan saw clearly and stated that in a competitive economy no business can long continue to provide good products and jobs unless it can sell products at prices that will enable it to make a profit. Business dollars to Sloan were like raw materials: they must be available in sufficient quantity, at the right time and place, if the industry is to operate effectively. One task of management is to keep dollars at work efficiently.

Quality people and efficient dollars — these two pillars of the General Motors strength operate within a concept of organization which Sloan clearly delineated. Policy formulation is separate from administration. Policy making divides itself into two governing committees, dealing with (1) operations and (2) finances.

The manufacturing units of General Motors operate much like an independent business. Each division designs, develops, manufactures, merchandises, and advertises its own products. It purchases the materials to supply its own needs, hires and trains its own employees. The general manager of each General Motors division is responsible for building his own organization, co-ordinating its efforts, and planning its progress. Unlike the manager of an independent small business, however, the general manager of a General Motors division has available to him the financial resources of the corporation as well as the staff facilities and "know-how" of the central organization.

For co-ordinating purposes the General Motors operations are grouped according to common relationships, a group executive with each such group.

The over-all responsibility for guiding General Motors division activities was assigned to these several *central office executives,* each group executive holding the rank of a vice-president. This group executive represented General Motors management and acted as adviser for the divisional managers of his group. In exercising this function he worked closely with the divisional managers and the executive vice-president to whom he reported.

Within the central office, the organization was divided into two major groups of staff activities — the general staff and the financial and legal staffs. The executive vice-president in charge of the finance and legal staffs was also chairman of the financial policy committee, and had in addition general supervision of the three subsidiary companies that made up the finance and insurance groups.

From this outline of the pattern which Sloan introduced and continually developed and improved, it can be seen that "strategy" is determined at the top and that "tactics" remain the responsibility of the field officers — with adequate provision for the flow of ideas and experience both ways. According to this pattern, the vice-president in charge of sales, for example, functions as a co-ordinating executive. He contributes his leadership of better and more advanced policies of distribution, arrived at by study and research. He exercises no direct authority over sales operations. The actual business of selling stands as the responsibility of the various divisional sales managers reporting to the divisional general managers.

When Sloan succeeded Lammot du Pont as chairman of the General Motors board in the spring of 1937, he pointed out that the management of an industry breaks itself down into two questions. The first is: What should be done? The answer to this question defines *policy.* The second question is: How should it be done? The answer to this question spells out the administrative structure, the program for carrying out the policy.

However much attention Sloan gave to this revolutionary organization of industrial activity, he was under no illusion that a mere pattern of decentralized activity alone would produce profitable industrial results. As his structure took shape, he placed enormous emphasis on the human factor. In the last analysis it is the human equation which determines total effectiveness of a corporation. That was why Sloan proposed to man General Motors from top to bottom with aggressive and "uncommon" men of outstanding ability. He sorted out the best of these superior men by vigorous competition driven hard by the men's hope and chance of promotion. This competitive climate focused ambition, sharpened talent, and increased loyalty. As a result of Sloan's practices, General Motors was invigorated by a steady upward movement of exceptional men. General Motors became the story of the development of good men to great leadership. Never did it become necessary for General Motors to "build into the top"; the system produced its own executives.

With clear policies and a coherent administrative structure staffed by capable executives, General Motors avoided the inertia, delays, frustrations of initiative, autocracy, and cumbersomeness which could have impeded the growth of so great a corporation. Under Sloan's pattern General Motors operated as a huge and far-flung enterprise, with amazing directness and dispatch.

In summarizing his administrative concepts, Sloan described scientific management as "a constant search for the facts to define the true situation, an intelligent and unprejudiced analysis of these facts, and the courage to determine policies and administrative practices upon them." He put down on paper a philosophy which guided him as the years went by. "Management," he said, "is the collective effort of imagination, intelligence, and experience. It involves the constant search for facts to show the truth, the open mind to base policy without prejudice upon an analysis of the facts, and courage defined as willingness to take a risk. Good management is equitable, respecting the rights of others. It is confident, exercising the courage of its considered convictions. It demands loyalty, defined as the willingness to make any sacrifice necessary to achieve a goal. It believes in progress and insists that there is always a better way. It recognizes hard work as the catalyst that energizes all these ingredients, and combines them into the promotion of a common cause."

It can be seen, therefore, that while General Motors was becoming the biggest corporation in the world, Alfred Sloan was guiding that growth on the basis of clear-cut organizational policy. Behind every decision, however, lay the fundamental concept of industrial profit: every dollar must make a showing for itself.

General Motors, under this pattern of concern for people and dollars, grew rapidly into a gigantic enterprise. By the fall of 1927 Sloan was fully aware of the awful responsibility which rested upon "the limited number of individuals who formulate the policies and establish the principles upon which the vast empire of General Motors revolves and upon which its future depends." "Millions of people," he said, "are dependent upon the establishment of sound principles of administration in General Motors and on the development of sound policies and wise programs, produced by sound thinking." By the third quarter of 1953 General Motors had 493,258 shareholders to whom management was responsible and for whom it acted as trustee. It had 557,261 employees. Allowing three and a half persons in the average worker's family, General Motors had a direct responsibility for the prosperity and happiness of almost two million individuals. It had more than eighteen thousand dealers. If each of these dealers employed an average of thirteen persons the dealer citizens dependent upon General Motors prosperity numbered over two hundred and sixty thousand. With their families, this number rises to almost a million people dependent upon the steady flow of income from General Motors.

In addition General Motors has some twelve thousand suppliers, who employ many thousands of workers. The prosperity of an enormous aggregation of "suppliers who supply the suppliers," in turn, depends upon the prosperity of those firms which serve the divisions of the corporation. The General Motors industrial web of relationships as a decentralized form of operation reaches into fifty-seven cities in the United States, and with assembly and manufacturing operations into nineteen countries of the world. Thus it is evident that what General Motors does affects the whole nation, as well as its relationships with other nations of the international community.

Recognizing the responsibility for economic statesmanship which inevitably falls upon the shoulders of General Motors management,

Sloan formulated a philosophy which he consistently emphasized in private and in public:

He began by saying that thinking moves toward decisions by the study of facts. Intelligent management, he observed, must develop the habit of being guided by facts. Under Sloan, General Motors operations became objective and fact-centered. Fact-finding was the number one General Motors procedure. Sloan next insisted that facts must be analyzed with the open mind unprejudiced by previous beliefs. "Nothing delays progress quite as much as too strict an adherence to history and precedent," said Sloan. "Progress is always tugging against the backpull of the human mind. Let us follow the course of analyzing any idea or suggestion," he proposed, "from the standpoint of the extent to which it means progress, rather than the usual way of approaching it from the negative side. I sometimes wonder," Sloan went on to say, "what we really could accomplish and to what heights of prosperity we really could rise if we were not limited by the inertia of the human mind. My experience in business convinces me that facts are too little considered in making decisions. It is difficult to get the facts, but it is worth every effort and General Motors puts forth that effort. With the facts before us, we try to approach the decision with an open mind."

Sloan secondly kept pointing out there is always a better way to do a job — "This restless urge toward perfection lies at the heart of progress." Essentially it depends on research and engineering. "A job well done today ought to be done better next week and still better next month," said Sloan. He laid it down as a principle that "we must make continual progress as the justification of survival."

Next he believed in hard work both for himself and for those associated with him. "Work" to him is the catalyst which makes the other virtues possible. "Our own success," he said, "is dependent upon the willingness of each of us to make the sacrifice of time, personal convenience, and effort to the achievement of the cause. We must have the ambition to serve and to serve with the best that is in us — both as individuals and as a group." Sloan recognized that this principle was "as old as the hills," but that out of the hard work of the past had come tremendous progress. Hard work which contributes everything a man has in him to the cause, as Sloan saw it, was a foundation stone of progress in the future, and a way to surmount difficulties. "I will go so far as to say," Sloan said, "that hard work is the only road to real happiness. There is no short cut." He practiced what he preached.

In the fourth place Sloan insisted on fairness to all the groups of the industrial process. He referred to the idea as "recognizing the equities of all concerned." To him this meant steady and reasonable dividends paid to shareholders, good wages paid to workers, stimulating incentives arranged for managers, a product of high dollar-value and rewarding usefulness for customers, a profitable relationship with dealers, a wholesome relationship with suppliers, and policies and products which command the respect of the public. General Motors, for example, did not beat the price of its purchases from suppliers down. It wanted them to make a reasonable return on capital employed, but it expected them to conduct their businesses with the highest possible degree of efficiency and effectiveness.

In the fifth place Sloan wanted action. "Too often," he said, "action is delayed or prevented by the lack of courage or the lack of willingness to deal with the facts. This reluctance to act may come from respect for the past or from some policy of the past or some individual relationship. If we believe in the facts, we must face them with courage and conviction. My experience has shown that irrespective of any other consideration, the equities of all concerned are more fully preserved by action with respect to the facts than by lack of courage in dealing with such facts."

Finally, Sloan asserted that the degree to which General Motors served the public by providing a constantly better product would determine the stature of the corporation. He recognized that companies must compete more and more in the individual's budget. He saw competition growing always keener. "We must not only work harder to get the same result, but we must work more intelligently," he said. He considered it the first duty of General Motors management to develop a competitive product and merchandise it profitably.

The degree to which Sloan's pattern for General Motors could succeed depended upon the spirit of cooperation and the dominance of loyalty to the General Motors idea. Sloan had to struggle against a prevailing belief that sooner or later General Motors must centralize its activities. There were of course personal and institutional jealousies. "The idea was prevalent, previous to our coming into the picture," he said, "that each division was God Almighty, you might say, and had no relation to any other division and was a law unto itself. That all had to be changed to a spirit of co-operation and a realization that after all we were all parts of the General Motors family." For his first two or three years Sloan experienced what he called "hard sledding."

With the experience of the years in good times and bad, he came to the conclusion that the fundamental policies and administrative practices in General Motors represented something of permanent and universal validity. "I have," he said, "come to the conclusion that they represent a philosophy of thought and action not only for industry, whether big or small, but for nations in their intercourse with nations."

While Sloan was doing fundamental organizational thinking, he had been participating in the major crises precipitated by the collapse of the world price structure and certain policy decisions which Durant had made prior to his retirement from the business. Sloan found it necessary to deal promptly with a whole series of problems all at once. Huge inventories had accumulated at high prices. Bank accounts were depleted. There was a large indebtedness to bankers. Products which were not entirely satisfactory in a competitive market had to be redesigned. A management staff, more or less unfamiliar with the corporation's problems, unacquainted with one another, had to be "introduced" and joined in teamwork. Each problem was in itself gigantic; Sloan had to face them all at once.

Perhaps the situation which alarmed Sloan most was the absence of control such as would be necessary to enable the corporation to adjust to any situation which might develop. He was determined to set up a system which would prevent the situation which he experienced in 1920–1921 from occurring again. To provide satisfactory control for a dynamic and decentralized business, Sloan proceeded to set up scientific operations whereby General Motors would be able to project its operations into the future and to discount changing trends and influences. Sloan wanted to be prepared at all times to alter the corporation's course as circumstances required. General Motors needed an apparatus for dealing with economic changes no matter how suddenly they might come, so that the influence of adverse trends could be reduced to a minimum.

From Sloan's concern for "control" developed a system of forecasting. This system indicated every detail of production, sales, overhead, profits, inventory, commitments, cash, and all the other elements that are involved. These forecasts were developed with considerable accuracy. On the basis of the projections General Motors was able to look forward and provide for the future with the assurance that management knew, to the extent that was humanly possible, where the corporation would stand four months hence. Explaining the system as a whole, Sloan said it could be described in two words: *proper accounting*. It was scientific bookkeeping providing a fact-control for management. It was accounting, however, concerned with tomorrow rather than with yesterday.

In Sloan's thinking the movement of merchandise into the hands of the ultimate consumer constituted the fundamental index of industrial activity. Up to 1920 General Motors had little regard for the number of unsold cars standing on dealers' floors. Sloan ended such a short-sighted policy. He established a system of reporting which summarized the dealers' experience three times a month. These reports gave the number of cars on hand, the models, the number of used cars, and the forward orders booked for future delivery. Upon these reports were based a manufacturing schedule involving hundreds of thousands of employees, thousands of suppliers, and operations at home and abroad.

The economic information which General Motors thus developed was no corporate secret. General Motors wanted this information to be generally useful. Each month up to the beginning of World War II it published the statistics to inform the whole world exactly what the experience was about the movement of motor cars to the ultimate consumer. The reports gave a specific, concrete record of the general business trends as General Motors sales found them. After the war, the corporation released production figures monthly.

Sloan had confidence in the system of control which had been established. "No matter what the future may bring forth," said he, "and no matter what changes may take place, irrespective of how suddenly they may take place, we have at all times the organization and machinery to deal with these changes in such a way that the adverse effects upon the great interests we represent will be reduced to the very minimum that human ingenuity can make possible."

The control system, so necessary to guide management in its policies of leadership of a great industry in its continuing dynamics in a free economy system, was a structural innovation in General Motors activity. Important as the control was, however, General Motors' purpose still was to manufacture good automobiles and to sell them at fair prices at a profit. The vehicles which came off the assembly line had to move into the hands of customers. Sloan was very clear about one sales fact: General Motors and its dealers were "partners" in a common enterprise.

Facing this fact frankly Sloan in 1924 began to visit thousands of dealers in person. While he knew that these dealers were in a sense independent merchants, he felt that their prosperity determined that of General Motors. Likewise he knew that every advance in General Motors products strengthened the position of the dealers in the highly competitive motor car market. Accepting a strenuous schedule for himself, Sloan set out to call on his outlets throughout the whole country. "In such a trip," he said, "you begin to realize how big America is." These field expeditions consumed weeks of time, involved constant travel on exacting itineraries, and required the hardest kind of mental and physical work.

According to his pattern on these trips, Sloan would drop in to see a distributor or dealer without notice. He would step into an office, introduce himself, and sit down opposite the dealer at the dealer's own desk. Then he would proceed to explore what was on the dealer's mind. They would exchange ideas, talk about common interests. But for the most part Sloan encouraged the dealer to talk; he was the good listener. He wanted to hear about all the criticisms of General Motors products. What Sloan wanted to find out was how to produce a better car which would be easier to sell. The whole idea of these face-to-face, nation-wide, over-the-desk conversations was so revolutionary and unusual that it often took Sloan most of the conference time to win the dealer's confidence.

Generally, therefore, the last half-hour — and often the last five minutes — became the most productive period of the interview.

On these trips Sloan visited from five to ten dealers a day in their own garages or salesrooms. In each conference he took notes. When he returned to his hotel room, he would analyze his notes to identify the key problems and then outline steps to capitalize on the suggestions. As these field trips developed into a sort of institution, dealers looked forward to the visits. They began to talk freely about their relationships with the corporation. They discussed customer reactions, consumer trends; talked about the future. Sloan was always concerned about the days ahead. He communicated a contagious belief that almost everything can and will be done better tomorrow than today.

From the dealer's office Sloan generally proceeded to call on the local banker and the newspaper editor. By means of these "field trips" he got to the roots of General Motors merchandising in a personal way, without any intermediary organization. Sloan believed that this strenuous field work contributed much to building the corporation into the great team of people which it became.

Out of these itinerant experiences Sloan came to the conclusion that the dealer was perhaps the weakest link in the General Motors chain. One of the greatest deficiencies which he found was the absence of sound accounting systems to insure that the dealer's business was operated profitably. Sloan was convinced by his observations that General Motors needed to help its dealers in their bookkeeping and accounting control. As an extension of his basic concept that business needs "proper accounting" to provide facts for management to plan and control operations, Sloan proceeded to organize a General Motors subsidiary known as the Motor Accounting Company. The whole function of this service agency was to help dealers establish proper accounting systems whenever and wherever they so desired. Through the Motor Accounting Company, Sloan developed a staff of expert fact-finders who specialized in the financial operations of the automobile outlets. Sloan preferred to consider the program one of fact finding rather than of accounting. He did not want the words which described the system to give the impression that men were dealing with the past. "A General Motors franchise," Sloan told the dealers, "is a profit-making opportunity. The establishment of facts, however, is a useless and unnecessary expense unless we effectively employ these facts and have courage to act in harmony with what they indicate." The Motor Accounting Company became a constructive instrument for helping dealers to merchandise General Motors products efficiently and profitably.

The outcome of these trips demonstrated the effectiveness of personal top liaison. One customer wrote to Sloan that he wanted a Buick but that the colors were "God-awful loud." Sloan replied with a letter which gave the factual reasons for the use of the colors. At a dinner one evening a dealer told Sloan that he had sold at least seven Buicks as a result of that letter. Some people in General Motors objected to the many letters which Sloan wrote. They felt that he was wasting his time. Sloan replied to his critics. "Each one of these letters," he explained, "while they may cost a little time and effort, are worth while. A page in the *Saturday Evening Post* would cost a lot of money too."

The field trips to visit dealers, like the many personal letters which Sloan so promptly wrote, expressed an idea which Sloan had about the gigantic General Motors Corporation. This idea was that a corporation is a network of human relationships and that these relationships should be as direct, forthright, and informal as those of a country storekeeper visiting at the cracker barrel. His approach was fact-centered but it was also personal and always humble. He studied criticisms with an open mind devoid of prejudices and gave answers that were courteous, straightforward, and factual. He applied his theory at the top and it spread throughout the organization. He urged his executives by example to give prompt and personal attention to "people."

In his close study of dealer problems, Sloan saw that General Motors needed to provide ways and means to finance the sale of the automobiles it manufactured. The corporation needed to make it easy to buy a motor car. From the very beginning of the industry, when an automobile would almost sell in a demonstration, it was clear that the industry needed to provide credit for the buyer. In the early days the dealer had to supply all the capital and credit necessary to stock cars pending their sale. His money was thus tied up and the burden became even larger when the dealer sold the car "on time." As installment buying became customary, finance companies sprang up to purchase paper from dealers on well-sold and well-insured automobiles. John J. Raskob studied the problem to see how a financing service could be developed which would help the dealer as well as the purchaser.

A year after Sloan came to the corporation, General Motors in 1919 set up the General Motors Acceptance Corporation. The purpose of this operation was, by means of the proper application of the credit function to the orderly distribution and sale of General Motors products, to promote sound and healthy manufacturing and merchandising conditions. In 1929 the General Motors Holding Corporation was formed to make it possible for experienced men without sufficient capital to enter the business as dealers. Sloan saw clearly the place which credit had of necessity to play in the development of the motor car market. As basic policy General Motors was determined to offer a complete service in the sale of cars — including financing.

The consumer financing operation raised questions of adequate insurance protection. In 1924 the corporation established the General Exchange Insurance Corporation, which every year since its founding has written more insurance than any other company. By fair and prompt settlements, the GEIC developed further respect for the General Motors name.

In explaining his position on credit sales Sloan said: "I firmly believe that the granting of credit to the consumer is not only sound if carried out under proper policies, but that the adoption of this principle has far-reaching influence on the amazing prosperity of the United States. I believe in placing a motor car in the hands of everyone where credit justifies our doing so. Such a practice advances large volume production and permits further expenditures for research and engineering." General Motors engaged the services of outstanding economists to assist it in developing and controlling consumer financing in such a way as to strengthen the national economy and to provide more transportation service.

From his concern with the development of General Motors in the United States, Sloan turned to the promotion of overseas business. He explained the objective of extending world activity by giving these reasons: "to bring a good return on the additional capital employed in the interests of the stockholders, to increase business, to earn additional profits, to lower the costs of all cars produced, and hence to provide greater value both at home and abroad."

The extension of General Motors overseas trade, which had been initiated in 1911, provoked a policy debate: Should the world be divided up by car lines, or by lines of geography? With his habit for spelling out clear policies Sloan soon worked out a plan under which geography became the basis for organizing regional and territorial authorities. He also advanced the idea of establishing assembly plants abroad. This revolutionary suggestion precipitated further policy controversy, but in the end the idea was accepted as a natural step for a big industry. Under the plan of overseas activity, as it clarified into policy, General Motors assumed wholesale functions and controlled inventions in each territory which was being penetrated by local dealers. The General Motors plants in foreign countries, as Sloan saw them, would provide a welcome opportunity for investment, for the employment of local labor, and open some degree of local purchasing — all extending good will toward General Motors. By 1926 plants were operating in fifteen countries.

Omens foreboding difficulty in international industrial activities were already on the horizon. Within the British Empire, the slogan "Buy British" was already spreading. Sloan sensed that the day was not far away when United States and Canadian export sales would decline as a result of tariff restrictions and exchange difficulties. To prepare to meet some such situation, Sloan proposed to establish General Motors units on a national basis. By 1928, General Motors was doing a million-dollar business in Great Britain and Continental Europe alone. "If Europeans could appreciate the fact," Sloan observed, "that automobiles create a greater value in business than any other industry in the United States, sales in Europe would increase at a tremendous rate."

With the collapse of world trade in 1929 and the enactment of the Hawley-Smoot Tariff Act in 1930, practically excluding the importation of foreign-made goods, General Motors discovered how wise the overseas development program really was. As trade barriers grew more complicated and currency problems more complex, the corporation was in a fortunate position. For the manufacture and sale of cars within the British Empire, it had acquired Vauxhall Motors, Ltd., and developed it as a thoroughly British concern. To meet the demands of the world which preferred a German product, it had acquired in 1929 Adam Opel, A. G., with plants located in Russelsheim and Brandenburg.

In October 1929 Sloan went to Russelsheim to meet the dealers who handled Opel cars in Germany. He told them that General Motors was conducting manufacturing and assembly plant operations in twenty-five countries outside the United States, that it had five thousand dealers abroad, and employed twenty-five thousand overseas personnel. Then he outlined policy at Opel. General Motors, he said, would develop Opel as a thoroughly German institution. It would employ German executives and German workmen, having only such American executives as might be necessary to guide policy. To the fullest possible extent Opel would purchase German materials produced by German workers. Pursuing the General Motors principle of competition, the corporation, he continued, would import American-made cars to compete with Opels. He set a production goal of fifty thousand Opels in the next five years and looked forward to the production of two hundred thousand a year for consumption in the Reich and for export. Such a program, he said, would require more German managers, German workmen, German machines, and German plant facilities. He pointed out that General Motors was the leading industrial organization in the United States and the largest individual manufacturing enterprise in the world. Such a high position, he explained, resulted from the highest possible business ethics and the adoption of operating policies along sound and constructive lines. "We have at all times advocated," he added, "the highest standard of living for our employees, have advanced the interests of our dealers, have maintained the highest standards of product quality, all for the purpose of supplying customers with the best possible motor car." Adam Opel, A. G., would become the "General Motors of Germany," and thus constitute an important part of German industrial life. "The motor car," he concluded, "contributes more to the wealth of the United States than agriculture. The automobile industry is a wealth-creating industry."

❈   ❈   ❈

The penetration of General Motors did not proceed without criticism. While the Hawley-Smoot tariff bill was being discussed in Congress, Senator Watson of Indiana attacked Sloan for manufacturing abroad when he had made his wealth in the United States. The overseas manufacturing operations, Senator Watson charged, were depriving Americans of jobs. International firms and international bankers, he alleged, wanted "free trade." General Motors, said Senator Watson, wanted "to produce where wages were only two-fifths those paid in the United States." By its cheap labor policy General Motors, he alleged, became the enemy of labor in the United States. Said Watson: "In other words, these great masters of production, after having enriched themselves and their corporations in this country, are using the wealth they thus obtained to set up competitive industry in foreign countries and to produce their products by men who receive from a quarter to a half the wages paid in their factories in the United States. General Motors wants free trade in these articles so that the corporation can compete in our market with the product of their own mills in this country where they pay 50 per cent more wages than in the competing production in foreign countries. General Motors wants to destroy the very conditions which made possible the accumulation of that wealth by transferring that production to foreign countries."

Sloan experienced similar attacks abroad. When he arrived in France in March 1929, French newspapers and industrialists began to suggest "American domination of the Old World markets." As the rumor spread that Sloan intended to buy Opel in Germany "for the mass manufacture of Chevrolet automobiles," Sloan made frank statements. "I was in Europe ninety days ago," he said. "I am back again because of the great importance these markets now have for us. The American car is coming into its own in Europe. The people over here are realizing more and more that automobiles are not a luxury but a necessity and an economic benefit. As this realization develops, so will the sale of our product." French interests indeed feared " economic invasion" and came forward with plans to restrict United States operations by quota programs.

By the end of 1929 General Motors' overseas operations were geographically like the realms of the British Empire on which the sun never sets. One writer at the time described the scope of the overseas operation by saying that "Japanese workmen in Osaka are putting on their sandals to go to work while in South Africa workmen are starting homeward from the factory in Port Elizabeth. General Motors salesmen travel by carabao-pulled sleds in Malatsia, by horse-drawn carts with seven-foot wheels in Argentina, by coolie-carried chairs in a Chinese bridal procession, by camel trains in the Sahara. Everywhere throughout the world General Motors carries forward its peaceful penetration of business. The General Motors overseas representative knows all the colorful scenes of this earth. General Motors families answer the call to move with little more concern than if they were moving to the next block. One family had four children, each born in a different country, each speaking the language of his or her early environment better than English."

While General Motors was confronted with the rising tide of nationalism in international trade, Sloan was forced to deal with an inter-industry struggle at home. The railroad industry was making a frontal attack on motor-vehicle transportation. Organized at national and state levels, the railroads promoted legislation to restrict and harass automobiles, and especially trucks. Railroads proposed to equalize competition by taking away what they called the "public subsidy" in the form of public highways used by freight trucks and passenger vehicles.

Aware of the danger inherent in a battle of giant industries, A. J. Brousseau, president of the Mack Truck Corporation, urged Sloan to head a movement to develop a Highway Users Conference. Sloan became the first chairman of the conference and continued in the office for sixteen years until in 1948 he was succeeded by Albert Bradley, executive vice-president of General Motors.

To the organization of the Highway Users Conference Sloan brought the same thoroughness for factual inquiry, sound policies, and good administration which he had brought to General Motors itself. He established a pattern for "highway statesmanship." Through the efforts of the conference, a joint Committee of Railroads and Highway Users sought to bring about a moderation and reconciliation of the differences of view between rail and highway transportation. "The highway," said Sloan, "is the point where many of our greatest industries converge. It is in the highway that they find the means to render the service upon which their existence primarily depends. Thus the significance of an adequate, comprehensive, and economical system of national highways and supporting secondary roads stands out crystal clear."

What Sloan was determined to achieve was an orderly and comprehensive system of highways at minimum cost. As Sloan looked forward to working out a highway policy, statisticians were predicting that by 1975 eighty-five million passenger cars, buses, and trucks would be on the roads. Motor vehicle transportation needed highway planning if America was to meet the needs of tomorrow. The National Highway Users Conference, organized in 1932 as an association to act for the public using the roads, included groups such as the National Association of Motor Bus Operators, the Automobile Manufacturers Association, the National Grange, the Milk Industry Foundation, the International Association of Ice Cream Manufacturers, the National Council of Private Motor Truck Owners, Inc., the Truck-Trailer Manufacturers Association, the American Cattlemen's Association, American Retail Federation, American Bottlers of Carbonated Beverages, National Automobile Dealers Association, American Bakers Association, American Trucking Associated, United Fresh Fruit and Vegetable Association, the National Sand and Gravel Association, the Rubber Manufacturers Association, the American Petroleum Institute, and such firms as the Ford Motor Company, the General Motors Corporation and the International Harvester Company. "Forward together," the conference urged. "Inform! Arouse! Encourage action where action counts." It was speaking for a segment of America which by 1952 was doing a thirty-billion-dollar annual business.

Some conception of the magnitude of the motor car industry as it had developed in America during the course of Sloan's life may be gained by the following facts. With 6 per cent of the world's population, the United States had almost four fifths of the world's automobiles and more than half of its trucks and buses. Directly or indirectly the automobile provided work for one out of seven employed Americans. It consumed more than four fifths of the rubber, nine tenths of the gasoline, three fourths of the glass, nine tenths of the lead, and one fifth of the copper and zinc. More than half of the families in America owned motor cars. Vast new job opportunities had been created by almost a quarter-million gasoline stations, finance companies, suppliers, and related industries. There was one registered motor vehicle for each four Americans.

The National Highway Users Conference, it should be noted, developed under Sloan's leadership in years of economic woe and international conflict. It was in the depression years, indeed, that Sloan's leadership of General Motors was given its acid test. The industrial depression which followed the collapse of the stock market in 1929 confronted Sloan with gigantic management and control problems which required prompt decisions and courageous action. The precipitous decline in sales resulted in an even more precipitous decline in production and profits. The situation required a contraction in operations and the introduction of wholesale economies. In 1929 General Motors net sales stood at 1,504,404,472 dollars. By 1930 in dollars they had fallen by more than 34 per cent to 983,375,137; in 1931 to 808,840,723, a decline of more than 17 per cent from the previous year. The calendar year of 1931 showed a reduction in net dollar sales from 1929 of over 46 per cent and a drop in net operating earnings of over 53 per cent. In the calendar year 1932 net sales fell off alarmingly to a figure more than 46 per cent below the 1931 low. In the corporation's annual 1932 report, Sloan discussed the economies and operating influence of the industrial depression. He pointed out that the net dollar sales for the whole automotive industry in 1932 were 78 per cent lower than those of 1928.

Yet, during three horrible years, at the trough of the depression, Sloan kept General Motors out of the red. The corporation realized a net income of 165,000 dollars in 1932, paid dividends, and maintained full depreciation charges. Meanwhile he aggressively promoted research and engineering. The cash position of the corporation strengthened, although working capital was slightly reduced. Salaries were reduced on a sliding scale from 20 to 30 per cent. Public confidence in General Motors products increased. Between 1929 and 1932 the number of General Motors shareholders increased from 198,600 to 365,985. By the end of 1931, one out of three cars on the road in the United States had been produced by General Motors. Ever since Sloan advanced to be president of the corporation, public preference for General Motors products had steadily grown. In 1924 General Motors in United States and Canadian plants manufactured one out of six cars sold by the industry, in 1925 about one out of five, in 1926 one out of three, and by 1927 — when Ford changed from the Model T to the Model A — one out of two.

The substantial world-wide growth which General Motors had steadily enjoyed for more than a decade, between the end of World War I and the collapse of the stock market, had confronted Sloan and his associates with entirely new problems. Later, circumstances put to the acid test the soundness of General Motors policies and administrative structure and control. To his industrial achievements Sloan now in depression years joined a clear and sober quality of industrial statesmanship grounded in an uncompromising faith in the future of America.

Perhaps Sloan's most revealing statement was made in 1930 when he asserted that industry is dependent for its prosperity upon the welfare of the community at large. "Sound measures," he said, "that will serve to maintain purchasing power on a more level line should have the support and co-operation of industry. Every effort should be made through scientific management to reduce unemployment, both seasonal and that resulting from the so-called business cycle." He amplified his conception by saying that the main objective of industry should be to produce always more things for more people everywhere. Its purpose should be to insure a constantly increasing flow of the material resources of nature through the avenues of commerce and the processes of manufacture, thus providing more and more comfort and luxury, raising the standards of living, and widening the horizons of enjoyment of the people and at the same time insuring an opportunity for employment for a constantly increasing number of people. "This concept means a constant increase in the production of wealth. The key to this increase is a continual improvement in efficiency made possible by the capitalization of technological progress which in turn results in lower prices for goods and services."

It became clear to industrial leaders that full production and full employment in an economy of abundance were goals toward which to work. Such full production was dependent upon a steady and increasing flow of spending. Sloan saw an increase in the standard of living as inevitable under the American system, to a large extent as a result of providing the worker with better productive tools and methods. Sloan was perfectly sure likewise that industrial statesmanship demanded not only technological efficiency, but a policy of maintaining the stream of spending. So clear was he about the importance of spending that he emphasized continually the importance of spending by General Motors itself. To be a successful manufacturer and merchandiser of motor cars, General Motors recognized that the corporation itself must be a good customer and consumer. In fact the automobile industry stood as an outstanding exponent of the principle that by capitalizing the gains from technological progress, more goods for more people in more places could be produced at fair prices and fair wages. "We must," said Sloan, "maintain the broadest possible spread between annual income and the cost of the necessities of life."

Likewise Sloan was certain that prosperity in the world exists as a result of a mutual enterprise. It could not be achieved or maintained by one nation to the exclusion of others. He felt that unrestricted trade was an industrial necessity. "All nations," he said, "should encourage the greatest possible volume of world trade by means of facilitating the exchange of goods and services."

Throughout the depression decade Sloan kept insisting that the most important job was to get people back into productive employment. "Whatever the depression did," said Sloan, "it did not deprive anyone of his inherent desire for a high standard of living. Modern industry has brought to Americans a multitude of devices which have made life more pleasant, more worth while for the masses of men. The farmer would not willingly return to the mud-bound isolation of a quarter century ago when roads and the motor vehicle had not yet come to make possible better schools, sanitation, and tractor power."

As he saw the economic depression, it stemmed from surplus, from huge production. This surplus, however, did not exist because consumers did not have need of products manufactured. Sloan's answer to surplus production was not less but more production. "When alongside surpluses in every community," he said, "we see on all sides all over the world millions of people who are deprived not alone of the comforts but of the necessities of life, then it becomes evident that a fault has developed in our system of distribution. In the laboratory and in the field we have learned how to produce at a lessened cost both in terms of dollar and of human energy. We have made these advances so rapidly that our facilities for getting these products into the hands of those who need and want them temporarily have broken down. I find no master plan, no set formula, no magic panacea which offers itself as a golden remedy for our troubles." He was, however, sure of a few things. Americans wanted more things; industry could produce them.

From day to day during the depression years Sloan was faced with immediate problems. On February 14, 1933, a banking moratorium was declared in Michigan. Detroit found itself without a banking system. With characteristic initiative General Motors arranged with the Reconstruction Finance Corporation for funds to open a National Bank of Detroit with an initial capital of twenty-five million dollars, to which General Motors and the Reconstruction Finance Corporation each subscribed twelve million, five hundred thousand dollars. General Motors was "in partnership with the United States." On March 24, 1933, Sloan wrote a letter to the people of Detroit. He said that after six weeks of moratorium, facilities were being opened in the city. The National Bank of Detroit, he pointed out, was "an entirely new institution, the most liquid bank in the United States, a Detroit institution, owned, directed, and managed by the people of Detroit."

In the face of immediate problems Sloan felt the need for more clear thinking, for uninterrupted planning on policy. To provide a means for getting the best minds away from daily routine to "think," he acquired a "floating conference room": this was why on February 15, 1930, Pusey and Jones Corporation of Wilmington, Delaware, delivered to Sloan a yacht which, with equipment and furnishings, cost two million dollars. Though actually owned by Sloan the papers said it belonged to the "Rene Corporation" which chartered the craft to Sloan. The yacht was a racy clipper-bow affair, two hundred thirty-six feet in length, capable of doing over fifteen knots an hour and equipped with gyroscopic stabilizers.

The depression, as he saw it, was a summons to great leadership. In private and in public, Sloan affirmed confidence in the future.

Economic recession had not changed human ambitions. "Man, no matter in what nation he lives," said Sloan, "is as eager to maintain and advance his standard of living as ever before in history. This — coupled with the fact that there is every reason to believe that man is willing to pay the price in working, to obtain that objective — establishes a foundation of confidence in the industrial development of the future and assures not only the maintenance of our present standard of living but justifies every reason for believing that the future will produce a standard of living as far in advance of our pesent standards as our present standards are as compared with those of twenty-five years ago. I maintain that man still has the desire to possess, the willingness to work to possess. The problem becomes one of ways and means to effectively capitalize these facts. The long-term trend is always upward. We go continually forward."

There was no doubt in Sloan's mind upon what this progress depended. "The only sound solution of the problem of a high standard of living, of reduced unemployment, of the expansion of business, in fact of opportunity in the future, lies in the aggressive capitalization of technological progress: increasing the productivity of the worker, enabling industry to pay higher wages and to reduce the prices of goods and services so that they may be brought within the reach of an ever-increasing number. *It is the only way.*" The sole question as he saw it was this: "How intelligently can we manage our affairs?"

One way to act unintelligently, Sloan said, was to handicap technological development. "The distinguished public official," he commented, "who suggested putting a tax on technological progress reached the absolute zero of economic intelligence. If it should be brought about, it would penalize, if not ultimately close, the only approach to industrial progress. "Fundamentally," he repeated, "there are just two approaches to accomplish all that all desire to accomplish — providing more things for more people in more places. These two ways lie in increased efficiency through the capitalization of technological improvement and in more work. Therein lies the answer and the only solution." The alternative to facing problems intelligently Sloan found in the continuation of riding on what he called "the economic merry-go-round." "After we have taken the

ride," he said, "we get back to just where we started from. The difference is that we are that much greater in debt. A change in half
a dozen policies affecting industry would change the whole economic picture."

Sloan saw no reason for young men to be discouraged. The challenge existed to advance technology and to supply industrial statesmanship. "The only way the standard of living of the less privileged
part can be advanced," he said, "is to improve the standard of living
of all the other parts." Charles F. Kettering stated Sloan's thesis well
when he said that the objective of industry, science, government,
and society was the same — "a better life, better living conditions,
better health, better food, better government, better houses — in
fact, for better everything. Our civilization as a whole is new. This
is the first time in the history of the world that such a civilization
has been in existence. It is itself an experiment. Just because
we have encountered difficulties is no cause for despair."

We have seen that as he studied the situation Sloan believed that
methods of distribution needed to be revolutionized. "I honestly believe American business would be appalled if it had a real measure
of the inefficiency that takes place in too many industries between
the manufacturer and producer and the ultimate consumer." But
this was just one of the areas which needed attention. The times demanded young men, fresh ideas. "I do not believe in the old idea
of young men for action and old men for counsel," said Sloan. "The
young men must be given full opportunity and charged with full
responsibility. The older men must step completely out of the picture. In no other way can the full measure of progress be maintained. By young men, I mean men irrespective of age, but young in
ideas, in intensity of effort, in willingness to sacrifice at all times personal comfort and convenience for the good of an organization. . . .
There is work to be done in the world today," said Sloan. "To my
mind those who will accept that type of thinking are the individuals
and organizations who will become the leaders in the next great
forward movement. This is not a time for discouragement. It is a
time for action. As a result of the readjustment and refinement that
is going on, our industrial machine will become more efficient and
effective from every standpoint than ever before in history. Let us

learn from the pages of history that our progress over the decades is always upward. Let us accept the philosophy that the world desires not less but more. Let us be willing to work for that objective. Let us have courage to deal aggressively with the problems of the moment."

To the Boston Chamber of Commerce Sloan said that "if each of us can go out of this meeting with greater confidence and greater courage and deal with the difficulties of the moment, a greater appreciation of the soundness of the future, a greater realization of the fact that we are in every sense of the word the most fortunate people in the world to live in such a marvelous country, that our difficulties are largely of the moment and stepping-stones to a wonderful future and if met with the courage of our convictions and with a proper attitude of mind, the results cannot help but add strength and ability to deal with that wonderful future."

As the depression continued there was a widespread belief, especially in academic centers, that progress had ended. Contradicting this thesis Sloan became the apostle of the idea that progress had only begun. On May 26, 1934, he invited six hundred leaders of industry, science, medicine, and education to a luncheon to combat the idea that progress was a concept which belonged to the past. "The next century," predicted Sloan, "will surpass the phantasies of Jules Verne." At the Century of Progress fair in Chicago, General Motors came forward with a "preview of industrial progress in the next century." "Is there any logical reason to assume that progress is to be halted at this particular point in our development?" asked Sloan. "No!" he answered emphatically. Progress had not ceased. It had broadened its base in industry and research and was producing a higher standard of living. The *New York Times* observed editorially that the "Jules Verne glimpse into the future of science and industry" combatted the "existing beliefs that progress in the world is finished."

The way to the "wonderful future" lay in industrial progress, Sloan said. He began to make it perfectly clear that the American system was the best approach to this future. In 1936, he talked to the Los Angeles Chamber of Commerce on the subject "Shall We Have More Or Less?" "Competition," he said, "offers the only solution to the perfectly natural desire and right of more people to have more things and especially provides the only approach to full employment of the workers in the production of wealth."

Never in depression years did Sloan entertain doubts about the soundness of the American system. Never did he fail to point out that the prosperity of all parts of the world could be "tremendously enlarged" through the gradual lowering of all tariff walls. Such an international economic policy, he held, would permit the various countries to produce the products which they were best fitted to market. "We cannot," he warned, "continue to enjoy a trading balance in our favor plus the invisible balance that comes from being a great creditor nation. There is just one way and only one way that the world can pay, and that is in goods and services or both. A full realization of this basic fact on the part of all will clarify our thinkthing and enable us to act more consistently in the future than we have in times past."

Although as a matter of principle, Sloan avoided public issues related to partisan politics, he accepted in the fall of 1932 the chairmanship of a committee to study the problems arising out of war debts owed by Europe to the United States. The group was known as the "Committee for the Consideration of Intergovernmental Debts." Sloan, believing that the purpose of the committee related to the economic welfare of America, invited seventy-six leading industrial leaders to join him in the study. "The problem of intergovernmental debts," he said, "is a problem of dollars and cents. It can be solved only by hard, strightforward business calculations. The American people cannot afford to leave a question so vital to their economic interests unsettled any longer. What will it mean in dollars and cents to America? What will it mean in jobs, increased production, enlarged markets? If business reasoning decides that insistence on payment is the best course, that then is the solution we want. If reduction or even outright cancellation is the answer, that, on the other hand, is the answer that will be welcomed."

Circumstances made it unnecessary for the committee to complete its study. At the beginning of 1933, Adolf Hitler came to power as the leader of the Third Reich; the tide of National Socialism in Germany had already begun to sweep the Continent toward World War II.

*　　*　　*

As the head of the largest manufacturing corporation in the world, Sloan began to discover that what he did and said in a public way was news. On all sides pressure groups sought his influence and the benediction of the use of his name. In the middle 1930's there were many organizations clamoring for a hearing. Sloan had to act with extreme care. On the one hand, Sloan felt that prohibition had brought industrial benefits. The forces seeking repeal of the Eighteenth Amendment, however, put pressure on him to support their efforts to "cure the big slump" by "Repeal" as the best road to temperance. The American Liberty League, headed by Jouett Shouse, enrolled him as a member. John J. Raskob's "grass roots" movement, known as the "Southern Committee to Uphold the Constitution," took a subscription from him to run a Georgia governor against Franklin D. Roosevelt in the 1936 election. By the time he had contributed to the "Sentinels of the Republic," Sloan balked and issued a frank and final statement: "Under no circumstances will I further knowingly support the 'Sentinels of the Republic.' The group was recommended to me as an organization constructively promoting a better understanding of our national problems, economic in character, and my contribution to it was with the objective of furthering that purpose. I have no desire to enter into any questions involving religious or political consideration."

As the depression continued seven hundred industrial business and civic leaders met at the Waldorf-Astoria in New York to promote a "share the work movement." The object of the program was to find jobs for some two million unemployed by spreading the available employment through the reduction of the hours of labor. Sloan attended the meeting; later at the San Francisco Chamber of Commerce he said that the proper attack was not to share the work, but rather should be a plan to rebuild the obsolete industrial plants of America. Commenting on Sloan's idea, the *New York Times* observed that "the idea that we must divide up, that we cannot expand, is a defeatist attitude. It is the philosophy of scarcity." If any economic philosophy was anathema to Sloan, it was the idea of scarcity. Such an idea was an anachronism in the age of technological industrialism. "Abundance" was the only word which could enable modern industrialism to survive.

Just as the depression years tested the soundness of Sloan's administrative leadership of General Motors Corporation, so it tested his industrial philosophy. Sloan remained consistent. He believed in America. He believed in progress. He believed in competition. He believed in the profit-and-loss system. He believed in more goods for more people in more places. He did not propose to permit loose thinking and panaceas which he felt were the "natural by-products" of a great depression, to misguide the public mind.

To the Los Angeles Chamber of Commerce he explained that those "industries which have been most successful in reducing the costs of goods and services and in expanding their markets" have continually raised wages. As a formula for further progress, Sloan proposed (1) constant lowering of costs and prices, (2) courage to employ more and more individuals, (3) acceptance of the idea of competition as the best instrument for regulating industrial relationships within various trades, (4) efforts to achieve a more economic balance through policies affecting the regulation of the wage scale, hours of employment, price level, and profits resulting from industrial production. In a word, Sloan insisted that the highest performance of management was to achieve the most economic use of labor and materials to bring prices with quality within the range of greater numbers of purchasers. "We must," he said, "develop the greatest numbers of purchasers. We must develop the greatest possible consuming power from within. Here lies the greatest opportunity — through the achievement of a better economic balance within the component parts of industry to stimulate consumption and to make every worker and wage-earner a maximum possible consumer."

In the summer of 1936, Sloan took steps to systematize his own philanthropy and extend his philosophy by establishing the Alfred P. Sloan Foundation. Subsequently he endowed it with forty million dollars. "Having been connected with industry during my entire life," he said, "it seems eminently proper that I should turn back in part the proceeds of that activity with the hope of promoting a broader as well as a better understanding of the economic principles and national policies which have characterized American enterprise down through the years and as a result of which its truly marvelous development has been made possible." He hoped, as he said, that the foundation would accelerate progress through a more enlightened understanding of the policies which bring about "more things for more people everywhere — an opportunity for achievement and greater security and stability as well." The Foundation made a significant impact on economic thinking. It gave assistance to educational institutions and provided fellowships for young men of promise.

An institution as gigantic as General Motors must inevitably have strong convictions on public policies which aid or hinder the industrial program of "more things for more people everywhere." Sloan had to define his position on politics. "Business and politics do not mix," he observed. "Although we have a right to our own thinking and our own position, politics should have no place in the General Motors scheme of things." On one subject, however, Sloan took a decided position. That subject was the cost of government.

Beginning with his annual report to stockholders in 1935, he introduced discussion of the "Cost of Government." His thesis was based on his major premise of "more goods for more people everywhere." His argument was this: Anything that tends to increase the cost of doing business lowers the productivity of industry in its important role of creating wealth. The cost of government is no exception to the rule. The reason is that as costs are increased, selling prices must increase. Thus less goods can be consumed and hence less can be produced. "The alarming increase in the expense of government, and its economic influence on industry, is reflected now, and of necessity must be reflected more importantly in the future, in the form of direct and indirect taxes." In 1935 Sloan estimated that the General Motors ascertainable direct tax bill amounted to $1.47 for each share of General Motors stock, $334 for each employee, and twenty-one cents of each payroll dollar. By 1952 Federal, state, and local taxes provided by General Motors amounted to more than half of the sum paid by the corporation in wages and salaries. In other words, for each dollar the corporation paid in wages in 1952, it contributed fifty-five cents in taxes. By 1952 the ascertainable direct taxes per share of General Motors Stock, which in 1935 was $1.47, had risen to $18.09 a share of common stock or four and a half times the amount paid in dividends on common stock.

In 1937 Sloan became chairman of the General Motors board.

William S. Knudsen succeeded him as president. Sloan, however, continued as the chief executive officer of the corporation. In his first report to the stockholders as chairman of the board, he pointed out that the road to more things for more people, to a higher standard of living, was through the increase of wages and at the same time the decrease in prices. General Motors had always believed in high wages, steady work, and high annual earnings. By 1938 General Motors was trying to even out and regularize annual employment. It wanted to provide more regular income distributed over the year and for the greatest number of employees. In fact, in 1935 General Motors had already set up a revolving fund of sixty million dollars to build up an inventory in periods of low seasonal consumer demand to maintain employment.

By this time a world emergency was making its impact on the American economy. For the depression problems the demands of war production were being substituted. In both research and production General Motors became a center of industrial strength in the world struggle for the free world. In comparison to its World War II performance the General Motors experience in World War I seemed small indeed. In the first global struggle General Motors had produced ambulances and trucks, officers' cars, artillery tractor engines, Liberty motors, and trench mortar shells. Eighteen of its twenty-three operating units were engaged in government contracts. At the end of World War I, General Motors had completed approximately thirty-five million dollars in orders and had another fifty million dollars of orders in hand. By 1941 in the second global struggle General Motors was producing civilian goods superimposed upon a rapidly increasing output of materials of war. By the last quarter of 1942 General Motors plants were producing 94 per cent of their output for war purposes and 6 per cent for civilian use. It had agreements with a network of nineteen thousand sub-contractors. The colossal production of General Motors in World War II represents an epic in research, engineering, management, and labor history.

In World War II General Motors became the largest producer of war materials. In the "gray period" of the long cold war which followed World War II it remained poised to enter full war production, while its plants were turned to civilian production. In the year 1952, it produced almost a billion and a half dollars' worth of defense production, which accounted for almost a fifth of its total sales.

A mere summary of the production of General Motors in World War II would show the importance of the corporation to the defense of the free world.

While Sloan was working on the long-trend problems of the industry and at the same time meeting the gigantic production and engineering demands of World War II, he was planning ahead for the postwar world with the same confidence in America and its future which had characterized his activities during the depression years. In his own mind he fixed a target date of 1944 toward which he should shoot. On that date, from the all-out wartime effort, General Motors should be ready to convert its plant to civilian manufacture. Whatever might be the role of General Motors as the largest manufacturer of implements of war, military ordnance was not the end goal of the corporation.

Three days before Pearl Harbor Sloan made this position clear. "Some," he said, "take the position that our every effort should be devoted solely to the objectives of the defense program. I do not subscribe to such a policy. I believe that we as industrialists and as citizens of a great democracy have two great responsibilities. We cannot afford to ignore either. First and foremost, there must be an all-out effort in the discharge of our vital obligations to the nation at this time of great need. The war abroad can be won only on the American industrial front. But second, we should keep in mind, in our determination to win the war, that this is *not* an end objective.' National security, the preservation of a representative democracy with free enterprise as an instrumentality of national progress — that is what we are fighting for."

Sloan was concerned with winning the war *and* winning the peace. "We should not deceive ourselves," he went on. "Even if such support should win the war, that does not insure the peace." He was of course clear — perhaps clearer than any civilian — about the role that General Motors must play in the winning of the war. "War," he said, "is a struggle between two opposing technologies. What does that mean? It means that we must have, if we are to use an airplane as an illustration, the plane that is superior in speed and superior in maneuverability. It must be equipped with superior instruments of destruction and it must be designed in such a way as to make it applicable to the processes of mass production in order that it may be produced in superior quantity. The military tells us that fifteen or twenty miles an hour will make a tremendous difference in the performance for victory of an airplane. That being the case, in order to maintain the superior technology, it must be supported by a virile and effective economy. So I make a second point. We must give consideration in the evolution of this plan to maintain at all times a virile and effective economy."

In war there was no question about where General Motors stood. "I stand and we in General Motors stand," said Sloan, "on a platform absolutely opposed to appeasement in every form. We do not believe in appeasement." This goal of unconditional victory, however, did not prevent Sloan from thinking about the causes and cure of war. "My feeling about war," he commented, "has always been that it emanates from an unequal distribution of the world's economic resources among the various nations. I do not believe that with all the problems that will arise we are going to be able to sit down and deal with these fundamental difficulties in a practical and realistic way. After the war I look for a continuation of the nationalistic spirit which has so greatly interfered with international trade and has reduced the standard of living of practically all the peoples of the world. My judgment is that whatever might be done among the peoples of the world from the standpoint of advancing their standard of living will require such great political statesmanship, such sacrifices of one nation as against another that we cannot for a great many years look forward to any real settlement of the world's problems of a character that might be construed as underwriting a peace. I think we are likely to see two or three spheres of influence which are very definitely restricted to the parties involved. However you figure it out, I cannot believe other than that as a result of the war, the American economy will be faced with serious problems. . . .

"In the last twenty years," he continued, "America has been losing its export position due to the development of nationalism. There was a time in the 1920's when the automobile industry exported hundreds of millions of dollars' worth of goods to Europe, tens of millions of dollars' worth of materials to Japan. All of that is absolutely gone. In those countries they have become self-sustaining in the manufacture of motor cars. In other words, we are exporting our technique, our mass production method, our machinery. We are no longer exporting our labor and our machines. I fear there is going to be a very strong demand for the contribution of great governmental expenditures in order to maintain the economy and prevent it from collapsing."

Sloan was sure that the wartime stimulation to industry was "synthetic" and came from the "urge of self-preservation." He pointed out that if men subscribe to the philosophy that there is no such thing as "something for nothing," then they can readily see how they should approach the solution of a problem if they wish to act intelligently. Looking objectively at the situation, Sloan saw these facts in the future — "clear as a crystal," as he was accustomed to say:

1. Greatly increased governmental debt, the continuation of high-level governmental expenditure to maintain the military set-up, far greater than America has before experienced. This means that government will take more of the national income through increase in taxes.

2. In the economy as a whole, profits at a minimum necessary to sustain our system of free enterprise.

3. Increase of the share of labor in the industrial product.

In short, Sloan pointed out, people who do not believe in the magic of "something for nothing" must expect increased taxes levied by government, higher wages for labor, and a minimum return for capital. Therefore the one chance to prevent prices from increasing and to stimulate a reduction in prices lies in increased efficiency. "We must have new and better instruments of production. We must also absorb the higher wage rates in the increased production of labor," he said.

Sloan was realistic about America's role in world affairs. "When real trouble comes around," he said, "we seem in some way to get into it and pay a good part of the bill, in some cases with the lives of our people and in some cases with our wealth." This situation meant to Sloan that America must take a position in world affairs commensurate with its responsibilities. He saw war no longer as combat between men but rather as conflict between machines.

Within General Motors, planning for the postwar period went on at feverish pace. On December 10, 1943, Sloan announced their postwar plan. It called for expenditure of half a billion dollars to reconvert operations from war programs to civilian production. His plans were based on the expectation that national income measured in prewar dollars would climb to a hundred billion dollars a year. General Motors was thus the first big corporation to come out with a postwar program. To maintain maximum postwar employment, Sloan felt that American industry must be invigorated by the pressures of competition in the free market system of profit-and-loss operations and be encouraged by reasonable profit incentives and constructive government policies. The situation demanded leadership and economic statesmanship. Included in such a program of statesmanship, Sloan felt these conditions to be imperative: maximum employment, a national defense policy designed to prevent a third world war, foreign trade moving on two-way streets, and no world WPA at the expense of the American taxpayer.

In summary of his position he pointed out that America must develop new things to produce and produce existing things at lower prices. "If we do not," he said, "there are certain to be fewer instead of more jobs available. Jobs, said Sloan, come from a combination of capital, management, and opportunity. The catalyst is possible profit. The foundation is confidence in the future of enterprise as determined by national economic policy. Expanding job opportunities are a social, political, and economic must. The sole instrumentality by which they can be opened up in a free economy lies in a virile and expanding system of enterprise. It is not "something for nothing" or "a rabbit out of a hat or a gift from Utopia."

Sloan never deviated from his conviction that technology is the great instrumentality that enables real gains to be made throughout the system as a whole. "The point can never be overemphasized," he said. "Engineering and research must be encouraged. There is no limit to their performance. But research should not be confined to the physical sciences. It must aggressively be applied to all the functional activities of enterprise."

Within this postwar system, Sloan was convinced that the issue of wages must be dealt with not as the predominant issue between two groups but as a function of cost and selling price and in a way to establish a proper balance among all groups.

As the largest manufacturing corporation in the world, General Motors had come to be, during the period of Sloan's leadership as president and board chairman, a trade name familiar to people around the globe. Everywhere GM products were respected for their quality. As an enterprise the corporation had performed a titanic service in developing the research in science and technology into assembly-line production. It continually demonstrated the genius of Big Business in producing new, more, and better things for more people at good value. In good years, bad years, and war years, it had maintained a sound financial position. Its size and world-flung activities had been directed according to policies which made the General Motors impart a positive, stabilizing, constructive, and liberal influence in national and international economic life. Its amazing achievement in supplying military matériel for the defense of the free world stood as a bulwark of industrial might in an age of technological warfare. The bigness, importance, and power of General Motors made the corporation a symbol of capitalism.

The behavior of General Motors, in an age when the American economy was under assault by forces and philosophies which would nationalize major industries, therefore, came to have an influence "by example" of serious importance. The economic system of which General Motors was a foremost example had in the long run no firmer foundation than the attitudes which people held toward it, and the stability and increasing productivity of the free economic system. With millions of customers, hundreds of thousands of employees and shareholders, and thousands of dealers and suppliers, General Motors had no choice about public relations: it had to create, maintain, and hold widespread confidence. General Motors was not only a superlative example of private enterprise in a system that Hoffman called "mutual capitalism"; it easily could become a major target for an attack upon that system.

Sloan understood this pivotal responsibility in the context of the times. He stated the task like this: "In the relatively new industrial order, geared so directly to communication through which minds meet over vast distances and in bewildering number and complexity, the use of media for all the senses becomes a necessity for any business enterprise which wants its message to reach all the public. Though the message itself may be simple, the means of spreading that message are many and complex. They include all the variations of communication through the printed word, the spoken word, appeal to the eye through color, form, and motion, and to the reason through logical presentation and detailed information."

Despite the huge size of the corporation, Sloan sought to conduct the vast enterprise with its mass publics in the same direct, courteous, and informal manner that is characteristic of small groups. Personal courtesy, humbleness, and thoughtfulness for people extended from Sloan down to the dealer who met the customer. Satisfaction with the product rose from the customer who drove the motor car to the research laboratory which worked on the development of new ideas.

Sloan believed in teamwork, group power, and face-to-face meetings. Not only did he go out to visit his dealers in person; he held to the idea that when a group of men gets together no one can predict what plus-values will come out of the discussions. On every level General Motors sought facts and group discussion in arriving at decisions. Once decisions were made, they became deliberate policies. Within General Motors under Sloan there were no hunches, no solo-playing, no emotional tantrums. The best men whom General Motors could employ were constantly searching for the best answers to problems. "Fine minds without a knowledge of how to make other fine minds work," said Sloan, "are wasted." Sloan had the capacity to bring out the best in the men with whom he was associated. "If Sloan were a chemical substance instead of a man," said one observer, "he would be a catalyst, because he releases a flood of unexpected possibilities in people." By his conception of executive growth to leadership, he created a favorable climate in which good men could become excellent individuals *on the team.* Up and down the line General Motors men knew that the success of the whole enterprise depended upon their sane and constructive decisions and actions. The General Motors type was, therefore, cut from a certain clear pattern.

These men had an objective: to manufacture a superior product and to merchandise it as a sound value — at a profit. Central in Sloan's thinking was the fact that General Motors manufactured a superior product at an intrinsic dollar value for millions of people. It was producing goods for use, and the user ought to be so served that with each purchase he became a witness for General Motors. "The quickest way to the permanent assurance of profits," said Sloan, is "to serve the customer in ways in which the customer wants to be served. Modern industry with its large-scale operations tends to create a gulf between the consumer and those responsible for guiding the destiny of the institution. A corporation can no longer depend upon casual contacts and personal impressions — the business is too big and the operations too far-flung. Furthermore, we are passing through a kaleidoscopic era characterized by swift movement — social as well as economic. Such conditions cannot fail to bring more rapid changes in tastes, desires, and buying habits of the consuming public. So it becomes increasingly important that we provide the means for keeping our products and our policies sensitively attuned to those changing conditions." A corporation "serves people." "General Motors consumer research," Sloan said, "takes the people just as it finds them. It makes no attempt to reform them and entertains no desire to change them. It studies them and gives them something that they should have. General Motors consumer research is based upon the same purpose which activates advertising and selling of its products: to stimulate business and to aid the buyer in spending his money wisely." Over and over again, in good times and bad, Sloan urged men not to "skimp on research supported by intelligent engineering. Such economy is not a good buy." To Sloan, consumer research was just as necessary to guide and control policy as was the system of control accounting which he introduced after the General Motors crisis in 1920 to hold the "ship in a steady course."

Sloan recognized that General Motors lived in a "goldfish bowl." Its products moved constantly before the public eye with high visibility. General Motors products became news, topics of household discussion. Small boys can name the products and discuss their good and bad points. If Principle Number One in Sloan's concept of public relations required the best man in the right place, Principle Number Two was the best possible product in the hands of the consumer. "Public relations," he said, "result from three things: good policies, good products, and good services. These three performances themselves result from good management, and they have a direct result on earnings and employe morale."

That people had confidence in General Motors was the testimony of many publics. When Sloan joined General Motors in 1918, the corporation had four thousand, seven hundred and thirty-nine shareholders. At the end of 1952 about one out of every three hundred and twenty men, women, and children in the country was a stockholder in General Motors. Sloan felt it to be a desirable goal that every American should become a shareholder in American industry. By 1952 about one out of every seventy Americans on the average were buying a General Motors car or truck. Both the investing and motor-car-buying public thought well of General Motors.

The task of directing public relations, however, became so gigantic with the growth of the corporation that Sloan found it necessary to put the work in the hands of a director. In 1931 he brought into General Motors the Phi Beta Kappa financial editor of the *New York Evening Post*. Paul Garrett, after a thorough preparation in governmental research and journalism, raised public relations to the level of a major concern of the corporation's executives on the policy level. As a vice-president in charge of public relations, he became a vice-president on the general staff, charged with the policy and service functions. A public-relations policy committee reports, through the administration committee through the operation policy committee, to the board of directors of the corporation. Through Garrett's leadership public relations in General Motors became a functional activity at the top corporate-policy level. Dividing the nation into eleven regions, Garrett maintained the quality and tone of Sloan's pattern and implemented it with the techniques and instruments of contemporary scientific communication.

As its public relations program developed, General Motors recognized that its task was not the comparatively simple one of making the corporation respected as a good manufacturer and a good citizen. It discovered that the structure of the kind of society represented by the General Motors pattern was under serious assault. General Motors research left no doubt about the determination of the leaders of the movement toward socialism. In the larger social context General Motors itself was under attack as a symbol of the kind of free society in which it had grown up. Sloan was clear about the issue. "Our civilization today is in a state of unstable equilibrium bordering on chaos," he said. "We are faced with great opportunities far in excess of anything heretofore thought possible. At the same time, we are faced with grave dangers. There falls upon our civilization the shadow of another event, a catastrophe motivated by an ideological conflict between the economic systems of the world's two greatest nations. The fundamental question before the leaders of the world today is: has it the will, the power, and the knowledge to rebuild its economies in terms of tolerant living standards before the people succumb in despair to the enticing appeals of the demagogue? And can this be done against the economic pressure of destructive and almost irresistible social forces? *The fundamental task before our country is so to manage its economic affairs as to demonstrate the basic truth that economic accomplishment and human happiness are determined by the extent to which men are permitted to exercise their initiative, their imagination, their individualism, and their leadership in the atmosphere of a free society.*"

In a politically and ideologically divided world, Sloan saw a series of problems. "Our economic burden," he said, "is great: inherent extravagance and inefficiency in government; increasing demand for social services; the burden of great debt. If we are to attempt to avoid war, we must develop and maintain at all times what will be accepted by the world at large as a predominance of military power expressed always in terms of the technology of tomorrow. This is a burden such as our country has never before had to accept in times of peace. The cost must be reflected in a continuing high level of taxation already at the point of confiscation, thus weakening incentive and limiting capital formation so essential to economic progress."

In such a setting Sloan saw many tasks facing management — tasks strange, new, and complicated. "The structure of the economy," he said, "is becoming more and more complex — a sequel of the industrial age. The interrelationships of one part of the industrial system with the others, the expanded role of government with its increasing interference with the economic process, and the ascendancy of labor and many other influences, have brought problems to management which require it to assume the role of economic statesmanship. Management must now consider the impact of policy upon the economy as a whole in terms of high living standards and of expanding employment with stability."

While General Motors in its operations was subject to such substantial control that it could adjust to almost any conceivable circumstance, no fact was clearer than this:

A highly industrialized technological society must maintain full production and full employment to provide more things for more people in more places. Full employment means full production, and full production means high-level consumption. Political and industrial policies which contravene these basic premises strike fatal blows at free society.

In exploration of the situation which he found in a free society under assault, Sloan saw some special points which needed attention. Two of these were (1) industrial bigness, (2) economic illiteracy.

Sloan had done personally a lot of thinking about industrial bigness in a competitive society. Opinion surveys verified the general impression that "large-scale enterprise" had become the "whipping boy of almost every social and economic reformer and many political propagandists." "These critics," said Sloan, "uncritically identify monopoly with mere size and condemn it. At the same time they may recognize that large entity is essential for the most effective utilization of managerial brains, investment, and production fairly required by the high standards of living that are inevitable in a society dominated by an advanced technology."

Sloan feels that the 1950's demand a reconsideration of the traditional assumptions about the relation of big size and monopoly. The traditional assumptions, he feels, were unrealistic. They were founded on premises of an economic system based on limited markets, little product diversification, a restricted rate of growth, and failure adequately to recognize the impact of technological progress. "A dynamic economy," he said, "is incompatible with such assumptions."

As one of the steps to encourage a reconsideration of these traditional assumptions, the Alfred P. Sloan Foundation and the Maurice and Laura Falk Foundation made grants to Brookings Institution in Washington to study the traditional stereotypes about bigness in business in relation to the facts of competition. On the basis of an elaborate statistical study extending over several years, A. D. H. Kaplan, senior staff economist on the project, made a summary of the relation of economic bigness to political freedom. "In our economy," he said, "Big Business undertakes the major role of co-ordinating individual effort and resources into collective achievement. Big Business has not merely been kept subject to this competitive control; on the whole it has also made an essential contribution to its scope, vitality, and effectiveness." In the world ideological conflict it was certain that a nonsocialistic nation with an advanced technology like the United States must inevitably recognize Big Business as a "fact" and deal with it realistically, just as Big Labor organized in industrial unions was a fact.

Another concern of General Motors as its activities related to the social order was economic illiteracy. By the use of such agencies as the Opinion Research Corporation and the Survey Research Center of the University of Michigan, Paul Garrett began to see statistically what people were thinking. The substance of the reports was that people felt General Motors lacked "human attributes." People, according to the surveys, felt that it lacked a soul, that it was reactionary in its policies, that it was concerned with profits rather than progress, that it looked upon the worker as a machine.

To deal with such misconceptions — which affected the welfare of General Motors as an important segment of free, competitive, technological society — the corporation faced the facts as it always did in shaping policies. To communicate its message that "profitable industry creates better products at lower prices," it proposed slowly to develop the technique of what it called "barnyard economics." By this it meant the simplification of economic information and its direction to particular publics. The corporation realized that it "must make haste slowly," "that it must creep" as it learned "to walk," but it proposed to "take its hair down" and talk to people informally on their own level in the same way that Sloan had visited his dealers in the 1920's. A mature corporation like General Motors found itself an amateur in the field of social policy where alternative patterns of social organization were being debated.

To take an example: youth was a public which needed cultivation. The corporation as policy felt that it should "leave no stone unturned" where it could strengthen the impression that General Motors has the interest of American youth genuinely at heart. "We can reduce many of tomorrow's problems if we pay more attention to youth today," its public-relations men said in conference. Another such public was composed of the sixty-five million women who live in cities and on six million farms, who hold 40 per cent of the titles to houses, who spend ninety cents of every dollar, who teach in schools, work in civic clubs, and who within the General Motors family number over two hundred thousand shareholders, seventy-five thousand employees, and wives of tens of thousands of General Motors employees, dealers, and suppliers. Women, so Garrett learned from studies, are the least informed of all publics concerning the objectives, policies, and purposes of business. General Motors wanted people to understand and to believe in the American system as the "only system that has ever produced for the individual the abundance of goods and services that Americans enjoy." An example of the kind of benefit which accrues to the individual in American society, it said, can be seen in the fact that between 1925 and 1940 the average price of passenger cars decreased almost a quarter, the average cost of operating a motor vehicle decreased a half, while wages went up and hours of work went down in the industry. In 1945 it took sixty-five hundred dollars to provide space, tools, equipment, and working funds for each General Motors employee to insure efficient production. Nearly 72 per cent of the General Motors investment has been earned by the corporation and reinvested in its plant and operations. The facts supporting the free enterprise system seemed to appear on every hand as they bounced around in General Motors public-relations policy groups which studied them. But how were these substantial facts to be communicated so that they would influence the public beliefs, attitudes, and actions?

General Motors saw the urgent need to counteract economic "fiction" with "fact." This need came sharply to focus in 1945, when the UAW–CIO was demanding a "look at the books" and asserting that General Motors could pay a 30 per cent increase in wages without increasing the price of its product. General Motors said that the fact was that the corporation had to increase its prices in order to pay a 16½-cent wage increase, and even then its earnings were below those of the depression year of 1938.

The need for economic literacy existed not alone because of the absence of information or the presence of misinformation; it was also the result of calculated "semantic" confusion. Ideas were being associated with symbols, General Motors public-relations men felt, in such a way as to evoke an unfavorable public reaction. Unions and others, social scientists reported to General Motors, for two decades have been associating such a word as "profit" with a bad symbol. Corporations were pictured as "profit-bloated." Industrialists were spoken of as "economic royalists" and pictured as men of "greed." That bad symbols stick in people's minds long after statistics are forgotten and affect people's attitudes, General Motors well knew. Thus another General Motors task was to find out how good symbols might be associated with the constructive concepts which belong to the competitive system of big technological industry — production of more things for more people in more places and continually raising real wages.

There were other concerns on the economic literacy front. What of Walter Reuther's interest in the co-operative movement? What consequences might the extension of co-operatives have for a free society? General Motors had to think of these things in an objective and hard-headed way. Top policy planning in big business had to take into consideration the attitudes and actions of "people" in relation to the pattern of social organization.

Leaders who know that high-level national income, increasing real wages, full production, and full employment are conditions of survival cannot remain aloof from participating in the democratic process by which public opinion is formed and public policy determined. Unless they so participate, everything which they represent through manufacturing more goods for more people in more places, through the creation of wealth, is threatened.

Top policy discussions in General Motors, in fact, soon became an advanced seminar in social economics. Executives were compelled to do fundamental thinking about the relation of industry to society. "We have never trained ourselves to think in these terms," said one General Motors executive. "We have taken our way of doing things for granted and assumed that everybody else understood." Sloan put it this way: "A great corporation must think at the policy level with a maximum of intelligence and understanding. It must become increasingly articulate as to what is to be done or undone in national economic policies to make the system operate more effectively. It must assume a leading role in the education of its own people on the economic facts of life, on the functions of enterprise, and on the processes of the production of economies. And all this must be done without fear or favor in recognition of management's great responsibility for the protection and perpetuation of a free economy. The measure of our accomplishment will be determined by our scientific progress, by its effective capitalization in the arts, by the climate of national economic policy created by government, and through the instrumentality of the American system of competition motivated by the freedom of the people."

To Sloan the national elections in 1952 were only a "conditional verdict." And as chairman of the Bonus and Salary Committee of the General Motors board, he did not intend to soften his conviction that "great leaders create great accomplishment and are entitled to corresponding economic rewards." The keystone of Sloan's General Motors system resided on rising above "mediocracy" on all levels by discovering and putting "uncommon men" to work with freedom to act and responsibility to produce. To maintain an equal purchasing power, he pointed out, an executive who in 1939 received a compensation of 50,000 dollars would need to receive in 1951 the sum of 365,000 dollars.

In the concern for public good Sloan and General Motors were not alone; they found a second area of danger in political apathy. "The right to vote without fear of reprisal is the keystone of free society," said Sloan, "but the tragic fact is that in 1948 hardly 50 per cent of the eligible voters went to the polls." Over the years the percentage had been growing less, he said, while in England over eight out of ten voters were going to the polls. In 1952 Sloan lent his active influence to overcome political apathy and to get out the vote. Economic illiteracy and political apathy to him were serious diseases in a free society. In fact General Motors applied these principles to carry out its own responsibilities in encouraging good citizenship. In January 1947 the Operations Policy Committee adopted a resolution which stated that "apart from any personal responsibility as a citizen of the community in which he resides, every corporation and divisional leader has an obligation to help maintain the position of General Motors as a good responsible citizen of the community. . . ." Paul Garrett pointed out: "Many years ago it was recognized in General Motors that good relations outside grow from good relations inside. What people think of us within our own organization, and in the communities where we operate plants, molds the opinion of General Motors held by people over the nation."

Through plant-city committees, and in other ways, General Motors local management in its dozens of plant communities over the country assumed a deep responsibility. As policy, General Motors encouraged its people to be a "friendly part" of the local community. The corporation encouraged its people to participate in civic affairs, to join and become active in business and service associations, to co-operate with local authorities in meeting community-wide problems, to use local sources of supply wherever possible, to sponsor youth activities, to promote the educational and cultural life of the community, to make its facilities as practical available for meeting rooms, to participate in local government, and *to vote*.

The corporation computed that a General Motors man who works a forty-hour week spends 27 per cent of his time in the plant and 73 per cent of his time outside the plant. The corporation took pride in a letter which it received from a professor following a plant tour and program arranged for a group of students. In part the letter read: "I was particularly interested in your introduction . . . as a businessman, civic man, and church man. It was an inspiration to many and to the young people that you are interested in all these activities. Would that more businessmen would set similar examples for young people to follow." In good citizenship in the local community General Motors found the foundation of free society — in citizens who take and perform the obligations of citizenship seriously.

❖   ❖   ❖

While General Motors was making its contribution to economic, literary, and community activity, Sloan was pursuing his conviction that in an industrial society "basic knowledge is the catalyst." With an unqualified faith in the future of America and in the progress which is created by science and industry in the service of a free people, General Motors proceeded to construct a brilliant symbol of the age of advanced industrial technology as "the General Motors Technical Center."

Twelve miles northeast of the Detroit City Hall, and thirty-five minutes by automobile from the General Motors Building, Sloan saw, on an 818-acre site at the junction of Twelve Mile and Mound Roads, the General Motors Technical Center take form.

This Technical Center, as Sloan says, is a "place for clear thinking." Perhaps no monument to the age of more-goods-for-more-people-in-more-places is as completely representative of the trinity of science, engineering, and industry as is this great development. It forms the bridge between the universities and industry, over which an unending stream of "uncommon" men with unorthodox ideas flows in the advancement of knowledge and the development of better products and better methods to increase quality and to reduce cost. It is the world's hugest and best-equipped nonacademic campus. The buildings themselves are grouped into four units which represent the pattern of the technological age of big industrialism. These units are known as the Research Laboratories, the Engineering Staff, Process Development, and Styling. The twenty-two acre lake which forms the center of the development, unlike a huge lawn, does not need to be mowed; at the same time it acts with the trees to cool the atmosphere. It joins beauty with strict economy! The landscape is arranged to provide ample motor vehicle parking and to "absorb" eleven miles of roads into the design. "Very often," says Sloan, "an idea can be substituted for an expenditure."

The architect for the Center was Eero Saarinen, the son of the distinguished Finnish designer. He joined interlocking forms, honest functional solutions, and structural clarity to express the American life of the industrial age. Saarinen was the same architect who designed the chapel at Sloan's alma mater, Massachusetts Institute of Technology — serene, windowless, cylindrical, a brick structure resting on arches in a circular moat, with light coming from a sky-opening above the altar, and from below, as it reflects through the arches from the water in the moat. The chapel in a technological institution, as the architect said, is intended to provide a retreat from frantic campus life, where an individual can "contemplate things larger than himself."

It was the capacity to comprehend bigness that had made General Motors great as, under Sloan's leadership, it had moved always forward and upward into the future with courage, imagination, and faith in America. In January 1954 Sloan, as chairman of General Motors, and Harlow H. Curtice, president of the corporation, entertained five hundred businessmen at a luncheon at the Waldorf-Astoria. The General Motors "Motorama" opened the next day. It was just fifty-one years before that Sloan had purchased the "Conrad" so that he could conduct research to develop a new market for roller bearings. In commenting that General Motors had made capital investments of two billion dollars in the eight postwar years from 1946 through 1953, Curtice took the occasion to announce a further billion-dollar expansion program to be completed within the next two years. The decision, he said, was "evidence of confidence in the immediate future, in the long-run growth of the market for General Motors products, and faith in the future of America." There is, he said, "no depression in my vision." Turning to statistics, he pointed out that the disposable per capita income in the United States was currently about 40 per cent above the level of 1940; by 1960 he expected that the average expressed in terms of buying power might well rise to 70 per cent. He rejoiced in the restoration of the foundations of a free economy by political leadership and was encouraged further by the fact that economic initiative had now passed to private industry. "Business leaders have the responsibility and must accept the challenge of building on these foundations an economy that will continue to be sound and dynamic," he concluded. "Those who see recurrent shadows of depression and recession falling across the nation's path of progress should also have faith. With a favorable economic climate, an enterprise system unhampered by controls, and a people willing to work for an improved standard of living, the responsibility rests with industry and business to keep the economy strong and, over the years, keep it expanding. . . . That is the challenge that faces us today. As far as **General Motors** is concerned, we accept that challenge."

Sloan, now seventy-nine, rose at the table. With his unquenchable faith in the future of America, he observed that in his opinion General Motors would probably spend a half-billion dollars more than Curtice had announced. "I never saw these things grow — except up," he said.

At the New York World's Fair, old-timers around the luncheon table recalled, William S. Knudsen and Alfred P. Sloan, Jr., were sitting in the Press Club of the General Motors Building, chatting after the opening celebration. Around them stood an array of products designed for better living, for widening horizons of contact, for increasing people's enjoyments. "Just think," said Sloan to Knudsen, "the wonder of it all is that we have only just begun. The opportunities for America are beyond the dreams of any man now alive, if we will only through persistent **work** and enterprise continue the **pattern.**"

IV

Walter P. Reuther

*President, International Union United Automobile,
Aircraft, and Agricultural Implement Workers of
America; and President, Congress of Industrial
Organizations*

Workers' Pressure toward Economic Security with Political Freedom

Paul Vincent

WALTER P. REUTHER

*"It is possible to build a world in which mankind can have
both bread and freedom."*

WALTER P. REUTHER SAYS:

OUR PROBLEM IS to achieve full employment and full production in peacetime without loss of democratic freedom. The unfinished business of this century is the problem of maintaining full employment in an expanding economy based upon the fair and healthy relationship between wages, prices, and profits. By common and sincere efforts we can provide for an ascending standard of living for everybody, through dynamic spending with high-velocity dollars pumping money into our economy, thus creating demand, jobs, and opportunity. Either we shall use our new machines and technology to help us create security and dignity in the construction of a brave new world, or the impact of jet propulsion technology upon a huffing-and-puffing Model T distributive system will dig our economic graves. ✍§In our complex industrial society, with science and technology providing us with increasingly effective tools of production, the majority of our people live in the shadow of insecurity and under the recurrent threat of unemployment. The more we learn to produce with lessened effort, the greater becomes our need to find the means of keeping our vast productive power at work maintaining and increasing the distribution of goods we are able to produce. ✍§By democratic means we must develop the social mechanism necessary to provide all people with a full measure of both economic security and political freedom. For the first time in the history of civilization, we in America have the human and material resources and the tools of abundance to conquer poverty and necessity. If we learn to use these tools we can build a world based on peace, plenty, freedom, and the brotherhood of man. If we fail in our great opportunity at this moment our epitaph will be simply stated: we possessed the ingenuity to unlock the secrets of the universe for the purposes of destruction, but we lacked the courage and imagination to work together in the constructive pursuits of peace. ৶§In our search for bread and freedom in the United States we must travel the middle democratic way. We must mobilize our full strength in the economic and political fields to plan, work, and fight for the positive ends of peace as we have worked and fought for the negative ends of war. Under the slogan of "teamwork in the leadership and solidarity in the ranks" we have been able to weld together the forces of our union around a constructive, militant trade-union program. The kind of labor movement we are building is not one committed to a nickel-in-the-pay-envelope kind of philosophy. It is a labor movement that says we have to mobilize workers in the economic field and then apply that power to the struggle in the political field as organized consumers. ৶§The relationship between the breadbox and the ballot box is close. What we win on the picket line they may take away from us in Washington. The surest way to guarantee that your icebox will be filled with good food is to see that the ballot box is filled with good votes on election day. ৶§On the economic front fact-supported bargaining under threat of strike exists as the major contractual device by means of which we translate technical progress into economic progress, human happiness, and dignity for man. ৶§We work to mobilize abundance for peace and for people, and to establish once for all the fifth basic freedom — the freedom from the fear of abundance. Technological logic now joins with moral sentiment to compel us to abandon antiquated, obsolete concepts of dividing up scarcity so that one man gets his share only when the other man is denied his. We are confronted with the necessity for the formulation of wise and sound economic policy which will generate a moral force throughout the world stronger than any H-bomb man can invent. ৶§Justice and peace and security and freedom are indivisible in the kind of world we live in. The million and more members of our union cannot win their own security in an insecure world. The road ahead leads not backward but forward, to full production, full employment, and full distribution in a social order which has achieved economic security with political freedom within the framework of political democracy.

৶§ ৶

Workers' Pressure
toward Economic Security
with Political Freedom

SOLIDARITY HOUSE STANDS ON THE EDGE OF THE DETROIT
River at 8000 East Jefferson Avenue on a site once occupied by
Edsel Ford's family. Three metal letters attached to a sandstone
gate pillar designate the entrance as the international headquarters
of UAW. In the entrance lobby of the highly functional building,
which is set off with lawns and terraced driveways, a bronze plaque
declares that

WITH OUR HANDS WE BUILD AUTOMOBILES, TRACTORS
AND PLANES

WITH OUR HEARTS WE BUILD A BETTER TOMORROW

STRENGTHENED IN THE SOLIDARITY OF HUMAN BROTHERHOOD
WE JOIN HANDS WITH PEOPLE EVERYWHERE TO WIN A WORLD
OF PEACE, SECURITY, DIGNITY, AND JUSTICE FOR ALL

The one-syllable verb WIN in the inscription connotes victorious
action in a contest. It thus implies the methods by which trade-
unions have advanced: their gains have been wrung in struggle
and strike as a result of determined effort, practical programs, militant demands, and theoretical positions.

The international union, United Automobile, Aircraft, and Agricultural Implement Workers of America, presided over by Walter
Reuther and known as UAW–CIO, occupies Solidarity House as its
headquarters. Since 1935, UAW has grown to be successively the
largest free trade-union in America, the largest free trade-union in
Canada, and the largest free trade-union in the world. Its more than
a million and a third members are organized in almost thirteen

hundred locals representing thousands of collective-bargaining units. The union "brothers" and "sisters" work in the nation's biggest industry, which consumes more steel and buys more basic and durable goods than any other segment of the American economy. Hundreds of accessory industries supply its specialized requirements. Upon its full production much of the stability and prosperity of the country depends. The products manufactured by the workers of UAW provide transportation for the American home, plow the farmer's fields, carry his produce to market, thresh his grain, move the goods of industry over the highways, haul railroad trains, and refrigerate food in the family kitchen. The assembly lines of UAW-organized industry turn out ultra-modern weapons ranging from jeeps to jets and from weasels to tanks. In peace or war, Walter Reuther's union members occupy a key position in the economy of the nation and the defense of the free world.

As trade-unions go, UAW is a rich organization. Its resources exceed sixteen million dollars. Its strike fund alone stands on the books at eight million and therefore represents a weapon to be wielded with telling effect in bargaining negotiations. With clear objectives in mind UAW earmarks substantial funds for the support of effective departments promoting fair employment practices, education, and recreation. Into its citizenship-fund "mite-box" drop five cents from each member every month. UAW spends this earmarked money to "strengthen democracy." It encourages members and citizens generally to register and vote in community, state, and national elections. It carries on organizational and educational programs directed toward the achievement of ever-higher standards of citizen responsibility. It crusades for active citizen participation in the affairs of democratic society.

In the heart of the automobile industry, which Dean Wallace Donham of Harvard University's Graduate School of Business Administration once described as the "grown-up baby of the science of thermodynamics" and a "triumph of engineering integration," Solidarity House stands as a milestone in the development of the labor pattern of a heavily industrialized society in an age of advanced technology. It represents the outcome of the assimilation of the craftsman through the introduction of automatic machines and standardized procedures into a routine worker attached to an impersonal apparatus where he functions as a standardized unit in a continuously moving assembly line. The UAW constitution describes the contemporary design by saying that "the complete subdivision of Labor in the development and operation of the industrial mass-production system imposes conditions under which the worker is gradually but surely absorbed and controlled by the machine." In such a mechanical environment of effort, UAW represents the auto worker placed in an urban, scientific, factory society; he earns his living with his human energies and emotions geared to the high-speed and high-volume output of metallic products.

Solidarity House, where Walter Reuther has his small but elegant office on the third floor overlooking the Detroit River, was dedicated seventeen years after John L. Lewis, coming out of an American Federation of Labor convention in Atlantic City in 1935, drove a decisive uppercut to the jaw of William Hutcheson, of the United Brotherhood of Carpenters and Joiners of America, for allegedly calling him a "bastard." The blow heralded the smashing of the ranks of craft trade-unionism as the labor front in America. A new "industrial" trade-unionism took shape as a social force in American life. "Let him who will," shouted Lewis, "be he economic tyrant or sordid mercenary, pit his strength against this mighty upsurge of human sentiment now being crystallized in the hearts of thirty million workers who clamor for the establishment of industrial democracy and for participation in its tangible fruits. He is a madman or a fool who believes that this river of human sentiment can be dammed or impounded by the erection of arbitrary barriers of restraint."

Making articulate the rumbling demands voiced by the rank and file in the American Federation of Labor conventions of 1934 and 1935 for industrial charters, Lewis berated the attitude of the AFL hierarchy and bolted the 1935 convention. By the end of the year he had joined eight defiant unions into a rump Committee on Industrial Organization with offices in Washington. Responding to this challenge to its authority, the AFL first gave warning, and then officially expelled the CIO unions.

Into American life the CIO promptly injected an aggressive new force. In organization it represented the industrial union, long regarded by many as the inevitable trade-union pattern in an industrialized society of big industry with technologically complicated and interlocking relationships.

Circumstances proved to be ripe for the encouragement of the new project of John L. Lewis. By its extension of assembly-line production, through the continuing installation of the automatic machine, management itself was tending to eliminate the crafts which had constituted a pillar of strength for the American Federation of Labor's aristocracy. With the stock-market crash in 1929, the national economy collapsed. In 1932 Franklin D. Roosevelt was elected to succeed Herbert Hoover; he looked with sympathy upon the aspiration of labor. Within trade-unions the activities of the Communist Party pressed along theoretical and practical lines for the advancement of the industrial unions. Within the UAW, a group of members organized around Walter Reuther were ambitious to take over leadership. They were imaginative, brave, and militant young men with substantial experience as workers, socialists, and agitators for an improved status of the laboring man. Finally, the demands created by the advent of World War II, a high-level prosperity in the postwar period, and continuing armament requirements in the cold war, swelled the ranks of employees in the UAW industries to unforeseen size.

For the group of progressives to which Walter Reuther belonged, the depression of the 1930's provided painful evidence of the results of uncontrolled capitalism. In his 1933 inaugural address, President Roosevelt reported that "a host of unemployed citizens ace the grim problem of existence and an equally great number toil with little return. Only a foolish optimist can deny the dark realities of the moment. Our greatest primary task is to put people to work." To create employment, Roosevelt came forward with a bold omnibus program passed by Congress as the National Industrial Recovery Act, NIRA, administered through an "alphabetical" agency called the NRA. The program aimed to encourage various industries to draw up and apply to themselves a series of self-developed codes. These codes sought to insure profits to industry by developing agreements to create a scarcity factor, to prevent unfair competition and overproduction, to assure the payment of a living wage, and to reduce unemployment by spreading available work through the establishment of shorter hours. By means of collective bargaining, organized labor was to share in the social planning of NRA, as it proceeded in its object of reducing irresponsible competition by approved codes of control. To win the support of labor for this kind of recovery program, NIRA included in its text the famous sections 7 (a) and 7 (c). These paragraphs recognized labor's right to organize, to bargain collectively through representatives of labor's own choosing free from interference, restraint, or coercion by employers, and guaranteed to trade-unions certain minimum functions. Thus the "New Deal" established as a government policy the right of labor to organize. At the same time, it restrained employers from interfering with organizing activities. Roosevelt promptly appointed John L. Lewis, of the United Mine Workers, and Sidney Hillman, of the Amalgamated Clothing Workers of America, to membership on the labor advisory board of NRA. From that moment these two union leaders used their positions to the utmost to exploit the new opportunities so favorable to the extension of trade-unionism. Beginning with the summer of 1933, the United Mine Workers undertook an intensive organizational drive. Lewis added drama and power to the campaign through a series of "spontaneous strikes" designed to show the workers' "enthusiasm" for the new order of affairs.

When the United States Supreme Court held NIRA unconstitutional, the National Labor Relations Act effectively superseded it.

Chief Justice Charles Evans Hughes, in holding the NLRB statute constitutional, took occasion to say that employees have a clear right to organize, to select their representatives for lawful purposes, to organize their own business, and to select their officers and agents. Long ago, he recalled, the court had pointed out the reason for labor organizations: a single employee was helpless in dealing with an employer. Being ordinarily dependent on his daily wage, the worker was usually unable to quit his job and thus to protest arbitrary and unfair treatment. Hence the union gave workers an opportunity to deal on an equal basis with their employers. The Roosevelt political policy created a "playing field" in labor relations and determined the rules of the game of collective bargaining between employers and employees. As a matter of fact labor now acquired an "umpire" in the NLRB, to see that the game was played according to the rules. Under these rules the United Mine Workers, the International Ladies Garment Workers, and the Amalgamated Clothing Workers in particular at once made substantial gains in membership.

Other circumstances contributed to the creation of a climate of opinion in the 1930's sympathetic to labor's goals. New Deal agencies were everywhere at work on the tragic human problem of unemployment. In every community new alphabetical agencies such as the Civilian Conservation Corps, the Federal Emergency Relief Administration, the Works Progress Administration, the Social Security Administration, a Fair Labor Standards Program, and the National Youth Administration were operating to mitigate the economic needs of people.

Examining into industrial policies, the La Follette Civil Liberties Committee was showing how big corporations maintained spy services and employed disciplined cadres of strong-arm men to keep labor under control. In fact, its report even identified industrial arsenal depots where munitions were stored for use, if necessary, in private industrial warfare. The Youngstown Sheet and Tube Company had in its armory, the committee said: machine guns, rifles, shotguns, and tear and sickening gas shells. Corporations, the committee suggested, were the largest buyers of munitions in the United States — law enforcement bodies not excepted. Senator La Follette pointed out that the two arsenals of the Youngstown Sheet and Tube Company and the Republic Steel Corporation alone provided adequate equipment for "a small war."

As the CIO entered the field after its break with the AFL in the fall of 1935, and became a permanent association in 1938, the Communists disbanded their Trade Union Unity League and directed comrades to work within the CIO. William Z. Foster described the realization of industrial unionism as the "greatest stride forward ever made by the American labor movement." When the CIO threw two hundred organizers into the field, Foster rejoiced, especially since he saw new vigor in the effort to organize the steel industry. This was a mission which had been close to his heart since his part in the great steel strike back in 1919. With its system of shop groups, shop papers, and trained fighters, the Communists offered a substantial core of support to CIO; John Lewis did not hesitate to draw upon their experience and skill.

Particularly within the automobile industry, the time was ripe for organizing activity. In the course of the next few years industrial trade-unionism was to find a new leadership in the collaboration of Walter Reuther and a group of younger leaders to which his brothers Roy and Victor belonged.

Walter P. Reuther, who in 1946 was to become president of UAW and in 1952 of CIO, was born appropriately on Labor Day eve 1907, in a brewer's home located on the outskirts of the steel manufacturing city of Wheeling, West Virginia. The family was German, Marxian, and alert to the relationship of economic problems to politics. In the Fatherland Walter's grandfather, a devout Lutheran and amateur theologian who wrote treatises on Lutheran faith (many of which were in sharp disagreement with the church hierarchy), was violently opposed to the kind of militarism that existed in Germany at the time. He came to the United States partly in order to prevent his sons having to be conscripted into the army.

Valentine Reuther, Walter's father, worked for a dollar and a half a day and ran the local brewers' union in his spare time. As he remembers events, his brewery workers never had to strike. He had the theory that the art of negotiation requires self-disciplined diplomacy and that two "hotheads," both steamed up at the same time, are bound to produce trouble. At the age of twenty-three he had risen to head the Ohio Valley Trades and Labor Assembly. The position was conspicuous if not too important, but it took courage for any man in those days publicly to act as a labor leader. It took double courage in Valentine's case, because in politics he was linked with Eugene V. Debs. Indeed, Valentine himself had run unsuccessfully for Congress on the Socialist ticket. Thus within the Reuther family there existed a climate of social awareness and economic rebellion which expressed itself in a liking for political action. To the Socialist position of the father, the mother added a touch of German piety and evangelical passion.

There were five children in the Reuther family, evenly spaced, except for a younger sister — two years apart, ranging from Theodore, the eldest, through Walter and Roy to Victor. Christine was seventeen years younger than Walter. With their father the boys hiked the West Virginia woods, went to union picnics on Wheeling Island, and attended socials in Drecker Hall. All the children went on from Ritchie Grammar School to attend the Wheeling High School for varying lengths of time, but their genuine education took place within the family circle. To the subsequent careers of his children, Valentine Reuther contributed a Socialist outlook and Mrs. Reuther a Christian motivation. Together the father and mother equipped their four sons and one daughter with a thorough, effective, and on-going kind of education which carried them forward with mental alertness, unquenchable curiosity, social sympathy, political insight, and economic understanding. In the educational environment of the family circle the Reuther boys together acquired the verbal skills necessary to communicate ideas cogently in group discussion, public debate, or formal writing. The Reuther home provided a continuous German type of seminar in which economics was always the core subject and trade-union organization and political action the channel of operation. The Reuthers habitually hitched economics and politics together, as Socialists of necessity must do; for they believe politics without economics has no orientation and economics without politics has no engine to propel and guide it toward the welfare destination of the workingman. In the Reuther system politics constituted the tool of economics. Because politics required active and informed citizens to watch and guide its course, the Reuthers made the affairs of state a family concern. As a group they read, argued, and thought things through together — all under the presiding leadership of Herr Valentine.

On Sunday mornings the family attended Zion's Lutheran Church. On Sabbath afternoons, when the dishes were done, the family formally convened in an upstairs bedroom of the farmhouse located on the side hill near the Schulbach brewery. Valentine Reuther moderated the weekly family town meeting. He pitted the brothers against one another on burning issues of the time, ranging from capital punishment to capitalism, from prohibition to woman suffrage, from pacificism to socialism, from child labor to the right of workingmen to organize trade-unions. The father assigned the topics; the boys did their studying in the public library. They wrote out their positions in substantial essays. The Sunday-afternoon debates were serious affairs; they were contests to be won. Under this private "tutorial" system the boys learned to study issues, search for evidence, marshal facts to support positions, and present ideas persuasively in orderly sequence. Together as a family the Reuther boys learned to think, to think on their feet, to outthink other people in their presence, to convince the moderator, and to relish the combat of ideas. They mastered written and oral English as tools for the persuasive communication of ideas — ideas, however, always conceived of in the context of orderly programs of social action. That their thinking was programmatic had important later consequences. Walter came to be known as the "young man with a plan."

The human and ideological comradeship which characterized the Reuther family when the children were growing up continued on through the years. When Walter became president of UAW he presented his father and mother to the convention. The convention record tells so much about the Wheeling home that it deserves to be read in the full text.

PRESIDENT REUTHER: Now, I want to do something that will take a couple of minutes. It is a personal matter with me and I ask your indulgence. Down in the hills of West Virginia there is a little working-class family with a redheaded mother who raised a bunch of boys. She knows the problems of every other working-class mother. She knows what it is to scrape and make ends meet. I remember one time when she bought a brand-new umbrella. We didn't have much money in our house in those days, and one of my kid brothers went out and tried to use it as a parachute and tore it apart. This working-class mother made a black shirt out of the cloth from that umbrella, because that's the way we lived in those days.

She has been a great inspiration to me, and at this time I want to present my mother to the Convention.

Mrs. Reuther was presented and acknowledged the introduction.

PRESIDENT REUTHER: The other member of my family I would like to present is one who is not unfamiliar with the struggles of the American workers. He is an old soapboxer, an old rabble-rouser who indoctrinated his boys when they were pretty young, and he told them the thing most important in the world to fight for was the other guy, the brotherhood of man, and the Golden Rule. In 1923 he was the President of the Central Labor Body in my home town of Wheeling, West Virginia. I advise you not to yell for a speech when I introduce this fellow, because he may make one.

At this time I want to present a good pal of mine, an old fighter in the ranks of labor, a Trade-unionist from away back when the going was rough. I give you at this time my father, Val Reuther.

I warned you fellows — I am not responsible for anything he may say.

MR. VAL REUTHER: Ladies and Gentlemen, Delegates to the UAW–CIO Convention:

Permit me to assure you that it has been a pleasure for Mrs. Reuther and I to spend the closing days of this Convention with you. It reminds me of my younger years. I can assure you I am extremely happy that the seed that I have tried to sow in the minds of our children as they grew up from childhood is bearing fruit. I am happy beyond the power of words to see that they are engaged in the trade-union movement that has always been dear and close to my heart, and I am extremely happy that this organization with which they are affiliated is a part of CIO, because they express the sentiment and the trade-union spirit that I believe in — the industrial form of organization. I am proud that your great organization has taken a definite and uncompromising stand against the question of discrimination against minorities. Those who take the opposite stand are on the wrong side. Their attitude is indefensible and inexcusable.

You can only build a strong labor movement by uniting every man and woman who works for wages, whether it is in the factory, in the mines, on the farm, or in the office.

POLITICAL ACTION

There is one thought, Delegates, if I may be permitted, that I want to leave with you, and that is this: organize your power as citizens — the power of the ballot. The ballot has been called the weapon that executes a free man's will. It can make and unmake Presidents, Congresses, and courts.

It can abolish unjust laws and return to private life those who enacted such laws. Remember that. Only when the workers, wherever employed, know how to use their ballot intelligently, will you ever be able to realize the dreams and the rights that are yours.

In conclusion may I urge you delegates, representing as I understand 900,000 members, to be constant in your loyalty and devotion to the trade-union movement, for it is not only the vehicle and the highway that leads to a better life, it is the beacon light pointing the way to a richer, a fuller, and a more abundant life. Be loyal to it.

Thank you.

PRESIDENT REUTHER: I am glad he is not a delegate to the Convention.

I want to say in all sincerity that in his day he was one of the best in the front lines of labor's struggles.

I will recognize this Brother at the rear mike.

DELEGATE FLEMING, LOCAL 34: I would like to move that we give the father of our leader, our great President, an honorary lifetime membership in our UAW–CIO.

The motion was supported.

PRESIDENT REUTHER: I will recognize that motion, provided it is distinctly and clearly understood he cannot run against me for President.

All those in favor of the motion to bestow on my father a lifetime honorary membership — which I deeply appreciate — all those in favor signify by saying aye. . . . Those opposed . . .

The motion was unanimously carried.

PRESIDENT REUTHER: It is so ordered; and thank you from the bottom of my heart.

At this time I want to take just a moment to call upon . . .

A delegate called out for the father of President Reuther to make another speech.

PRESIDENT REUTHER: I am afraid to get him back here again. I know him much better than you fellows do. My mother will say, "There he goes again, when you get the old fellow wound up he never knows when to stop."

Despite the happy life in the Reuther home in Wheeling, economic necessity forced Walter to quit high school in his third year.

He went to work as an apprentice tool and die worker in the Wheeling Steel Corporation's corrugating plant, where his older brother Ted was already employed. While still an apprentice, Walter's skill in labor agitation and organization became apparent. His employment in Wheeling Steel denied him the privilege of attending the Sunday-afternoon family debates, since his work schedule demanded a seven-day-week performance. Walter decided to mobilize a protest against Sunday and holiday work. For his pains, Wheeling Steel promptly fired him and he thus became a well-identified youthful labor agitator. Further employment in Wheeling was out of the question.

Without a job and without a recommendation, Walter migrated north in 1926 to the automobile manufacturing city of Detroit. He found himself to be a part of the stream of white and Negro workers which had been flowing to Michigan from the South ever since 1914 when Henry Ford first announced his five-dollar-a-day wage. Over the years the movement continued as a consequence of the activity of industry's recruiting agents. Year by year personnel operators encouraged so-called "hillbillies" and Negroes, from Kentucky and West Virginia south to Alabama and Mississippi, to move North to work in Michigan factories. To the city of Detroit more than a half-million Southerners migrated. There they mingled with a quarter-million Negroes from their own states and with a third of a million men and women joined by strong European cultural ties. (World War II was to intensify the demand for labor, and recruitment in the South then became even more active.) The resulting urban social pattern in Detroit produced a clash between Southern folkways and a mechanical urbanism.

Within the industrial city, the factory existed as the center of people's lives. Its schedule determined the organization of their time. Its machines commanded their energies. Its assembly lines, substituting automatic monotony for the heavy labor of former times, created a new kind of nervous fatigue which came neither from manual nor from muscular strain. Workers lived in constant fear of a "lay-off" which could stop their pay-checks. They likewise dreaded the "speed-up," by which industry accelerated assembly-line movement to increase output.

At the age of nineteen, Walter arrived in this kind of Detroit, in the era of Coolidge prosperity. Without difficulty he got a job with the Briggs Manufacturing Company and went to work on a night shift for a thirteen-hour stretch, at a wage of eighty-five cents an hour. From Briggs, Reuther moved on to Coleman Tool and Die Company, and finally settled down for five years as a tool and die craftsman employed by the Ford Motor Company. At Ford he earned an hourly wage of one dollar and ten cents. From the ranks he rose till by 1931 at twenty-four he was foreman in the tool and die room in charge of a complement of forty men.

Ambitious to "get on in the world," Reuther voluntarily continued his education. Nights he worked in industry. Days he attended Fordson High School in Dearborn as did also his brother Victor. As a student activity he organized some of his classmates into a "Four C's Club" representing the ideals of (1) Citizenship, (2) Confidence, (3) Comradeship, and (4) Co-operation. He completed his work in three years. Upon graduation from secondary school, he shifted his schedule to a daytime job so that he could pursue evening courses in labor and industrial problems offered at Wayne University, Detroit's municipal college. As a student, his inclination to agitate, to organize, to develop plans for reform, and to improve conditions found adequate outlet. He organized and became the first president of the Social Problems Club. He mobilized cadres of fellow students and paraded his elite in picket lines.

When Norman Thomas ran for President of the United States as Socialist candidate in 1932, Walter and his brother Victor, who had joined him in Detroit two years earlier, mounted the soapbox. With an avowed admiration for the Soviet experiment in Russia, the Reuther boys castigated Wall Street capitalism with all the vocabulary which Marxism so richly provides. Together Walter and Victor led a campaign against the establishment of a Reserve Officers Training Corps on the Wayne campus, and forced the university administration to give up the idea of an ROTC unit.

As a part-time undergraduate, Walter enjoyed Wayne; the university did not forget Walter. He continued his relationship, with a warm and constructive interest in the university's phenomenal growth as it became a major American urban institution. (At the 1953 commencement, Wayne conferred upon Walter Reuther the honorary degree of Doctor of Laws. Thus he was to receive, finally, a diploma from the institution from which he was separated by economic circumstances in the 1930's, more than two decades before.)

Wayne students as well as Ford workers recognized Walter as a militant trade-unionist with Socialist affiliations.

Within the Ford plant his class-conscious reactions meanwhile were heightened as he experienced a sort of feudalistic paternalism administered through "Ford Service" by Harry Bennett, who among his other duties exercised personal supervision over employees and attended to plant protection. Under Henry Ford's directive, Bennett bore the responsibility of preventing the organization of labor unions among Ford employees. Further, he had the task of identifying Communists in the working force and dealing appropriately with them.

Within the Ford plant a small group of militant Communists had organized the Auto, Aircraft, and Vehicle Workers of America. As an underground operation among Ford employees, it was closely related to William Z. Foster, the militant advocate of industrial unionism. *The Ford Worker*, a spicy little one-penny sheet issued by this group, was first distributed at the Ford plant gates and then found its way by subterranean channels to the rank and file. Among the items circulated in this publication was a version of the Lord's Prayer edited for the benefit of Ford workers. It ran like this:

Our Father who art in Dearborn, Henry be thy name.
Let payday come. Thy will be done in Fordson as it is in Highland Park.
Give us this day our six bucks (plus forty cents?)
And forgive us our laziness as we forgive thee for speeding us up.
Lead us not into intelligent thought or action
But deliver us from all Freedom, for thine is true slavery,
Thy power over us forever and ever. Amen.

When the Auto Workers Union disbanded in 1933 upon the organization of an industrial union affiliated with the American Federation of Labor as Federal Local 19374, Bill McKie became the unit's first president. A Scottish sheet-metal worker with extensive British trade-union experience, McKie as a young man had joined the Salvation Army, migrated to Detroit in 1927, and found a job with Ford. In the winter of 1928, at fifty-two, he had joined the Auto, Aircraft, and Vehicle Workers of America, and was to become one of this Communist-dominated union's most active operators. To achieve the union organization of Ford workers came to be McKie's life passion. In his Scottish brogue he would sing:

> We're going to roll the union on!
> If Henry Ford gets in the way,
> We're going to roll it over him,
> We're going to roll it over him . . .

In 1935, at sixty, McKie officially joined the Communist party.

Henry Bennett had reason to be concerned about the threat of union activity which it was his task to stamp out. Detroit was jittery. By 1932, at least a third of the wage earners in the city were estimated to be without jobs. Relief agencies were not yet adequately organized to cope with the magnitude of the problem of feeding men who have no work. For the alleged purpose of presenting a formal petition to the Ford management, making specific demands on behalf of the unemployed for jobs or relief, unemployed workers — among whom operated a hard core of veteran Communists — organized a march on the Ford plant. William Z. Foster, on parole from a New York penitentiary, arrived in Detroit to address the mass meeting. In the scuffle which ensued at the main entrance to the Ford Rouge plant after Foster's address, Bennett was hit on the head with a flying brick. Guns fired into the mob. Afterwards, elaborate ceremonies were arranged to bury the dead. A cortege ten thousand strong moved from the Detroit Institute of Arts down Woodward Avenue to Grand Circus Park, then reversed its course and paraded five miles to the cemetery. Behind the red-draped caskets "mourners" carried banners with slogans such as: JOIN THE AUTO WORKERS UNION! DOWN WITH JIM-CROWISM! A SEVEN-HOUR DAY AND FULL PAY! WE DEMAND UNEMPLOYMENT INSURANCE! STOP THE DEADLY SPEED-UP SYSTEMS! FREE THE SCOTTSBORO BOYS! HANDS OFF CHINA! Huge cartoons pictured tractors equipped with machine guns mowing down workers; they were labeled THE NEW 1932

MODEL. Demonstrators dressed in gray clothes followed this cartoon. A chorus outfitted with red armbands and neckties chanted a litany:

Ford . . . gives
Bullets for bread.
Ford . . . gives
Bullets for bread.

JOIN THE AUTO WORKERS UNION

Ford . . . shoots
Workers with bullets.
Ford . . . shoots
Workers with bullets.

JOIN THE AUTO WORKERS UNION

Smash the bloody terror.

Orators urged the masses to join the trade-union. The crowd responded antiphonally:

We . . . want
Bread not bullets!

At Woodmere Cemetery pall bearers wearing red berets lowered the four red caskets into graves. In single file, mourners dropped red roses into the holes while demonstrators sang as the band played:

Arise, ye prisoners of starvation,
Arise, ye wretched of the earth!
For justice thunders condemnation,
A better world's in birth!

A strike at the Briggs Body Corporation's Waterloo plant, which manufactured V–8 bodies for Ford, followed to add to Detroit's jitters. In January 1933, five hundred workers walked out. Within two weeks ten thousand other Briggs workers struck. Ford, which depended on these factories for supplies, was forced to shut down and lay off a hundred thousand workers.

Harry Bennett's Ford Service reacted to all these developments with alarm and firmness. Walter Reuther looked on quietly, as a Ford foreman. Within the plant he had been active in signing up members for the trade-union. But both his job with Ford and his pleasant evenings as a Wayne University student ended abruptly in 1933. Ford fired Walter Reuther. The company gave no reason for his dismissal. He was twenty-six.

Thus unemployed, at the bottom of the depression, Walter sat down with his younger brother Victor to hold a caucus to decide what should be done. Always ready with a bold program of action, Walter proposed that they embark upon an odyssey that would take them around the world as a project in "social engineering." In the Soviet Union in particular, Walter anticipated, they could witness at first hand the experiment of socialism as a way of life. The grand tour would give them, the brothers thought, a fresh understanding of the world. As young men, they owed it to themselves and to the future to turn Walter's momentary misfortune into an educational opportunity. With a travel fund of nine hundred dollars between them, Walter and Victor left Detroit to study European industry, trade-unions, and political action abroad.

Embittered by Walter's dismissal and aflame with youthful radical ideas, the brothers set out for New York. Before sailing they had dinner in Manhattan with Paul Porter and a group of intellectual liberals connected with the *Nation.* In the next three years, they circumnavigated the globe. They traveled on foot and on bicycle. They slept in farmhouses, cheap *pensions*, hostels, and haystacks. They cooked their meals or bought them at the cheapest cafés. Everywhere they mingled with working people, found out what they were thinking about and what were the problems of their lives. Avoiding abbeys, museums, and general tourist thoroughfares, they first crisscrossed England. They visited the Austin, Ford, and Morris automobile factories. They went through textile mills. They studied the coal mines. In France they saw what economic autocracy means when they observed the overbearing ways of French managers. Overnighting in German hostels, they heard at first hand how National Socialism regimented thought. They arrived in Berlin the day after the Reichstag fire and inspected the smoldering ruins. With German students they joined in underground activities by which anti-Nazis were smuggled into Switzerland. They visited their mother's birthplace at Scharnhausen near Stuttgart. When after a year they finally obtained a visa, they traveled on to the Soviet Union. They arrived late in 1933.

Walter and Victor remained in Russia sixteen months. Soon after arrival, Walter got a job making tank dies in an automobile factory constructed near the Volga city of Gorki by the Ford Motor Company. He was quickly promoted to a post as leader of a labor brigade of sixteen workers. For his production ideas he won bonuses. With a talent for mastering languages, Victor learned to speak, read, and write Russian. Walter, with no such aptitude, stuck to English. With Victor's interpreting they penetrated the Soviet worker's mind. They prepared stories for a Moscow newspaper on ways to improve production. Among the workmen they found craftsmen from many nations — including a good many American workmen who lived together in a hostel constructed in an "American village" for the Ford plant construction workers. The brothers listened to the Russian workers and peasants discuss their problems. They were thrilled by their eagerness to improve their standard of living. Their fondness for the workers, however, was clouded by their growing disillusionment about the political activities of the Soviet government. When it was time for them to leave, they both felt that the Soviet experiment was not the answer to their quest for the kind of society which could provide economic abundance with political freedom.

With the "bushels of rubles" which Walter had earned, they then proceeded on through Soviet Siberia eighteen thousand miles toward home. In the cities and rural districts of India they witnessed the efforts of the people to achieve political independence and to promote the economic development of their country by throwing off the yoke of British imperialism. They took note of Gandhi's effective method of passive resistance.

They saw China. Going down the Yangtze River at the height of the 1935 flood, the brothers observed Chinese evacuating flood refugees from one side of the river to the other. As they watched, the boat on which the Reuther brothers were sailing collided with a junk. The jolt hurled three or four dozen Chinese men, women, and children into the water. In the face of such a tragedy Walter and Victor protested to the Chinese captain of their boat. He laughed and replied philosophically: "You don't understand China." Walter replied: "We may not understand China, but it's wrong to let people die when not a finger is raised to save them." The captain answered that six million people would starve in China that year. "When we starve in China," commented the captain, "it's because there's nothing to eat. In America you starve because there is such an abundance that the farmers destroy their little pigs to create scarcity." Victor observed to Walter that it might take fifty years for China to produce what its people needed to wear, to eat, and to enjoy. Chinese industries were not operated, he said, to give the Chinese people the things thy needed. Instead they operated with cheap labor to flood the markets of other countries which already had higher standards of living. Always ready with a program, Walter commented: "I say, build up Chinese industries. Build up the industries of India. Let the people in these countries get the benefit of production instead of using manufacturing to exploit the people of these countries. . . . Think of it," he went on, "one third of the people of the world live on less than a dollar a week. The second third lives on less than four dollars a week. It must be possible to build a world in which mankind can have both bread and freedom."

The brothers traveled on to Japan, where they witnessed feverish industrial and military activity.

As a result of their grand tour, Walter and Victor returned with a fresh view about what was going on in the world. They possessed about as comprehensive an orientation as two young men with energy, curiosity, and imagination could obtain.

Although they had been absent three years, employers had not forgotten Walter's union activities at the Ford plant. He began to hunt for a job; he found one at the Brothers tool and die shop and later at the Ternstedt unit of General Motors. During the absence of Walter and Victor on their tour, their brother Roy had migrated to Detroit to work in the Chevrolet gear and axle plant. He had served on the faculty of Brookwood Labor College, and soon became a full-time union organizer. Employed at General Motors, Walter felt the same urge to advance union organization. He volunteered to serve as an organizer of the UAW West Side Local 174. His membership in this local has continued.

When it came time to select a delegate to go to South Bend to attend the UAW convention, Reuther was chosen. With five dollars in his pocket, advanced from the union treasury, he started for Indiana.

The automobile workers who assembled in South Bend, with the Studebaker and Bendix locals as hosts, were determined, rough, and radical. The delegates included seasoned Communists, backsliders from the I.W.W., militant left-wingers, and experienced agitators — together with young men like Walter who had decided to make trade-union leadership their careers. The delegates were mostly men of vigor, youth, courage, and idealism. They were men who had been through the depression and who were seeking any kind of answer to the problems which confronted them as heads of families. As a whole they arrived at their convictions, not through any kind of ideological contemplation, but through their own personal experience with the economy in which they lived. When Walter presented himself as a duly elected delegate, the convention refused to seat him. Reuther contended that he was the regularly elected representative from the Ternstedt plant of General Motors on Detroit's West Side, but the name of "Walter Reuther" seemed to be quite unknown, even to Ternstedt workers themselves. After the credentials committee of the UAW convention had studied the dispute, the chairman delicately reported that Walter had taken an assumed name to cloak his identity in the plant. To operate under the name of Walter Reuther, the committee explained, would have been folly; management would have fired him point-blank.

The convention faced a fundamental issue: would the delegates elect a president and an administration of their own choosing or a representative of the American Federation of Labor who had served as president of UAW since it was granted an AFL charter in 1935? The AFL had granted UAW what it called a probationary charter as an International Union. This meant that AFL appointed its officers and executive board members.

Meanwhile the Committee for Industrial Organizations had been set up. The issue of whether UAW would elect its own officers was now joined with a second issue: should UAW affiliate with CIO? Reuther lined up with those delegates who wanted autonomy for UAW, affiliation with the CIO, and an aggressive drive to organize the industry. The victorious group included a broad cross-section of the union membership which cut across most of the factional and political lines which developed later.

Reuther ended his attendance at his first international trade-union convention as a member of the UAW international board. He was twenty-nine.

Walter now set himself up as a union organizer in a cubbyhole office at Thirty-Fifth Street and Michigan Avenue and proceeded to amalgamate the scattered West Side locals into one substantial unit, chartered as West Side Local 174. Walter's position was a one-man job. He typed his own letters, wrote his own leaflets, drafted his own speeches, issued his own press statements, buttonholed members, and organized — always organized. He liked professional trade-union activities. As he saw his job in the perspective of his grand tour and his growing membership, he began to feel a sense of personal mission and strength. Walter had found his lifework.

With the exception of Theodore, who remained in Wheeling on his old job, all the Reuther children found their way to Detroit and established their homes. In March 1936 Walter married an auburn-haired trade-unionist named May Wolf, who had been active in a teachers' union. A year later Victor married a wife, who, while firm in her support of trade-union activities, was engrossed in the administration of her home. Several years later Roy married a young woman who was engaged in union work among retail clerks. Victor joined the Reverend Henry Hitt Crane's Central Methodist Church and became a member of the board of stewards. Christine, the only sister, after completing her training as a registered nurse at Ford Hospital, fell in love with an ordained minister, and moved to Boston where her husband served as the industrial secretary of the Y.M.C.A.

In the sustaining environment of the Reuther family circle, thus re-established in Detroit, Walter found constant encouragement in his activities.

When Reuther began his West Side organization work the membership of the Local had been seventy-eight; shortly his roll stood at thirty thousand. To a large degree, this monumental achievement resulted from the sit-down strike called in December 1936 at Kelsey-Hayes Wheel Company.

Before calling the strike, however, Reuther had approached the Kelsey-Hayes management and asked them to negotiate some grievances which workers had filed with the union. The management replied that Walter did not represent the workers.

The time had come, therefore, for the union to demonstrate its strength. Plans for the operation were laid at a strategy bull session which Walter called at his home. According to the order of well-timed and perfectly executed assignments, a Polish girl fainted on the assembly line. Upon this signal Reuther's men pulled switches, while the members of Local 174 shouted "S T R I K E!" Outside the plant a loud-speaker mounted on a truck called orders to the men at the gates inside the plant.

With tactical finesse, the union men took their places on the assembly line and sat down. For ten days, union aides fed the strikers with supplies hoisted over the fence and smuggled in through passageways. Day after day the workers "sat." Under the unyielding pressure of this kind of sit-in strategy, Kelsey-Hayes capitulated. It recognized Walter's Local 174 as the bargaining unit. At once management and workers saw Walter as a new force, a master mind of the sit-down strike technique.

The achievement at Kelsey-Hayes, which among other benefits included a minimum wage of seventy-five cents an hour — a rate well above the minimum wage previously paid at Kelsey-Hayes and throughout the industry generally — was a practice exercise in the militant organizing drive upon which UAW–CIO had embarked. From Kelsey-Hayes the organizers turned their attention to General Motors. The outcome of this campaign did much to determine the future of UAW *and* CIO.

The leadership and membership of UAW recognized that if the automobile industry was to be organized, General Motors, as the company responsible for nearly half the industry's production, would have to accept the union. UAW felt a pressure from workers themselves with an impetus which, according to UAW leaders, "had been frustrated over several years of the depression through the repressive measures of intimidation, discrimination, and labor espionage on the part of the company." The realization that the organization of General Motors was a first step in any successful unionization of the motor vehicle industry also made it obvious that Flint had to be organized, if General Motors was to be organized, because Flint was the location of the largest and most important concentration of General Motors plants and workers. Flint was the heart of the General Motors empire.

By this time, as Eddie Levinson, labor editor of the *New York Post* and later UAW's chief editor until his death in 1945, said, the "auto workers felt their oats." To prepare the ground for the 1936 General Motors campaign, UAW assigned Robert Travis (a left-winger well-known to workers and Communists) and Roy Reuther, as organizers. To Bob's experience in strikes Roy added a capacity to see an immediate campaign in its whole industrial setting. These two advance agents were supported by Wyndham Mortimer, a labor leader who likewise commanded a Communist following. The mission of this elite corps was to lead and direct a strike in the Fisher Body, Chevrolet, and other plants in Flint as a condition precedent to paralyzing the whole General Motors automotive division.

At the start, the outcome of the assignment did not look promising. Bob Travis and Roy Reuther, however, were men not easily discouraged. Bob knew how to handle the men; Roy knew how necessary victory in this campaign was to move American labor in a new direction. Together, Bob and Roy hammered at a few simple themes. They reported the facts thus: that General Motors had earned a quarter-billion dollars in profits while the average worker's wage for a whole year added up to scarcely eleven hundred dollars; that in two years General Motors had spent nearly a million dollars for intra-plant labor espionage, and that speed-ups constantly recurred. On its part, General Motors was quite as clear as Roy Reuther about the importance of this Flint strike. Hence it stood adamant in its refusal to recognize and negotiate with the union.

The strike came before the union wanted it to begin. UAW officials wished to hold the strike off until after New Year's 1937 when Frank Murphy, the newly elected Michigan governor, would take office. The union was unable to restrain the workers; the workers called the strike themselves.

After Christmas on December 28, 1936, UAW officially ordered workers to strike and sit down. Flint quickly became the center of one of the bitterest and most decisive struggles in labor history. To defend its interests, General Motors sought protection by injunction. After the strike had been in progress a little more than a month, General Motors obtained a court order directing UAW to cease and desist from its picketing operations and to withdraw its men from the plant. The court threatened imprisonment and a fifteen-million-dollar fine for noncompliance with the order. The union refused to budge. Employers formed themselves into the "Flint Alliance" to present a united front against UAW and to encourage a "back-to-work" movement. UAW on its part called for union reinforcements. Workers, revolting against conditions in the industry, responded. The more experienced men, including a group of Communists and other radicals, helped to make the demands articulate. The determination of the union, supported by the resentment of the men against the corporation, brought events quickly to a focus.

Reinforcements poured into Flint from major industrial cities such as Detroit, Cleveland, Toledo, and Akron. Civil war settled over the city. When the municipal government attempted to halt the movement of food to the men in Fisher Body Plant Number 2, police engaged workmen in hours-long hand-to-hand combat. Guns fired. A bomb discharged tear gas. Stones, lumps of coal, steel hinges, bolts, and milk bottles flew at police and company guards. Outside the plant, a union sound truck manned by Victor Reuther and other experienced leaders called out orders. As the situation got out of hand, Governor Frank Murphy summoned the National Guard. At the same time, he attempted to persuade General Motors to negotiate with the union. While John Barringer, Flint city manager, tried in vain to restore order, Roy and Victor conferred with Governor Murphy in the Durant Hotel.

In the meantime the union was building up food reserves in Fisher Body Plant Number 2 for a long ordeal. Further union reinforcements continued to arrive. Picket lines patrolling the streets lengthened. Sound trucks moved about giving instructions. It was at this point of crisis that Travis, Roy Reuther, and a group of seasoned associates worked out a bold new strategy. They recognized the fact that the union strength inside the plants was inadequate to win a victory. The few members were not evenly spread throughout the plants. For this reason, the leaders determined to seize Chevrolet Plant Number 4, which housed the motor-assembly division. In labor history "Chevrolet Number 4" stands as a sort of landmark, like the Fourth of July. If Number 4 shut down, the act would paralyze General Motors and at the same time bring courage and fighting morale to the union ranks.

When forces were ready, the UAW Women's Auxiliary began demonstrations in front of Chevrolet Plant Number 9. At this signal, the union men inside Number 9 engaged company guards in combat. The ruse operation created the impression that this plant was going to be seized. Number 9, however, was not the objective. While these diversionary activities were going on, workers themselves seized Chevrolet Plant Number 4 and sat down. Governor Murphy, thwarted by these activities in his plan for compromise, threatened to order the state militia to clear the plant. He ordered the guard to interrupt the food shipments to the two thousand men inside the plant. The workers inside had two alternatives: they could fight or they could starve. They chose the former course.

By this time the strike had grown to such huge proportions that the Flint strategists sent for John L. Lewis to take personal command. Knowing that the future of CIO might well depend upon the outcome, Lewis at once boarded the train at Washington Union Station for Detroit with the classic comment: "Let there be no moaning at the bar when I put out to sea."

When the sheriff had read the order to the UAW men to vacate Fisher Body, the strikers calmly proceeded to draw up a statement directed to Governor Murphy. If "the militia, armed thugs, and armed deputies" entered the plant, the workers warned, a bloody massacre would ensue. While Governor Murphy hesitated, the deadline for vacating the premises approached. Again union reinforcements from all over the Midwest began to pour into the city. Among these was Walter Reuther's flying squadron from West Side Local 174. Armed with bricks, baseball bats, and billies, union recruits came to Flint in such numbers that they soon blocked traffic. With their sound trucks, Victor Reuther and his strike leaders took over traffic control. Windows were barricaded with steel plates. Unionists took fighting formation.

Still Governor Murphy hesitated. As an alternative to the enforcement of the court order, he pressed General Motors President William Knudsen to negotiate with John L. Lewis. Then the Governor unexpectedly ordered Lewis to take his men out of the plant. Lewis replied: "Your Excellency, I do not doubt your ability to call out your soldiers and to shoot the members of our union out of these plants, but let me say that when you issue your order I shall leave this conference and I shall enter one of those plants with my people." At this moment President Roosevelt urged General Motors by wire to meet once more with the union representatives. The suggested conference resulted in a compromise. The strike, which had affected a hundred thousand General Motors hourly workers, ended.

As a consequence of the struggle, General Motors recognized UAW as a bargaining agent for the plants which had been closed by the strike. Union membership jumped from a hundred thousand to two hundred thousand. At the end of March 1937, UAW demonstrated its power in a rally held in Detroit's Cadillac Square. A hundred and fifty thousand people joined in the demonstration. Sitdown strikes spread throughout Michigan. On April 6, 1937, Chrysler signed with John L. Lewis. By September, UAW had contracts with four hundred companies; a year before it had held only sixteen. The union had asserted its place.

The third UAW–CIO convention convened that August of 1937 in Milwaukee. Walter Reuther was there as a delegate from General Motors Ternstedt plant. Victor Reuther was there as a delegate from Kelsey-Hayes Wheel, and Roy Reuther went as a delegate from Chevrolet Forge. With Wyndham Mortimer, Ed Hall, and Bob Travis, a Communist leader, the Reuther brothers formed the "Unity Caucus" as a common front opposed to the policies of UAW's president, Homer Martin, a former Baptist minister who had been named a vice-president of UAW by the AFL and who was elected president in 1936 by a coalition of pro-CIO forces. After the General Motors and Chrysler strikes in 1937, Martin began a vendetta against those who were even mildly critical of his policies. The constructive opposition included not only Walter Reuther and such Communist forces as existed, but many other individuals and groups in the union. Martin characterized all his opponents, without any regard for the truth, as Communist or pro-communist. The factional feuding which raged at the Milwaukee convention continued for ten years, until Walter Reuther achieved undisputed leadership at the November Convention in 1947. This decade of intra-union quarreling was guided by Reuther's determination to establish a program for trade-unionism with a broader context than that which theretofore had existed. It was made bitter by Reuther's struggle to oust Communist and Stalinist influence from UAW.

Although Walter had dropped out of the Socialist Party after his return from his world tour, the Reuther brothers were commonly identified at the Milwaukee convention as Socialists. Mortimer and Travis followed the Communist party line in the Unity Caucus. Communists held party caucuses and issued orders for the conduct of party members on the floor. While the "Unity Caucus" was made up of men who were experienced public speakers and parliamentarians, Reuther distinguished himself at Milwaukee in a speech from the convention floor pointing out the undemocratic character of a proposal designed to give small local unions an advantage over the big locals in the next convention.

Back from the convention, Reuther joined in efforts to organize Ford. The drive on Ford continued over a period of four years, until in June 1941 the company signed a contract with UAW. With Chrysler, General Motors, and Ford organized, the union felt that it would be headed for permanent success. Ford, however, was a formidable adversary to engage, as union organizers well knew. Henry Ford himself was a man of stubborn will; he was determined never to recognize a labor union. "Labor union organizers are the worst pest that ever struck the earth," he commented. Harry Bennett now directed three thousand men in Ford's private militia in the Ford Service Department. His force included released convicts, pugilists, ex-policemen — in fact Bennett himself described his corps "as a lot of tough bastards but every goddam one of them's a gentleman."

By the time the organizers moved from General Motors to Ford, Bennett had observed how the union applied its new strike strategy. He was ready for the attack. Among his assets he counted a disciplined plant leadership, an efficient espionage service, and an iron determination not to recognize a union. On its part UAW knew that within Ford there was a strong nucleus of union sympathizers who could be depended upon in the drive. At the request of UAW, the CIO in 1940 set up a Ford organizing committee. John L. Lewis appointed Michael F. Widman to direct the drive. UAW contributed most of the funds necessary for the organizing campaign. The organizers from UAW were strengthened by veterans assigned by John L. Lewis from the United Mine Workers and CIO. Among the organizing group was Emil Mazey, later to become UAW secretary-treasurer under Reuther. Briggs had fired Mazey for union activity in 1936. Subsequently he became president of Briggs Local 212, an office which he held when he joined the Ford organizing staff. He became a key figure in the Ford drive and in the negotiations of the first contract with the company at the end of the successful organizing activity.

As the union organizing campaign proceeded, the tension between the company and the UAW increased. Ford, who consistently refused to negotiate, terminated what gestures the company had made toward collective bargaining at the beginning of April 1941. Wholesale discharges and failure to negotiate grievances, which had arisen in the rolling mill, led to a strike even before UAW was ready for it. After some hesitation, resulting from a feeling that the strike was premature, the organizing committee authorized the walk-out. In a few hours it spread from plant to plant, until the whole huge River Rouge plant stood paralyzed. It became obvious to UAW officers that the time had come to clinch the organization of the Ford plant.

As the news was whispered from mouth to mouth that "Ford is shut down," Detroit quivered with anxiety. Union officials met promptly. Shortly after midnight they called the strike, which already was in full swing. In Union Hall that evening the discussion was long and frank. Emil Mazey remembers the session as one of the most interesting in his labor experience. Among those who spoke was Walter Reuther. Union men milled around the halls. They held informal caucuses. They entered the meeting to speak their minds. In the early morning hours of April 2 they reached a decision. Equipment was made ready for a long siege. A soup kitchen was set up. A union hospital moved in. Flying squadrons were instructed. Next morning, Harry Bennett's Ford Service men held the gates ready for action; but union men used a new strategy. This time they barricaded all approaches to the Ford plant to shut off communication. Then they seized control of the Dearborn drawbridge, to prevent delivery of supplies by water. At seven o'clock in the morning fighting broke out. Union men began by hurling nuts and bolts. Outfitted with bars and knives, Ford Negroes charged out of the main gate to assault union pickets. When the union men were attacked from the plant the second time, they slugged with baseball bats, fists, billies, and clubs. Ford meanwhile branded the union campaign a Communist conspiracy.

In the midst of this drawn battle, Ford and the UAW accepted an offer of the governor to work out a settlement. Ford history infers that Mrs. Henry Ford persuaded her husband to negotiate. However the armistice was achieved, something actually did compel Ford to consent to a National Labor Relations Board election to determine the proper bargaining unit and to negotiate a contract if UAW won. Out of eighty thousand votes cast, UAW received fifty-eight thousand. In a complete reversal of its position, Ford agreed to a union shop, dues check-off, grievance machinery, seniority, overtime pay, and other benefits. With the UAW Ford then negotiated an agreement which, according to union figures, in the next year brought an additional fifty-two million dollars in wages to Ford employees.

As the citadel of the nonunion shop, Ford had fallen. Ford Local 600 became the largest local union in the world, and continued to be one of the major centers of Communist trade-union activity in the automobile industry. Ford victory gave UAW–CIO its first union shop and its first check-off contract in the industry. With General Motors, Chrysler, and Ford organized, UAW now moved forward from plant to plant, in a mop-up campaign.

From the automobile industry UAW turned to the aircraft business, which by this time was adding thousands of workers to its rolls to meet World War II armament demands. The aircraft organizational drive won victories in the plants of Curtiss-Wright, North-American Aviation, Douglas, Goodyear Aircraft, Vought-Sikorsky, and others. The records of UAW show the results of these campaigns. In 1939 UAW had three hundred and twenty plants under contract. Four years later the number had increased five times, to nearly fifteen hundred. At the end of April 1941 the paid membership was over four hundred and fifty-three thousand. By October of the same year, it had risen to six hundred and forty thousand.

Meanwhile both the government and the union had taken official note of the sit-down strike. A UAW constitutional convention resolution described the "stay-in strike" as a weapon of "singular effectiveness in stopping the very heart of an industry" as well as "the only method" of compelling employers to enter into real collective-bargaining relationships. "It will," said the convention, "remain labor's most effective weapon against the autocracy of industry." The United States Supreme Court felt otherwise. On February 27, 1939, it declared the use of the sit-down strike to be "an illegal seizure of buildings in order to prevent their use by the employers in a lawful manner." In reviewing the sit-down experience, an observer asked a sit-down leader why the simple defense strategy of having the city shut off the water had not been used by management. "Such action," said the unionist, "would have been impossible. The act would have been against the law."

During the years of the Ford organizing drive the CIO organization suffered severely from internal policy differences and the political tactics of John L. Lewis. In the summer of 1938 four powerful unions withdrew from CIO. Lewis, who had supported Franklin D. Roosevelt for President in 1936, in 1940 declared that he would withdraw from the CIO if Roosevelt should defeat Wendell Willkie. Lewis kept his word.

While Reuther and the Unity Caucus were active in all the union feuding, Walter was developing his own concept of what a responsible trade-union movement should be like. For one thing, he felt that UAW should completely divorce itself from Communist and Socialist Party activities. In economic philosophy he felt that the militant objective should be to obtain a generous share of the productive benefits of the American capitalistic system for the workingman. Without in any way surrendering his fighting spirit, Reuther began to accept a maturing sense of responsibility for the leadership of a liberal, democratic trade-unionism. This concept gradually enlarged with Walter's own widening experience into a sense of personal obligation to champion the American liberal tradition in national life and in the international structure of the free world.

Although Walter had become a member of the UAW executive board in 1936, his influence until 1940 remained small. As he moved forward with his own ideas, he was compelled to "play by ear," through difficult periods of union squabbling. The game of politics within UAW was neither nice nor easy. It involved face-to-face contest with experienced labor leaders. From the very center of the struggle Walter Reuther alone emerged as a permanent force in American life.

It was a tough schooling which seasoned Walter for subsequent leadership. In the struggle, he developed a kind of operating procedure which served as a major source of his strength. He was always discussing ideas and programs. He discussed them at home, in coatrooms, in washrooms, in hallway alcoves, in rented auditoriums, and in union halls. He persistently carried on an urgent adult education program wherever he went.

His discussion of policy, however, was part and parcel of his union political activity. He proposed to see to it that delegates of his own stamp were elected to the international conventions. His objective was to gain control of the executive board. He wanted political control so that he could have freedom to exercise a responsibility for the formulation of union policy. It was the programmatic appeal of Reuther's leadership that lifted UAW to its point of outstanding social significance in the practice of American democratic government and the evolution of free welfare capitalism.

To the caucus, the policy, and the program, Reuther contributed a final technique of which he himself — thanks to his father — was a master. This was the technique of the "oral cadre." The oral cadre comprised people who knew how to use the English language and were committed to a sound policy and a proper and militant program. Such men know how to think in groups, operate in caucuses, write letters, handbills, and leaflets, speak in public, debate from the platform or the floor, and argue and persuade in the shop and washroom.

As his program of leadership began to unfold, Reuther incorporated the techniques of oral cadres into the union educational

program. UAW designed its program to make men articulate —
thoughtfully articulate. With huge posters captioned LET HIM
SPEAK, UAW quoted John Stuart Mill to the effect that "If all
mankind, minus one, were of one opinion, and only one person were
of the contrary opinion, mankind would be no more justified in
silencing that one person than he, if he had the power, would be
justified in silencing mankind." In another poster UAW declared
that THE GREATEST UNUSED RESOURCE IS PEOPLE. Under Reuther
UAW opposed programs which sought a "predetermined automatic
reaction." It encouraged men to analytical skepticism. It urged
them to beware of people who sought to shake them from their
position until, by forthright inquiry and objective search for the
correct facts, they arrived at the right policy. As the years went by,
UAW popularized simple manuals for shop stewards and members
on effective discussion methods: how to speak, how to conduct a
union meeting, how to say what you mean by understanding the
science of semantics, and how to analyze propaganda and lies scientifically. For ten cents any steward could obtain an authoritative,
simple, and job-related manual applying the latest findings of the
social sciences. In *Semantics for Shop Stewards* UAW told members
that "quicker than the eye, faster than the mind thinks, words don't
always mean what they pretend." The union told its men "how to be
semantic." In the shop manual on *How They Lie Scientifically* the
UAW educational department dealt with propaganda analysis and
statistical misrepresentation. It discussed, in a popular way, such
concepts as glittering generalities, hysterical history, black and
white, name calling, positive and negative transfers, identification,
plain folks, old wooden virtues, pocketbook appeals, scares, band-
wagons and card stacking. The effect of this kind of instructional
program for the development of oral cadres became increasingly
important; workers became more thoughtful, more articulate, more
poised, more participant. As the communication skills matured, the
role of the union became more significant in national and international action and the task of leading such a union became broader,
deeper, and more difficult. Everybody had to keep growing! In fact,
Valentine Reuther's domestic Sunday-afternoon debating society
had extended to hundreds of thousands of workingmen's homes of
all colors and creeds.

By the summer of 1941, the Reuther faction felt it necessary to face and to end the Communist domination in the UAW. When the international convention met in 1941 the Reuthers were ready with a resolution which provided that no member of a local union was eligible to hold any elective or appointive position in the union if he was also a member subservient to any political organization which owed allegiance directly or indirectly to any foreign government. For two and a half hours, the convention engaged in turbulent debate over the proposal. Its adoption meant that the union would not countenance Communists, Fascists, or Nazis. The convention immediately divided on Communist and anti-Communist lines, with the principal attack centering upon the Reuther brothers. A Communist amendment proposed that Socialists likewise be included in the inventory of international "untouchables." Indeed, a minority report on the resolution said that "The real question here is whether the Socialist Party in the form of the Reuthers is going to have a privileged position in the union." In the heated floor discussion, Walter Reuther was described as a "draft dodger." Taking the floor as a matter of personal privilege, Walter explained that his deferment had been the action of the local draft board upon the official request of Philip Murray and President Thomas. They felt that if young labor leaders were put in military service, war production would be handicapped. Reuther had consented to have his case serve as a "guinea pig." The local board had deferred Walter under rules of selective service. "This is the story," he said frankly, "and I hope it will end this matter at this convention."

Victor Reuther spoke in support of the majority report on the anti-Communist resolution. "This union," he said, "is at the crossroads. We cannot preserve democracy in our ranks for those who use the strength the union gives them to advocate the destruction of freedom." Another union man observed that "We believe that anyone has a right to be a Communist or a Holy Roller or whatever they choose, but in the trade-union movement they must give their first loyalty to their unions and not attempt to use the union to further the end of any political party."

When the roll was called at the end of the discussion, the Reuther proposal to oust Communists from union leadership was ratified by the convention delegates by a two-to-one vote. At the end of the convention the Reuther group had control of twelve of the twenty members of the executive board, and two hundred and thirty-three out of three hundred and fifty-three votes which the board could cast.

The intra-union battle had been turned against the Communists. The struggle, however, continued on into 1949 when, at the CIO convention, under the leadership of Philip Murray and Walter Reuther, action was taken which led to the expulsion of eleven unions including the United Electrical, Radio, and Machine Workers; the United Farm Equipment Workers; International Union of Mine, Mill and Smelter Workers; Food, Tobacco, and Agricultural Workers; United Office and Professional Workers; United Public Workers; American Communications Association; International Union of Fur and Leather Workers; International Longshoremen's and Warehousemen's Union; National Union of Marine Cooks and Stewards, and the International Fishermen and Allied Workers. When the 1950 CIO convention convened in Chicago in 1950, not a single left-wing delegate was in attendance. William Z. Foster commented that "the process of transforming the CIO top bureaucratic machine into a tool of the State Department was complete."

The struggle to hold trade-unions free from Communist domination was also taking place on the international front. During World War II, trade-unions had experienced throughout the world an enormous growth. At the end of the war it had seemed therefore beneficial, while world organizations were taking shape, to tie the workingmen of the world more closely together. Plans for such a world organization were formulated at preliminary conferences at London, Paris, Washington, and San Francisco. On October 3, 1945, at a session called in Paris, the World Federation of Trade Unions (WFTU) was organized to represent sixty-four million workers in fifty-two countries. Although the American Federation of Labor did not participate — "true to the Wall Street spirit of its top leadership" as William Z. Foster said — the CIO, under the leadership of Sidney Hillman, was fully involved and committed. With the establishment of WFTU the old International Federation of Trade Unions, largely dominated by Social Democrats, was dissolved, and the WFTU became the largest international labor federation. It included more countries and, as the Communists liked to say, "more colonial and semicolonial lands," than any previous society.

Before the WFTU had existed three years, it too faced a crisis — as a result of which the world labor movement split into free and Communist segments. In the spring of 1948, James B. Carey, on behalf of the United States representatives, proposed to the executive bureau of the WFTU meeting in Rome that it endorse the Marshall Plan. British and Dutch representatives supported the American suggestion. The bureau decided, nevertheless, that each affiliated national trade-union ought to take its own position on the issue. In January 1949 Carey propose in Paris that the WFTU suspend activities for a year. When this suggestion was disapproved the CIO, British, and Dutch delegates withdrew. The CIO took official action to terminate its participation on March 2, 1949. The Americans were certain that the WFTU had become a tool of international Communism.

The American Federation of Labor then joined with the CIO and other national unions to hold a conference in London in November 1949. This meeting gave birth to the International Confederation of Free Trade Unions (ICFTU). William Z. Foster observed that it was created with the "usual litany of anti-Soviet charges" under State Department guidance. Walter Reuther headed the twenty-man United States delegation sent to the ICFTU organizing conference in London. He took a leading part in drafting the London 1949 Manifesto of the International Confederation of Trade Unions. The manifesto asked for:

Bread: economic security and justice for all.
Freedom: through economic and political democracy.
Peace: with liberty, justice, and dignity for all.

The manifesto addressed its appeal to the workers of all countries, races, and creeds. It summoned the workers in factory, field, and office to "unite with us to achieve a world in which men can be both free and secure and in which people of all nations may live in peace with each other." It called upon the free and democratic trade-unions of the world to build "a just and lasting peace," and declared that "human dignity rests on the broad foundations of freedom of thought, speech, and assembly; freedom to organize trade-unions, to bargain collectively with employers regardless of the character of ownership or management, with the right to strike when necessary; freedom of all peoples, including those in colonial or semicolonial status, to determine or change their own political, economic, or social institutions by democratic means." The free trade-unions, said the document, "will support with all their strength the efforts of the peoples suffering under police-state rule — such as those of the Soviet Union and its satellite "popular democracies," Franco Spain, and all forms of military dictatorship in Latin America and throughout the world — to free themselves from totalitarian oppression."

The manifesto defined the task of the free trade-unions as that of mobilizing the "tools of abundance possessed by the industrially advanced nations of the world to assure full employment, security against want, old age, and sickness, and to provide ever-rising standards of living and a richer and fuller life for people everywhere" — especially for peoples in the colonies and economically underdeveloped areas. As a personal comment Reuther told the delegates that "people of the world want neither Stalin nor Standard Oil."

While Reuther was in the midst of these struggles against the Communists he and his brother Victor experienced a series of personal attacks. On the night of April 20, 1948, Walter had returned home late from a meeting of the international executive board in downtown Detroit. As he was eating a late supper in the kitchen of his modest brick-frame house, he finished a plate of stew and rose from the table to get a bowl of fruit salad from the icebox. As he moved, he turned his head to hear what his wife was saying. From the darkness outside a charge of buckshot blasted through the storm and regular kitchen window and struck Walter in the arm and chest. The assailants fled in a maroon Ford sedan. Walter was rushed to the hospital. For three months his body remained in a cast; he never recovered the full use of his right hand. The executive board immediately offered a reward of a hundred thousand dollars for information leading to the arrest of the assassins. It declared that the attempted murder was an "attack against the whole labor movement and against the democratic principles for which it stands

and fights." A CIO former vice-president of Local 400 at Ford Highland Park plant, who had been defeated for office when his criminal
record was exposed, was tried on charges of having fired the shot at
Walter. He was acquitted, but later sent to prison on other charges.

Thirteen months went by before the next attack came. This time
it was made upon Victor, director of the UAW–CIO Educational
Department.

On the evening of May 24, 1949, Victor sat quietly reading with
his wife at home. Toward the end of the evening an assassin fired
through a window. The shot fractured Victor's collar bone, wounded
his face and neck, and crushed his eyeball. He was given four
blood transfusions; next day surgeons removed his eye. The executive board of UAW now doubled its reward for information leading to the arrest of the assassins involved in the crime.

The third attempt came as a 1949 Christmas present. A gaily gift-
wrapped parcel was delivered to the basement of UAW–CIO headquarters. It contained thirty-nine sticks of 50 per cent dynamite,
with a fuse which had gone out just a fraction of an inch below the
cap. Again the executive board offered a reward — this time of
twenty-five thousand dollars — for the arrest of the thugs. None
was ever apprehended.

Early in 1954, the Wayne County Prosecutor made a statement
that he was "convinced the shooting of Walter Reuther in 1948"
had been solved. A series of arrests was made in what promised to
be a startling conspiracy. Then the wheels of justice bogged down
in the tricky mud of Detroit's underworld. The shooting of Walter
Reuther still remains unsolved.

Despite the substantial victories over the Communists in UAW,
Reuther still experienced difficulties from their activities. Two examples will suffice. In the winter of 1949 a flying squadron of three
hundred goons, organized for violence at the John Deere plant in
East Moline, Illinois, attacked a UAW international representative
who was handbilling the International Harvester plants with facts
concerning labor unions among farm implement workers. The assault
was an open demonstration of the tension existing between UAW
and the United Farm Equipment and Metal Workers of America.
In June 1949 the CIO revoked the charter of the latter union. Again,
in Ford Local 600 there was trouble. Although the historic 1947

convention had set up the slogan of solidarity in the ranks and team-work in the leadership, the idea had not percolated down to the Ford Local. In Local 600 there existed a well-disciplined Communist cadre which exerted an influence sufficient to subvert the policies, programs, and publications of the Local to Communist ends and, so the international executive board said, "against the best interests of the union membership." The UAW was thus faced with a fundamental problem in the biggest local in the world. It had to end Communist influence and disruption. It had to do this to meet and solve the problems of Ford workers, to provide for a flow of "truth and facts" to the membership, and to "stop irresponsible action" which was doing great harm to the whole union. After thirteen hours of deliberation, the international executive board by unanimous action, on March 15, 1952, established an administratorship over Local 600 UAW–CIO, to insure that the local would carry out its obligations under the international constitution. The six-man board of administration was headed by Walter Reuther, and included the two international vice-presidents, Emil Mazey, the international secretary-treasurer, and two other members. The administration extended over a period of seven months.

From this experience the international officers discovered that the amendments to the constitution taken in 1941 were no longer adequate to deal with the problem of Communists in the ranks. The administrators pointed out to Local 600 that the responsibility rested squarely on its shoulders to eliminate the Communist influence. In making the UAW position clear, the international executive board said that it proposed to "make no compromise with the Communists, either as an organized subversive force or an individual within our ranks. Organizationally and as individuals, Communists are against our union, against our country, and against everything that free men stand for throughout the world. Communists are not just people who may have a different point of view on how things ought to be done. They are an organized conspiracy with only one loyalty, and that is blind service to the Soviet Union."

Reuther's maturing discipline in the leadership of UAW was further shown in an action taken in relation to in-plant gambling. Reuther holds not only that gambling cuts into the pay envelope which a worker carries home, but that its existence opens the channel for the entrance of gangsters into union operations. Reuther takes the position that in-plant gambling cannot take place without the tacit assent of management and the active collaboration of employees at least on the foreman level.

In General Motors in-plant gambling exists much less than in other plants; management does not tolerate it. UAW likes to cite GM as an example of the beneficial results which come when a corporation refuses to tolerate in-plant gambling. The Union gives to management its fullest co-operation in this struggle. Reuther has sought to encourage other companies to adopt this policy. For example, Local 669 at the Wright Aeronautical Company in Paterson, New Jersey, opened war on gamblers and racketeers who infested the plant. A web of illicit bookies covered the huge factory. Within the plant, handbook operations were highly organized and obviously in direct contact with the Costello and Willie Moretti gangs. Gambling offices were set up in hideaway places such as toilet cubicles. There bets were taken both from plant workers and company supervisors. Within the factory, runners picked up bets at fixed points. Although these runners were on the payroll, the collection assignment seemed to be their only duty required to earn their wage. Because the gambling network had such full access to the plant, the union felt that operations were conducted with the knowledge of management. With the election of a new president of the Local 669, the union took steps to end in-plant gambling.

When the United States Senate Crime Committee was scheduled to look into the plant gambling, Bergen County police arrested a man who had been discharged for picking up bets outside the plant. They found gambling paraphernalia on his person. Union officers told management that the employee who had been dismissed was merely a front to cover up the management before the Kefauver Committee. The union asserted that the management knew who the gambling ringleaders were and that the union wanted such men apprehended, not the small fry. The union took the case of the discharged employee to arbitration, and proved that he had nothing to do with the organized "bookie" operation at the plant. The fired man came back to work with full back pay. The next step came quickly. Management made a thorough investigation, and issued instructions to all supervisors that any of them who aided the handbook enterprise would be summarily fired. At the same time the local ran a front-page editorial in its newspaper to explain the case of the discharged employee. The union editorial pointed out that anyone gambling in the plant would not be defended by the union. By the co-operation of the union and management, organized in-plant gambling ceased. UAW–CIO, organizationally, was in a position to take a stand.

While UAW was cleaning its own house of Communists and their influence, and Reuther was rising to undisputed leadership, world events were creating situations which demanded of labor a broad policy. The outbreak of World War II, with Hitler's march on Poland at the beginning of September 1939 and Japan's declaration of war on the United States on December 7, 1941, had confronted labor with the patriotic duty of achieving maximum industrial production. From 1939 on, Reuther had provided a series of programs and publicized them so successfully that UAW was now known as a new and important force in American life. Increasingly, his demands were to have important consequences in economic practice and in political theory.

As the United States mobilized for World War II, Reuther began to get intimately acquainted with Washington. He served as a labor representative with the Office of Production Management, the War Production Board, the War Manpower Commission, and in various capacities with the Joint Labor-Management Production Committee. As he observed the capital in operation, he began to feel that the idea of labor participation on production councils and plant committees received only lip service from management and from the War Production Board. Belatedly the WPB consented to appoint two labor men as vice-chairmen in June 1943. Reuther's outlook on the role of labor in world affairs had been widened in 1942 when he went as a United States Delegate to the International Labor Organization Convention in Montreal. Now in the perspective of his wartime experience at top level, he began to see his own labor program in broader outlines.

It was in wartime Washington that Walter Reuther began to lay the foundations for a new kind of labor statesmanship. He was just thirty-four in 1941 and flushed from victory in the UAW advance. He was militant, skillful in group conferences such as those that form a good part of Washington activity, and something of a new breath in the circle of Washington policy makers and social leaders. During the confusion of war years Reuther began to develop a coherent philosophy, a skeleton which he proceeded to clothe with bold and colorful plans.

Industrial unionism was so young it had never existed in a wartime situation. How industrial unions were to behave in the national emergency was a question which concerned the leadership of the CIO quite as much as it did the industrial managers of the nation. In October 1942, UAW began to clear the atmosphere by coming forward with a "Triple Victory Program" which established three cornerstones of union wartime policy. The first was to win the war. The second was to maintain democratic institutions at home. The third was to win the peace. At the end of the war, UAW came forward with a fourth policy defining its postwar program. Finally, shortly after the aggression in Korea, in late June 1950, Reuther was to produce a plan which can only be described as "stupendous" for coupling an adequate military defense program with a positive offensive for peace.

In his first war months in Washington, Reuther was horrified by the indecision and delay in the leadership of government and industry in launching an all-out mobilization. In full-page newspaper advertisements, UAW blasted away in "An Open Letter Addressed to Mr. O.P.M." on the apparently inadequate speed of preparation. To get thinking started on the problem, Reuther as early as the summer of 1940 had proposed the utilization of the idle capacity, machinery, and man power in the automobile industry to produce five hundred planes a day in addition to keeping up the manufacture of motor cars. Management in the industry contended that the plan was impractical. In order to produce aircraft and other war materials, industry said, it would require a different type of plant and different types of machines from those used in automobile production. William S. Knudsen, in charge of OPM production problems, said that "if Walter is interested in production, we'll give him a job with us." After Pearl Harbor, however, when the government curtailed automobile production, industry found it possible to convert its plant capacity; more than nine tenths was thrown into the production of aircraft and other war materials. From the beginning of the war Reuther and UAW stood for prompt and full mobilization of all America's resources.

In further definition of this policy UAW, as its own contribution to total mobilization immediately after Pearl Harbor, established a policy of refusing to authorize strikes for the duration of the conflict. At a special emergency conference held in the spring of 1942, it adopted a nonstrike pledge and scrupulously maintained the position. As a result, the basic war industries in which UAW locals operated retained uninterrupted labor performance. General Motors in particular enjoyed, appreciated, and later tried to preserve this steady industrial peace.

As a still further contribution to the war effort, UAW, largely under Reuther's guidance, volunteered (after furious debate within the union) to withdraw demands for overtime premium pay on Saturdays, Sundays, and holidays as such. This meant that in any work week of forty hours which included a Saturday, Sunday, or holiday, or two or all three, the worker would still get paid straight time. The union would insist only on time-and-a-half for all work over eight hours in any one day, or over forty hours in any seven-day work week period. UAW further provided that the overtime pay should be paid in the form of non-negotiable special defense bonds. All of these proposals were conditional upon the acceptance and adoption of a ten-point program known as "Victory through Equality of Sacrifice," in which the overtime proposal was the tenth point.

In substance the "Equality of Sacrifice" program, as Reuther saw it, provided a scheme to end war profits, to curtail war luxuries, to prevent war millionaires, and to guard against wartime inflation. What Reuther proposed to do was to take the profit and romance out of war and to encourage the American people to settle down to the grim, disciplined, and sacrificial life which war imposes upon men in the armed forces. While the ten-point program never was approved, Reuther's concern for a plan bold enough to win the peace grew stronger over the years.

*　　*　　*

When Korean fighting broke out in the summer of 1950, Reuther showed how his thinking had expanded. He came forward with a bold and detailed *Proposal for a Total Peace Offensive to Stop Communist Aggression by Taking the Initiative in the World Contest for Men's Minds, Hearts, and Loyalties.* He wanted "a combination of adequate military defense plus a positive peace offensive." He proposed the plan, as he said, not as a "finalized" schedule of action, but as an effort to awaken thinking and discussion of the problem. "The announcement of the existence of the H-Bomb," said Reuther, "has created a moral vacuum in the world. In the great emptiness in the world, men's hearts are filled with a hollow uncertainty. This moral vacuum must be filled with positive, democratic, human values, by the mobilization of positive spiritual and material forces greater than the negative power of the H-Bomb. Such a program will provide hope against despair and promote revolt against rule by terror." Reuther saw a compelling necessity for quick, positive, daring action to take a paralyzed world, hypnotized by negative values based on men's fears and hatreds, off dead center. Since 1945, the Soviet realm had increased from one hundred and eighty million to eight hundred million to supply a vast reservoir of slave labor and military man power. To him it was clear that freedom's fight for Asia must be "won in the rice fields," as he put it, "not by the incantation of pious slogans about democracy's supposed virtues."

Reuther's later plan for a total peace offensive was incorporated into a nine-point program. Its dollar computations were based on Paul Hoffman's estimate that World War II lasted forty-four months with a final cost of one trillion, three hundred billion dollars; Reuther reckoned that one-hundredth of that sum was thirteen billion dollars, and that thirteen billion dollars was less than 5 per cent of America's current annual output. On the basis of these figures, he proposed that the American people through their government make a fixed commitment to the peoples of the world for the next one hundred years between 1950 and 2050 to make available through the United Nations an annual sum of thirteen billion dollars which over the next century would equal the final money cost of World War II to the American people. Other nations would be asked to make similar investments, according to their ability, but the United States investment would not be conditional upon the payments into the United Nations fund by other nations. This huge annual sum would be deposited in a special "United Nations Fund for Economic and Social Construction" and would be used solely to help people in other nations help themselves by developing and expanding the economic resources and facilities of participating nations and for other purposes which would contribute to the improvement of living standards, including nutrition, housing, health, and education. An annual report would be made to the people of the world listing expenditures and specific results achieved. Reuther proposed that the fund be made available to all nations, including the Soviet Union and its satellites, on equal terms. Upon the adoption of this program by Congress, the President would submit it to the peoples of the world through the United Nations. Upon acceptance of the plan by a majority of its member nations, the United Nations would convene an international conference for the purpose of achieving total disarmament, establishing universal inspection and other appropriate security controls, and creating an international police force. A mutual defense program was to be developed by the United Nations among all the co-operating states until the disarmament program was universally accepted and all participating nations were to agree not to employ their armed forces outside their boundaries except at the direction of the United Nations.

Reuther suggested that after the acceptance of the idea in principle by a majority of its member states, the United Nations convene a "Peoples' World Assembly for Peace" to discuss the proposal in detail and to make recommendations to the United Nations for its implementation. In this assembly each United Nations member state would be represented by eighteen delegates functionally representative of groups in its population: dirt farmers, industrial workers, housewives, youths, veterans, educators, scientists, professional persons, businessmen, and religious leaders. When this assembly presented its recommendations to the Secretary-General of the United Nations he was to forward the plan to the governments of member states for official action by the United Nations Assembly. The "People's World Assembly for Peace" was to reconvene annually to hear reports on expenditures, projects, and achievements, and to discuss and make recommendations concerning future operations and projects of the peace program. The bold program was to be one which would work through the United Nations to give it a genuine economic task and to penetrate the Iron Curtain by the "facts of performance."

"This is no time for little faith," Reuther declared. In summarizing his plan for winning partners in peace and allies if total war comes, he said:

Instead of taking, we propose to give. Instead of reducing the living standards of other people, we propose to help them raise their living standards. Instead of confiscating their crops, we propose to help them modernize their agriculture for production of more food. Instead of drafting men and women for forced labor, in the service of the Soviet war machine, we propose to free them and assist them in the building of a richer life. Instead of draining their countries of mineral wealth and other natural resources, we propose to help them develop and use these resources for the fulfillment of their own needs. Instead of driving their bodies in speeded-up production for the Soviet war machine, we propose to assist them in achieving decent wages, hours, working conditions, and the right of collective bargaining, and obtaining medicine, hospitals, and schools for them and their families.

The peace plan, like the "Equality of Sacrifice" program, as a whole did not prove to be acceptable. Reuther's policy on overtime pay never became effective, and as yet his hundred-year plan for peace has not received serious discussion in top State Department circles.

Within UAW during the war years Reuther had taken another stand which arrayed the Communist faction squarely against him. Under Earl Browder's leadership, the Communists attempted to encourage output in World War II, chiefly, to aid the Soviet, by tying wages to production through what Browder called an "incentive wage." He felt that through the establishment of the "payment-by-results" system production could be doubled in six months and that this increased output would count heavily in supporting the Soviet-American coalition against the Nazis. Opposition to piecework, of course, was deeply ingrained among automobile workers, and few of them were willing to go back to the pre-union system which they had so bitterly fought in the organizational days of UAW. The Communist faction within the union, however, promoted the idea, making its appeal that this method was one way of increasing wages during wartime. In a newspaper advertisement, Browder charged Reuther with a policy of "wrecking" the automobile and airplane industry. He implied that Reuther's opposition to the establishment of incentive pay was the kind of crime for which men in Russia were shot.

When the UAW met in convention at Buffalo in 1943, the incentive pay system was hotly debated. The Reuther forces felt that the Communist-inspired position on piecework and other matters provided a good occasion through which to oust George F. Addes from his position as secretary-treasurer and to replace him with a Reuther man. Addes was supported in his position on the incentive wage by Richard T. Frankensteen. At Buffalo, Reuther forces worked day and night to convince delegates that the position of Addes and Frankensteen on incentive wage was sufficient to "toss them out of office." Among Reuther supporters there sprang up a popular song sung to the tune of "Reuben and Rachel" with words entitled "The Gruesome Twosome." Two verses of the song ran like this:

> Who are the boys who take their orders
> Straight from the office of Joe Sta-leen?
> No one else but the gruesome twosome,
> George F. Addes and Frankensteen.

> Who are the boys that fight for piecework,
> To make the worker a machine?
> No one else but the gruesome twosome,
> George F. Addes and Frankensteen.

Delegates snake-danced through hotel corridors to the tune. Men would stick their heads out of a window or hotel-room door and sing the first two lines. Down the corridor would come the antiphonal response:

> No one else but the gruesome twosome,
> George F. Addes and Frankensteen.

When the incentive wage issue came to the floor of the convention, Reuther took his stand against piecework pay; Addes and Frankensteen supported the Communist-inspired scheme. The convention supported Reuther and his position.

In the year which followed the Buffalo convention workingmen were suffering from rising prices in wartime inflation. Men in the shops began to question Reuther's position on the pressing issue. At Chrysler, men walked out and booed Reuther when he attempted to persuade them to return to work. Within the UAW a new faction began to make itself felt. This movement came to be known as the "Rank and File Caucus." Its supporters urged the repeal of the no-strike pledge, the adoption of a militant action program, and the election of new leadership to carry out these two objectives. When in 1944 the UAW convention met in Grand Rapids, Reuther faced formidable opposition. Whenever in his remarks he would mention labor's obligation in the war effort, the Briggs local delegation would wave small American flags as a silent chorus.

The Rank and File Caucus was a "bread-and-butter" movement. Within the union Reuther was now confronted by a group of hard workingmen who wanted to see results promptly in the take-home-pay envelope. President Roland J. Thomas wanted to see the no-strike pledge kept exactly as it was until the war was over. Walter Reuther wanted the pledge withdrawn only as war production was cut back, in plants which were not operating defense contracts. The Rank and File Caucus wanted the pledge immediately and completely abolished. The convention finally decided to take a referendum to determine the union's position. In this referendum, the membership voted by a very substantial majority to support the Thomas position and to keep the no-strike pledge fully intact. The ending of the war soon made that issue academic.

The end of the war, indeed, precipitated a cry among union members for "action." Union reports showed that retail prices were more than 50 per cent over those of 1939. General Motors wartime profits were so huge, so UAW said, as to make the union rank and file feel that wartime sacrifice had not been evenly spread throughout the nation. Although government reports showed that during the war strikes in General Motors plants had been reduced to a fraction of 1 per cent of time worked, the public increasingly accused workers of having hindered wartime production. UAW pointed out that man hours lost in just a single one-week shutdown ordered by General Motors caused ten times the loss in man hours as all the strikes and work stoppages in the corporation's plants for a period of twenty-seven war months prior to V-J Day. Union members mobilized their venom against the "do-nothing record" of the international officers.

Reuther knew the temper of the men demanded action. He came forward with a program which set union sights above the usual picket-line operations. He took the problem personally in hand and on June 30, 1945, submitted an economic brief to the Office of War Mobilization and Reconversion, the War Labor Board, and the Office of Price Administration. He contended that wages could be increased without increasing prices. Following the lines of the Truman ruling, which permitted wage increases on the condition that such increases did not result in price increases, Reuther at once began negotiations with General Motors for a 30 per cent wage increase without any increase in the price of motor cars. Side by side with this demand, Reuther won the support of the UAW executive board for a "one-at-a-time" strike strategy. He knew that if General Motors hoped to win its place in the postwar market it would have to come forward with new cars promptly. This situation placed the union in a strong position to negotiate.

Reuther expressed his willingness to General Motors management to lower his demands if inspection of the company books showed that the company was unable to meet the demands. "The Look at the Books" became a fighting formula. General Motors managers charged that the UAW proposal to inspect accounts was a union interference with the prerogatives of management. The real significance of the demand was deep indeed. It was not participation in management which the union sought at the moment. It was the tying-together of prices, wages, production, and profits, as a package at the bargaining table. Labor was moving toward a new kind of action philosophy which implied a new form of capitalism.

The outcome of the dispute was that on November 21, 1945, two hundred thousand General Motors employees in ninety-six plants began a hundred-and-thirteen-day strike. Both the company and the union appealed to the public. President Truman set up a fact-finding board. In the process of the negotiations, Reuther and his staff undertook an exhaustive presentation of economic facts. His brief was immediately given nation-wide circulation in a booklet entitled *Purchasing Power for Prosperity: The Case of the General Motors Workers for Maintaining Take-Home Pay.* As Reuther delivered each section of the brief to General Motors, the UAW public-relations offices worked feverishly. They mailed out copies of the brief by sections, clipped the text to press releases, and fed material to newspapers, magazines, broadcasting stations, Federal agencies, and leaders in Congress.

Clayton Fountain, one of Reuther's publicity men, described the UAW performance as "departure from unionism as usual." "UAW–CIO," said Reuther, "does not base its demands on short-run selfish considerations, but is basing them on enlightened long-run considerations which identify the true interest of the union with the general interests of the public." To this kind of position a General Motors representative in the conference room observed to Walter: "Why don't you get down to your size and get down to the type of job you are supposed to be doing as a trade-union leader, and talk about money you would like to have for your people, and let the labor statesmanship go to hell for a while?"

Despite the prodigious effort which UAW made in the presentation of its case, the general labor front began to crumble in its support of the Reuther formula. Other CIO unions accepted wage advances of eighteen-and-a-half cents an hour without tying the increase to Reuther's program for simultaneously checking the price spiral. In the end, UAW had to settle for eighteen-and-a-half cents without action on its principle of "ability-to-pay." UAW, however, felt that its position was confirmed by the Fact Finding Board's report to the effect that General Motors could have paid an eighteen-and-a-half cents an hour increase without increasing prices.

While the full goals of the strike were not attained, Reuther's handling of the negotiations gave him enormous newspaper publicity. His personal staff saw to it that the crisis was fully utilized to strengthen his position within UAW. Reuther men said that the Communists and General Motors were not far apart in their strategy, "Both were out to get Reuther!" It seemed to some the proper time to clip the young man's wings.

❈   ❈   ❈

The 1946 UAW convention convened in Atlantic City at the end of March, ten days after the settlement of the General Motors strike. It was pretty clear that Walter Reuther, aged thirty-nine, was going to run for president. The Reuther boom had been kicked off in Detroit while the General Motors strike was still in progress by a committee composed of the presidents of seventeen large local unions. On the evening of the opening of the convention, Reuther forces held a mass caucus. His candidacy created the first real contest for president in the eleven years of UAW's existence. Reuther's publicity men worked tirelessly. Knowing that his oratorical ability would win the delegates, his men issued a pamphlet challenging President Thomas to debate Reuther. The Reuther campaign urged a "dynamic unionism" extending beyond the bargaining table into the community.

The convention as a whole was a wild and raucous affair. Communist forces were active, seeking to create shifting coalitions to defeat Reuther. Thomas, with the advantages which come from being in office and controlling the international staff, appeared to hold a safe command of the delegates. The Association of Catholic Trade Unionists, determined to oust Communists from UAW, supported Reuther. So did a few Socialists. The roll-call vote on the election of the president came on March 27, 1946. The occasion was a tense and dramatic moment. Delegates figured the score on their tally sheets. Suddenly a group of men, convinced by their arithmetic that Reuther had achieved mathematical majority, swarmed to the platform, picked him up, and began shouting "victory." In a close-fought election Reuther had become the president of the largest labor union in the world. His victory had been won on a platform which dealt with programs and philosophies. The Reuther forces proceeded to clinch the victory. They elected Emil Mazey, at the time of the convention an army sergeant in the Pacific theater, *in absentia* to the executive board.

By the time of the 1947 convention Walter Reuther was in full control of UAW. He had a supporting staff which was loyal to him. Victor, after the 1946 convention, had become director of education. Frank Winn advanced to become publicity director. UAW at last was rid of intra-union factional warfare. With "teamwork in the leadership and solidarity in the ranks" it now advanced to new power in labor, national, and international affairs. In an open contest on alternative policies, UAW under Reuther's leadership had lifted itself to a new role in American life. It promptly expanded its activities, as the union approved policies which departed from the dollar-in-the-pay-envelope kind of program. Its action now became a thoughtful, continuous, and provocative policy of economic and political action. On both the economic and the political fronts UAW proposed to participate in goal-planning.

Underlying UAW activities lay a fundamental economic conception which makes the union a major influence in promoting a stable economy: the conception of insuring full employment by providing mass purchasing-power capable of making a stable market for the products of a heavily industrialized society in a stage of advanced technology. Reuther was determined to break down what he likes to call the "disparity between the B-29 technology and the huffing and puffing Model T distributive system." Gone from Reuther's mind were ideas of inevitable class struggle, general crises, and the ideologies of Marxism. Under the technological conditions which make abundance possible, Reuther saw the conditions emerging for a stable and liberal capitalism. He thus felt himself engaged in laying the groundwork necessary for the maintenance of a liberal political democracy. Like his father before him, and his brothers around him, he saw economics and politics joined together at the assembly line as one condition of freedom. But make no mistake about one fact: the UAW–CIO broadened outlook was deeply rooted in militant courage to call strikes to further its program, as necessary.

Shortly, Reuther was to see another advance in the theory of the liberal welfare-capitalism of abundance. In 1948 Charles E. Wilson proposed what he called "progress sharing." This concept was an outgrowth of the General Motors conviction that collective bargaining must be based on a definite philosophy to insure industrial peace — one that is understood and accepted by both parties. A vision of strikeless years encouraged General Motors to suggest a standard-practice wage formula. In the futile bargaining negotiations which had been conducted up to the late spring of 1948, General Motors identified two major workers' problems. First, workers wanted to maintain the steady purchasing power of an hour's work. Second, workers wanted this purchasing power to increase as the nation's industrial efficiency increased. To satisfy the first requirement, General Motors recognized the need to establish a standardized means by which a dollar would continue to buy a dollar's worth of goods. To satisfy the second requirement, Wilson felt compelled to place an enormous faith in the future progress of America.

General Motors and UAW reached a historic agreement on both propositions, and on May 25, 1948, signed a two-year contract. The contract worked so well that upon expiration it was extended for a five-year period — to May 29, 1955. The new formula on the one hand linked an hour's wage to the cost of living, thus maintaining the stable purchasing power of an hour's work. On the other hand, the worker had assurance that his purchasing power would increase with the nation's increase in industrial efficiency. Under the agreement wages were to be adjusted every three months according to a Bureau of Labor Statistics index. This procedure of lifting and lowering wages according to the cost of living came to be known as the "escalator clause." Although labor has historically been opposed to escalator clauses, the General Motors agreement provided a floor below which wages cannot drop, regardless of any decline in the cost of living. It was this feature that distinguished the plan from those which labor shied away from.

Wilson was very clear in his description of the progress factor. The reason America has developed a vast mass market, in contrast to Europe, he said, is because of the constant increase in real wages which share industrial progress with workers as a result of greater productivity. This factor has come to be known technically as the "annual improvement factor." Over many decades, said Wilson, productivity had increased at the rate of about 2½ per cent a year. The epoch-making clause in the GM–UAW agreement needs to be quoted in full. It reads:

> The annual improvement factor recognizes that a continuing improvement in the standard of living of employees depends upon technological progress. It further recognizes the principle that to produce more with the same amount of human effort is a sound economic and social objective.

UAW was enthusiastic about the agreement on the major principles, but continued to say that while the principles are correct, the annual improvement factor should be fixed at a higher rate. Constant union pressure in the next five years pushed the improvement factor from three to five cents an hour.

Reuther continued to press for further upward considerations, and in the spring of 1953 achieved a "flexibility" in the long-term contract by introducing what UAW called the "living document principle." In substance, this concept means that collective bargaining contracts are not legalistic, static documents, but living documents which obligate both parties to work out and adjust any problems and inequities that develop during the life of the contract and that could not have been anticipated at the time the original contract was negotiated. UAW's demand for opening of long-term contracts as "living documents" was a result of the Korean affair, which broke out a month after General Motors and UAW had signed a five-year contract. The amendments to the 1950 contracts were made according to the "living document" theory. Reuther felt "happy."

The next important Reuther-led advance in UAW policy was unfolded at the fourteenth constitutional convention at Atlantic City at the end of 1952. UAW had selected a guaranteed annual wage as its next major collective-bargaining goal. Under the slogan of FULL PRODUCTION AND FULL EMPLOYMENT IN A FREE SOCIETY IN TIMES OF PEACE, UAW launched its determined drive.

In the Atlantic City convention hall, huge thirty-five-foot banners declared that the guaranteed annual wage was the road to abundance, peace, progress, and freedom, and the necessary next forward step to provide full employment, full production, and full distribution. "We live in an economy of potential abundance," said Reuther, "yet only at war and under the threat of war have we been able to keep our factories steadily producing and to keep ourselves steadily at work. Up to now the workers have borne the brunt of the cost of unemployment — a cost exceeded only by the cost of prolonged all-out war. The time has come to consider labor costs as annual costs, to pay the employee as the employer pays himself — by the year. The annual wage attacks the problem of unemployment at its root. It shifts to the employer, where it belongs, the cost of unemployment. We have seen repeatedly how financial responsibility can convert management to social responsibility. A sound guaranteed annual wage plan will arouse management's social conscience and stimulate its social ingenuity by putting pressure on its pocketbook nerve."

The introduction of the annual wage demand added something new to the bargaining pattern — something more than the annual improvement factor as a share in the progress of America. It placed new financing, new scheduling, new planning, upon the shoulders of management — with Reuther and UAW perfectly willing to help think through the problems whether such participation be called a share in management or not. The demand for the living wage was essentially a statement of goals for management to meet. "Goals for management" have a familiar ring when one talks of the management function.

When one takes the pattern of postwar UAW negotiations as a whole piece, and joins them with the forward outlook of General Motors, one discovers two concepts of momentous importance. The first is a deep faith in America and its future. The second is that human labor is not a commodity. *Taken together these ideas — an America with a great future, a human being as a participating partner in the progress of America — lay solid foundations for a liberal democracy.* Perhaps it was fortunate that UAW should have grown up within the motor vehicle industry, because the whole structure of its automatic assembly lines expresses the philosophy which must of necessity belong to the management of the industry: more things for more people in more places — everywhere.

But UAW was already on the march again. Paraphrasing the Ford advertising slogan, UAW workers began to parade the theme THERE'S A PENSION IN YOUR FUTURE, BUGAS. HOW ABOUT OURS? To John S. Bugas, industrial relations director for Ford and former head of the FBI in Detroit, Reuther pointed out: "Workers are determined to put an end to the unreasonable double standards by which high-paid industrial executives pay themselves generous pensions while denying even a minimum security to employees." The UAW had begun a drive to win retirement security for its members back in 1949. At that time pension plans in industries within UAW jurisdiction were scarce. UAW followed its preliminary explorations with a drive for a UAW-negotiated health program, to give members a substantial means of security against the hazards of physical illness and disability. Outraged because insurance companies with workers' money have been engaged in the fight to limit and often to reduce the benefits under the Social Security Act, UAW plans to establish a nonpolitical and nonprofit insurance company to provide a low-cost adequate insurance coverage adapted to the workers' needs.

Solidarity House, on the edge of the Detroit River, thus represents a new kind of phenomena in America — it is the headquarters of a corporate labor spokesman for what may well become a fundamentally new, liberal, democratic welfare-economy; it is the center of an organization representing not labor bought and sold in the market, but citizens: partners in America's wholeness. The policies of UAW–CIO require a huge organization for their administration. In his position as president, Walter Reuther is, therefore, the chief administrative officer of a complicated organization whose whole business is dealing with people.

This organization is supported by dues-paying members. According to the constitution, locals pay to the international union a monthly dues of one dollar and a quarter a member. Parts of this payment are earmarked. Twenty-five cents is tagged for an International Strike Fund to be drawn upon exclusively for the purpose of aiding local unions engaged in authorized strikes or suffering from lockouts. Five cents is set aside as a special Citizenship Fund to be used for the purpose of strengthening democracy by encouraging members and citizens generally to register and vote in community, state, and national elections and to carry on organizational and educational programs directed toward the achievement of an ever-higher understanding of citizenship responsibility and the need for active participation in the affairs of a free and democratic society. Three cents is set aside in a special International Education Fund. One cent is earmarked as an International Union Recreation Fund, which is apportioned among the regions on a per capita basis. One cent a month is set aside as a Fair Practices and Anti-Discrimination Fund. Five cents a month per member is earmarked as a special fund to circulate a copy of the *United Automobile Worker* every month to each union member.

The Strike Fund, as Reuther often points out, gives support to bargaining activities. Under Reuther, the organizing and bargaining operations are closely directed by the top international officers. International Vice-president John W. Livingston, for example, serves as director of the General Motors Department and the National Aircraft Department. International Vice-president Richard Gosser serves as director of Auto-Lite Department, Borg-Warner Department, the Competitive Shop Department, the Die Casting Department, the Foundry Department, the Skilled Trades Department. International Secretary-Treasurer Emil Mazey directs the Briggs Department. International President Walter Reuther at the moment heads the Office Workers Department, in which an especially strong campaign is being waged to organize white-collar employees. Under his aggressive leadership, initial gains have been made into the office workers field. From this distribution of departments at top level, it can be seen that UAW–CIO is militant in its effort to extend union organization to more people in more plants in more ways. It moves from strength to strength.

As policy, UAW proceeds to "organize the unorganized"; to catch up with and to conquer UAW "Enemy Number One," the "runaway plant" which moves to an area where it expects to avoid union recognition. UAW also seeks to win the "competitive plant," which when operating in competition with union plants exists as a constant threat to the welfare of the union workers. In organizing work, the union men feel that the Taft-Hartley Act "inflicts titanic handicaps upon them."

It is interesting to note in this connection that public-relations organizations have sprung up whose sole business it is to advise manufacturers, facing a representation election, in anti-union tactics. These firms provide management with standardized materials to influence workers against the union. For a heavy fee, these experts lay out a whole program, including anti-union speeches, for the company officials. These speeches are often so cleverly done that they are effective in swaying the opinions and votes of many workers. In addition to these difficulties, UAW organizers suffer further from comments arising from factional disputes during organizing campaigns in the form of rumor, papers, letters, and pamphlets. The UAW recognizes that the heyday of mass organizing is past. Easy plants are in; the holdouts are tough. This means that in the future long and bitter campaigns will be required, where formerly only a short time elapsed between the beginning of an organizing campaign and its successful conclusion. The cost of such organizing campaigns constantly rises. Reuther makes organization the first business of the union. And the UAW is equipped to do the job, even against the formidable odds which it faces.

Next to the Strike Fund, the most important earmarked operation is that of citizenship and political action. Walter Reuther himself directs the UAW–CIO Political Action Department. His brother Roy, one of his four administrative assistants, works with him at this job. The department carries on intensive campaigns to register union members and to get out the vote in every community where UAW has locals. It co-operates with city-wide registration drives and get-out-the-vote campaigns. In Detroit it joins in the work of the Ballot Battalion Committee. Over 90 per cent of the local unions have political action committees.

Under Reuther's Political Action Department legislative conferences are held in almost every region throughout the United States to discuss pending bills and to acquaint political action committee members and the local union leadership with the CIO legislative program. In the various states and many cities, government institutes are held in co-operation with the Education Department and CIO councils to acquaint members with the actual operations of the various city, county, and state agencies. In co-operation with the Education Department, political action classes are conducted for union members in local unions and in summer schools to emphasize the importance of participation of members in the political life of the community. In Washington the department holds a legislative conference to acquaint local union leaders with the functions and operations of the Federal government. All of these activities mean that UAW intends its members to be politically conscious. It does not intend to have the gains won at the bargaining table lost by default at the ballot box or wiped away by action in Washington.

Reuther explains his general idea about the need for labor leadership in Congress by telling a story about the Eightieth Congress. Walter was flying into the capital in a sixty-passenger DC–4. As the plane went over the Capitol dome, it "bounced about five hundred feet in the air and then settled down and landed." When Reuther asked the pilot the cause of the bump, he replied that he "should have known better. Every pilot has been warned not to fly over the Capitol dome when Congress is in session because the political hot air and gas come rushing up." Reuther turned to his seat-mate Martin Wagner of the CIO Gas, Coke, and Chemical Workers Union.

"Martin," he said, "your union has jurisdiction over gas plants; you ought to go down there and organize them; Congress is the biggest political gas plant in America."

In the area of political action it can be said that UAW works for an informed membership which understands issues. The union wants its members to take their duties of citizenship seriously at the polls. It wants them to express their opinions through appropriate channels in ways which will make their voice effective between elections.

In its practical politics UAW is wholly pragmatic. While it supported Franklin Roosevelt, Harry Truman, and Adlai Stevenson for president, it maintains that it would be ready to back a Republican who offered superior assurance to labor. Its position in everyday politics is based on a principle: labor must share generously as a right in the abundant productivity of American enterprise, and that association must be maintained as a free and competitive activity. UAW is neither for nor against socialism in the technical sense of the word. If nationalization is necessary in some instances, it favors such nationalization as may be necessary to break down the monopoly and scarcity policies of industry. UAW insists that American industry must produce abundantly, and to its fullest capacity, and that it must do so with a policy which will insure full employment and a broad purchasing power necessary to provide for the consumption of the annual product. UAW feels that "yard-sticks" may have to be set up along the line — TVA's which will compete with private enterprise so that competition will be a reality. It does not want to freeze the *status quo*. Both UAW and CIO were born in revolt against the routineer and they do not propose to withdraw from the leadership of the rebellion when an industrial and technological society can bless men so generously with plenty.

Nor does the UAW anticipate the development of a labor party. In fact, its leadership dislikes the idea of any political alignment of labor against industry at the polls. What it does want — and works to promote — is the development of a genuine liberal party, achieved by a reconstruction of the liberal and conservative forces in existing parties. It would like to see this liberal party supported by a thoroughly liberal daily newspaper. Leadership has been playing with this idea very seriously. At one time recently plans were well under ways to begin publication. A skeleton staff had been engaged. The project was to have been a joint activity of the AFL and the CIO. In the present thinking leadership would like to encourage the publication of a labor-oriented newspaper of the general type of the *St. Louis Post-Dispatch*. Such a newspaper would be committed thoroughly to liberal policies but it would not be edited or directed by the labor groups. Labor would merely supply necessary initial financing and share in the corporate ownership.

UAW has reason to believe that its political leadership of its members really counts. While its support of Adlai Stevenson for President in 1952 did not assure his election, UAW polls show that seven out of ten members followed the recommendations of the international convention.

Side by side with political action stands UAW's educational work. By constitutional provision education is a "mandatory" part of the business of the international union and of each local union. Instruction in such subjects as labor history, labor problems, and the objectives of the international union is encouraged.

From the beginning UAW had an extremely active and effective educational program. During part of the period before Victor Reuther took over the directorship in 1946, the Educational Department was under the direction of people sympathetic to the Communist Party and allied with factions opposing Walter Reuther. When Victor went to Europe as the representative to the Continent of CIO, Brendan Sexton took over his educational post. While the department stands in its own right, it works closely with other UAW service departments including the Community Service Department directed by Emil Mazey, the Fair Practices and Anti-Discrimination Department co-directed by Walter Reuther and William H. Oliver, the Political Action Department likewise directed by Walter Reuther, the Radio and TV Department, and the Recreation Department.

In its educational activities UAW is a pace-setter in the American labor movement. By its policies, methods, and materials as well as by its trained cadres of leaders, UAW establishes patterns for adult education even beyond the labor movement. It has introduced into its work the most recent developments in the field of adult education, and has adapted the principles of group dynamics to further the involvement, participation, and continuing growth of its membership.

In general UAW educators use the conference method. From October 15 to April 15, week-end educational institutes regularly take place. They are held on the county, state, and international level. When summer comes, UAW sponsors sessions of one- and two-week durations at leading universities and resorts. The department inaugurated a National Education Conference in Cleveland which the *New York Times* called a "milestone in the history of American adult education."

From the International Headquarters in Detroit there flows a series of educational pamphlets – about one new issue a month. *Ammunition* magazine devotes itself to educational methods and materials. It is widely used not only by the union leadership but by schools, universities, churches, and community organizations. Some local unions subscribe to bundle orders and place copies in dentists' and doctors' offices, barbershops, and other places where people have time to read while they wait.

The UAW Education Department also utilizes the tools of mass communication. Fully equipped sound recording and broadcast rooms greet the visitor when he enters the public-relations offices at Solidarity House. The UAW film library owns more than four hundred film prints. One of its films describes the "Union Buzz Groups," another the "UAW's Big Round Table." Still another deals with the work of the union's Skilled Trades Department. UAW visualizes its programs.

The Radio and TV Department works closely with the Education Department in its use of mass-communication media. The nightly broadcast "Labor Views the News" covers an estimated potential of eight out of ten UAW members. A weekly Sunday half-hour television program entitled "Meet the UAW–CIO" reaches an estimated audience of a hundred and twenty-five thousand. In 1953, the union took steps to develop a television station of its own to be owned by

UAW–CIO Broadcasting Corporation of Michigan. The union makes available platters and tape recordings of convention and institute proceedings. To train a cadre of mass-media specialists in the rank and file, the Radio and TV Department holds summer schools, weekend institutes, and technical workshops.

As a part of the educational program staff members undertake training courses for the locals they represent in dealing with management. Stewards and committeemen meet locally for seminars dealing with their problems. From the inside, educational activities reach out. At more than two hundred county fairs throughout the country the UAW puts up exhibits. A steady stream of overseas trade-union groups coming to America to see democracy in action is routed through UAW summer schools and plant and shop meetings, union offices, and workers' homes. The entertainment of visiting foreign guests requires the full time of a person who does nothing else but schedule the visits of the groups.

Side by side with the educational program stands the Recreation Department, directed by Olga Madar. Its program is designed to develop leisure-time activities for workers and their families. The shorter work day and higher wages have provided both time and money for leisure. UAW feels it has an obligation to help members and their families enjoy to the fullest this opportunity. The impact of the international policy on local leadership is reflected in developing programs appealing to a variety of interests and skills at all age levels. Locals have instituted Saturday-afternoon programs for the children at local union halls. As never before, local unions are sponsoring Boy Scout and Girl Scout troops and union members increasingly serve as troop leaders. The UAW recreation program is comprehensive. It ranges from children's camps to carefully planned programs for retired members, from area golf tournaments to bowling leagues, from ball clubs to archery, from group sewing classes to dancing schools and dancing parties, from camera clubs to fishing and hunting contests, from sports clinics to moonlight carnivals, from card clubs to hobby shows and talent nights. UAW recreation programs begin with a member's interest where that interest now lies. From this point, the recreation program seeks to develop a desire to lend support to activities which will enable him to enjoy a constantly improving standard of living. A fundamental policy of the recreation programs is that the activities must be open to *all* Americans.

As one of its projects, the Recreation Department at the direction of the international executive board and its officers undertook to initiate a movement to break down the discrimination existing in bowling contests conducted under the auspices of the American Bowling Congress. The bowling congress exercised a virtual monopoly on tournament bowling in the United States, since bowlers could compete only in tournaments conducted in "sanctioned" alleys. Only the congress could qualify an alley, and its players, for participation in ABC tournaments. Until recently the constitution of the American Bowling Congress included a clause which limited participation in its tournaments at sanctioned alleys to "white Caucasians." The UAW, with the aid of religious, civic, and other groups, formed a committee for "Fair Play in Bowling." By appearances before the conventions of the ABC, by publicity, and even by threats of anti-monopoly suits, the committee finally got the congress to eliminate the objectionable clauses from its constitution. Bowling is now open to all who wish to bowl regardless of race, creed, sex, or color. UAW is thus having an influence on the recreational activities of America.

Recreation like education is, however, only one functional part of the whole UAW mechanism over which Walter Reuther presides as executive officer. To discuss each special phase of UAW activity would be to isolate a service activity which belongs to the whole. In any detailed discussion it would be necessary to include important activities such as the Collective Bargaining Department and technical services such as compensation, law, research, engineering, social security, and women's affairs.

From the moment it begins an organizing campaign until its members attend the funeral of a brother or sister, UAW as a process *is* education. Its whole structure rests on a framework of experience, research, policy statement, mass information and communication, and the activities of trained cadres of elite leadership which leaven the operations of the whole rank and file.

A legend has it that after a heated bargaining session William Knudsen said to Walter Reuther:

"Young man, I wish you were selling used cars for us."

"Used cars?" Walter asked.

"Yes," repeated the General Motors president, "used cars. Anybody can sell *new* cars."

Of the fact that the Reuther brothers sold education to UAW there can be no question. More staff members of UAW are directly involved in instructional and other educational activities than have ever been involved in the educational program of any other union.

Article 25 of the UAW constitution sets up in the international union a Fair Practices and Anti-Discrimination Department. Besides earmarking a fund for this, it makes it mandatory for each local to set up a fair practices and anti-discrimination committee. The purpose of the department is to educate the membership and to end discrimination chiefly among three groups of the populations whose energies are not fully utilized: woman power, Negro workers, and older workers. The international committee to implement the anti-discrimination clause is headed by Emil Mazey and includes all the international officers.

Walter Reuther, who with William H. Oliver directs the department, says that America either means what it says about equality or it does not, "when it blows the whistle for the freedom train." UAW intends to mean it. In the face of the world struggle, Reuther predicts trouble for the United States if it continues to countenance the "raw deal" in the shop, the "you can't work in my factory" line, the "you can't eat in my restaurant" discrimination, the "you can't vote in my election" exclusion act, the "you can't live on my street" snobbery, the "you can't study in my school" dualism, and the "you can't be sick in my hospital" medical treatment.

Article 2 of the UAW constitution states an objective of the union to be the uniting "in one organization, regardless of religion, race, creed, color, political affiliation, or nationality" all employees under the jurisdiction of the international union. Reuther's Fair Practices and Anti-Discrimination Department, since 1946, has been putting teeth into this principle. Its activities reach from the local union to Congress and to the President of the United States. On the national level, Walter Reuther is a member of President Eisenhower's Commission on Discrimination.

The local union fair practices committee of five or seven members typically includes one member from the education committee, because fair practice embraces education. It includes a woman worker because women suffer much from discrimination. It includes a member of the bargaining committee who can give support in negotiations and avoid suspicion that the fair practices committee seeks to serve as a bargaining agency for minorities. It includes a member of the political action committee since city, state, and Federal fair-practice laws are a concern of the department. To these committees the international union gives a leadership which puts teeth into the ideal. It provides standard procedures by means of which members can raise complaints against management alleging discrimination on the basis of religion, race, creed, color, sex, national origin, or political affiliation. The local committee must meet bi-weekly.

Not only does UAW mean business with management; it deals with its own members by suspension and expulsion and with its locals for violation of the principles of the international. When the local at the Braniff Airlines in Dallas, Texas, refused to admit to membership Mexicans and Negroes, the local officers were ordered to show cause why they had not complied with international policy. The local officers claimed they were impotent to make the provisions effective. The local was expelled from the international; its charter was withdrawn.

At the International Harvester plant in Memphis, Tennessee, a group of welders protested the upgrading of a Negro worker. The company, asserting that it could not operate the plant without welders, closed down. UAW's international executive board, in session at the time, directed Walter Reuther, upon his recommendation, to dispatch wires both to the company and to the local union officers informing both groups that the international union would not protect the jobs of any member who quit his job or struck on grounds of the upgrading. In his telegram to the company management Reuther said: "Our union completely supports the principle that any worker entitled to promotion on the basis of seniority and ability to handle the job shall not be denied promotion because of race, creed, color, or national origin. Under the terms of the Taft-Hartley Act we are prevented as a union from disciplining our members in terms of their employment. The responsibility for discipline in such cases rests exclusively with management. You have our assurance that we shall not stand in the way of your meeting your responsibilities by appropriate disciplinary action." To his own UAW local Reuther wired: "The international executive board directs the members of Local 988 to return to work and to co-operate with the international union and management of the International Harvester Company in implementing the provisions of the UAW–CIO International Harvester agreement which provides for promotion based upon seniority and ability without regard to race, creed, color, or national origin. America cannot be a symbol of freedom and equality in the struggle against Communist tyranny and at the same time tolerate double standards in employment opportunities." As a result of these telegrams, the white welders went back to work and the Negro held his promotion.

The year after the international at its tenth convention adopted the program of putting teeth into fair practice at the hiring gate it negotiated its first contract with the standard anti-discrimination clause. On October 20, 1947, Local 72 incorporated the principle in the contract with Nash-Kelvinator. The standard anti-discrimination clause reads as follows:

> The company agrees that it will not discriminate against any applicant for employment or any of the employees in their wages, training, upgrading, promotion, transfer, lay-off, discipline, discharges, or otherwise because of race, creed, color, national origin, political affiliation, sex, or marital status.

Since the tenth convention, twenty-eight municipalities have enacted fair employment practices legislation; a dozen states have taken steps to deal with the problem. UAW has been less successful at the Federal level.

In striking at the failure of Congress to act on fair practices Reuther came face to face with the filibuster problem in the United States Senate, which he believed resulted from the existence of Rule 22. By the exercise of this rule, Reuther holds, a Senate minority can betray the "moral obligation of America." In commenting on "rule by filibuster" Reuther says that it is "morally wrong to have two sets of standards, one if your skin is white, another if you are dark." He says that in terms of the basic struggle in the world, when we need allies on our side, we must remember that "the great majority of the people in the world are not Caucasian, they are people of dark skins. The Senate minority is giving the Communist forces in the world a tremendous advantage which is being used in areas where dark-skinned people make up the overwhelming population."

Reuther's fight against Senate Rule 22, which he calls the "unconstitutional roadblock to democratic legislation," shows a matured and somewhat presuming method of political action. He appeared in person before the Senate Committee on Rules and Administration to talk to the members about their "own" rule, which he alleged was both unconstitutional and dangerous to American interests in the global struggle. Quoting Senator Henry Cabot Lodge, Sr., he said that "We ought to have both voting and debate — debate certainly in ample measure . . . the right of action must prevail over the right of discussion. To vote without debate is perilous, but to debate and never vote is imbecile." To the Senate Committee Reuther submitted two proposals for breaking the filibuster. He ended his presentation by issuing a UAW brochure which ended with the statement that "We must not permit the right of free discussion to be undermined by unlimited talk."

Realizing as always that the ultimate solution of democratic progress must stem from education of the rank and file, Reuther's Fair Practices and Anti-Discrimination Department has joined in the development of a film entitled "The Challenge," a simple, straightforward story about the many facets of discrimination which minority groups encounter in their day-to-day activities in the struggle to achieve freedom and democracy. Further, the department brings its war on discrimination to the living room of the American home through broadcasts and telecasts. At the end of 1951, in co-operation with the National Association for the Advancement of Colored People, the department launched an attack on the "Amos 'n Andy" television show. The objection was that the program depicted the Negro in such a way that viewers inevitably reached the conclusion that Negroes are "inferior, lazy, dumb, and dishonest." "Television," said Reuther, "is unmistakably the most powerful medium which we have today, and that medium can certainly do irreparable damage to the furtherance of human rights, civil rights, and the entire fight for democracy." It is obvious that UAW means business on the fighting front in the war against discrimination.

It is inevitable that the Washington office of UAW should exercise a powerful role in the program of labor. Every administrative, legislative, or judicial act of the Federal Government may have serious implications for labor. Conversely, the goals of the labor movement assume that Government is a necessary instrumentality for promoting its interests. The Washington office is in charge of Donald Montgomery, a man who has devoted his life to the advancement of the consumer interest and who knows Washington and its folkways thoroughly. Through this Washington office, Reuther operates at top level. He meets with the President, with his old opposite number in General Motors the Secretary of National Defense, with the Secretary of Labor, and with the Secretary of State — in fact he is everywhere where the interests of labor are affected — and the ramifications of labor's interest are broad indeed as Reuther deals with them.

Between Donald Montgomery and Walter Reuther there exists a very close and deep intellectual and spiritual understanding. Their hearts beat together and their minds stimulate each other. Both believe in research, facts, education, and action. Montgomery represents UAW's chief national intelligence officer alert to uncover the plans of the "enemy" of the economy of abundance. He stands ready to propose attacks and counterattacks. To him the "colossal difference" in the Capitol after the election of 1952 was that "the American people no longer have a President prepared to act as a blocking back to veto raids upon the people's riches for special private interest and gain." He feels it more important than ever that liberals distinguish between good and bad administration policies and be quick to support the good and oppose the bad. All along the home front, nevertheless, he finds "betrayal" of the consumer interests, the advancement of which he believes to be so necessary to stabilize the American economy at the levels of full production and full employment.

Montgomery's influence on the UAW since he joined the staff in 1944 has been to assert a deep-seated and fundamental theory of consumer interest within the framework of technological abundance.

It is this theoretical orientation which perhaps gives the UAW movement an importance in social history which rises above its other achievements. To the productive performance of capitalism Montgomery has developed the theory of the consumer base, so necessary for the preservation of the economy of abundance; Walter Reuther has in part become the policeman for the enforcement of this idea. The meaning of this simple statement is momentous.

Perhaps the clearest vision of its full significance was glimpsed by a member of the Association of Catholic Trade Unionists, an organization which has played a thoughtful if not conspicuous part in the American labor movement. Beginning as a local group in New York in 1937, it grew to national scope in 1940. It seeks to express the Catholic outlook firmly based on the social encyclicals of the Popes. On the labor front the association has opposed the Communists, supported Walter Reuther, and been skeptical of Reuther's radical allies. From a hundred Catholic labor schools it graduates as many as seven thousand students annually into the union movement. For a time its newspaper, the *Wage Worker*, was brilliantly edited. In each association of Catholic Trade Unionists a priest acts as an adviser. On October 26, 1945, the *Wage Earner*, seeing the theoretical implications of UAW's direction, observed that if Walter Reuther was able to compel General Motors to recognize his demand to raise wages without raising prices "every union will then insist that the profit and price structure be examined in collective bargaining and wage increases be absorbed out of profits as far as possible. *The result may not be the end of capitalism but it will certainly be the beginning of a new kind of capitalism.*" At this time the association of Catholic Trade Unionists supported the Reuther program because it rejected the theory implicit in General Motors negotiation that labor was merely a commodity which enterprisers buy in the market like pistons and Fisher bodies. The Catholics recognized the worker as a partner entitled to share as a right in the productivity which he joins in making.

In the same connection a Socialist position held that the linking of prices, profits, and wages meant the intervention of labor in running the economy as a whole, and that if corporations are unable to face the demands made upon them, competitive capitalism becomes bankrupt and nationalization must follow.

Both of these positions need to be taken seriously within the consumer-interest context which holds that, by higher wages and welfare benefits, lower prices, and reasonable dividends, provision must be made for the annual consumption of the annual product. This concept does mean that America stands at the threshold of a "new kind of capitalism." It does not mean — but it could mean — that labor will as necessary act to nationalize industry. It does mean that UAW proposes to exert a sustained pressure to distribute the national income in such a way as to consume the product of industry, to guarantee full production, full employment, and constantly rising standards of living. It is perfectly clear that the UAW alone, acting with teamwork in leadership and solidarity in the ranks, can paralyze American industry and precipitate civil war.

In all his discussion Reuther emphasizes UAW's determination to close the gap between production and distribution, which he believes dries up purchasing power among the masses, makes the economy unstable, and thwarts the potentials inherent in the economy of abundance.

The constitution of the UAW contains this language:

> We believe that Organized Labor and Organized Management possess the ability and owe the duty to society of maintaining, through co-operative effort, a mutually satisfactory and beneficial employer-employee relationship based upon understanding through the medium of conference. The worker does not seek to usurp management's functions or ask for a place on the Board of Directors of concerns where organized. The worker through his Union merely asks for his rights. Management invests thousands of dollars in the business. The worker's investment in the business is his sinew, his blood, and his life. *The organized worker seeks a place at the conference table, together with the management, when decisions are made which affect the amount of food he, his wife, and family shall consume; the extent of education his children may have; the kind and amount of clothing they may wear; and their very existence.* He asks that the savings due to the inauguration of machinery and changes in technical methods shall be equitably divided between management and the worker. The organized worker asks that those who may be discharged be paid adequate dismissal wages to enable them to

start afresh in another field; that society undertake to train them in new skills and that it make provisions through amelioratory social laws for the innocent and residual sufferers from the inevitable industrial shifts which constitute progress.

At the heart of the industrial age, therefore, stands the bargaining table, the conference method, and the weapon of the strike. It is pretty clear that the contemporary industrialist, despite all his wealth of capital apparatus, managerial skill, public relations experts, and command of science and technology, stands at the mercy of the organized workingman who may for what he believes to be provocation "when the speed-up comes, just twiddle his thumbs" and "sit down! Sit down!"

In less than twenty years Walter Reuther had become the acknowledged leader of the industrial union in heavily industrialized America. At the 1953 CIO Convention Reuther was re-elected president by acclamation. In his acceptance speech he declared that the "tools of production" can "dig our own economic grave and that of the whole free world if used only for the benefit of the few."

When the 1953 UAW constitutional convention raised Walter's salary to the "annual wage" of eighteen thousand dollars, Reuther protested. "I am not in the union for what you put in my pay check," he said. "I am in this thing for what is in my heart. The union must have dedicated leadership; it must believe in the labor movement. You can't buy that kind of leadership with money. We have something that leaders of industry cannot buy with all their millions and that is the loyalty and support of a lot of honest workers in this country."

For the eighteen thousand dollars a year, as he did when he was an unpaid volunteer organizer back in 1936, Reuther gives everything that he has. With his wife and two daughters, Linda Ann and Lisa, he lives modestly in a section of Detroit unpublicized for security reasons. He avoids business luncheons, preferring to work through the noon hour with a glass of milk, a pot of tea, or a fruit salad from the cafeteria brought to his desk. More than half of each month he spends away from Detroit — in Washington, New York, Cambridge, or anywhere in the country, or in Europe.

His work serves as his recreation. Once when he was talked into taking a two-week vacation, he began to pack papers and documents into his briefcase in quantity sufficient to carry him through the ordeal. When Frank Winn, UAW public-relations officer, inquired what he was going to do with all that material, Reuther replied: "I'm just taking some stuff along to work on during this vacation." When Winn protested that such preparations were out of place in planning a vacation trip, Reuther said: "Tell me, Frank, what can a man do on a vacation?" Winn suggested that Walter might fish. He did. Shortly, from the vacation camp, Winn got a note from Reuther instructing him to assemble some material. Walter ended the note by telling how many fish he had caught in the morning, how many he had caught in the afternoon. He added a postscript: "Going out this afternoon to catch the rest of the fish in the lake."

Despite his drive, Reuther requires a good deal of sleep. He gets what he needs by taking advantage of every opportunity to catch up on lost sleep. He snoozes in airplane seats, snoozes in breaks in meetings. Walter lists as his hobby "the development of economic and production plans." His mind reaches out with enthusiasm into many fields. On a plane one day he sat chatting with a man about the marvelous developments in the cattle business. He described in detail artificial insemination, feeds to finish up cattle for market. As the plane landed, his listener said shortly, "Yes, I'm a rancher!" So much does Reuther like to talk that his associates have to guard him from answering his telephone. The phone rang in a hotel room one day; he was quick to answer. He proceeded to talk forty minutes to a woman who was inquiring about her husband's pay check. Over the bargaining table Reuther can be tough, profane. But he likes conferences — especially in his office.

At his desk, in meetings, on planes and trains, he is constantly reading correspondence, reading periodicals, making memorandums for speeches and discussions. He wears down and wears out his associates and then goes on with fresh zest. He does not shy away from problems; he likes them, relishes them. To him every problem is an opportunity to work out a solution — and he likes the idea of proposing solutions. He works with pencil and paper. Even when he is talking with individuals he makes notes and draws diagrams constantly to keep a running picture of the discussion.

On one fact all UAW men are agreed: nobody can ghost-write for Walter Reuther. His memorandums, speeches, and articles are "produced by Reuther." When he begins work on an idea or assignment, he thoroughly canvasses it with his associates and specialists and sets forth his ideas on the subject clearly in conference. Then his staff goes to work and submits a preliminary draft. Reuther goes over this draft, sentence by sentence, with the person or persons who are engaged in writing. Sometimes there are several drafts. When the final draft is ready, he thoroughly overhauls it, rearranges the sequence of ideas to suit his own meticulous pattern of orderliness and logic, and polishes up the paragraphs and sentences. There is nothing casual, accidental, or unstudied which leaves UAW under the by-line or with the signature of Walter Reuther.

Although Reuther takes no active part in organized religion, he is recognized widely, by the Protestant churches in particular, as a Christian liberal. Personally, he finds his satisfying fellowship within the corporate structure of the UAW–CIO where men and women, as in the church, call one another "brother" and "sister" as a workingman's united family concerned with the promise of liberal values. When the President of Boston University conferred upon Walter Reuther the honorary degree of Doctor of Laws at the age of forty-three, he described the UAW chief in the citation as "a man who knows both intellectually and experimentally the Christian ideals of America — a man whose civic stature is well-proportioned and whose American patriotism is unimpeachable."

V

Francis Cardinal Spellman
Archbishop of New York, Roman Catholic Church

The Holy Tradition

FRANCIS CARDINAL SPELLMAN

*"I shall pray as if everything depends upon God. I shall work
as if everything depends upon me."*

FRANCIS CARDINAL SPELLMAN SAYS:

*I BELIEVE IN GOD, Father, Son, and Holy Ghost. I
believe in the Holy Roman Catholic Church as the Church which
the Blessed Son of God founded upon the spiritual rock which was
then Peter and is now Pius. Believing in God, I believe in man, in
the fundamental goodness of the creature because of the goodness
of the Creator. ◅§I believe in America, in the fundamental righteousness of our Constitution, the basic righteousness of our people
in their sincere desire to live in harmony, helpfulness, and peace
with their fellow men and in obedience to her laws and the Commandments of God. I glory in my American citizenship. I believe in
America's high destiny under God to stand before the people of the
earth as a shining example of unselfish devotion to the ideals that
have, under God, made us a great nation: in the Christian ideal of
liberty in harmonious unity, builded of respect for God's image in
man and every man's right to Life, Liberty, and Happiness. I
pledge myself to maintain and defend our fundamental liberties. In
this America I believe; for this America I live; for this America I and
millions of others stand ready to die. ◅§God in His infinite wisdom, mercy, and justice implements His plans for man's welfare
through human efforts. Labor and Capital are His especial instruments impelled by God's guiding hand to lead and to help man on
the Road to Happiness. If Labor and Capital are to thrive and
survive, they must serve as members of one social body, with sin-
gleness of purpose and diversity of functions, united in the strong
bonds of service for the good of mankind, spirited by reverence
for and love of God, working to do God's will on earth as it is
done in Heaven. ◅§Constant and courageous prayers are mightier
than atom bombs. God is our only hope. He alone will not fail us,
for He came to abide in our midst as one of us if we will but open*

[277]

our hearts to receive Him. He came to glory in our glory, to suffer in our suffering. He is yoked to the same plow as we. God is no stranger to our lot. ⮐§*Teach us that only by exemplifying in our everyday lives the love and service of Thee, Creator and Liberator of Mankind, and the love of our fellowman, be he white or black, yellow or brown, may we hope to achieve that peace for which the brokenhearted human race now yearns, that peace which is the tranquility of order, that peace which is the product of justice, that peace which can come only to men of good will.* ⮐§Dear God who rules the heavens and the earth, enkindle within all men the fire of Divine Love. Keep it forever aflame within men's hearts. Preserve our precious heritage of Faith. Grant to this great bewildered world another resurrection, that all men may know that in Thee rest our life and hope, and through Thy Risen Son, the peace that all men crave. AMEN.[1]

---

[1] All these excerpts are from different prayers by Cardinal Spellman.

The Holy Tradition

In the spring of 1939 Pope Pius XII named his close friend Francis Joseph Spellman to the See of New York to succeed Patrick Cardinal Hayes. In his first public statement the Archbishop-elect stated a formula for his activity. "I shall," he said, "pray as if everything depended upon God. I shall work as if everything depended upon me. My completely absorbing interests will be the salvation of souls — including all — and the welfare of my fellow man — excluding none." Such robust faith, coupled with strenuous practical activity and tempered with common sense, earned for His Excellency the high personal favor of the Holy See, the affection of a third of a billion Catholics around the globe, the friendship and confidence of leaders of world affairs, and the affection of priests and faithful alike.

Spellman came to his position of high leadership through a series of experiences which thoroughly prepared him to play a first role in the struggle of ideas and institutions characterizing the last half of the twentieth century. In a life of continuing growth in usefulness and single-minded service as a Catholic man, he has shared the highest offices, grappled with grave issues during turbulent decades, and remained in spirit an humble parish priest.

The Spellmans were Irish to the core. Both the paternal and maternal grandparents of Francis Spellman came to America from Ireland in what he later described as "no very fine ship." One of five children, Francis was born in Whitman, Massachusetts, on May 4, 1889. More of a New England village than an industrial city, Whitman manufactured shoes in two major plants producing two trade-named products — the Regal and the Bostonian. The town, twenty miles southeast of Boston, was predominantly Protestant.

William Spellman, the father, was a well-to-do grocer, who lived in a spacious white house set off with lawn and trees and equipped with a neighborly big front porch. Behind the house was a three-story barn where the grocery wagons and horses were kept. To the happy Irish-Catholic family circle the father contributed economic security, and a companionship spiced with Irish wit. "Son," he used to say to Frank, "always associate with people smarter than you are, and you will have no difficulty finding them."

Francis attended the public grammar and high schools in Whitman, delivered daily newspapers, waited on customers in the grocery store, drove the delivery wagon, wrote a prize essay in the ninth grade on the Battle of Gettysburg, and became the town's champion horseshoe pitcher. So happy were his memories of his school days that years later he established an endowment fund in the Whitman High School in memory of his mother, Ellen Conway Spellman, whose picture hangs prominently in the Cardinal's office.

Immediately upon his graduation from the Whitman High School in 1907, he proceeded in good Catholic tradition to Fordham University in New York. His academic record was not distinctive although he showed special competence in English composition, Latin, and scientific studies. He proceeded through his four years inconspicuously, achieving no unusual record in either scholastic or extracurricular activities. He failed to make the baseball team because he was too short and light. Occasionally he wrote a poem like many other college men. The really important event in his life at Fordham was his decision to enter the priesthood. William Cardinal O'Connell selected the young Fordham man as an outstanding candidate for the priesthood from the Boston Archdiocese. Upon graduation, Francis traveled to Rome to begin his studies at the North American College.

Francis Joseph Spellman, A.B., Fordham 1911, arrived in the Eternal City with a camera over his shoulder and the jaunty air of a college man who had quite recently received his diploma. His native curiosity and love of adventure during the next five years led him up and down the streets and lanes of Rome, studying both architecture and people at first hand. With the zeal of an amateur photographer, he took pictures until he could describe in detail almost any building or location and refer to his album for visual authentication.

It was in his studies at the North American College that Spellman struck his stride and began to exhibit qualities which subsequently marked his career as both priest and prelate. His interest in scholarship deepened. His memory showed a remarkable capacity to store away facts and names and to recall them at the proper time. His genius for organizational leadership began to unfold. His capacity for human friendship ripened.

Receiving the degree of Doctor of Sacred Theology from the University of Propaganda, he was ordained to the priesthood on May 14, 1916, in St. Apollinaris Church, by Archbishop Giuseppe Ceppetelli, then vice gerent of the vicariate of Rome. On July 16, 1916, he celebrated his first mass in America in the Lady Chapel of St. Patrick's Cathedral where his father and mother years before had brought him as a child. Returning to Boston, he took up his duties as an assistant at the Church of All Saints in Roxbury, Massachusetts. In 1918 he became director of diocesan literature at Boston's Cathedral of the Holy Cross, with special duties on the *Pilot*, official journal of the diocese. Four years later he became assistant chancellor of the archdiocese, and three years afterwards was an editor of the *Pilot* and archivist of the Archdiocese of Boston. Thus in a period of hardly a decade he had gained experience in parish work, the functions and problems of religious journalism, and procedures in diocesan administration.

His career in Boston terminated in an unexpected way as a result of a pilgrimage to Rome, which he made in the Holy Year of 1925. As a consequence of his presence in Rome, his linguistic skill, and his personal friendships, the Boston priest, with the consent of Cardinal O'Connell, was named by Pope Pius XI as an assistant to Cardinal Gasparri, papal secretary of state. In the next few years he received thorough orientation to the operations of the Church in world affairs, and emerged from the experience as a matured churchman well equipped to play a role in international life. Father Spellman had come to Rome as a Boston pilgrim; he remained seven years as the first American ever officially to be attached to the Secretariate of State.

During these years he lived in a single room in the modest Minerva Hotel, usually said his mass in the nearby Church of St. Mary, and then walked over the Tiber Bridge to the Vatican. Mornings he performed secretarial jobs. He copied orders, translated encyclicals, arranged broadcasts, and drafted documents. No education in the daily routine of diplomacy or in the detail of negotiation could have been more adequate. He enjoyed the work especially because he served directly under his beloved professor, Monsignor Borgongini-Duca, deputy secretary of state. To his duties in the Vatican the young priest brought a buoyant American emphasis. He suggested the practice of distributing press releases. He proposed the idea of issuing official statements with translations into various languages for the convenience of correspondents. He encouraged the mechanization of the offices and created a respect for American ways and know-how.

As a result of his diplomatic apprenticeship, Spellman obtained a world-wide perspective on ecclesiastical affairs. He made the acquaintance of the leading prelates of the Roman Curia, the central government of the Church. During the course of seven years he met every American bishop who had occasion to visit Rome.

In addition to his duties as deputy secretary of state, Monsignor Borgongini-Duca served as the chaplain of the boys' program which had been recently established within the Vatican area as a result of a million-dollar gift made by the Knights of Columbus in the United States. The Monsignor chose his old pupil, Francis Spellman, as his assistant chaplain and athletic director. Afternoons and evenings Father Spellman played with the boys on the field. The boys watched their "coach" play tennis. They joined in soccer and other games which he directed.

In these busy years, while Father Spellman was serving his diplomatic apprenticeship and acting as a part-time coach, historical issues were being worked out between Rome and the Vatican. The priest from Boston was in the center of them, since Monsignor Borgongini-Duca was Cardinal Gasparri's principal assistant in negotiations being carried on with the Italian government looking toward the Treaty of the Lateran and the related domestic concordat and financial convention. Spellman witnessed the steps which led to recognition by Italy of the international sovereignty of the Holy See with sole and absolute jurisdiction over the state called "City of the Vatican." The establishment of this "real and visible evidence of temporal power" was fundamental in the theory and vital to the practice of the Roman Catholic Church. In November 1926 Spellman was raised to the rank of papal chamberlain with the title of Monsignor.

Through his work, Monsignor Spellman formed an intimate friendship with Cardinal Pacelli, whom he had met for the first time when the Cardinal was Nuncio to Germany. In 1929 the Cardinal was named secretary of state. (Later he became Pope Pius XII.)

Because of Monsignor Spellman's linguistic ability, he was chosen to translate into English the radio message of Pope Pius XI in the first radio broadcast beamed from Vatican City station built by Marconi. For this service he was awarded one of the three commemorative gold medals.

It was in the summer of 1931 that Spellman performed an unforgettable service to the Pope which completely established his position. During the spring Benito Mussolini's Fascist government had initiated an aggressive campaign directed against Catholic Action organizations in Italy. Fascists considered Catholic Action to be an interference with Italian politics under the cloak of religion. In the course of the quarrel, Mussolini's operators singled out Monsignor Spellman for special attention, because he brought to Paris, for publication to the world, the Pope's Encyclical against Fascism. They gave him special mention in news comments. They caricatured him in cartoons as an American meddling with Italian politics. They stereotyped him as a United States propagandist, determined to deliver the Vatican to American interests. Sleuths shadowed him. On one occasion he turned quickly around and confronted his pursuer. "What do you want?" Spellman said sharply. The surprised and startled sleuth was speechless, and bothered him no more.

Mussolini finally dissolved Catholic Action. Fascist squads invaded Catholic Action clubhouses shouting "Down with the Pope!" They beat Catholic Action boys with clubs. In protest, the Pope issued a letter to his Italian bishops exhorting them to protest the arbitrary dissolution of the society and to protect what remained of it. Then, with the support of Cardinal Pacelli, Pius XI took the offensive. He decided to issue a message to the whole world denouncing Mussolini's interference with spiritual matters; he thus proposed to combat the internal difficulty with external public opinion.

To Monsignor Spellman, Cardinal Pacelli entrusted the hazardous task of secretly carrying the encyclical letter out of Italy to Paris. In the French capital Monsignor Spellman translated and distributed the letter to news services such as the Associated Press, United Press, International News Service, Havas, and Reuters, and to broadcasting networks. As a result of this and other incidents Cardinal Pacelli and Monsignor Spellman were drawn closer together in friendship and mutual respect.

Monsignor Spellman's experience continued to broaden. In 1932, as secretary to Lorenzo Cardinal Lauri, papal legate, he attended the Eucharist Congress in Dublin, Ireland, and translated the messages of the Pope's representatives to the congress.

In August 1932 Pope Pius XI appointed Monsignor Spellman auxiliary Bishop of Boston and titular Bishop of Sila. In September he was consecrated at the altar of the Chair of Saint Peter, in the Basilica of St. Peter's in Rome. In keeping with his own modest ways, the Bishop-elect performed the work preparatory to his consecration himself, without the help of secretary or valet. He arranged the guest list to be invited to fill the apse of St. Peter's, sent out his own invitations, and supervised the arrangement of the chairs and tribunes. For the members of the American embassy and their wives he provided a special tribune. To each guest he issued a booklet describing the entire procedure and giving the meaning of the forms and symbols used in the service. Just as Father Spellman was the first American to hold an office in the Secretariate of State, so now he was the first American to receive episcopal consecration at the high altar of the Basilica. As an expression of their esteem, the children of Rome presented Bishop Spellman with two mitres, one white and the other embroidered in gold, as a farewell gift on the occasion of his departure to enter upon his duties in Boston.

As auxiliary of Boston, Bishop Spellman performed his duties with characteristic organizational skill and wisdom, showing special interest in Catholic Action, youth, and education. In 1933 Cardinal O'Connell added to his duties by appointing him pastor of the Sacred Heart Church in Newton Center, a residential suburb of Boston. In this parish he found himself confronted with a debt of nearly seventy thousand dollars. While he was ministering to this parish he was awarded, in 1934, the Grand Cross of the Military Order of Malta, the highest ecclesiastical rank within the order. For service to Italy and its children he was further decorated by the Italian government with the Grand Official Cross of the Crown of Italy.

To the Newton Center rectory a stream of Catholic leaders made their way. In 1936, when Cardinal Pacelli as papal secretary of state visited the United States, it was Bishop Spellman who arranged his itinerary and accompanied the future pope on his historic aerial tour of the United States. Two years later Bishop Spellman flew twenty thousand miles through Latin American countries to study the progress and problems of the Church.

On March 2, 1939, Cardinal Pacelli was elected Supreme Pontiff. Six weeks later, in one of his first major appointments as Vicar of Christ, he named Francis Joseph Spellman to succeed the late Patrick Cardinal Hayes as Archbishop of New York, the richest and most influential See in America. The appointment came at the moment when circumstances in the deepening world crisis combined to require of Archbishop Spellman a high leadership in global affairs.

Archbishop Spellman had been in office scarcely three months when on September 1, 1939, Adolf Hitler's Third Reich declared war on Poland. On September 3, 1939, Great Britain declared war on Germany. As conflict spread around the world, Pope Pius XII entrusted to Spellman the task of mobilizing the colossal ministry to the armed service of the United States. On December 11, 1939, he became military vicar. Up to the time of that appointment he had been the archbishop of the third largest archdiocese in the United States. Overnight he became the directing chief of the largest See in the World. With a specialized ministry now spread across the face of the globe, Spellman proceeded to divide the world into twenty-three zones and place each zone in charge of a vicar delegate through whom the chaplains reported to him. In the administration of this work he kept in close touch with every corner of the globe. It is often said that he made the acquaintance of more Catholic lay and political leaders and of more political figures and military officers than any other person in history.

From the beginning of the struggle, Spellman was clear in his position that the military might of the United States was to be the decisive factor in its outcome. To the American Legion convention in Boston he observed: "It is better to have protection and not need it than to need protection and not have it." His prayer for "peace with justice after victory" became a slogan throughout the nation. Immediately after the news of Pearl Harbor, he pledged the entire facilities of the Archdiocese of New York to the government and encouraged the participation of the religious of the archdiocese in Red Cross first-aid courses to insure their readiness in the event of emergency. "As Archbishop of New York," he said, "I place all our resources, hospitals, institutions, and personnel at the disposition of our Government. As an American, and one of the twenty-five million Catholic Americans, I follow the identically glorious tradition of my country and religion." Immediately he proposed that there be no work stoppage for any cause until the war was won. He was one of the first to offer his blood to the Red Cross and continued to be a frequent donor throughout the war years. For the benefit of armed service personnel he opened the Catholic Canteen under the auspicies of the National Catholic Community Service and assigned the proceeds from his book *Action This Day* to its support. Presently at the Canteen he said: "Americans: we have prayed for peace with justice. We shall continue to pray for peace with justice, but peace with justice now can come only through victory. What will it profit us to emerge victorious over attacks from abroad if at the same time we do not preserve the ideals of democracy at home and their indispensable supports of religion and morality? The answer is: it will profit us nothing because democracy without the props of religion and morality collapses into anarchy and tyranny."

Archbishop Spellman saw in the world conflict a challenge to American democracy and Christian faith. His speeches, his poems, and his prayers expressed his conviction. He wrote:

O God, give us a victory that is just, merciful and wise,
For Thou hast chosen America to be the vessel of Thy justice,
   The medium of Thy mercy,
   The instrument of Thy wisdom.

Let all nations know that our justice comes from Thy spirit,
   Our mercy from Thy heart,

Our wisdom from Thy mind,
Our victory from Thy strength.

He saw the cause of freedom as worthy of the sacrifice of life:

The night breeze moves above our dead to-night,
To-morrow's light with warmth will touch their graves,
Yet none of them so silently shall sleep
But that the angels' lips shall o'er them breathe
The Master's benediction: Greater love
Than this no man can have, that he lay down
His life that other men may live in peace.

The Archbishop decided to administer his global vicarage "in person." He dedicated himself to the personal visitation of Catholic chaplains and the men and women they served. After flying visits to various camps in the United States, he began a series of notable trips to the armed forces abroad. In August 1942 he flew to the Aleutian Islands. In February 1943 he was in Spain and traveled on to Italy which was at war with the United States and met with the Holy Father.

Under the provisions of the Lateran Treaty, which assures safe passage to any cleric traveling to Vatican City to pay homage to the Supreme Pontiff, he landed at Guidonica Airport in Rome and was escorted by Italian police to the Vatican. Back on sovereign Catholic ground, he prayed with the Holy Father in his private chapel and attended the weekly meeting of the pontifical commission dealing with prisoners of war. After a farewell audience with Pius XII, he was off next day for Africa, Syria, Iran, and Iraq. His was a kaleidoscopic experience — one day an audience with the Pope, the next luncheon with General Mark Clark, then dinner with King George, next a meeting with Field Marshal Alexander, a week later saying mass on the camouflaged hood of a jeep and broadcasting to troops in North Africa with a relay to the United States.

In his spiritual odyssey he circled the globe by plane, boat, train, and jeep. Laying aside his role as Archbishop of New York, he served as a humble priest moving about companies, battalions, depots, and hospitals. He spurred his priests to greater activity. He encouraged soldiers and chaplains alike. His visits were "man to man" affairs. He spoke the GI language with its short-cuts and phonetic economy. He met with kings in their palaces, generals in their headquarters, and wounded men in field hospitals.

Over the air his voice spoke out:

SOLDIERS AND SAILORS OF THE UNITED STATES IN NORTH AFRICA:
. . . Your destiny is not alone to live protected under the folds of the Star-Spangled Banner and to sing in chorus its soul-stirring verses. Your vocation is something infinitely more noble and responsible, for you are writing again in imperishable glory its immortal stanzas —

"Then conquer we must when our cause it is just, and this be our motto: In God is our trust." . . .

And to all soldiers looking upwards to the black, star-studded African sky, the same sky into which St. Augustine gazed and from the same places in which he lived, I pray that Almighty God will give the same blessings and the same answer that He gave Augustine through the stars when to his silent questioning they answered: "We are not the God whom thou seekest — He made us."

Yes, the stars proclaim in luminous, unerasable language the existence of God, for they navigate the firmament in a certain, definite way, and the order in their movement presupposes an intelligence that cannot come from matter or from chance. And the first great Cause, Who regulates celestial orders, Who designed our bodies, resulting from the union of a hundred perfectly co-ordinated masterpieces, we know by the name of God. Every fiber of our bodies, every power of our souls, proclaims the existence of God, and to that God and Creator, our Ultimate End, we wish to be faithful and loyal.

From the microphone in North Africa the Archbishop hastened to visit a Red Cross club, to view torpedoed ships, and to pray with the sick and wounded in hospitals. Scarcely a month before the same airborne vicar from New York had dined in Madrid with the Nuncio and a group of prelates. During the dinner Spellman had kept thinking of a statement: *Twenty-four hours of disorder in Spain could mean the assassination of every bishop, priest, and man that could be found.* Later the Bishop of Madrid showed His Excellency a crucifix above his bed with bullet holes through the Body of Christ.

On Good Friday, 1943, Spellman was in Jerusalem following from station to station the footsteps of Jesus Christ as He endured the agony of His Passion and Crucifixion. On the Monday after Easter, at five o'clock, he celebrated mass in the chapel of the Nativity in Bethlehem. "This humpty-dumpty world has had a very great fall," he wrote in his notes. It was still dark when he left Jerusalem for Bethlehem, and stars studded the sky. "I was thinking . . ." he commented, "of that night on yonder hillside, in that little village, when Christ was born. The Scriptures say, 'The world knew Him not.' Nor does the world know Him today."

From the Mediterranean the Archbishop flew to London where he met American troops preparing for the Normandy invasion. When he returned to New York in August 1943 he had traveled, mostly by air, forty-five thousand miles. From the trip he brought back to his Madison Avenue residence fourteen thousand requests which he had collected from GIs, as he moved from company to company, to write to parents, sweethearts, and friends, and in the next weeks he wrote fourteen thousand personal letters!

Back on the home front he threw his support behind the Third War Loan. Concerned with the possibility of an allied bombing of Rome, he begged for "prayers that Rome, the city of the soul, eternal Rome, be spared destruction." To President Roosevelt in Washington he expressed the hope that "military ingenuity would overcome military necessity." After another visit to the White House, when it appeared that Rome had been spared, he said that he was grateful that "military ingenuity had displaced military necessity." To inaugurate the Fourth War Loan Drive, he wrote *Prayer for America,* which included this stanza:

> Bless us, O God, with manifold graces,
>   To give freely of what we have,
>   To give fully of what we are,
>   In victory to give ourselves alone to Thee.

Expressing his conviction that American sacrifice was necessary to achieve the historic destiny of the moment, he wrote in *An American Creed:*

I believe in America:
In her high destiny under
God to stand before the people of the earth as a
shining example of unselfish devotion to the ideal
that has made us a great nation: The Christian
ideal of liberty in harmonious unity, builded
of respect for God's image in man and every
man's right to life, liberty, and happiness. . . .

In this America I believe; for this America, I live;
for this America, I and millions of others stand ready
to die.

On July 19, 1944, Spellman was off from New York again to visit chaplains overseas and to meet in audience with the Holy Father. He visited Fifth Army Headquarters in Italy, confirmed thirteen Americans in St. Peter's Basilica, made a five-day tour of hospitals and military installations in Sardinia and Corsica, and visited virtually all the Mediterranean coast installations held by the Allies. In September he toured England and then visited American hospitals in Paris and the First and Third army sectors along the German border. In ten days he covered six different countries including France, Belgium, Germany, Luxembourg, and Italy. In middle October he returned to New York after a nineteen-thousand-mile tour of the European war theater. With the horrors of his experience fresh in his mind, he composed a *Prayer for Children* which was reproduced in poster form and placed in many schools throughout the nation. In part it read:

We do not sense the toll of war, the price
Man pays for putting faith in force of arms,
Till we have seen war's children and their woe,
The innocent who reap of Herod's wrath.
It is the children; they are lambs of God,
They are our generation's sacrifice
For immolation on the altars raised
Not to the loving fatherhood of God,
But to the cold and cruel cult of Mars.

The global travels of the military vicar to the armed forces and the heavy responsibilities of his office did not prevent Spellman as

Archbishop of New York from sending food to the Vatican during the middle years of the war nor from supporting the vast Catholic welfare activities made necessary by wartime circumstances. Mindful of the physical needs of the Holy Father and the residents of the neutral Vatican City, Spellman assumed a special task to see that the inhabitants were properly fed. Shipments of bacon, hams, smoked fish, and canned goods moved from New York to Lisbon. From the Portuguese port the supplies were carted on trucks over the Pyrenees, across southern France and the Riviera to Rome. Catholic relief extended its work to forty-three countries. By 1943 one ship was leaving the United States every ten days for areas of need. In all, foodstuffs and clothing valued at thirty-five million dollars were dispatched to Catholics abroad. The shipments included milk and cod-liver oil for babies, bedding, shoes, soap, hospital equipment, and supplies. The relief service even included provision for the transportation equipment such as motorcycles, trucks, tractors, and trailers, necessary for the distribution and delivery of the goods. American Catholics were united in their world crusade and clear about their world obligation. The air-borne military vicar everywhere made people mission-minded.

The news of the death of President Roosevelt on April 12, 1945, came to Archbishop Spellman as a personal sorrow. In St. Patrick's Cathedral he presided at a votive mass for the nation as thousands crowded the edifice to express their grief.

V–E Day came in early May, 1945. In the Cathedral and throughout the Archdiocese, the Archbishop's *Prayer for Thanksgiving after Victory* was read. In part it ran:

O God of Destiny!
Our nation, still bleeding from the wounds of war,
Thanks Thee for the Victory of this hour,
Won by our valiant dead,
Our soldiers' blood,
Our country's tears.
We were not alone when we groped through the night of war,
When we drank the cup of grief,
Thou, Lord God of Hosts, wert with us,
For we were with Thee.

As the summer wore on, he published in August a poem entitled *No Greater Love* which once again expressed his conception of the war as a necessity and a holy crusade. In part it read:

> Some say our dead were born expendable;
> In this sense only speak they true: There is
> No wiser spending of this earthly span
> Than, like the Master, greater love to prove
> By dying for the cause one holds most dear.
>
> The night breeze moves above our dead to-night,
> To-morrow's light with warmth will touch their graves.
> Yet none of them so silently shall sleep
> But that the angels' lips shall o'er them breathe
> The Master's benediction: Greater love
> Than this no man can have, that he lay down
> His life that other men may live in peace.

As peace came to the European front, military activity concentrated in the Pacific theater. Shortly before V–J Day, the Archbishop left on a tour of the Oriental outposts. On the Feast of the Assumption Day he celebrated a military mass at Pearl Harbor in thanksgiving for victory. He traveled to Guam, Saipan, Okinawa, the Philippines, Kwajelein, Tinian, and Iwo Jima. He entered Korea with the occupying forces, spent nine days in Japan, visited Hiroshima, and offered mass on a battleship in Tokyo Bay. He flew from China to India and on his way home made stops at Cairo, Rome, Paris, and the Azores. On this fourth wartime journey he traveled thirty-two thousand miles by air in a world-encircling trip climaxed by another visit to the Holy Father.

With peace Archbishop Spellman began to see the war years in perspective. In a poem entitled *We Are Free Men* he began:

> Today we stand on the top of time,
> On the summit of the ages,
> Looking down the steep slopes
> Which humanity has scaled
> From base slavery to rightful liberty . . .

Yet with the thought of the destructive potential of the atom bombs in mind and with hope in the United Nations, the Archbishop wrote a *Prayer for the United Nations* which concluded with this stanza:

Into man's hands, O God,
Thou hast placed power for his salvation or destruction.
Seek he peace, life grows abundant;
Seek he war, death dooms the world!
Merciful God of Nations, Spirit of Peace, Thou shalt prevail!
Reign Thou supreme among all nations;
Banish hates from peoples, root out wars from earth!

In *America Reborn*, Spellman saw the spiritual victory which could come. He concluded:

We are a single host of grateful love for Thee,
A single will for universal peace for men,
A single soul of righteousness to come!
Lord, lift this mighty host that is America,
Reconsecrate us now in Thy Son's holy Name. Amen.

With the war ended and the world faced with problems of reconstruction, Spellman was overwhelmingly convinced that the conquest of the Soviet menace could only be achieved by the united action of Washington and Rome. He became increasingly concerned lest the Communists impose a *Pax Sovietica* with a single goal: "One world — Theirs." "Soviet Russia," he said, "is building an empire. Communists, like vandals, vaunt in the desecration and destruction of all that is noble and sound. Every Communist is a potential enemy of the United States. Will we be lax, lazy, and cowardly, or crazy enough to permit the Soviets to trace their carbon copy of communism upon our land? . . . Spiritual diseases are the symptoms and effects of totalitarian tyrannies and the greatest of these is the worship of false gods. . . . *This is the only lesson that will save humanity: Love God and serve your fellow man."*

Up to 1940, Francis Joseph Spellman had been an enormously effective Catholic diplomat, priest, and administrator. In the 1940's he became an acknowledged spiritual and public leader. On August 27, 1945, United States troops had landed on Japan's home islands and raised the Stars and Stripes over Atsugi Airfield in Tokyo, just three weeks after the first atom bomb had been dropped on Hiroshima. The declaration of war by the Union of Soviet Socialist Republics on Japan on August 8 had introduced a new and dangerous force into the power vacuum in the Orient. Just before Christmas, General Douglas MacArthur abolished Shintoism as Japan's national religion. America had assumed new responsibilities in the Far East — to fill spiritual, political, and economic vacuums which had been created by victory. Archbishop Spellman understood these problems. He knew the geography of the world. He knew world leaders and was sensitive to the obligations of the Christian Church in the Orient as well as in the Occident.

The Archbishop had been back from his trip through the Pacific theater and around the world hardly three months when, at Christmas 1945, word came to New York from Rome that Pope Pius XII had chosen him as a member of the Sacred College of Cardinals, the fourth New York Archbishop to be so honored by the Vatican. "My life," said Spellman when he heard the news of his appointment, "I think, will not change in any way, and my activities or the purposes of life, which are to do everything I can do to help in the salvation of souls; to promote all humanitarian causes through the supernatural and natural forces of religion; and to further in every way possible the interest and welfare of my country."

In February the Archbishop flew to Rome for his elevation. On February 19, 1946, he was clothed in the red robes and white ermine cape symbolic of tongues of Pentecostal fire and the dove of peace. When His Holiness made Archbishop Francis Joseph Spellman an ecclesiastical prince of the Roman Catholic Church, he placed upon his head the same Red Hat which he himself had received as Cardinal Pacelli, papal secretary of state. He presented to the new cardinal his own Pectoral Cross. He assigned to him the Church of Saints John and Paul on Caelian Hill, which had been the Holy Father's own titular chair before his election to the throne of Saint Peter. The late Pope Pius XI had chosen for him the motto *Seguere Deum* — meaning: "Follow God."

In verse, His Eminence expressed convictions which were close to his heart:

And now,
Amidst the ruins of a world that strove

To prosper and to live apart from what was bought
On Calvary, by Christ, Thy Son —
Now we come back by that well-trodden way
That prodigals of every age have walked,
Back to our higher destiny — to Thee,
Our Father and our God.
And, kneeling in the valley of our grief, . . .
Rededicate ourselves to the great task that still remains,
That on the altar of our common victory,
Not to a god of war,
But to the Lord of Peace,
We give ourselves anew within the wounds
Of Him in Whom all men are one —
For all may yet redeem their faulty past,
Held in these wounded Hands of Christ, our Great High Priest.

We are a single host of grateful love for Thee.
A single will for universal peace for men,
A single soul of righteousness to come!
Lord, lift this mighty host that is America,
Reconsecrate us now in Thy Son's Holy Name. AMEN.

When Francis Cardinal Spellman returned from Rome to New
York on March 5, he was met at LaGuardia Field by the auxiliary
bishops of the archdiocese, the chancellor, the diocesan consultors,
and a delegation of the clergy. The Catholic War Veterans, the
American Legion, and other veteran groups formed an escort for
His Eminence from the airplane to the airport terminal, where he
was met by the Mayor of New York and his staff. Cheering crowds
lined the streets as the Cardinal's motorcade traveled over Tri-
borough Bridge to Cardinal Hayes High School, where Spellman
was greeted by the student body and school band. He proceeded
down Seventh Avenue to 110th Street and went to Central Park
West, across 57th Street to Fifth Avenue, and south to St. Patrick's
Cathedral. When his motor car approached the Cathedral, he
stepped to the pavement and continued the journey on foot, resplen-
dent in the Cardinal's robes of scarlet. As he passed, many faithful
dropped to their knees.

Cardinal Spellman entered the great Cathedral under huge
American flags which hung over the entrance and under a newly

painted and gilded shield which bore his coat of arms. At the door he was welcomed by the administrator of the Cathedral, who presented him a Crucifix. Kneeling, Cardinal Spellman kissed it. Then, preceded by seminarians, acolytes, priests, prelates, and attendants, he walked slowly up the center aisle to the sanctuary as more than five thousand school children sang "The Star-Spangled Banner." In the sanctuary the Cardinal was escorted to a prie-dieu in front of the altar. Following a simple ceremony conducted by Monsignor Joseph F. Flannelly, the Cardinal ascended the archiepiscopal throne, which had been decorated in cardinal red. Two school children read addresses of welcome to which the Cardinal responded. The children also presented him with a spiritual bouquet as witness of the many prayers and acts of piety performed for his intention while he was in Rome. This offering included a hundred thousand Holy Communions, a hundred thousand masses, a hundred thousand rosaries, a hundred thousand visits to the Blessed Sacrament, and a hundred thousand ejaculations.

At the Metropolitan Opera House a great public reception followed. It was attended by more than sixteen bishops. For the State of New York Governor Thomas E. Dewey brought greetings. Mayor William O'Dwyer welcomed the Cardinal on behalf of the City of New York, while Postmaster Robert E. Hannegan represented President Truman. On March 7 more than fifteen hundred sisters, six hundred priests, and a hundred monsignori, one archbishop, and twenty-five bishops participated in a pontifical mass of thanksgiving in the Cathedral. Two days later parochial and high school students of the archdiocese attended a pontifical mass. On the next Sunday, March 10, the Cardinal celebrated a pontifical mass for all the people and charitable works under his jurisdiction.

The strenuous life which the new cardinal had lived is perhaps indicated by the fact that in the ten years, 1936 to 1946, between his flight with Cardinal Pacelli throughout the United States until his return from the seven-thousand-mile round trip for his elevation to the Sacred College of Cardinals, he had traveled more than one hundred and fifty thousand miles, or the equivalent of six times around the equator.

Despite the burdens of his wartime activity, Spellman as the administrator of the vast archdiocese of New York, with its gigantic spiritual and public responsibilities, had given a dynamic and effective leadership to his See. With an archdiocese embracing Manhattan, the Bronx, and Staten Island, in the City of New York, and the seven counties above the Bronx — Westchester, Putnam, Dutchess, Rockland, Orange, Sullivan, and Ulster — Cardinal Spellman was the spiritual leader of more than a million and quarter Catholics. His metropolitan authority extended over the suffragan sees of Brooklyn, Albany, Buffalo, Rochester, Syracuse, and Ogdensburg. He had responsibilities for a parochial school system enrolling more than a hundred and fifty thousand students, a system of higher education of national and international importance, and vast Catholic charities. During all the years of his active archiepiscopal leadership, the archdiocese had grown both in spiritual and material strength.

In the summer of 1946, in a solemn pontifical mass commemorating the canonization of the Blessed Frances Xavier Cabrini as the first citizen of the United States to become a saint, Cardinal Spellman expressed his primary concern when he said that "the chief call of the hour is not for statesmen, generals, scholars, diplomats, or economists. All of these have their places, but they alone cannot be agents of peace. *The essential need is for saints.*"

From the moment that Archbishop Spellman had assumed his office in 1939, New York knew that it had a spiritual leader and ecclesiastical administrator determined to give the Church an effective organizational program for advance with renewed spiritual and material strength. Spellman's motto "Follow God" became the central fact in his ministry. By personal example and official program he communicated spiritual strength to his priests in their ministry. He exhorted them to faithful effort in their parishes. He himself set the example. WORK — WORK FOR GOD became the watchword throughout the archdiocese. Spellman wanted his priests and his people to have a deep and continuing spiritual experience, a vision of the great commandment to preach the gospel to the whole world. He insisted on a Catholic educational system in quantity and quality adequate for the needs of the youth of the archdiocese. He wanted institutions sufficient to discharge the responsibilities incumbent upon the Church.

Shortly after his installation he inaugurated a ten-million-dollar school and hospital building program. In the Bronx the Cardinal Hayes Memorial High School rose. In White Plains the Archbishop Stepinac High School was dedicated to the memory of the imprisoned Yugoslavian Roman Catholic prelate. In 1947 he announced the inauguration of a twenty-five-million-dollar archdiocesan building program with the statement that he expected the program to be a wholesome stimulus to postwar recovery, since it expressed "confidence in ourselves, in our economy, and in our country." His planning for Catholic schools demanded foresight and courage. The facts spoke for themselves. In 1940 the number of boys and girls in elementary and Catholic schools in the archdiocese numbered one hundred and nineteen thousand. By 1950 the number had increased to over one hundred and fifty thousand. His statistical projection showed that by 1960 he would need facilities for over one hundred and eighty thousand. At mid-century 55 per cent of the elementary school population and 35 per cent of the secondary school population in the Archdiocese of New York was enrolled in parochial schools. The policies necessary for construction, instruction, and finance required leadership of the kind which the Cardinal supplied.

With the thrifty habits of a New Englander, Spellman wanted to see each Catholic dollar produce the fullest possible value in goods and services. Likewise he wanted to see that the real estate of the archdiocese was kept in first-class condition. Soon after he became archbishop he launched a program to refinance, fund, and amortize the indebtedness within his jurisdiction. For the convenience of his parishes he set up a centralized insurance advisory service so that they could verify rates, standardize coverage, and make savings on premiums. He established a central diocesan buying agency to advise parishes on procurement, building problems, maintenance, and repairs. Like a railway system president, he made inspection tours of Catholic properties. His eye quickly spotted leaking roofs, worn-out floors, doors that needed paint, and waterspouts that required the services of a plumber. He gave the physical plant the attention which modern building operational efficiency demands.

He began at home by undertaking a large and varied program of restorations and improvements at St. Patrick's Cathedral. The program called for the installation of new stained glass windows, including a new rose window; the erection of a new high altar; a new altar and statue of Our Lady of New York in Lady Chapel; the rebuilding of the great organ, and exterior renovations, costing in the neighborhood of three million dollars. In December 1949 he blessed the massive new bronze doors of the Cathedral at the Fifth Avenue entrance. Six statuettes symbolized how the redemptive mission of Christ had been carried forward by the Church in the State of New York. These figures represented:

1. Saint Joseph, portrayed as a workingman
2. Saint Patrick, patron Saint of the Cathedral and of the archdiocese
3. Saint Isaac Jogues, first Catholic priest to visit Manhattan
4. Saint Frances Xavier Cabrini, founder of Columbus Hospital, Mother Cabrini High School, and Mother Cabrini Home, the first American citizen to be canonized as a saint
5. Blessed Catherine Tekakwitha, the "Lily of the Mohawks"
6. Mother Elizabeth Bayley Seton, native of Manhattan and founder of the Sisters of Charity of Saint Vincent de Paul

The statuettes symbolized the universality of the Church. They emphasized that Saint Joseph was Jewish; Saint Patrick, Celtic; Saint Isaac Jogues, French; Mother Cabrini, Italian; Catherine Tekakwitha, native Indian; and Mother Elizabeth Bayley Seton, native Anglo-Saxon. Between the figures of Catherine Tekakwitha and Mother Cabrini were placed the coats of arms of Pope Pius XII and Francis Cardinal Spellman. Surely Manhattan culture had joined America with the Catholic tradition of the ages.

Often, Cardinal Spellman found himself compelled to deal with issues relating Catholic policy to general public interest. Three such situations will be sufficient to illustrate the difficulties which Spellman faced in the administration of his See as a result of the impact of Catholic culture on the whole community. The first relates to tax support of parochial education, the second to labor union policy, and the third to the application of Catholic standards to the arts.

The issue on Catholic education was brought to focus by Eleanor Roosevelt in her column *My Day*. Mrs. Roosevelt referred to a suggestion made by Cardinal Spellman to the effect that Catholic schools should share in Federal aid funds. She pointed out that the Cardinal's position confronted citizens with a perplexing decision in public policy. In part she said that:

> Those of us who believe in the right of any human being to belong to whatever church he sees fit, and to worship God in his own way, cannot be accused of prejudice when we do not want to see public education connected with the religious control of the schools, which are paid for by taxpayers' money. . . . Many years ago it was decided that the public schools of our country should be entirely separated from any kind of denominational control, and these are the only schools that are free, tax-supported schools. . . . The separation of church and state is extremely important to any of us who hold to the original traditions of our nation. To change these traditions by changing our traditional attitude toward public education would be harmful, I think, to our whole attitude of tolerance in the religious area. . . . If we look at situations which have arisen in the past in Europe and other world areas, I think we will see the reasons why it is wise to hold to our early traditions.

In a subsequent column Mrs. Roosevelt observed that

> If we want our children in school to receive some particular sectarian church education, then we should pay for that education and it should not in any way lessen our interest and support of the public schools, which are attended by the vast majority of the children of our country and can be attended by all of our children if they so desire. . . .
>
> I do not want the public school system to be dominated by Federal Government. . . . Neither do I want church groups controlling the schools of our country.

In a letter promptly dispatched to Mrs. Roosevelt Cardinal Spellman pointed out that her record of "anti-Catholicism stands for all to see — a record which you yourself wrote on the pages of history — documents unworthy of an American mother." He clearly defined his own position in these words:

> You say you are against religious control of schools which are paid for by taxpayers' money. That is exactly what I too oppose. But I am also opposed to any bill that includes children who attend parochial schools for the purpose of receiving

funds from the Federal Government while it excludes these same children from the distribution and benefits of the funds allocated. I believe that if the Federal Government provides a bottle of milk to each child in a public school it should provide milk for all school children. I believe that if Federal funds are used to transport children to public schools they should be used to transport parochial school children. I believe if through the use of Federal funds the children who attend public schools are immunized from contagious diseases that all children should be protected from these diseases. 'Taxation without representation is tyranny' was the cry that roused and rallied our pioneer Americans to fight for justice. Taxation without participation should rouse today's Americans to equal ardor to protest an injustice that would deprive millions of American children of health and safety benefits to which all of our children are entitled.

Mrs. Roosevelt replied. She said that "spiritual leadership should remain spiritual leadership and the temporal power should not become too important in any church."

The day after the Cardinal's letter was dispatched, Governor Herbert H. Lehman issued a comment to the effect that "the issue is not whether one agrees or disagrees with Mrs. Roosevelt on this or any other public question. The issue is whether Americans are entitled freely to express their views on public questions without being vilified or accused of religious bias." The Cardinal insisted that the issue was but one: whether or not children who attended parochial schools were to be denied auxiliary services such as health care, which are provided for children who attend tax-supported schools. For her part Mrs. Roosevelt observed: "I reiterate that I have no anti-Roman Catholic bias. I am firm in my belief that there shall be no pressure brought to bear by any church against the proper operations of the government and that there shall be recognition of the fact that all citizens express their views freely on questions of public interest." After the controversy was over, Cardinal Spellman, accompanied by Monsignor Joseph A. Nelson, made a gentlemanly courtesy call on Mrs. Roosevelt, without in any way retreating from his original position.

* * *

The second situation of wide general interest which Cardinal Spellman faced arose from a crisis within the archdiocese when gravediggers in two Catholic cemeteries struck. The experience introduced the Cardinal for the first time into the painful difficulties involved in labor negotiations. The nine trustees of Saint Patrick's Cathedral operate two cemeteries — Calvary in Queens and the Gate of Heaven in Hawthorne. On January 3, 1949, two hundred and forty members of the United Cemetery Workers Union CIO, Local 293, called a gravediggers' strike after the trustees had refused to meet their demands for a five-day, forty-hour week with wage increases and overtime payments. According to the trustees' calculations the demands would increase the diggers' weekly pay check from fifty-nine dollars to seventy-seven dollars and twenty-two cents. They felt that they could not find funds to meet the demands without adding considerably to burial costs. On February 10 the strike was extended to the Gate of Heaven Cemetery, and union members began to picket the chancery of the archdiocese at Madison Avenue and 51st Street. Although the union members opened no new graves, people in New York continued to die as usual. When the bodies awaiting burial numbered seven hundred, Cardinal Spellman felt compelled to act. One night he went quietly to Yonkers to St. Joseph's Seminary, the training center for the priesthood in the archdiocese. He attended benediction with the seminarians, and the next morning issued a call for volunteers to perform a "special kind of task" which he specified as a "corporal work of mercy." All the seminarians volunteered. Enlisting the senior hundred men who responded to his appeal, Cardinal Spellman, with Monsignor John J. Fearns, president of the seminary sitting in the front seat of the first of a caravan of three buses, conveyed the men to Calvary Cemetery. There he organized them into fifty two-man teams, handed out shovels and assignments, and proceeded to oversee the work in person. The Cardinal walked around among the men, admonishing them in their enthusiasm not to overstrain. At the same time he officiated at twenty committal services supplementing the work of parish priests. At noon, box lunches were distributed and at the end of the day the Cardinal mounted the bus and rode back to the seminary at Dunwoodie, Yonkers. The two hundred and forty union workers on strike had regularly opened forty-two graves a day; the one hundred seminarians had opened ninety.

To Cardinal Spellman the strike was "illegal," "immoral," and conducted along the lines of Communist tactics. The union replied that "with all reverence and respect it is more important to recognize the right of workers to organize and bargain collectively in unions of their own choosing and to pay a living wage than to bury the dead." Thus the issue was sharply drawn. The seminarians, said the union, were nothing more than "strikebreakers." The CIO condemned the "union-busting tactics of any employer — including the Catholic Church when it acts as an employer." As the strike dragged on, it was clear that the Cardinal intended to bury the dead, that his seminarians could dig the graves as necessary, and that the strikers intended to hold out until their demands were satisfied.

"Morally unjust?" asked the Cardinal as he took note of the union comment. "A strike that leaves all these people unburied? If they think that's decent, I don't." He made his position clear. "I admit," he said, "to the accusation of being a strikebreaker and I am proud of it. If stopping a strike like this isn't a thing of honor, then I don't know what honor is. I've had a problem confronting me for several weeks and know of no other way to solve it."

With a handful of exceptions, the striking gravediggers were Roman Catholics. Indeed the strike itself was being approved by some members of the Association of Catholic Trade Unionists to which Cardinal Spellman had been a generous contributor. The association had been organized in 1937 to provide an educational and religious unit to work with and alongside the established unions in America, according to the suggestion in *Quadragesimo Anno* that "side by side with these unions there should always be associations zealously engaged in imbuing and forming their members in the teaching of religion and morality so that they in turn may be able to permeate the unions with that good spirit which should direct them in all their activities."

In joining the association members had to swear that they were practicing Catholics, that they were faithful members in good standing of their labor unions, that they would familiarize themselves with and faithfully carry out the duties imposed upon them by the Papal Social Encyclicals, and that they would do their utmost to oppose Fascists, Communists, Nazis, and racketeers and their philosophies.

While the Cardinal was being advised by an attorney who was recognized by ACTU (as the association is known) as a "tough union buster," ACTU was guiding the strategy of the CIO union strike against the Cardinal. Union members proceeded to meet in the Democratic Club in Queens. They opened their meeting with the Lord's Prayer, said a Hail Mary, and then joined in the "Prayer of the Worker" which reads:

> LORD JESUS, Carpenter of Nazareth, You were a worker as I am, give to me and all the workers in the world the privilege to work as You did, so that everything we do may be to the benefit of our fellowmen and the greater glory of God the Father. Thy Kingdom come into the factories and into the shops, into our homes and into our streets. Give us this day our daily bread. May we receive it without envy or injustice. To us who labor and are heavily burdened send speedily the refreshment of Thy love. May we never sin against Thee. Show us Thy way to work, and when it is done, may we with all our fellow-workers rest in peace. Amen.

The prayer had been published under the imprimatur of the late Patrick Cardinal Hayes, Archbishop of New York. The gravediggers read it from a hand card illustrated with a woodcut of Christ kneeling at His carpenter's bench.

Following the prayer the chairman of the negotiating committee asked the union members to rise and raise their right hands as they joined in this pledge:

> We here as Catholic gentlemen solemnly declare that we are opposed to Communism and all that it means in all walks of life. Be it recorded, however, that Communism is not the issue here.

The union men then proceeded to approve a resolution severing relationships with the international affiliated with the CIO and to become a local of the AFL. A settlement quickly followed. Wage adjustments were made, the Cardinal recognized the new union, reversing his previous stand that he would permit the men to return to work only as individuals. He had been initiated into the problems of labor conflict. The Cardinal, to show his good will and sympathy, gave one full week's wage to every employee.

"True it is," said the Cardinal in analyzing what had happened, "that there have been at stake economic principles, policies, and practices. But it is just as true that there have been souls at stake — confused, misled souls — and I am a priest of God, striving to live in imitation of Him, the Forgiving Shepherd of Souls. If I had yielded to the union demands I would have been unfair, unfaithful, and a hireling, rather than a shepherd. Therefore I choose to protect the rights of millions of Catholics, living and dead, as well as the rights of the cemetery workers themselves — all entrusted to my care as their shepherd."

Looking back upon the strike, which lasted more than two months, the Cardinal observed that the strike confronted him with "one of the most difficult, grievous, heartbreaking issues that has ever come within my time as Archbishop of New York, and it will be my daily prayer that if ever again the working men of this Archdiocese must make their choice between following their Faith or faithless leadership, they will of their own free and immediate choice, choose — God!"

The third situation which evoked widespread public interest resulted from the showing of the motion picture *The Miracle* in New York. In his encyclical letter "On Motion Pictures" Pope Pius XI discussed the principles entrusted to the Hierarchy and to "The Legion of Decency" for implementations, pointing out that the essential purpose of art, its *raison d'être*, "is to assist in the perfecting of the moral personality which is man. For this reason art must itself be moral." The Pope called on the bishops of the entire world to recognize that no more potent means of influencing the masses exists than the cinema. By means of vivid and concrete imagery, the motion picture, he said, speaks to the mind, which takes in its communication with enjoyment and without fatigue. He wanted the motion picture to become an "effectual instrument for the education and elevation of mankind." He wanted the bishops of the world to assume their share in the exercise of painstaking vigilance over the motion picture. He wanted to protect the morality of the people during their moments of leisure and recreation to the noble end of promoting the highest ideals and the truest standards of life.

In carrying out his duty in relation to motion pictures, Cardinal Spellman took note of a film which opened on December 12, 1949, at the Paris Theater at 58th Street. The story, as summarized in a United States Supreme Court Report, told the experiences of a poor, simple-minded girl tending a herd of goats on a mountainside.

One day when a bearded stranger passed, the idea struck her fancy that the man was Saint Joseph, her favorite saint, and that he had come to take her to heaven where she would be happy and free. While the shepherdess pleaded with the stranger to transport her, the wayfarer quietly plied the girl with wine and apparently ravished her. The girl awakened later to find the stranger gone. She climbed down from the mountain not knowing whether her experience was real or a dream. As she walked along, she met an old priest who told her that it was quite possible that she had seen a saint. A younger priest scoffed at the idea. "Materialist," the old priest explained. A brief symbolic picture sequence followed, in which the girl was reverently seated with other villagers in church. Moved by a whim of appetite, she snitched an apple from the basket of the woman next to her. As the girl left the church, a cackling beggar tried to make her share the apple with him but she chased him away and munched the fruit contentedly. Then one day while tending the village youngsters as their mothers worked at the vines, the girl fainted. Women discovered that she was going to have a child. Frightened and bewildered, the girl murmured "It is the grace of God!" In excitement she ran to the church, sought out the statue of Saint Joseph, and prostrated herself on the floor before it. Thereafter she meekly refused to do any menial work. Housewives humored her, but the young people were not so kind. In a scene of brutal torment, first they flattered and then laughingly mocked her. They shoved her, beat her, and clamped a basin on her head as a halo. Abused even by beggars, the poor girl gathered together her pitiful rags and sadly departed from their village to live alone in a cave. When she felt her time coming, she started back toward the village, but when she saw the crowds in the street dark memories haunted her. She turned toward the church on a high hill and instinctively struggled toward it, crying desperately to God. With a goat as her sole companion, she drank water dripping from a rock. When she came to the church she found the door locked, but her goat guided her to a small door. Inside the church, the girl braced herself for the labor pains. There came a dissolve and when the girl next appeared on the scene, spectators saw her sad face in a close-up, full of tender light. There was a cry of an unseen baby. The girl reached toward it and murmured, "My son! My love! My flesh!"

The film, which was one of a trilogy entitled *Ways of Love*, had been produced in Italy by Roberto Rossellini. It had been shown at the Venice Film Festival and had been freely exhibited in Italy, although without great success. It had been examined and licensed by the motion picture division of the New York State Educational Department. During the first eight weeks of its exhibition at the Paris Theater, the New York State Board of Regents received hundreds of letters, telegrams, post cards, affidavits, and other communications protesting and defending the public showing of the film. The Legion of Decency described the picture as a sacrilegious and blasphemous mockery of Christian religious truth. On December 23, 1950, the New York Commissioner of Licenses declared the film, "officially and personally, blasphemous" and ordered it withdrawn under threat of suspension of the license to operate the Paris Theater. The issue was promptly taken to court and the New York Supreme Court ruled that the New York City License Commissioner had exceeded authority since power to censor motion pictures was not one of his prerogatives. The Paris Theater resumed showing the film. On Sunday, January 7, 1951, Cardinal Spellman condemned the picture and called on "all right-thinking citizens" to unite to tighten censorship laws. His letter was read at all masses at St. Patrick's Cathedral. On the next day the *New York Times* quoted the Cardinal as saying that the film was a "vile and harmful picture," a "despicable affront to every Christian." "We believe in miracles," he said. "This picture ridicules that belief." Then he concluded: "We, as the guardians of the moral law, must summon you and all people with a sense of decency to refrain from seeing it and supporting the venal purveyors of such pictures."

The issue received widespread public attention. On two different evenings the Paris Theater was emptied on threat of bombing. Coincident with the criticism of the film, the theater experienced difficulties with the New York Fire Department. The *Commonweal* questioned the wisdom of transforming a church dogma which Catholics may obey as a "free act" into a "state-enforced censorship for all." Allen Tate, the well-known Catholic critic, observed that "in the long run what Cardinal Spellman will have succeeded in doing is insulting the intelligence and faith of the American Catholics with the assumption that a second-rate motion picture could in any way undermine their morals or shake their faith."

Roberto Rossellini, who with Vatican approval had previously filmed the "Life of Saint Francis," using as cast members of the Franciscan Order, cabled Cardinal Spellman protesting the boycott. "In *The Miracle*," he said, "men are still without pity because they still have not come back to God, but God is already present in the faith of that confused, poor, persecuted woman; and since God is wherever a human being suffers and is misunderstood, the 'miracle' occurs when at the birth of the child the poor demented woman regains sanity in her maternal love." To the Cardinal the theme of the seduction of an idiotic woman, regardless of race, remained "revolting to any decent man or woman" and represented "art at its lowest." He said that the film should have been entitled *Woman Further Defamed*.

Catholic organizations began to picket the Paris Theater. The Catholic War Veterans carried signs declaring that the film was "blasphemous." Three thousand men of the New York Holy Name Society joined the demonstration and then marched from the theater plaza to St. Patrick's Cathedral to attend a vesper service. The Ancient Order of Hibernians and the ladies' auxiliary joined the decency crusade, as did also members of the New York Chapter of the Knights of Columbus, who expressed their "displeasure and indignation."

Meanwhile the New York State Board of Regents reviewed the picture and in middle February determined that the film was "sacrilegious." The Board directed the Commissioner of Education to rescind the license which had been issued authorizing the exhibition of the picture. A series of court actions followed. The Appellate Division upheld the revocation of the license as ordered by the Board of Regents. The New York Court of Appeals affirmed the judgment of the Appellate Division. The case was appealed to the United States Supreme Court, because of issues raised under the First and Fourteenth Amendments. The case of *Joseph Burstyn, Inc.* v. *Wilson, Commissioner of Education of New York, et al.* came up for argument on April 24, 1952, and was decided in late May. The American Civil Liberties Union filed an *amici curiae* urging reversal of the decision of the New York courts. The New York State Catholic Welfare Committee filed an *amici curiae* urging that the prior decisions be affirmed. In a decision overruling the New York State Courts, the United States Supreme Court recognized motion pictures as a significant medium for the communication of ideas and concluded that expression by means of motion pictures is included within the free speech and free press guaranty of the First and Fourteenth Amendments.

"The State," said the Court, "has no legitimate interest in protecting any or all religions from views distasteful to them which is sufficient to justify prior restraints upon the expression of those views. It is not the business of government in our nation to suppress real or imagined attacks upon a particular religious doctrine, whether they appear in publications, speeches, or motion pictures." The New York Court of Appeals had looked at the problem differently. "No religion," it had said, "shall be treated with contempt, mockery, scorn, or ridicule."

The effect of the discussion provoked by *The Miracle* was to create a respect for the Crusade of the Legion of Decency in its program to encourage public morality, to revitalize the ideals of natural and Christian rectitude, and to advance the cinema "on the road to artistic significance." The incident likewise was important in setting bounds to the activity of any group seeking to use legal weapons to prevent the free expression of ideas.

The issues which arose between the Cardinal and Eleanor Roosevelt, between the Cardinal and the gravediggers' union, and out of the boycott of *The Miracle* set in motion currents of searching discussion and mutual criticism. By his criticisms of the cinema, Pius XI had emphasized the positive affirmation that recreation, which has become a necessity for people who labor under the fatiguing conditions of modern industry, must be worthy of the rational nature of man, must be "morally healthy," "must be elevated to the rank of a positive factor for good, must seek to arouse a noble sentiment." The Cardinal, while grieved by his experience with the cemetery workers, had said in his address at his investiture with the Sacred Pallium that "despite the need for proper readjustments and equalizations of our economic burdens, despite the necessity of providing much greater opportunities for work for men and women who need work and wish to work, despite the need for more hands fraternally clasped and fewer fists menacingly clenched, despite the need of a renewal in our midst of the Christian concepts of life and Christian discipline of living in which our liberties were conceived and enfranchised, despite the need of strengthening our moral fiber grown weak through prosperity and indulgence, still I believe in America, in the fundamental righteousness of our Constitution, the basic righteousness of our people, in their sincere desire to live in harmony, helpfulness, and peace with their fellow men, and in obedience to her laws and the Commandments of God." In an address to workingmen in Buffalo he expressed a "Creed of Capital and Labor" by stating that he believed "in a system of government which encourages Labor and Capital to function freely under God, giving full measure of deed and devotion for the common good of the common man, in loyal, concerted service to our common country — America!"

In his address at the investiture, Spellman as Archbishop had pointed out that paramount among his interests was his desire to follow the example of Patrick Cardinal Hayes in his devotion and service to the poor and suffering through the agency of Catholic Charities. In his official capacity as Archbishop of the New York See, the Cardinal was president and treasurer of Catholic Charities. This organization ministers to the spiritual, social, and economic needs of the vast metropolitan community. In a single year its hundred and eighty-five agencies serve a half-million human beings — men, women, and children of every race and faith. Catholic Charities works in close co-operation with the three hundred and eighty-seven parishes in the archdiocese and with the lay neighborhood work of the members of the Saint Vincent de Paul Society, of which the Cardinal is state spiritual director. Under the leadership of Catholic Charities, the Church provides specialized services to help people at the point of their most personal and immediate need. It provides sports, dances, and marriage forums for youth. It arranges for cultural activities, lectures, courses on guidance, and offers psychological and psychiatric counseling, and employment services. In family case work, professional social workers join with the parish priest to help individuals find the cause of their problems and to work them out for themselves. Catholic Charities provides maternity care for unmarried mothers and fights the "black and gray" market in adoption practices. It maintains homes for the aged. It maintains family service for the Puerto Ricans who have come in such numbers to New York. It provides counselors in court actions. Legions of Mary Volunteers visit homes to encourage people to return to their religious practices. The Church provides residences for the blind, the homeless, the delinquent, and the orphans. It operates day nurseries. Some fifteen general hospitals with annual budgets running into the millions minister to the health of the people. Cardinal Spellman's New England prudence makes him proud that Catholic Charities operates at one of the lowest overhead costs of any comparable organization in the United States.

In thinking about Catholic Charities, the Cardinal likes to refer to Holman Hunt's portrait of Christ standing in the dark, lantern in hand, outside a house. The picture bears the inscription: "Behold, I stand at the door and knock." Hunt, as Spellman tells the story, was standing before the portrait one day when a visitor remarked: "Surely you forgot something in this picture. Look, there is no handle on the door." "It is not a mistake," replied the artist. "The door represents the human heart, and *it opens only from the inside.*" The Cardinal's heartfelt concern for the welfare of his people resulted in a vast development of Catholic Charities.

Francis Cardinal Spellman lives in the graystone residence at Madison Avenue and 50th Street behind St. Patrick's Cathedral. His home is a friendly, human place with nerves that touch every section and problem in the world. In a fifteen-to-eighteen-hour working day beginning at seven o'clock in the morning he moves through a kaleidoscopic series of activities which range from the simplest friendly greeting to the most difficult institutional and policy decisions. Work and human friendship constitute the content of his long day. An old Jesuit who taught Spellman at Fordham University used to say that the "three S's" of Spellman's ministry are his simplicity, his sympathy, and his sacrifice. His associates — priests, bishops, and personal friends — corroborate one another in describing his humility, his native kindness, his thoughtfulness, and his generosity. John Cifrino, a Boston provisions merchant who sailed with Father Spellman on the Holy Year pilgrimage in 1925, remembers the young priest as "errand boy for everybody." "Someone lose baggage," said Cifrino, "he find it. Someone need hotel room, he get it at low price. He friend of everybody on ship — Protestants too." Prince Lobkowicz of Croatia records in his notes that at the conclusion of a Vatican conference Spellman in person helped him on with his coat and escorted him to his car. As a young priest he was so highly regarded by the managers and waiters of La Rosetta Restaurant in Rome that they hung his portrait, taken in the garb of a priest, on the wall. As one commentator observed, "This is no small distinction in a city where priests are almost as plentiful as parishioners." There is also the story of how, on the day before he flew to Rome to be elevated to the Sacred College of Cardinals, while he was vested to preside at a solemn pontifical mass with China's new Cardinal Thomas Tien he stopped to greet a lady unknown to him, who was waiting in his parlor in the hope of receiving his blessing.

On one occasion the Cardinal was going up the Hudson River on a boat with a group of priests. En route to the dock, the Cardinal climbed in the front seat with the driver. Opening his briefcase he went to work while the priests visited in the back seat. During war trips he insisted on shining his own shoes and was always quick to offer his seat in crowded vehicles to others. For himself and his staff he has two general rules. Rule number one is this: *Help everybody you can.* Rule number two reads: *Never become impatient.*

The Cardinal's direct, human approach expresses itself in his gregariousness. He likes people, likes to have them around him, likes to walk and talk with them. At the large oval table in his dining room he entertains guests sometimes at breakfast, sometimes at lunch, and sometimes at supper. Some days there may be less than ten; on others over twenty. Diplomats, businessmen, heads of government, governors, priests, GIs, writers — the people at his table represent all callings and all levels. He makes every guest feel at home by directing conversation to touch each person's interest. Like a parish priest, he is always concerned with the problems which concern his people — the faithful and priests alike. Some times he will say to a priest who is waiting to see him, "Let's walk around the block together and talk it over in the fresh air." His conversation is enlivened by Irish wit. When an old friend in Ireland reproved him for not staying longer with him, the Cardinal observed that he was "becoming accustomed to reproofs of this kind. They are preferable to hints that I am not moving along fast enough."

In the same spirit that Spellman decided to conduct his military vicarage "in person," so he performs personally functions which are his duty. He has written thousands of individual letters to parents and sweethearts of GIs. No letters go out under his signature which he has not personally read and signed. To the many commencements in the archdiocese he sends no deputies; he appears in person and hands out the sheepskins; he signs the college diplomas. When the exercises are over, he climbs down from the platform and shakes hands with the graduates and their parents. He considers attendance at meetings of boards to which he belongs a sacred trust; he is present, and on time. He has never missed a meeting of the board of the Catholic University of America in Washington. When the commencement season is over toward the end of June, the Cardinal withdraws to Dunwoodie for a week's retreat to pray, meditate, and rest.

Once, while attending a baseball game, a ball struck the Cardinal's knee. "Never mind," he said to the player, "the knees of a priest should be the toughest part of his body. . . ." The Cardinal's private chapel, located on the third floor of his residence, is fitted with oak paneling and a small oaken altar with the statues of the Blessed Mother on one side and Saint Joseph and the Christ Child on the other. Each evening after supper the Cardinal, the members of his household, and any guests of the evening withdraw to the Chapel to recite the Rosary.

While his daily calendar must of necessity be kept flexible, he attempts to reserve mornings for personal work with his staff and on appointment days for private consultation. Afternoons he likes to devote to board meetings and visits to the hundreds of institutions which are entrusted to his care. Early evenings are taken up with public meetings and ceremonial functions.

In the middle of the evening he takes a leisurely walk. Sometimes he goes alone; sometimes a priest accompanies him. He greets people, stops on the curb to visit and shake hands with them, and then returns to his residence to continue with his work.

It is about midnight when the Cardinal pushes aside the official work of the day and sits down at the old board-of-directors' table in the Consultors' Room which adjoins his office. Here in his "workshop," he writes — always in longhand — addresses, poems, articles, and prayers. During these early morning hours of the new day, when he retires to his own private world, he has time to think and compose. The income from his writings has exceeded a half-million dollars — all of which he has dedicated to charitable institutions, including USO Canteen, Foundling Hospital, and the Lighthouse for the Blind. His first novel, *The Foundling*, published in 1951, opened a new field for literary effort. The story has now been reissued in pocket size and is on sale at almost every newsstand and drugstore where paper-covered books are on display. The first Catholic bishop to enter Hollywood circles, he sold the motion picture of his volume *The Risen Soldier* to Metro-Goldwyn-Mayer. As an expert radio and television performer, he knows how to write good script. He is equally at home at the conference table, the dinner table, the forum, the pulpit, the microphone, and before the television camera.

Whether the Cardinal puts in a strenuous day at his residence or is aflight on a global tour, he occasionally devotes some time to his postage stamp collection, which he began when a fellow priest of his North American College days taught him the educational and recreational pleasure which a collection provides. Like thousands of other amateur philatelists, he began by buying packets of stamps and taking others from envelopes received in the normal ecclesiastical correspondence. Within a few years, his interest matured into that of a collector. He specializes in United States stamps issued since 1847, but also works on a secondary collection which includes the stamps of any country in the world in which persons or scenes directly related to religion or literature are depicted. He is said to have every stamp portraying Christ, the Blessed Virgin, and the Saints. He has stamps which picture cathedrals, churches, basilicas, and shrines, stamps issued to honor noted poets and authors. His collection has been sent to international exhibitions for display in shows in the United States, Canada, Switzerland, Spain, Luxembourg, the Netherlands, Argentina, and the Philippines. Each time the United States issues a new stamp, the Post Office Department sends the Cardinal a full, unused sheet, autographed by the Postmaster General and mounted in a specially prepared folder. Courvoisier-Helio, a Swiss concern which manufactures postage stamps for a number of countries in different parts of the world, likewise sends the Cardinal folders of all new issues. His albums, which are added to almost daily, are technically the property of Regis College in Boston, to which institution he has donated his collection in memory of his late aunt, Sister Mary Philomena of the Sisters of St. Joseph, so that his stamps may be permanently available for examination by interested collectors. The actual work of mounting the Cardinal's stamps is performed by Sister Mary Fidelma, of Regis College. She elaborates the Cardinal's rough layouts, which are illuminated by sisters who are artists, giving the album the appearance of a rare medieval work of art.

No words can adequately describe the scope, variety, and quality of the experiences which constitute the Cardinal's life. The kaleidoscopic events of which he is a part begin with New Year's Day. They end only with the passing of the old year. A quick look at a few typical activities will perhaps indicate the range and fantastic nature of his routine.

On New Year's Day the Cardinal's reception takes place in the Archbishop's Room of the Chancery Offices, in the old Whitelaw Reid mansion across Madison Avenue from Spellman's residence. The richly appointed room is stimulating with its rare books, medals, coins, stamps, and other items which have at various times been presented to Cardinal Spellman and his predecessors. The faithful, coming to bring greetings, kneel and kiss the Cardinal's episcopal ring as he stands by an ivory inlaid desk on a rare Persian rug. The room is outfitted with gold brocaded wall covering and Italian-style ceiling, with wood wainscoting of the French Renaissance period. From a gold balcony above the Cardinal hang the flags of the United States of America and the State of the Vatican. The faithful inspect items which represent the varied interests and personal friendships of the Cardinal — the Red Hat presented to him by the Pope and many decorations bestowed by Papal authority and by various governments; a set of breviaries bound in fine leather, a white linen amice presented to the Cardinal by the Pope, a fifteenth-century illuminated Book of the Hours, a fourteenth-century illuminated Bible, a set of journals of the Continental Congress autographed by some of the signers of the Declaration of Independence, a leaf from a Gutenberg Bible, the Cardinal's huge collection of wartime "short snorter" bills, including the signatures of Winston Churchill and President Truman and a badge of an honorary deputy fire chief of the New York City Fire Department.

On another day the Cardinal opens a new home for children, the Joseph P. Kennedy, Jr., Home, remodeled at an expense of two million, five hundred thousand dollars contributed by the Joseph P. Kennedy, Jr., Foundation.

The Cardinal dedicates the Alfred E. Smith Memorial Building of St. Vincent's Hospital. By the bust of the Happy Warrior and beneath the inscription FELLOWMAN TO EVERY MAN Cardinal Spellman reads his tribute in verse:

> We must not think of this high lifted mass
> In terms of steel, concrete and carven stone,
> Of rooms and corridors, of halls and clinic space.
> This building is a living thing, it has a soul,
> It breathes the spirit of a man who walked
> A friend of all, an enemy of none —
> For bigotry — the realm of little men —
> Too great; in vision — for the grasp of time —
> Too large. And so in this memorial
> Al lives again, extends to those in need
> His friendly hand and lends a willing ear
> To every human woe. Here may he soothe
> The fevered brow, his smile again give light,
> His courage steel the spirit wavering,

His charity and faith sustain us all.
No lifeless stone today we dedicate
But that wide spreading of a great man's soul,
That seedling upwards from a city street
And nourished by the deep-thrust roots of faith
Did reach its branches to a grateful state,
And dying, lives again within these walls
That breathe Al's spirit and proclaim his creed —
God made us all, God loves us all, and we
As brothers must within these troubled years
Protect, maintain Al's heritage and ours
Devotedly in service to our fellow men.

In dedicating the former building of the Russell Sage Foundation to be the central office of the Catholic Charities of the Archdiocese of New York, the Cardinal in gay mood says: "I take the deed to this fine property from my pocket as Archbishop of New York and put it in this other pocket which is that of president and treasurer of the Catholic Charities." Shortly Cardinal Spellman is at Lincoln Hall, a home and school operated for problem boys. The institution, occupying 839 acres of rolling countryside in northern Westchester County, provides farm experience for youths eleven to sixteen. The Cardinal presents to each of the 260 boys a string of rosary beads which had been blessed by Pope Pius XII.

On the century anniversary of the establishment of the Archdiocese of New York, the Cardinal leads a procession of clergy and members of religious orders from the Rectory of Old St. Patrick's, on Mulberry, to Prince Street, to Mott Street, and on to the Old St. Patrick's Cathedral, while the bell rings from the old tower. From the pulpit of the Old Cathedral, the Cardinal deplores the fact that "we have once again failed ourselves and youth — beguiled, deceived, betrayed, defeated by Communists, fellow-travelers, apathetic and guileful people and public servants." The world could have found peace, he continues, if it had followed the true road "marked by the signposts of the Ten Commandments, the road back to Christ and His teachings in personal, national, and international life." He adds an observation on the support of Catholic education. "What fair-minded American," he asks, "can fail to see that it is discriminatory to demand that one citizen pay taxes to help another citizen's children, yet deny his own child a cup of milk, a little lift along the common way because some say that this would promote the union of Church and State? Do they ask us who only yesterday gave, as today again we give of our flesh and blood in common defense upon the battlefield, do they ask us to accept this Red-Fascist treatment of our American children? We only ask a citizen's fair share of our common wealth."

When New York faces a water crisis, the Cardinal directs his parishes to avoid any waste of water and to pray for rain.

On Easter Sunday the Cardinal broadcasts a Voice of America message to "friends of freedom, lovers of liberty, everywhere." He says: "We free Americans live in a country conceived in liberty and dedicated to the ideal that all men everywhere are created equal, free to live, labor, love, and worship under the laws of a just God administered by a free government of just men." To the peoples behind the Iron Curtain he proclaims: "Free men in soul you still stand, and free men you will ever be, as long as your eyes look upward toward God and forward toward freedom. Remember that God, your Creator, is also your Saviour — for those who fail Him not, shall not be failed by Him!"

The Cardinal's days continue. Three hundred and fifty children from the Guardian Angel Parish greet him at Pier 54, North River, with a drum corps as he returns from a thirty-two-day Holy Year pilgrimage to the Vatican and European shrines. He pushes a point for Catholic education. "Now," he says, "they are attempting to keep American children off public transportation facilities. Tomorrow they will try to keep us out of the public libraries, the public gardens, and perhaps off the sidewalks if they continue using the same logic they are using in the matter of bus transportation."

He is in Vatican City in 1950 presenting six hundred pilgrims personally to the Pope for his blessing on the occasion of the eleventh anniversary of the reign of Pope Pius XII. Twenty-five years before Father Spellman had gone to Rome as a pilgrim from Boston. When Cardinal Spellman's party enters the Holy Door at St. Peter's Basilica, the Cardinal himself is carrying the Cross while Michael Mahoney, a New York policeman, carries the Stars and Stripes by his side. (The Communist newspaper *L'Unità* remarks that the performance is "more American than the Americans.") Today he studies the issue of marriages between Catholics and non-Catholics in the light of policy set at the Third Plenary Council of Baltimore in 1884. Tomorrow he is in Rome at a gathering of Cardinals to hear reading of the Papal Bull defining as a truth revealed by God that "the immaculate Mother of God, Mary ever Virgin when the course of her life on earth was finished, was taken up body and soul into heaven." Back in New York, he receives a detectives's miniature gold badge and a certificate of membership in the Detectives' Endowment Association, and observes that while he is an honorary fire chief in both Boston and New York, the new honor is the first to give him membership in the Police Department. From his home he dispatches a letter to the *Washington Post* praising an editorial endorsing the naming of an American Minister to the Vatican, and emphasizes that "no argument stronger than prejudice" can be found for not sending a Minister to the Holy See. In another talk he points out that the Holy Father is not alone the supreme head of the Roman Catholic Church. He is also the head of a Sovereign State. He points out that one of the first Sovereign States to recognize the United States after the Revolutionary War was the Papal State at a time when the separation of Church and State was recognized as an American principle. At an hour-long liturgical service he blesses five new bronze doors at the Fifth Avenue entrance to St. Patrick's Cathedral. But no language can adequately portray the prodigious variety of events in which the Cardinal is a participant.

Occupied with the affairs of his archdiocese, Cardinal Spellman was rudely jolted but not surprised in the summer of 1950 by the news that the Republic of Korea had been invaded from the north. He immediately issued a pastoral letter asking special prayers on behalf of the "unfortunate populace of Korea which has been so brutally assaulted." At a Thanksgiving mass observing the centenary of the Archdiocese of Old St. Patrick's Cathedral, the Cardinal spoke his mind and minced no words: "Throughout the years since 1939 I have pleaded for peace with justice for the small nations and little peoples of the world," he said, "I have worked for a peace grounded on faith in God and respect for our fellowman, recognizing that all

men are created equal by God in God's own image, a peace builded
by strong, loyal, truly united nations — for any other peace is coun-
terfeit peace, a Soviet-pagan-peace! This is the menace which we
have listlessly, appeasingly permitted to develop and spread over
the major portion of the world, as during these years of pretended
peace, the forces of our satanic Soviet foes have crushed out the
liberty and life of one small country after another."

Once again, as military vicar of the armed forces, the Cardinal
called for volunteers among the priests to meet the need for chaplains in the armed forces so rapidly expanding after the Korean
aggression. To Korea the Cardinal flew, to spend Christmas with
the boys in their bunkers. Again in 1952 he was with the men in
Korea for Christmas, following a global itinerary which indicates
how small the world has become:

Thursday	December 18	Lv. New York	TWA #93	1000
Thursday	December 18	Ar. Los Angeles	(Super Connie)	1815
Friday	December 19	Lv. Los Angeles	PAA #805	2359
Saturday	December 20	Ar. Honolulu	(Boeing)	0830
Saturday	December 20	Lv. Honolulu	PAA #3	2230
Monday	December 22	Ar. Tokyo	(Boeing)	1300

By Army to Korea, and Return to Tokyo.

Saturday	January 3	Lv. Tokyo	NWA #843	1700
Saturday	January 3	Ar. Okinawa	(DC–4)	2230
Monday	January 5	Lv. Okinawa	NWA #863	0715
Monday	January 5	Ar. Taipeh	(DC–3)	0850
Tuesday	January 6	Lv. Taipeh	PAL #403 °	1900
Tuesday	January 6	Ar. Manila	(DC–3)	2300
Thursday	January 8	Lv. Manila	PAA #1	0730
Thursday	January 8	Ar. Hongkong	PAA #5	1130
Saturday	January 10	Lv. Hongkong	PAA #5	1030
Sunday	January 11	Ar. Beirut	(DC–6)	0650
Monday	January 12	Lv. Beirut	BOAC #783	0435
Monday	January 12	Ar. Rome	(Comet)	0850
Friday	January 16	Lv. Rome	TWA #931	1430
Friday	January 16	Ar. Paris	(Connie)	1745
Saturday	January 17	Lv. Paris	PAA #119	2000
Sunday	January 18	Ar. New York	(Boeing)	0925

° Advanced Departure of Scheduled January 7 Flight

12/12/52

The Cardinal's deep understanding of the problem of Korea, and of the importance of United Nations success on the peninsula to the stability and freedom of all the Orient, has built a deep affection in the hearts of Syngman Rhee and the Korean people. On his first visit to spend Christmas with the GIs, he gave to President Rhee his personal check for five thousand dollars to be used for the assistance of war sufferers without regard to religious affiliation. Recognizing the practical nature of the Cardinal's interests, the Korean President used the fund frugally to purchase fifty-eight American-made sewing machines. The machines were mostly sold at a fifth of their market price to tailors selected through the Korean Tailors Association. The proceeds of the sale were used to assist North Korean war victims who had fled South from above the thirty-eighth parallel. Through President and Mrs. Rhee, a grateful Korean wrote a note from an Inchon refugee camp. "May God bless you forever," it read. On his visit to Korea in 1952 the Cardinal left a second check for ten thousand dollars.

In the beleagured outpost of the free world the Cardinal drafted a poem entitled "Christmas in Korea" which concluded with these words:

> With faith unshakeable we pray
> That God's cause will triumph,
> And that man will abide with God
> In love, and His will be done
> On earth, as it is in heaven.

On Heartbreak Ridge, Korea, he was inspired to write a Christmas meditation which began:

> One morning, on a hill, I saw the Christ,
> Beheld Him there all wounded and forlorn,
> The day was Christmas and the place Korea,
> And mine the privilege to offer Mass,
> To the strange choiring of batteries
> And stuttering guns, amid the quiet ranks
> Of men whose business was to play with Death,
> To gamble Life — of men who knew the stakes
> But still in wonder and bewilderment,
> Must ask the value of their sacrifice.

On New Year's Day in Korea he wrote "A Message to America from America's Soldier-Sons" which ended with these words:

> There ain't no peace for anybody anywhere until
> We've got this war finished over here.
> And when you talk to God, please tell Him, Father,
> That His Little Son is needed now as much
> As when those shepherds first found Him in His cave.

When Cardinal Spellman spent his fourth Christmas with the GIs in Korea, he offered mass in the chapel of the 67th Tactical Reconnaissance Wing. He said to the men: "You have come to serve your country in patriotic loyalty, and I have come to serve you in love and loyalty." He inspected the area of the city of Pusan, which had been laid waste by the worst fire in Korean history, donated funds to clinics, and spent an hour with President Syngman Rhee. Flying by helicopter from the *U.S.S. Toledo*, to flagship *Yorktown*, he made a night broadcast to all the ships of Task Force 77. "The freedom of nations hangs in the dignity of man with his God-given rights," he said. He was up at dawn to celebrate mass for the marine airmen. Then he visited an orphanage that the First Marine Aircraft Wing had adopted.

On the Sunday before Columbus Day, 1953, the Cardinal presided at a two-hour mission rally conducted at the Polo Grounds by the Roman Catholic Archdiocesan Union Holy Name Society. He was just recovering from a virus infection that had confined him to his residence. The rally was a dramatic occasion. As a "living rosary," fifteen hundred girls from the Roman Catholic high schools in the Archdiocese formed the decades, the links, the cross, and the medallion. Grammar school children, dressed in miniature versions of the garb worn by the religious orders that serve the New York archdiocese, paraded the grounds, the center field of which was dominated by a twenty-seven-foot statue of the Virgin Mary. "Except through the grace of God," said Bishop Fulton J. Sheen in the sermon, "materialism and Communism will never be overcome."

The Cardinal quickly withdrew at the end of the service. Guided by lights from a police emergency truck and a police launch standing by, he hurried to a small parking lot, boarded a Sikorsky S–55 helicopter, shuttled in a fifteen-minute lift to Idlewild International

Airport, and boarded a Rome-bound Pan American Airways Strato-cruiser. The next morning he celebrated mass in Shannon, Ireland, and by evening celebrated mass once more in Vatican City. "I believe," said the Cardinal, "in miracles." The next morning Pope Pius XII received the Cardinal in private audience at Castel Gandolfo. At the conclusion of his audience, he introduced a group of forty persons from New York to his Holiness. They included ten priests, knights and ladies of the Holy Sepulcher, and some college students. In the afternoon the Cardinal administered the Sacrament of Confirmation to a group of sailors from the United States Sixth Fleet, in a ceremony in St. Peter's at the altar of Pope Pius X. At the end of the confirmation he spoke to each sailor and to the chaplain who accompanied the group.

The Cardinal had flown to Rome to attend the opening in the Pope's presence of the new seminary of the pontifical North American College — which Francis Spellman had entered as a student back in 1911, more than forty years before. In a message to Bishop Martin John O'Connor, rector of North American College, the Supreme Pontifical said that the enlarged facilities would result in great benefit to the American nation where "by the grace of God, the strength and prestige of Catholics are constantly on the increase." In congratulating Bishop O'Connor on the construction of the new seminary, the Holy Father observed that "we have such a great and well-deserved affection for this nation of yours that we never omit to do anything that may turn to its advantage."

In the spirit of a humble priest vividly aware of the problems of the world and of the need of sinful man for the mercy of God's grace, Cardinal Spellman serves with the spirit which he expressed when he was named Archbishop in the spring of 1939:

> I shall welcome the participation of all in the doing of good things for God, for Country, for the poor, the sick, the suffering, and the underprivileged. *For my part I shall give my all and do my best.*

VI

James B. Conant

United States High Commissioner for Germany; and
President Emeritus, Harvard University

Emergence of a Coherent and Unified Culture for Free Men

JAMES B. CONANT

"The goal which we desire is a unified, coherent culture suit-
able for an American democracy in this new age of machines
and experts."

JAMES B. CONANT SAYS:

THE GOAL WHICH WE DESIRE is a unified, coherent culture suitable for an American democracy in this new age of machines and experts. America's unique contribution lies in a demonstration that a certain type of society long dreamed of by idealists can be closely approached in reality — a free society in which the hopes and aspiration of a large part of the members find enduring satisfaction through outlets once reserved for only a small minority of mankind. ৶Because the educational process lies at the heart of the existence of democracy as a special kind of organism, citizens must pay attention to their schools, hold a true reverence for learning in the community, and see to it that future generations have a high regard for the activties of the human mind. Universities are the trustees into whose hands the fate of the future of human knowledge is committed. Hence the man who enters a university walks on hallowed ground where the ideals of free discussion, unmolested inquiry, and reverence for the American tradition of dissent prevail. Because teachers are members of the high calling by which the foundations of a free commonwealth are secured, a heavily industrialized society must rely upon their work as more and more the nation itself and the different groups within it look to specialists for guidance in handling basic social and economic problems. ৶Contemporary technological society can prosper only if the professions are filled with capable, imaginative, and forward-looking men. Today a working partnership of science with industry joins a maximum development in the natural sciences with a maximum application of the results of research to the production of those things which civilization can employ. The scientist, the engineer, and the industrialist have become a fruitful team producing good things for the use of man. If science is to benefit from the unending zest of adventure inherent in its method, groups of able men must be set up to compete with one another. The discovery and preparation of such men becomes a task of education. ❧*A requisite for the flowering of democracy is the existence of a ladder of opportunity which can be climbed by able young men. A path to the top should always be open to all of exceptional talent. Hence the educational system must operate to rectify the accidents of birth and geography so that at no level will a qualified individual in city or country be thwarted by insurmountable economic barriers in the attainment of the kind of education suited to his aptitudes and interests. By provisions which encourage a high degree of social mobility, society moves in the direction of a free and nonstratified community.* ❧*Within such a society of free men the private citizen occupies the most important of public offices. He must live among his neighbors with an informed civil courage. In the words of Horace Mann each American must "be ashamed to die until he has won some victory for humanity." When such citizens exist, America in spite of whatever troubles may lie ahead will remain free and continue to play a brilliant part in advancing a significant civilization. Only by the best labor of each citizen can democracy be made responsive to the needs of a free nation in a divided world. Who could ask for more than to be given an opportunity to live in an open society at a time when such possibilities of carrying forward ideals and aspirations lie ahead?*

❧ ॐ

Emergence of a Coherent and Unified Culture for Free Men

EVENTS TAKING PLACE ON THE SAME DAY IN TWO universities on two sides of the Atlantic Ocean showed how wide a gulf can exist between the ways men deal with ideas. On the Monday of October 9, 1933, National Socialist students in Adolf Hitler's Third Reich, in preparation for a huge political bonfire, were piling thousands of books on the Unter den Linden pavement in front of the University of Berlin. The operation was designed to secure the foundations of Germany through the incineration of thoughts which the volumes contained. "As you watch the fire burn these un-German books," said the Minister of Public Enlightenment Joseph Paul Goebbels, "let it also brand into your hearts the love of the Fatherland."

In Cambridge, Massachusetts, a quite different ceremony was taking place. Late in the afternoon, the Sheldon Emery Professor of Organic Chemistry at Harvard University cut short his usual routine of the day and walked into the faculty room of University Hall. In less than fifteen minutes, James Bryant Conant, at the age of forty, was installed as the twenty-third president of the first collegiate foundation to be established in the Anglo-Saxon settlements of North America. He held in his custody the silver keys, the charter dated 1650, and the two seals of the most generously endowed independent university in the world.

At Professor Conant's request his installation was tailored after the modest pattern set in 1707 by President John Leverett. The university remained in session without interruption of regular schedules. Classes met as usual. Quite in contrast to the thirteen thousand distinguished guests and alumni who had come to Cambridge to attend the installation exercises of President A. Lawrence Lowell, there were this time only one hundred and fifty persons in the room which had once served as the Harvard chapel. This number included the members of the corporation (the President and Fellows of Harvard University), the deans of the various schools of the university, forty senior members of the faculty, and representatives of the Commonwealth of Massachusetts and the City of Cambridge. There was no inaugural address. There were no elaborate luncheons, dinners, and receptions customarily included in the order of events attending the installation of a university president. After a prayer by the dean of the Divinity School, the chemistry professor responded to the charge with Yankee terseness. "May I," said he, "have skill and patience to continue the bold advance and courage and steadfastness sufficient for my duty in these uncertain times. I promise to govern according to the statutes of the university and in conformity with that spirit of freedom which has marked our past and must guarantee our future. I pledge my entire strength and devotion to the leadership of this community of scholars and students that knowledge and understanding may be increased and transmitted to the youth of our country."

Following tea, served according to custom before Harvard faculty meetings, President Conant, dressed in a plain black robe with only the gold tassel on his hat adding a touch of contrast, seated himself in the president's chair. The university choir, according to the tradition of Harvard ceremonies, sang the seventy-eighth psalm — "so he led them according to the integrity of his heart; and guided them by the skillfulness of his hands." The ceremony was over. By 5:30 most of the guests had left. With his wife President Conant walked across the yard, past Widener Library, and retired quietly to 20 Oxford Street. As the legend runs in Cambridge, an optimistic professor stopped Alfred North Whitehead by the Memorial Church to observe that Charles W. Eliot had also been a chemist and that he had made a good president. "Yes," replied Professor Whitehead, "but Eliot was a bad chemist. There is a difference."

The new president belonged to the New England tradition. He was born on March 24, 1893, at historic Dorchester, five miles east of Cambridge in an elm-shaded mansion standing on Bailey Street near Peabody Square. On the broad lawn which ran down to the avenue, Bryant played football with the boys of the neighborhood.

Although the *Boston Social Register* did not include the name of James Bryant Conant until two years after he was elected president of Harvard University, and although the Conant family was no part of the tight Boston aristocracy to which the Eliots and the Lowells so definitely belonged, the Conants on both sides of the family ran their lines of descent to Massachusetts pioneer stock. James Scott Conant, the father, traced his ancestry back to Roger Conant, founder of Salem. In such a line of succession James Bryant Conant stood ninth in direct descent. Jennette Orr Bryant, the mother, in the line of John Alden who arrived on the Mayflower and of William Bradford, second governor of Plymouth Colony, likewise reached back to old colonial stock. Thus on both the paternal and the maternal sides "Bryant," as the family called him to distinguish the son from his father James, belonged to the whole length of the New England tradition.

In both lines there was no want of civil courage. James Scott Conant, the father, had enlisted as a captain's boy in the Twenty-ninth Massachusetts Volunteers in the Civil War. Grandfather Seth Bryant was so determined in his political views that he arose from a sickbed to vote for William Jennings Bryan. He was a man of firm convictions and vigorous action, as much interested in politics as in industry. He held the opinion that free trade and free silver were good news for the American businessman.

On both sides the Conants were moderately well off. Seth Bryant, born in 1800, was one of the most prosperous of the wholesale shoe manufacturers at the time of the Civil War in the South Shore industry, but in the 1880's he lost his money. James Scott Conant, a pioneer in the wood and photo engraving industry, founded his own firm in 1876. For thirty years he conducted profitable enterprises serving the trade.

In the fall of 1898 Bryant entered public kindergarten at the age of five and a half. After a brief experience in a private school, he entered Miss Baldam's third grade in the Bailey Street Public School in 1901. Miss Baldam quickly discovered that the boy suffered from two academic handicaps: he was slow in reading and poor in writing. In time he overcame the former weakness, but one day he came home in tears to report that he had flunked the spelling section on the entrance examination for the Roxbury Latin School. This deficiency was appropriately made up, for in the autumn at the age of eleven he enrolled in the private academy.

From the day that Jim arrived at the preparatory school he knew that he belonged there. Because he liked to participate and to do things with other people, he entered into the spirit of the academy. He enjoyed being around where things were going on; the boys enjoyed having him around. The general appraisal of the unassuming new pupil was that he was a "damned likable kid." He plunged into student activities as well as into his studies. He made the scrub football team and in time became captain of the second crew. He worked on the *Tripod,* and during his last year served as editor in chief. People who read the paper under his management recognized a new organizational hand at work; new ideas were in motion. Conant became treasurer of his class, the senior who arranged the class dinner, and a member of the committee to select the class gift to the Latin School. With a flair for acting which hitherto had been chiefly expressed in a liking for charades, he went out for dramatics. The senior play cast him as the fair and vivacious heroine in *Lucille.* He became the hit of the show when the audience recognized the editor in chief of the *Tripod* delicately dressed in skirts holding the crew captain in his arms. In looking into the future, the class prophet predicted at graduation that the best he could see for Conant was a druggist's job "serving, as a premium on all sales over three cents, a guaranteed chemically pure prussic acid ferrocyanide milkshake."

Although he found student activities delightful, Jim Conant discovered in the science department of Roxbury Latin School what a teacher can mean to a student. He experienced the kind of educational climate which creates a partnership of minds and opens the road for the maturing of youthful talent. Newton Henry Black, Harvard '96, science master at Roxbury — with whom the boy was later to co-author a basic chemistry textbook — recognized Conant in his section as "the towhead with a Dutch cut and broad collar." "N. Henry," as the class labeled their science master for short, had the habit of watching for young men of promise. He was quick to see young Jim's inclinations and aptitudes. Black was known to have no patience with shirkers, but possessed an ability to pass on knowledge and to inspire and encourage good students to do exceptional work. Jim Conant became one of his chosen pupils, not only because he displayed an aptitude for understanding science, but also because he knew how to construct apparatus and could work experiments with increasing confidence and independence.

As a matter of fact Jim had been at the business of experimenting and constructing apparatus at home for a good part of his eleven years before he arrived at Roxbury Latin School. Recognizing his son's inclinations, James Scott Conant had constructed a lean-to on the family house to provide space for a private laboratory. He assigned an allowance of five dollars a month to his son for the purchase of supplies and equipment. Whether the project was rubbing a hot-water bag over the fur on the back of a live cat or detonating an explosive, Conant had a natural itch to experiment and the skill and craftsmanship necessary to execute the operation.

To his delight and embarrassment N. Henry soon found out how Jim Conant relied on evidence. One afternoon in Roxbury's science laboratory Black differed with his pupil over the characteristics of a certain compound. The boy asserted that the mixture would explode; the science master declared that it would not. Thereupon the pupil, observing that the only way to settle an argument is by recourse to facts, set up an experiment. In a few minutes a small blast rocked the laboratory.

Despite his outstanding work in science Conant was not regarded as a scholar of high rank. Because of his scientific reputation in the school, however, the faculty selected him to give an oration at his commencement in 1910. In preference to delivering a conventional speech, he proceeded to demonstrate to the audience a complicated experiment in combustion. He performed it with such confidence and serenity and explained the operations so lucidly and so accurately that even his professors, N. Henry excepted, were amazed. In commenting upon the commencement exercise the *Tripod* observed that "James 'Bailey' Conant then tried to blow up the building with some examples of combustion."

On an autumn day in 1910, three months later, two young graduates of Roxbury Latin School rang the doorbell of a house on Cambridge's Linden Street. With their valises they climbed up three flights, to begin two years of residence as roommates in a private dormitory known to Harvard students as "Miss Mooney's Pleasure Palace." One of the new freshmen had been the editor in chief of the Roxbury Latin School *Tripod*. The other was the same captain of the crew whom this editor had embraced so amorously in the senior play. Now, as Harvard men, Charles H. Crombie was studying to be an architect and out to row stroke oar on the crew; James B. Conant was deep in chemistry and headed for the editorial board of the *Crimson*.

Harvard at the time provided a system of voluntary examinations by which students could anticipate courses. If they passed, they earned credits toward the bachelor's degree and were excused from formal study. Conant promptly presented himself in freshman chemistry, solid geometry, logarithms, and plane and spherical trigonometry, thus clearing the way for the study of advanced chemistry in his first year. Although he had a course in philosophy with George Santayana and another in economics with Frank Taussig, his love remained with chemistry. At the end of his third year he completed his undergraduate studies, took his baccalaureate degree in 1913, was elected to Phi Beta Kappa, and became an honorary John Harvard Scholar.

The strenuous demands of the chemistry laboratory, it should be noted in passing, did not smother Conant's enjoyment of college life. With John P. Marquand he developed what was known as the "two-beer dash," a sprint from Miss Mooney's Pleasure Palace via subway, from Harvard Square to Boston and back, drinking the grog in the quickest possible time in the Hub city. He was a fairly regular patron of the stated Friday-evening parties at Brattle Hall, where sub-debs came to dance with documented freshmen. When he moved up to become an upperclassman, he graduated from that group, referred to as "Baby Brats," and pursued the company of the debutantes proper at the regular "Brattle Halls." On occasion, he demonstrated practical skill in handling chemical equipment by such stunts as running a rubber tube from a punch bowl on the table to the mouth of his sleeping roommate Crombie. (At dawn, he remembers, the bowl was empty!) He practiced catching a baseball while standing on a beer barrel, once set up a knight in armor on the third-floor landing of the Pleasure Palace to greet late-returning residents, and on a Christmas holiday traveled with Crombie by coal barge from Providence to Newport News. When the time came, he joined the literary-minded dining club known as the "Signet" where a man was supposed to sit at the table next to "somebody of intelligence."

His work as an undergraduate in science headed him toward his professional career; his election to the board of editors of the *Crimson* increased his command of language. Chemistry and English combined to serve him well in later years.

It was in his relationships with a Harvard science instructor that Conant found an experience worthy of his mettle. Just as in Roxbury Latin School he had become the working associate of N. Henry, so in Harvard as a freshman he by good fortune fell into the hands of George Leslie Kelley, who introduced him to organic chemistry — the field in which Conant was soon to achieve distinction. When Kelley became chief chemist of the Midvale Steel Company in Pennsylvania, where Frederick Winslow Taylor was putting ideas of scientific management to work, Conant decided to follow him. Immediately after graduation, in June 1913, he went to work in the Midvale laboratories. Under Kelley's guidance he learned electrochemical methods used in steel research. The interest so developed formed the research basis for his Doctor of Philosophy dissertation.

From the standpoint of education it is worth noting that the close student-teacher association between Newton Henry Black and James Conant had started the boy on his real career in chemistry, and a close partnership in the laboratory with Kelley gave his interest matured direction. Meanwhile Professor Theodore William Richards, Nobel Prize winner and chairman of the Harvard chemistry department, taught Conant physical chemistry (incidentally providing the channel through which Jim met the professor's daughter Grace). Conant thus experienced the kind of comradeship and teamwork which seemed to him, when he became president of Harvard, to represent the substantial fact in the educational process.

Without stopping for a master's examination Conant took his Doctor of Philosophy degree at commencement in 1916. He had begun his teaching career at Harvard two years before.

Conant had held his doctor's degree less than a year when on April 6, 1917, the United States declared that a state of war existed with Germany. From his very actively war-hating Quaker mother, Conant had inherited some ideas about the success of war as a method for adjusting human differences. Like most other Harvard men, however, he began to investigate to see what useful part he could play in the national effort. He imagined himself in the role of a top sergeant directing a crew repairing gas masks for the American expeditionary forces in France. One day, after he had pretty well convinced himself of the nature of his mission, by merest chance he bumped into Professor James Flack Norris, one of the great chemists of the world and director of the organic research laboratory at Massachusetts Institute of Technology. Conant confided to Norris that he was planning to join the army to work as a gas-mask repairman. "That's not the best way to serve," said Professor Norris. He proceeded to describe the greater need for trained scientists in government service working in secrecy on the development of poison gas. For an hour Norris pleaded with Conant.

The outcome of this chance discussion was that Conant went to Washington to undertake work with the Chemical Warfare Service on mustard gas research in a laboratory located in the Ohio Building on The American University campus. Quickly he rose to head of a division and proceeded to develop the method used by the government to produce gas for field operations in France. The use of a poison gas in an attack launched by the Germans in the second battle of Ypres at the end of April 1915 had led strategists to believe that this new weapon might possibly determine the outcome of the war. From the military point of view, the development by the Allies of a newer poison gas, in 1918, played much the same role in World War I thinking that the development of the atom bomb did in the early 1940's in World War II. Both the gas and the bomb were to be secret, powerful, and decisive weapons with which to surprise and overwhelm the foe and to bring him to surrender with a minimum loss of American lives.

By midsummer 1918 it was clear that G-34 (later to become well known as "Lewisite" gas) could be produced in the laboratory. On July 19, 1918 — just a week after the practicality of commercial manufacture seemed certain — Conant was assigned from Washington to Willoughby, Ohio, a village east of Cleveland. Here, in a factory taken over from the Ben Hur Motor Company, Conant set up his laboratory. Of the twenty-two officers and five hundred enlisted men who reported for duty at the plant, Conant was one of the two or three who understood the nature of the secret mission. The men at Ben Hur named their project "Operation Mousetrap" as descriptive of the situation which confined them to their plant. Electrically charged barbed-wire fences enclosed the factory area. Searchlights swept the premises at night. Sentinels patrolled the grounds. Personnel themselves marched back and forth from their quarters to work under military command. The pattern of the operation was one with which Conant was to become very familiar two decades later: intercontinental warfare, scientific competition to perfect new weapons to produce a military advantage, science called to the service of government, the scientist turned inventor under conditions of great urgency and pressure, a frantic effort to achieve mass production in a race against time, all the operations carried forward under the veil of complete secrecy.

At Harvard Conant had been accustomed to rapid and sustained work. At Ben Hur he arranged a cot for himself so that when he broke off his experimentation at midnight he could throw himself down on the mattress to sleep. At daybreak he was up and at the task again. Within the operations staff Conant's influence was positive. He could dispel the temperamental tensions among his fellow workers with a laugh. To his associates he was that same "damned likable" guy the boys had welcomed to Roxbury Latin School. He smoothed out personal differences which developed within the staff, identified himself with no cliques, and engaged in no personality disputes. He was good-natured, diplomatic, and kept his eyes purposefully on the goal which had been set for the mission. His one all-mastering pursuit was to discover a gas weapon "in time" to hasten the end of the war, and to bring about the defeat of the Kaiser and all the totalitarian *Kultur* for which he stood.

When differences of professional opinion arose, Conant purposed to find the right answer. He did not allow himself to be drawn into heated debate about assertions whose validity could be established by experimental test. He remembered, as on the occasion when he had demonstrated to science master N. Henry in Roxbury Latin School how to look for the right answer, how a search for facts can end an opinionated discussion. Conant dramatically proved this again at "Mousetrap." To run a pilot production-operation, the Ben Hur staff requisitioned large amounts of hard rubber pipe and containers to be used in place of steel, which it was believed would be corroded by acids used in the manufacturing process. When the hard rubber supplies could not be delivered in time and in sufficient quantity, the staff fell into a violent and frustrating argument. Conant, taking no part in the debate, set up an apparatus from available steel to find out what really would happen in efforts to use steel for the operation. "The answer to an issue is the answer — not an argument," he said. Through this experiment, Conant found that the addition of a foreign substance to the acid would change its corrosive powers, and thus that steel could be used! It was Conant's open mind, his habit of adventuring to find out, his operating belief that old answers do not solve new problems, that made Ben Hur operations successful. He was always willing to give a possibly good idea a quick try. In the field of science, even at this early point in his career, colleagues recognized him as a "calculated gambler."

By 1919 Conant had completed a two-and-a-half-year tour of duty and returned to Cambridge. The major from the Chemical Warfare Service changed hats and became an assistant professor of chemistry. Behind him lay an invaluable experience. In government employment he had seen how science serves the military arm of the government. He had witnessed how the scientist becomes an inventor, and how the scientist and the engineer can team up together.

For the next fourteen years Conant built his own career as a capable, busy, and active professor. On April 17, 1921, he married Grace Richards, daughter of the chairman of his department. One son they named James after the paternal grandfather, the other Theodore after the maternal grandfather. It was now that the young professor, who had begun to write textbooks as soon as he got back from the war, joined as co-author his old science master from Roxbury Latin School, Newton Henry Black — now an assistant professor of chemistry at Harvard. Together they published *Practical Chemistry*, which through successive editions by 1942 became *New Practical Chemistry*. In 1928 Conant alone wrote *Organic Chemistry: A Brief Introduction*. In 1933 he published *The Chemistry of Organic Compounds*. Meanwhile he had found time to edit two volumes of *Organic Synthesis*.

*   *   *

In 1925, at the age of thirty-two, Conant with his wife took his first trip abroad, spending eight months in Germany studying methods of research and instruction in leading German universities. During this period he gained a reading and speaking knowledge of the German language, a skill which almost three decades later he was to turn to diplomatic advantage. Upon his return from the Weimar Republic, Harvard promoted Conant to the rank of associate professor. Two years later, in 1927, the university advanced him to full professorship. In 1929 he was elected to the Sheldon Emery Chair of Organic Chemistry. In 1931, at the age of thirty-eight, he became chairman of the department.

Conant meanwhile was distinguishing himself in the field of research and original investigation. His operations as a scientist were characterized by thoroughness, broad vision, wide knowledge, and willingness to depart from hackneyed methods. Between 1926 and 1933 he published over eighty papers in various scientific journals on such subjects as chlorophyll, hemoglobin, hemocyanin, free radicals, dyes, absorption, and the spectra of organic compounds at liquid air conditions. In the laboratory he was making significant discoveries in his studies of the green substance in plants and the red coloring matter of blood in cells. As an extension of his university work, Conant had become adviser and consulting chemist to important corporations. In the single year of 1932 he received both the Charles F. Chandler Medal at Columbia University and the William H. Nichols Medal of the American Chemical Society. His distinguished work in the laboratory called him to the notice of the Corporation of Harvard University.

One day a graduate fellow asked him this question. "Professor Conant," inquired the student, "what is the first requisite of a good chemist?"

Conant answered quickly: "The first requisite of a good chemist is breadth of vision — to pick out the problem on which to work."

This observation applied with equal appropriateness to the performance of a good executive, and Conant the chemist was about to become Conant the administrator. In the late spring of 1933 the Corporation of Harvard University proposed to the Board of Overseers the name of James Bryant Conant for election as president of Harvard University, to succeed the distinguished President A. Lawrence Lowell, who was about to retire.

With his election to the presidency Conant abdicated from the laboratory. He was compelled, as he said, to "shut off chemistry into a small and little-used corner" of his mind. A Harvard legend records the tale that on a Saturday afternoon a wiry and youthful individual with steel-rimmed spectacles was seen tossing pebbles against the window of Converse Chemical Laboratory off Oxford Street in a frustrated attempt to return to complete the exciting experiments which were being carried on by the assistants. He no longer possessed a key to the Converse door. Conant says that the pebble-on-the-window simile may be allegorical, but the truth of the matter is that "since 1933 I can't claim to have advanced the barriers of science one millimeter." Whatever claim Conant might have made for a Nobel Prize for chemistry ended when he moved from Converse Laboratory to the university administrative offices in Massachusetts Hall.

From President Lowell, Conant inherited a definite educational pattern for Harvard College. He recognized that the development of this pattern by his predecessor had wrought a "marvelous change" in the attitude of the undergraduates toward scholarship. The whole university, he said, rejoiced in the "free and vigorous intellectual atmosphere" which Lowell's policy insured "even in times of great stress." The Harvard College design stood on three foundation stones: the tutorial, the general examination, and the residence house plan. Conant struggled during his entire twenty years of administration to infuse this magnificent educational structure with a contagious intellectual enthusiasm which would justify the whole lavish apparatus which Cambridge provided.

Basic to the Harvard system was the tutorial plan established by President Lowell in 1912. It operates in this way. At the beginning of his sophomore year, a student is assigned a tutor in the field of his concentration. Throughout the year the student meets regularly with the tutor, usually in residence house groups. The tutorial work comprises individual reading on topics in the student's field, the writing of essays, and the problems raised by them. The tutorial thus provides a highly individualized and expensive form of instruction. A student is forced to read and think for himself, to express his own ideas orally and in writing, and to have them criticized by both fellow students and teachers. Thus through an intellectual partnership each student has the opportunity to develop his fullest powers. Such is the theory of the tutorial system.

Four years after the introduction of the tutorial plan, Harvard in 1916 added the general examination. Its purpose was to provide a means for testing a student's grasp of his major field by going beyond the bookkeeping mathematics of merely adding up individual course credits as the visa required for graduation. Conant liked the idea of the general examination for two reasons. It set up a strong incentive for intellectual competition among undergraduates, and established a distant goal toward which a student must move during his undergraduate years. "To accomplish the ideal of self-education and to stimulate competition," said Conant, "a goal must be found remote enough to require long-sustained effort, but not so remote as to be out of sight. The goal must be tangible and capable of measurement."

Conant was especially proud of Harvard's residence house plan. He discovered in his reading that back in 1684 Cotton Mather explained that "the Government of New England was for having their students brought up in a more collegiate way of living." By that Mather meant an educational program organized around a small residential college patterned after England's Cambridge, where most of Harvard's founders had been educated. Under such circumstances, students live together in close contact with teachers.

Harvard's answer to the problem of providing the "collegiate way of living" in a college of four thousand under modern conditions had come as a result of a gift of thirteen million dollars by Edward Harkness in 1930. Under the house plan, Harvard is divided into seven small undergraduate colleges. Except for the first year, when freshmen live as a class in residence halls in the historic Yard and take their meals together in the Union, men live in the houses. Each house is a self-contained college community of about three hundred and fifty men and faculty. Each student lives in a suite with one or two roommates; together the men have a study, fireplace, and bath. Each house is in charge of a master and a senior tutor known as the dean, who serves under him. Ordinarily eight or ten tutors out of a house faculty of about forty live in. Each house contains a dining room, common room for students and faculty, a library of about twelve thousand books for tutorial, course, and general reading, music rooms, and special rooms for varied activities. Under this residential house system student problems can be approached on a well-informed and individual basis, since the house provides an ideal situation for friendly and informal student–teacher relationships so helpful in furthering a liberal education. For most undergraduate social, athletic, and extracurricular activities, the house serves as the center of operations.

This Harvard system of education based on the tutorial, the general examination, and the residential house plan was the completed undergraduate pattern which Conant inherited from Lowell. No other institution in the Western Hemisphere except Yale had such apparently adequate provision for undergraduate life. Conant recognized this fact, but as he looked at Harvard and continued his own educational reading he became more and more concerned with "a personal something" which no external apparatus, however lush, could provide. The nature of that "something" seemed to elude him; he was convinced that it constituted the essential element of education. As a young university president, Conant began a search for a deep, personal, inner motivation which would make a man want to learn in Harvard College and continue to learn throughout life. He expressed the idea by saying that he wanted to devise ways and means to "infect students with the virus of ongoing intellectual activity." This ideal of injecting a contagious germ of educational desire into the lives of Harvard men became a primary concern of the new president during his twenty years of office. He held the position that "a liberal education which is not self-perpetuating is of no enduring value. The only worthwhile liberal education is one which is a continuing process going on throughout life. Whether a liberal education has been a success or failure should be measured by the student's breadth of vision twenty years after graduation. Has the smattering gained in college worn thinner with each succeeding year? If so, it has been of little value. Or has it provided a basis for continued intellectual and spiritual growth? In this case the momentum to self-education continues as the most significant part of college training."

It bothered Conant to know that, despite all the educational effort Harvard put forth, students in their own vernacular were still "taking courses" rather than "studying subjects." He said: "The college graduate is only too apt to feel that the only road to knowledge is through formal instruction administered by a college or university. The possibility of education through self-directed study by reading in hours snatched from a busy life seems to be only dimly appreciated by those who enter a business or profession fresh from the atmosphere of a university."

Side by side with his concern for the injection of the "virus" of an "on-going education" into the intellectual veins of Harvard men, Conant was thinking about an issue which he believed to lie at the root of all current academic controversies. The root problem of a liberal education as Conant saw it was this: "How can a student acquire a breadth of view, so much admired and desired as an ideal and yet which one so rarely finds in this age of specialists?" At the very beginning of his administration Conant thus was searching for answers to the most fundamental and perplexing issues in education.

Eliot and Lowell as Conant's predecessors had in their time dealt with the same fundamental educational problems. Both had done basic pedagogical thinking. In addition to his amazing ability to raise funds for Harvard and his vision in expanding the university, Eliot had introduced the elective principle. It seemed axiomatic to Eliot that a college must attend to the individual characteristics of many different minds. A boy of eighteen or nineteen, he thought, should study what he likes best and what he is best fitted for. College should provide a curriculum which gives free play to natural preferences and inborn aptitudes. In fact, Eliot looked upon the free elective as a historic development in the general pattern of human freedom.

Quite aside from concern for academic principles, Eliot felt pressure from parents, alumni, trustees, and benefactors to enlarge the Harvard curriculum so as to provide courses that would meet the increasing competition of technological schools. Through the introduction of the elective system he hoped to extend the scope of academic offerings by drawing upon specialists throughout the whole institution. He further saw how the industrial climate was influencing academic tradition and was causing questioning about the classical concepts which had theretofore characterized a liberal arts education. Eliot, practical administrator that he was, started educational theory toward a pragmatic adjustment to what he believed inevitable in the trend of the times.

When Lowell had succeeded Eliot he had led a movement to "reform" the elective system. A study of student habits revealed that many Harvard men felt that they were dissipating their energies in too many different fields or were specializing too exclusively in one narrow field. It showed that students were studying less than three and a half hours a week for each course, were choosing subjects haphazardly with choice being determined too largely by the convenience of the hour of class sessions. Students were "guiding" fellow students into notoriously easy courses, called "snap" subjects. Some students were rushing through Harvard — as Conant himself did — in three years. President Lowell proposed to stiffen up the "snap" courses, make honors work more difficult, and provide a system by which students would be required to specialize more thoroughly in one "major" field and at the same time broaden its base by taking work in several other "minor" fields.

In 1910 Harvard had put into effect the plan of "concentration and distribution," which reoriented the whole fabric of American undergraduate education. Lowell proposed to encourage students to plan their courses seriously and to plan them as a whole. Distribution in studies was to encourage breadth and concentration to develop depth. Under the Lowell revision of the Eliot plan, a student still had considerable latitude to arrange his curriculum; relatively few programs of study were identical. The concentration pattern continued from Lowell's day without serious challenge or important change.

The fate of the distributed studies was otherwise. Between the two World Wars the discussion of what and how many distributed studies constituted a proper breadth for a student, "majoring" in chemistry for example, came to be a nation-wide concern for faculties. When Conant assumed office, academic tinkerers had a variety of proposals for the new president to act upon. At the very beginning of his administration Conant continued the search to find the magic formula which would make a genuine educational process.

Throughout the country, educators were discussing various formulas. Perhaps the most popular pattern in the 1930's was the "survey course." The advocates of the survey course and requirements of "an elementary knowledge of this or that" maintained that in the complex world of today every educated man must have at least an acquaintance with many diverse subjects. "If this be true," said Conant, "and with only four college years available, can we provide more than a bowing acquaintance? So runs the argument heard in many different forms. It is generally assumed that only a casual meeting is preferable to no introduction whatsoever."

To get perspective on the issue Conant turned to the reading of English educational history as a part of his own "on-going intellectual education." The statesmen who laid down the principles of the competitive examinations for the English civil service, he said, from the very beginning took the position that "nothing can be further from our wishes than to hold out premiums of knowledge of wide surface and small depth." "A candidate," said the British administrators, "ought to be allowed no credit at all for taking up a subject in which he is a mere smatterer." "Unless the smattering acquired in college is the small beginning from which great things develop," said Conant, "it seems to me a hopeless task by four years of college work to provide a complete and finished liberal education suitable to this century."

By observing what was taking place in his own experience since he left Converse Laboratory and moved into Massachusetts Hall, Conant felt there was another approach to the issue worthy of consideration. He now opened his one-man campaign to provide "incentives to self-education." "Would it not be possible," he asked, "to experiment with methods of inoculating Harvard students with that educational virus which alone maintains its potency throughout life — the virus of a self-perpetuating liberal education?" In his early years as president Conant played with different schemes for putting that virus to work. He would begin, he thought, by inculcating in a large number of Harvard men the habit of reading and intensive study apart from courses and entirely outside the field of major interest. A certain number of men were already finding the time necessary for this type of activity, he said. These men arranged their programs during the college term to provide time to pursue work for which they received no formal credit. They ordered their vacations so that their study suffered no interruption. Such men on graduation carried with them not only the knowledge thus acquired but the key to a future education. "How can their numbers be increased?" This was the educational question which Conant asked when he became president of Harvard, and he was still seeking the answer twenty years later when he became president emeritus. Harvard had not found the magic formula! In a somewhat disillusioned mood Conant commented later that "undoubtedly there are still many people who believe that education would work miracles if only the perfect pattern could be found and the proper persons engaged to execute the design of a philosophy of education. But even the most optimistic believer in the power of formal education to transform thistles into figs would recognize that gathering the fruit from the usual source would be more economical."

In his own reading and thinking, and from the many suggestions offered to him for improving the opportunity for a man at Harvard to get a liberal education, Conant began to see the possibility of a core study *independently and individually pursued* which would deal with the historical, political, social, and cultural development of the United States. He appointed a committee to draw up a report on the possibility of extracurricular study in this field for undergraduates. He felt the importance of a knowledge of American history for every citizen was self-evident. He would not make such a course compulsory because he felt that a course taken under compulsion represents something quite different from true education. In explaining the idea Conant said that "it seems clear that it would be desirable for every college graduate to have a knowledge of the cultural history of the United States in the broadest sense of the term." He wanted the faculty committee to prepare an interesting and comprehensive statement of the scope and value of the general field of United States cultural history and to indicate by lists of suitable books how a partial mastery of such a field could be obtained by systematic reading carried on during term time and vacation periods.

The more Conant thought about this the more he came to the conclusion that such extracurricular study might serve as an *inte-*

grating discipline. For Conant personally as a mature scientist it did. Although pressures on academic life in World War II buried the program in the graveyard of ambitious projects, its idea gave sharp direction to Conant's own thinking. "It seems to me possible," he reasoned, "that in the study of our national cultural history we may find the principle that is needed to unify our liberal arts tradition and to mold it to suit the modern age. A true appreciation of this country's past might be the common denominator of any educated man's equipment so that men could face the future united and unafraid." "Such a possibility," he added, "does not narrow the breadth of vision in either time or space. On the contrary, starting with a keen interest in his own past, a student is necessarily drawn into an ever-widening field." Such a student would master the "decisive and characteristic views" that have welded "our present civilization in the United States."

Of course Conant in this statement was not suggesting a program for students already concentrating in history. He was talking about history as part of general education for the nonhistorian. "Here," he said, "is a vitally important aspect of his liberal education which a man might at least start developing during his college years." Somehow the student interest which Conant had imagined did not appear, but he went on dreaming just the same. He imagined an added stimulus being given to the independent study of the students by offering a few lectures on special topics during the college year. He played with the idea of initiating an annual fall competitive prize examination for those who had interested themselves in the field and yet had not taken formal courses of instruction. Conant was aware of the fact that he was merely sticking his toe into the academic water. "Any attempt," he said, "to rescue the liberal arts tradition from its present dilemma must be extremely tentative. Almost any reasonable approach to the problem seems worthy of trial. It is in this spirit that the efforts of those interested in the extracurricular study of American history must be viewed." Administrative pressures at this point diverted Conant's energies to other problems, but they did not dilute his interest. In the midst of World War II he continued his quest in a slightly different frame of reference. His own probings, however, equipped him personally with an understanding of the role and meaning of America as his

whole previous Harvard experience had not done. This outcome of
his own "extracurricular" academic thinking had far-reaching consequences.

Conant had indeed been carrying forward his own "independently
and individually pursued" studies. He intensified his reading as he
was compelled to think about the plans and program for the celebration of the Harvard tercentenary in the late fall of 1935 two years
after his installation. He extended his readings in American history
to include the history of Harvard and the educational histories of
British universities as well. It was in the thinking, planning, and ar-
ranging for this tercentenary that Conant, the chemist, was compelled as Conant, the president, to give detailed consideration to
the glorious traditions of Harvard within the much longer historical setting of universities as a movement in the Western world. His
conversation, speeches, and writings began to reflect his broadened
horizons and his deepened understanding. His "extracurricular" studies forged his own appreciation of the university as an institution
and sharpened his awareness of the role of his own leadership.

As he saw the tercentennial celebration approaching, he felt that
it provided an opportunity to dramatize the varied activities which
characterize a university in all times and places. He wanted the program to cut across conventional lines of academic interest, to demonstrate the "all too rarely appreciated fact that however separate
and lonely individual investigators may appear, they are in reality
close neighbors." In that sense the tercentenary performance to
Conant became much in the nature of a "reunion of old friends, a
renewal of the intellectual ties which had their origin many years
ago."

"The joint labors of university scholars," said Conant, "proved
once again that it is because of specialization that knowledge advances, not in spite of it, and that the cross-fertilization of ideas is
possible only when new ideas arise through the intense cultivation
of special fields." Thus the tercentenary caused Conant to see the
role of the university as that of increasing specialization, but, at the
same time, increasing unity through knowledge of the ancestry and
relationship of ideas. He felt that much of the "academic fencing"
between departments could be avoided by an appeal to a "common
family tradition." The line of descent was the same for all. The classi-

cist, he said, reaching into educational history, can proudly claim as his ancestor such sixteenth-century giants as Scaliger and Casaubon; but so can the physicist and biologist. Everyone in the modern university, he said, should be aware of the historical importance of such men as Isaac Barrow, of Cambridge University, a noted theologian and scholar who in 1663 exchanged his professorship of Greek for a newly founded one of mathematics and in 1669 resigned once again to make way for his favorite pupil, Isaac Newton, who thus became the second Lucasian professor of mathematics. Said Conant: "If we understand the spirit animating such men who labored within the academic walls before the rise of modern science we can comprehend the fundamental unity which binds together the professors in the twentieth century university. An appreciation of this unity is essential if higher learning is to flourish in periods of uncertainty and social change."

From his studies in university histories Conant came to a working definition which gave further direction to his administration. "A university," he said, "is an independent, self-governing community of scholars concerned with professional education, the advancement of knowledge, and the general education of the leading citizens." From his reading he was convinced that universities flourish when four elements stand properly in balance — namely: the cultivation of learning for its own sake; an educational current that supports specialization making possible the professions; a core of general education sustaining the liberal arts; and a "never-failing river of student life carrying all the power that comes from the gregarious impulses of human beings." Inherent in each of these four components of a university Conant from his studies found certain dangers, elements which might impair the breadth of the whole academic organism if given overemphasis. The cultivation of learning alone, he reasoned, produces not a university but a research institute. Professional education if left to itself results in nothing but a trade school. An institution concerned chiefly with student life in these days produces "an academic country club or a football team maneuvering under a collegiate banner." Concern with general education alone, even in the best liberal arts tradition, when divorced from research and training for the professions admittedly exists not as a university, but as a college. The task of a university administrator must always be to keep a balance between the four traditional elements of a university's strength.

Upon the university considered as a community of scholars Conant now began to look with increasing reverence. Harvard Yard, like other university soil, became hallowed ground. "Universities," he said, "are now the residuary legatees of many of the spiritual values which were guarded by the church three centuries ago. Our responsibilities are correspondingly increased and our ideals must be clearly defined. If future generations are to have that high regard for the achievements of the human mind which is essential to civilization, there must be a true reverence for learning in the community. A university's first job is the guardianship of eternal values." From his reading Conant committed to heart the statement of President Charles W. Eliot in his inaugural address in 1869 to the effect that "the only conceivable aim of a college government in our day is to broaden, deepen, and invigorate American teaching in all branches of learning." Since universities, in Conant's mind, "are trustees into whose hands the fate of human knowledge is committed," the man who enters a university walks on dedicated ground where the ideals of "free discussion, unmolested inquiry, and reverence for the American tradition of dissent prevail."

For his twenty years as Harvard's president Conant persisted in the working conviction that the three requisites for the successful operation of a university were and would always be financial solvency, a student body of high quality, and an outstanding faculty. To each of these three components he gave specific attention.

He proposed first of all to maintain the university's financial solvency. By any standards Harvard is big business. At the end of Conant's term in 1953 the market value of Harvard's endowment had risen to three hundred and eight million dollars. While Harvard carries no property or equipment account — for who would be so bold as to value its priceless resources or to propose an amortization on buildings many of which have stood for centuries and some of which have been rebuilt several times? — a good guess would put the university's net worth at around a billion dollars. Its annual gross expenditures at the end of Conant's term stood at thirty-five million dollars, a sum almost three times the budget when he took office.

At the time Conant succeeded Lowell, a generally pessimistic feeling was prevalent that the day of private giving had come to an end. And the corporation had nominated Professor Conant for the consideration by the Board of Overseers only two months after President Roosevelt ordered the "bank holiday." To the question of what future the endowed colleges might expect, a Washington official had bluntly observed: "I didn't know that they had a future." The record of annual gifts and bequests to Harvard promptly showed Conant the hard facts, which seemed to verify the financial pessimism circulating in the climate of the depression years. From 1923 to 1932 the total annual gifts and bequests for capital and immediate use had never fallen below six million dollars. In fact, the annual benefactions had averaged nearly ten million. In the fiscal year 1932–1933, however, the total fell to three million, eight hundred thousand dollars. In the next two years the figures sank to three million and to two million, six hundred thousand dollars respectively. Even with the depression as an excuse for the steady decline, a treasurer's report which showed that philanthropy had been sliced in half under the administration of an "organic chemist" was none too palatable an accounting report for the faculty to swallow.

Yet the record after two decades of Conant's service to Harvard showed how wrong was the impression that private giving in America had ended. During every twelve-month period after the tercentenary year gifts and bequests to Harvard, except in the war years, never fell below six million dollars. During the twenty Conant years, ninety-seven million dollars were added to capital and forty-eight million more were received and currently spent. These two sums added together mean that the philanthropy to Harvard from 1933 to 1953 totaled one hundred and forty-five million dollars, as compared with the one hundred and twenty-eight million received in the relatively stable twenty years of Lowell's leadership preceding the Conant administration. Despite war, depression, and the dismal chant that the day of private giving had terminated, the Conant years showed a seventeen-million-dollar increase over the Lowell period. For the two cataclysmic decades under which Conant served, Harvard's annual benefactions averaged seven and a quarter million dollars a year!

Money serves only to support educational activity and Conant was firm and determined to act upon the principle that "solvency for a university depends on far more than balancing the dollar budget each year — essential as the dollar balance is. . . . Solvency," asserted Conant, "depends on a stable personnel policy. No business can stay solvent without a careful and continuous inventory of the materials in hand and in process of manufacture. A university at root is men — men of unchallenged excellence." Conant kept driving at this point: a university could be bankrupt even if the annual auditor's report showed a neat dollar surplus.

"A university," he declared again, "is a group of men, a community of scholars and students. Here is the real problem in regard to the future of all institutions of higher learning. Harvard's success will depend almost entirely on our ability to procure men of the highest caliber for our student body and for our faculty. Harvard must endeavor to draw to its staff the most able investigators and teachers of the world. We have today a faculty of which we may justly be proud, but we cannot ignore the fact that it is increasingly difficult to attract from other universities and research institutes the outstanding men whom we desire. I need not stress the necessity of our having at Harvard great scholars and investigators. Our ultimate contribution to society will depend on their scholarly output and their stimulating teaching. What they accomplish and those whom they inspire will be the measure of our success. If we have in each department of the university the most distinguished faculty which it is possible to obtain, we need have little worry about the future. If we fail in this regard, there are no educational panaceas which will restore Harvard to its position of leadership. We have at Harvard unusual advantages for scholarly work: libraries, museums, laboratories, and special institutes. In some fields we can provide opportunities for investigation which are unequaled in this country. It is clearly our first duty to see that our permanent staff is composed of those who can use these facilities most effectively and wisely. We must provide every opportunity for the ambitious, brilliant young scholar to come to Harvard and demonstrate his worth. In order to obtain such men for our Harvard family, the academic life in Cambridge must be made more attractive in a number of ways. Sufficient time should be allowed for writing and investigation. A satisfactory balance must be struck between teaching and research."

To insure "personnel solvency," Conant painfully over the years developed a cool, deliberate, and discriminating personnel policy. After twenty years of effort he confessed that the administration of the policy was highly difficult. "Except in periods of great expansion," he said, "there is little hope of building a distinguished faculty unless there is a long-range plan for continual recruitment of the most promising young men." Because general-use income is limited, tenure definite, and qualifications high, university personnel policy must be hard-headedly projected.

Harvard's personnel policy under Conant grew out of his own ideals, out of faculty controversy, and out of circumstances which made action urgent. At the beginning of his term Conant inherited what came to be known as the "young man problem." During his office Lowell had installed a large number of tutors. The prosperity of the 1920's, coupled with the expansion of the tutorial system and the establishment of the seven residential houses, had swelled the ranks of the young instructors and assistant professors in almost every department. Unlike most other colleges and universities, Harvard did not cut faculty and staff salaries during the depression years. Indeed in 1930, as it had in 1927, the corporation raised salaries. Naturally the young men wanted to remain in Cambridge! The impact of the depression on institutions of higher learning had been so serious that the normal flow of young men from the large universities to other institutions had almost ceased. New academic jobs were practically nonexistent. Colleges were attempting to reduce their staffs, not enlarge them. When by 1935 the worst of the lean years had passed, pressures from the departmental chairmen to promote some of the young men increased. An inventory of the faculty of arts and sciences showed that a major problem was at hand. Each year the situation was growing more unhealthy as instructors and assistant professors with temporary appointment stayed on in the hope of being promoted to permanent rank. A glance at the president's chart giving the distribution of the staff by age and rank, however, showed that Harvard could not possibly finance a faculty of the size that would result if any considerable proportion of the hopefuls were made full professors.

Conant began to deal with the staff surplus department by department. At first he suggested, then he demanded, that young instructors must leave after a short period of service. Unfriendly critics — and there were plenty of them — labeled the policy "up or out." Conant admitted later that he pursued the task "perhaps with more vigor than finesse." A legend around the *Crimson* office has it that this conversation took place between Conant and an applicant for a job. Conant: "Can you throw a man downstairs?" Candidate: "Yes, sir." Conant: "Fine! Can you make him like it?" Conant's problem was throwing men downstairs and out and making them like it.

By 1942 Harvard's "personnel solvency" policy became effective. In pattern it begins with the principle that the total number of permanent appointments is fixed, subject only to enlargement as new endowment becomes available. Vacancies are allocated to departments at the associate professor level — the first level of permanent appointment. The frequency intervals at which vacancies will occur are then determined. Upon this schedule a twenty-year program is built which shows the opportunities as they will open up for the introduction of young men. To make this system work Harvard enforces the rule without compromise that no assistant professor can continue appointment for more than five years. If such a holder is not a successful candidate for a vacancy in the permanent ranks should there be one, he can receive no further appointment of any kind from Harvard.

The permanent appointments themselves result from the recommendations of *ad hoc* committees, a system introduced by Conant. These committees are composed of experts in the field in question chosen from outside the university and a few members of the faculty from departments other than those whose recommendations are being reviewed. Conant considered his chairmanship of these sessions the most sacred obligation of his office. The chairmanship of the *ad hoc* meetings by the Harvard president gave them importance and made the outstanding specialists of the country honored to serve.

In the deliberations of these committees no sentimental considerations stand in order. Neither a departmental recommendation nor good performance as an assistant professor becomes a controlling factor. The single question before the committee is this: what person in the world gives promise of bringing to Harvard the best intellectual leadership? The recommendation is based upon the application of this criterion.

The maintenance of personnel solvency requires collateral policy on related issues. Attention to one of these will indicate their nature. To Conant, research chemist become administrator, it was perfectly clear that on the Harvard faculty there should never be a separation of personnel "into those who teach and those who carry on creative work." No line should be drawn between teaching and research. Harvard's strength in the past had lain in the fact that the spirit of scholarship had pervaded teaching and that teaching led to the advancement of knowledge in specialized fields. Conant was clear that "it is only by advancing learning that it is possible to perpetuate it. When knowledge ceases to expand and develop, it becomes devitalized, degraded, and a matter of little importance to the present or the future. The community loses interest and the youth of the country responds to other challenges. Able young men enlist in an enterprise only if they are persuaded that they too may contribute by creative work. A zest for intellectual adventure should be the characteristic of every university. In the future as in the past, our teachers must be scholars who are extending the frontiers of knowledge in every direction."

An administrative policy so clearly stated meant that Conant would have to take a position on the "extra-mural activity of certain professors." Before he became president, he had been one of these. He faced the issue head-on. No one who understands modern science, said Conant, will propose that chemists, physicists, and engineers shut themselves off from the ever-changing problems of modern industry. Similarly the economists must be constantly in touch with the life of the nation. No reasonable person objects to the undertaking of work for the city, state, or nation by a social scientist or to a chemist's serving as adviser to the chemical industry. *No retirement to a lonely hilltop is desired.* But the whole life of a scholar must be dominated by his desire to further a branch of learning — and here lies the great responsibility for all those who are teachers in a university. The university cannot and should not impose any limitations upon outside activities as such. The question is whether, over a period of years, this work is incidental to a man's teaching and research or vice versa. Where is his primary field of interest?

If Conant was determined to procure men of the highest caliber for the faculty, he was equally concerned that the professors should have students worthy of their efforts. Moreover, he asserted an obligation which Harvard must assume: the responsibility for providing a Harvard education for men of high ability even when such men cannot finance their own education. "In the future, even more than in the past," he said, "we should attract to our student body the most promising men throughout the whole nation. To accomplish its mission Harvard must be a truly national university drawn from no single locality and no single class. We should be able to say that any man with remarkable talents may obtain his education at Harvard whether he be rich or penniless, whether he comes from Boston or San Francisco."

In his first report to the overseers, Conant had stressed the need for making the student body of Harvard College more representative of geography and family income. He wanted Harvard to be a cross section of the nation. "No Eastern Seaboard college," said Conant frankly, "wants to be a local institution." When as a result of the tercentenary activities funds were available for scholarships, Conant openly earmarked them to recruit students from the West and South. These new "National Scholars," first appointed in 1936, were dubbed "Conant's boys." By the end of Conant's term Harvard in 1953 was granting fifty national scholarships to men entering as freshmen from thirty different states. Conant recommended to Harvard alumni the mission of informing potential applicants in faraway communities about Harvard College. He was disappointed to find that national scholars did not bring with them to Cambridge other students from the same locality, thus broadening the geographic base of the Harvard student body.

The National Scholars — and the president openly confessed his disappointment about his failure to raise more funds for their support — provided something more than mere class and geographic

diversity. Conant held the theory that the privately endowed institution needs to keep a path to the top open for the gifted youth of
limited means. "It is," he said, "quality and not quantity in which
Harvard is interested, and to this end we must give financial aid in
larger amounts to more carefully selected men." When judged
from the point of view of this aim — discovering needy and highly
competent youths to encourage "social mobility" — the National
Scholarship program accomplished the ideal which Conant was
pursuing. Three fourths of the national scholars came from public
schools, predominantly from the Middle West. An analysis in 1945
at the end of World War II showed that three out of four recipients
came from families with incomes of less than three thousand dollars,
and one out of three from families with incomes of less than two
thousand dollars. In geographic distribution, Harvard was becoming a national institution; the number of students from New England declined while the number from the rest of the country increased. More students were entering Harvard from public schools
as a result of a more liberal and flexible admissions policy.

Given substantial financial resources, a great faculty, and a student body carefully selected to profit from the opportunities offered
by the institution, an administrator has the materials for educational
leadership. President Lowell used to be fond of reminding Conant
in the early years of his administration that "a college president
often gets credit for things he has no hand in, but this is only fair
because he also gets blamed for many things with which he has had
no connection." One of the developments at Harvard which was
Conant's very own was the inauguration of the one-year graduate
program leading to the degree of Master of Arts in teaching. This
program, designed to prepare young men and women for work in
public or private secondary schools and junior colleges, was offered
jointly by the faculty of arts and sciences and the faculty of education with provision for apprenticeship experience in co-operating
schools. It provided an arrangement by which women of Radcliffe
College could enter the program with degrees conferred by Radcliffe College upon the recommendation of the Harvard Faculty
of Arts and Sciences and certification by the President and Fellows
of Harvard College. Conant liked to refer to the "infiltration" of the
Radcliffe women into Harvard programs as "the silent revolution."

The program, which presently set a new design for teacher preparation, was the result of fundamental educational thinking on Conant's part and the discarding of the stereotyped pattern. It was first offered in 1936, three years after Conant took office, and represents his profound interest in the secondary school at this early point in his administrative career. To assure the better preparation of teachers for the secondary schools and junior colleges, Conant proposed to unite training in scholarship with development of professional understanding and personal fitness for teaching. These three elements of preparation, he felt, must be suitably tested through apprenticeship performance.

To the administration of the program Conant brought an inter-faculty co-operation, the kind of teamwork he held to be so important in the life of a university. By the establishment of the program Harvard recognized a vocation of great potential importance for the life of the nation as having claims on the attention, not of a separate professional faculty alone, but also of the older Faculty of Arts and Sciences. The needs and standards of the program became a matter of general university policy. The establishment of the program made it clear that at Harvard there was a unity of purpose. The plan for teacher preparation committed the university to a general ideal of teaching.

In advancing this program Conant was charged with a "surrender to vocationalism." Academic orthodoxy, at the time, felt that a university should pay no attention to the application of knowledge, but should devote all its resources and energies to the pursuit of learning as an end in itself. Conant held this division of matter and method to be a wholly superficial view of education. He was not apologetic in the least for proposing to facilitate graduate work in secondary education so that young men could earn their living by doing an outstanding job in teaching. In fact, Conant had his private doubts about the advantages of keeping all learning "pure." "The problems of life," he said, "should not be kept apart from the institutions of learning. It is not vocationalism as an ultimate principle that the American university ought to fear, but a truckling to popularity and the service of present need, at the expense of standards and ideals." Conant's conception of "standards and ideals" for the preparation of teachers was quite as unorthodox as the inter-faculty co-operation in its administration. He lifted teacher-preparation entirely above the college level, to the higher plane of the university. "For the sake of teaching" Conant advanced the radical proposal that the direct study of education should be postponed until the graduate year. A student who completes his bachelor's work in a field of concentration with honors and comes on to the university, Conant asserted, is no longer a young learner. He can think in terms of the subject, use its methods, understand its relationships with other subjects, and make sound application of its results. Teaching is better done, as Conant saw it, when the teacher candidates have a general education as broad and thorough as it can possibly be made before they begin to concern themselves with problems of instruction, the program of studies in the school, or educational policy. Teachers, he held, have a peculiar need for an intellectual breadth which is not attained at the price of superficiality.

Personality as a chief factor in good teaching, Conant felt, was best fostered by a generous interest in the problems and values of life. The greatest growth of such a personality, he held, takes place when studies inspired by such interest remain as long as possible undistracted by questions of methods in teaching or issues of school administration. When he finally comes to these professional subjects, such a student then has a maturity of mind and a breadth of outlook not normally attained before graduation from college. Such a teacher candidate has developed a clearer grasp of values and a steadier view of social and ethical ends.

At this point Conant found both his program and himself facing the fundamental problems of educational philosophy. What should teachers teach? Whom should they teach? Under what condition, standards, and control should they serve? What values, ends, and social goals should concern them? What picture of economic life should teachers present to youth?

Conant considered these questions. As the years went by, his interest in secondary education deepened and matured. When in 1937 the educational world observed the centenary of Horace Mann, two years after the celebration of the Harvard tercentenary, Conant as president of the university was presiding over an inter-faculty committee directing policy concerning the Master of Arts in the teaching program. Within Harvard he had substituted co-operation for the competition of faculties. He had made the preparation of teachers a legitimate function of professional graduate work. He had given an answer to the question of what kind of education Harvard wanted American society to have. He had set a standard which was to have an influence on the "pot-boiling," "money-making" courses in education, which some people were referring to as "rackets." He had established contact between the university and the educational life of the community which the secondary school touches. He had lifted the vocation of teaching from being considered a "job" to recognition as one of the most important social functions, requiring clear thinking about the goals in common life.

While Conant was working on the program for the Master of Arts requirements in teaching, he was taken completely by surprise by the announcement that Agnes Wahl Nieman, widow of the millionaire publisher of the *Milwaukee Journal,* had in her last illness executed a will bequeathing a five-million-dollar "Lucius W. Nieman and Agnes Wahl Nieman Fund" to Harvard broadly to promote and elevate the standards of journalism in the United States and to educate persons deemed especially qualified for journalism. The Niemans had had no connection with Harvard. The bequest was unsolicited and unexpected. (When the fund was paid to the university, however, Wisconsin taxes took such a large slice that the final endowment actually amounted to one million, four hundred thousand dollars.)

Mrs. Nieman came from a family which had fled from Germany in the revolution of 1848. The story of the heroes and patriots of liberalism were a part of her bringing up. "Lute" Nieman, as her husband was known in the newspaper profession, was two years old when his father died. He had gone to work as a printer's devil at the age of thirteen in Waukesha, Wisconsin. He had worked his way up to the ownership of the highly profitable Pulitzer Prize winning *Milwaukee Journal,* which he edited for fifty-three years. He had spelled out the personal policy of his life as a determination to build the *Milwaukee Journal* into a newspaper of independence and force, devoted to the maintenance of high ideals in the civic and normal life of the community.

Here in the Nieman family was the epic of America — hunger for political freedom, social mobility, civil courage. As a university president Conant had almost a free hand to write the policy of the use of the income from the fund. Again he was faced with the question of vocationalism. Harvard offered no courses in journalism, yet Conant welcomed the opportunity to tie the profession of journalism to a high level of scholarship and to infuse it with a deep sense of social values as well as professional responsibility.

To work out a policy Conant proceeded according to his usual pattern of operation: he sought the advice of the most respected journalists, and then invented his own program. The plan as developed involved no new building nor additional expenditures for staff. The Lucius W. Nieman Fellows at Harvard, first appointed in the academic year 1938–1939, became a group of mature "in-service" young men appointed on generous stipends from among working journalists of at least three years' experience. The Nieman Fellows came to Cambridge for a period of study. Their work was individually planned to develop breadth and at the same time to further special competence in the specialized areas of journalism. Young men, for example, who wanted to be financial editors concerned themselves with courses and contacts in their field. Reporters interested in diplomatic correspondence paid attention to the field of international affairs. Labor editors studied economics and industrial relations. In the appointment of the fellows Conant saw to it that selections were distributed in the West, Middle West, the Southwest, the South, the Middle Atlantic States, and the Northeast. He wanted to promote the pattern of Harvard as a national institution.

Thus Harvard assimilated a vocational program without in any way lowering standards of scholarship. By managing this Conant had built another bridge between Harvard Yard and the professional life of America. More than that, he had brought to Cambridge a stimulating group of men whom he felt would make a valuable contribution to the kind of "informal education" which proceeds from the personal association of different kinds of men within the university environment.

The Nieman Fellows program initiated a series of professional adult-education programs. In 1943 the School of Business Administration inaugurated its advanced management program under which business executives came to Cambridge for thirteen weeks of study. In 1945 a program of Trade-Union Fellowships was patterned on the Nieman Fellowship. In the School of Public Administration, with grants from Carnegie Corporation and the United States Department of Agriculture, a program in agriculture and conservation brought such diverse operators as county farm bureau agents, foresters, and soil conservationists to Harvard. Harvard was building more bridges between vocation and education on the level of breadth and standards, not narrow specialization.

While a university president is concerned with substantial issues such as those involved in the development of programs for teachers, journalists, businessmen, and farm experts, he is aware of the task for which a university primarily exists — the inspiring of students. A university president is expected to establish rapport with all the students for whose benefit the organization exists. He usually finds his most difficult relationships with undergraduates, in the College of Arts and Sciences. Conant began his administration with a series of acts which won him the confidence of this undergraduate student body. His first official move after being installed earned the amazed thanks of the entire freshman class: he saw no good reason, he said after careful study, for continuing the seven o'clock rising bell in Memorial Hall. The *Crimson* welcomed the decision as a sign of a "New Deal" on the campus.

In his first talk to the entering class of 1937, Conant spoke modestly and man-to-man. "You and I," he said to the first freshmen to enroll under his administration, "are both facing unfamiliar conditions and heavy responsibilities. The essential feature of a university has always been a small group of distinguished, learned men and a community of students drawing inspiration from their teachings. In my opinion one of the greatest values of a university education is that for four years one is living in a free and vigorous intellectual atmosphere. A spirit of tolerance based on reason is in the air. Dogmas are courageously examined, compared, attacked, and defended. For many of you who will go out into the world of affairs, the last three years of your college life may be the only time when you will have the privilege of indulging in a whole-

hearted interest in some purely intellectual activity. If you are fortunate enough to have the experience of a real intellectual passion,
you will, to my mind, have gained what is best in a university
education."

The month after repeal of the Federal prohibition laws Harvard
applied for a liquor license and set up a bar in the dining hall. For
the first time in over a hundred years the university served liquor
to undergraduates. The *Crimson* welcomed alumni back to the 1934
commencement by saying that they would not find the "New Deal"
absent from the Yard. Conant had started some "bold experiments
of his own," the newspaper said, which permitted undergraduates
individually "to blossom forth in formerly restricted paths."

Conant also placed much responsibility for learning directly on
the students, where it belonged. Gone were cram examinations,
midyear probation, and compulsory attendance at classes. "It is,"
commented the *Crimson,* "wise to equip the student with independence and initiative so that he can sail before the wind on this sea
of confusion with his spinnaker set."

To maintain liaison with the student mind Conant met regularly
with top *Crimson* editors every two or three weeks; but the feeling
spread that scarcely one out of a thousand undergraduates had any
contact with him. A public figure in a sphere outside the ordinary
undergraduates' life, he became a glossy image to the average Harvard man, a sort of wandering scholar who journeyed around the
country living on Harvard prestige while "some people" over in
Massachusetts Hall ran the university. Many students resented the
distance between them and their president. They felt that the president should take a greater interest in them.

Relationships with the undergraduate students became increasingly strained as a result of administrative actions taken to meet the
"young man problem" and as a result of Conant's position on public
issues. Alumni joined with articulate student groups in voicing
their opinions. Conservative students denounced Conant for his
failure to denounce the New Deal. Others compared his stand with
the conservatism of President Lowell, who had opposed child labor
laws. Some criticized him for the citation which accompanied the
honorary degree awarded to Henry A. Wallace when he was Secretary of Agriculture. Conant described Wallace as a "public servant

of deep faith and high integrity who finds courage to attempt an uncharted journey in our modern wilderness." It was a fact that Conant had supported Al Smith for President in 1928; that he had at one time stated his politics in *Who's Who* as a Republican and had later withdrawn the line; that he maintained that how he voted was a personal matter. "Even my closest friends have to guess how I vote," he said. Some students and alumni referred to him as the "cold-fish chemist." Leftist students denounced him as a "tool of Wall Street." H. V. Kaltenborn, '10, charged that he was neglecting the "social sciences." One alumnus even bragged that he had thrown a pie at Conant at a dinner held in a social club.

Agitation against Conant rose to a high point in the spring of 1937 and continued at the boiling point until he was drawn to Washington to advise the government on matters of scientific warfare. Among other charges he was accused of violating the principles of academic freedom. This issue arose when a hundred younger members of the faculty joined in a petition addressed to eight professors requesting them to investigate the action of the administration in executing the "up or out" policy. They requested a review of the whole "young man" problem. The professors wrote to Conant recommending the appointment of a committee of inquiry. Conant immediately named the eight men who had written to him, and the group came to be known in Harvard history as the "Committee of Eight." For the next three years Harvard Yard smoked with tensions and unpleasantness.

For their part the undergraduates organized a "Student Committee to Save Harvard Education." They proceeded to wage a drive to bring about the reinstatement of ten assistant professors, some of whom were members of the Teachers Union, whose appointments had been terminated. They conducted mass demonstrations. They met with Conant to discuss budgetary limitations. The students saw little value to them in "high salaries" paid to "bigwigs." The middle-rank men who had been discharged, they said, were the real teachers who worked with students.

In 1939 the "Committee of Eight" reported. By 1942 a new faculty policy became effective. Out of the controversy, said Conant, there emerged "a strong fair wind" that enabled the faculty of arts and sciences to "sail a new and better course." As a means of dealing with the personnel problem and providing a placement service for the younger men who did not obtain permanent appointment, Conant created the post of personnel assistant in his office and called to the position the assistant to the president of the Carnegie Corporation.

Looking back on his administration, Conant later felt that his clarification of the personnel policy, including the establishment of the *ad hoc* committees, was his most significant and original contribution.

The issue of athletics raised problems quite as thorny as the tenure problem. Consistently, as president of Harvard, Conant was determined to maintain the scholastic integrity of the historic university. He faced many pressures — not all "ideological in nature," as he pointed out — which attempted to divert Harvard from its primary purpose. Universities engage, for example, he said, "in the public entertainment business" in so competitive a fashion as to generate public scandal. If Lowell had not stood fast, alumni pressure would in the gay twenties have forced the university to enlarge its stadium on "borrowed money." After World War II, Conant took steps to straighten out Harvard's athletic policy and to put it on the same basis as other university activities, which were largely supported by endowment. He intended to break the vicious connection between football gate receipts and expenditures for the athletic program. "A student," he said, "takes part in college athletics because of the value of the experience for him. He has the same obligations as other students and assumes responsibility for solving his own financial and educational problems. Any other view seems a distortion of educational and moral values." Such an administrative policy on athletics was bound to stir up animosity among certain circles.

There were, also, issues "ideological in nature." In the fall of 1939 the John Reed Society invited Earl Browder to address the organization. The secretary of the Harvard Corporation refused a permit to allow the general secretary of the Communist Party of the United States to speak in a university building. His presence, said the Harvard secretary, would be "in bad taste." Students branded the denial "a violation of the rights and liberties guaranteed by three hundred years of Harvard tradition." At a meeting protesting the corporation's action Carliss Lamont, '24, son of the distinguished alumnus who later donated Lamont Library, declared that Harvard was "smothering free speech," that his alma mater had become a "one-horse Midwestern college," and that the university was "afraid of the guilt of harboring a Communist through association with Browder." "The issue," said Lamont, was "whether students had liberties and rights to listen to whomsoever they want to hear." The *Crimson* paid its respects to Harvard's "Supreme Command — the Corporation" by describing it as a "self-perpetuating board" made up of corporation lawyers, a physician, a broker, a financier, others, and Conant." The *Crimson* was suspicious that Browder was *persona non grata* "for more reasons than his passport peccadilloes." "The liberals of the nation," it declared, "are on the war path and it is hard to see how the Corporation could have ignored this." Yale allowed Browder to speak; he made a far from persuasive appearance.

The Harvard Corporation's refusal to allow Browder the privilege of speaking on university property was tied together with the failure of the administration to give Granville Hicks, who had served the year of 1938–1939 as a fellow, an academic appointment. Hicks, the first avowed Communist on the Harvard staff, resigned from the party at the time of the Soviet aggression on Poland in 1939, after his appointment at Harvard had terminated. To Conant the Hicks incident was a routine operation quite outside the interest of the president's office, but to the students here was another situation which "threatened freedom."

By this time faculty members as well as students were expressing their own opinions of Conant. Some considered him "overbearing." Others characterized him as "ruthless." Still others referred to him more respectfully as the "slide-rule administrator." The deepening world crisis fed the fires of anti-Conant feeling. His ardent support of intervention in European affairs, especially by giving aid to Great Britain, created widespread comment. He was accused of supporting Franklin Roosevelt in "getting the United States into war." When he supported the first peacetime draft, undergraduates felt that he was trying to force them into the army "to get shot at." Students began to picket halls where Conant spoke. (In reviewing his stand on world affairs, Conant's critics later said that in 1935 he was enthusiastic, in 1937 cautious, in 1938 fearful, in 1939 despairing, and in 1940 tyrannically jittery.) By the fall of 1939 the *Crimson* observed that Conant was "earning an unenviable place in the road-gang that is trying to build for the United States a super-highway straight to Armageddon." It pointed out that Conant's lofty position gave "weight to his words beyond their worth."

Between the halves of the 1940 Yale game, Conant recalls with a touch of bitterness, a group of students rushed to the field to present a skit representing their president as engaged in a solitary military drill. Presently a chemical retort was substituted for the gun he was carrying, reminiscent of World War I, and a sign appeared. It read BOOKS NOT GUNS. When Conant became active in the Committee to Defend America by Aiding the Allies, Professor F. O. Mathiessen violently criticized his "warmongering philosophy." Many Harvard alumni shared the Mathiessen point of view.

When the United States joined World War II, however, such criticism of Conant weakened. Students were being drawn into the armed services. Harvard became a huge training camp for various kinds of officer candidates and specialists. The student body, which when Conant took office stood at eight and a half thousand, by January 1, 1944, had dropped to eighteen hundred. By 1947 the enrollment had jumped to fourteen thousand; by 1953 declined again to ten thousand. During the war Conant turned over the president's house at 17 Quincy Street to the Navy as an administrative head-quarters and moved across the street to a small yellow frame house. He did not occupy his official residence again until May of 1947.

Despite the kaleidoscopic problems which Conant faced in meeting wartime programs at Harvard and despite his brilliant and strenuous national service, he was still seriously at work thinking through educational policies which presently were to point a new direction in Harvard instruction. He had, however, as a result of a series of events, been drawn into controversy on public policies. The story of his excursions into public affairs became a significant part of his career as a citizen. Soon after he became president of Harvard, he had fixed a policy for his comment on public questions. He would, he said, make statements only about issues on which either he had very deep personal conviction or on which he was particularly well-informed. While he was preparing for the tercentenary, a situation arose which required him to apply this policy. He was compelled to think of Harvard in its immediate setting in relation to the State of Massachusetts. For the remainder of his administration his public life was defined by the co-existence of two worlds. The first of these worlds respected the traditions and obligations of the university in American democracy; the other existed as a police state insisting on its dogmatic cultural program. Europe has experienced much tragedy at the hand of such a society.

On January 26, 1935, the General Court of the Commonwealth of Massachusetts passed an act requiring teachers to take and subscribe to an oath before they undertook their fall work. The text of the oath read: "I do solemnly swear that I will support the Constitution of the United States and the Constitution of the Commonwealth of Massachusetts and that I will faithfully discharge the duties of the position according to the best of my ability." As far as Harvard was concerned, the law was clear: the corporation could not allow any citizen of the United States to teach who failed to take the required oath. The passage of the bill had been opposed by nearly all the presidents of colleges and universities in Massachusetts as an "unnecessary and unwise" piece of legislation. Conant indeed had been especially outspoken in his position. After careful consideration the Harvard Corporation, however, decided not to enter into a legal controversy concerning the mode of enforcing the law. "Therefore," said Conant, "much as I dislike this measure, I express the hope that all members of the faculties will take the oath." All members did.

Compliance with a law, however, does not prevent a citizen from disagreeing with it. And Conant did disagree. "Such a piece of legislation as the Teachers' Oath," he said, "is merely a reflection on the general wave of intolerance which has been rising in this country. Those who understand the true nature of the functions of an institution of higher education have always stood firm in their support of the principle of free inquiry. If the tenure of office of full professors is held sacred and the administrative officers are zealous in maintaining the right of the teacher as a citizen of free speech, then the professors in turn may be relied upon to form a responsible opinion within each academic community. The collective attitude of the college teachers toward their obligations as members of a learned profession will determine the future course of higher education in this country. If the country is convinced of the sincerity of the purpose of professors, of their selfless dedication to the advancement of knowledge, I feel sure that the attacks on academic freedom will fail to find support."

A committee report had already gone to the Corporation which stated that in the recruitment of new faculty members the question of views on controversial public issues should not constitute a subject for question. The committee saw no wisdom in trying to judge a candidate by the criterion of whether his conclusions conformed with opinions of the existing faculty or of the governing boards.

However, the wave of intolerance represented by the enactment of the Teachers' Oath statute did not recede. A decade and a half later Conant reported to the Harvard Board of Overseers that the "proponents of the ridiculous charge that our colleges are subversive receive a wider hearing today than at any time in recent history." One of the reasons, he felt, was the "failure of the colleges by their collective action to demonstrate the nature of their primary task." He hoped that an atmosphere would not be created in which professors would be afraid "to speak freely as private citizens on public issues."

In chapel Conant clearly stated his position. He told the students that Harvard itself was founded by a group of vigorous dissenters from the Church of England. Before a generation had passed there was dissent from the first dissent. By the beginning of the eighteenth century the orthodoxy of Harvard was considered highly questionable. Conant had no fear of heresy in religion, science, or any other field. He felt strongly that any barrier to the expression of an opinion opposed to a commonly held doctrine froze society into a *status quo* which threatened life with stagnation. For his part he did not propose to see the future frozen to the past.

"If a university is to be alive for generation after generation," he asserted, "the institution in question must be in close touch with the life of the community which it serves. The essential motivating force behind a university's scholarly work and research in all times and places when universities have flourished has been the connection between the scholars' activities and the burning questions of the day. If this be the case there is bound to be public discussion of what some scholars may write or say. The world cannot have it both ways: either the professors live in ivory towers and their teaching and thinking have no relevance to the times in which they live or the professors are going to have views that somebody will not like. Sometimes one part of a university, sometimes another is criticized. The idea that a university is some kind of ivory tower seems to be a pure myth that has grown up only in recent times."

As to the charges that some professors held unpopular political opinions, Conant said frankly: "Of course they do. It would be a sad day for the United States if the tradition of dissent were driven out of the university. For it is freedom to disagree, to quarrel with authority on intellectual matters, to think otherwise, that has made this nation what it is today. Indeed I would go farther, and say that our industrial society was pioneered by men who were dissenters, who challenged orthodoxy in some fields and challenged it successfully. The global struggle with Communism turns on this very point."

There was thus absolutely no doubt about Conant's position on the Teachers' Oath: the Massachusetts statute violated the autonomy of the university as a free community of scholars, and it violated the principle of a free democratic society by setting up a kind of operation characteristic of the totalitarian regimes.

The next public issue to draw the Harvard president's fire was the proposal of President Franklin D. Roosevelt to "pack" the United States Supreme Court in such a way as to encourage decisions which would support the legislative program of the New Deal. In March 1937 Conant joined the controversy by directing open letters to his two Massachusetts Senators. Although he admitted that he felt the decisions of the Supreme Court confronted the country with serious problems, he feared "the gravest consequences" when an administration proposed to bring about "a constitutional change without submitting it to the voters of the country." He felt that such a high-handed interference with the judiciary, however well intentioned, might eventually jeopardize the liberties guaranteed under the Bill of Rights.

❊　❊　❊

Two more years went by before Conant came forward to take a stand on another major issue. This time he was fired by a consuming passion which dominated his thinking and planning for the remaining years he served as Harvard's president.

Europe was collapsing. On September 1, 1939, Germany declared war on Poland. Two days later Great Britain declared war on Germany. By June 4, 1940, the retreat of the British Expeditionary forces from Dunkirk had been completed. By July 10 Nazis had begun the bombing of Britain in earnest. For weeks the invasion of Britain was warded off only by the determination of the British people. To President Roosevelt it was clear that if the Nazis were to be defeated, England must be saved. England could be saved, he was sure, only by the all-out support of the United States. To overcome a strong isolation and neutrality sentiment among the American people and to generate a public opinion which would support America's entrance into the war, Roosevelt felt that a citizens' movement for the mobilization of opinion was necessary.

The initiative toward the formation of such a movement was taken by William Allen White, editor of the Emporia, Kansas, *Gazette*. By telegram he had invited several hundred prominent Americans to join a national Nonpartisan Committee for Peace through Revision of the Neutrality Law as such revision was proposed by the administration for Senate action. The theory was that by repealing the arms embargo, the United States would no longer be aiding Hitler to the disadvantage of the democracies which were resisting the spread of dictatorship. Actively promoted, the organization spread from state to state — while its name changed from "The American Union for Concerted Peace Efforts" to "The Nonpartisan Committee for Peace through the Revision of the Neutrality Law" to its final name as "The Committee to Defend America by Aiding the Allies."

Five days before White dispatched his telegram, President Conant, on September 28, 1939, had already written a letter to Alf M. Landon as a representative of forces reluctant to make a full American commitment to aid the European democracies. "I am personally strongly in favor of a modification of the so-called neutrality law so as to permit the sale of implements of war to France and England," Conant told Landon. "I believe that if these countries are defeated by a totalitarian power, the hope of the free institutions as a basis of modern civilization will be jeopardized. To depart from our historic policy and by so doing handicap those who are fighting for ideals we share, seems to me inconsistent and unwise." The *Crimson* referred to Conant's letter as a "moral fire alarm."

While large numbers of educators and clergymen immediately endorsed White's program, nearly eight months went by before Conant, almost on the eve of Dunkirk, joined the committee. In doing so he broke the precedent of refusing to join "front" committees which he had set up when he became president of Harvard. He now did so, he explained, because of the urgency of the situation and the necessity for all-out American participation in the defense effort. From that moment Conant became a foremost voice urging total American involvement; for the rest of his administrative career at Harvard he continued to be such a spokesman. He became honorary chairman of the Committee and its most effective publicist. From his deep personal conviction he kept hammering on one theme: "Fear of war is no basis for a national policy." The *Crimson* called this sentence his favorite refrain. In the face of Conant's position the *Crimson* observed that its own editorial stand in support of American neutrality was not "an easy one to uphold."

On May 29, 1940, the week before the German forces reached the Channel, Conant spoke to the nation over the Columbia Broadcasting System. "A total victory of German armies," he warned, "is now well within the range of possibility. Can we as a free nation, considering first and foremost our own best interests, tolerate the overwhelming destruction of the British Fleet?" He urged "rearmament at lightning speed." "I believe," he said, "the United States should take every action possible to insure the defeat of Hitler. I shall mince no words. The actions we propose might eventuate in war. But the fear of war is no basis for a national policy!"

Conant was ready to do his part in World War II as he had in World War I. At the beginning of June 1940 he was back in Washington on scientific assignment as he had been in 1917. This time he was the chemical member of the National Defense Research Committee headed by Vannevar Bush. President Roosevelt had assigned to this group responsibility to deal with the exploration of possibilities of the utilization of atom energy for military purposes. Events made the activity of this committee urgent. On June 10, 1940, Italy entered the war. The evacuation at Dunkirk was completed. On June 12 Conant declared that the "issue before the United States is: can we live as a free, peaceful, relatively unarmed people in a world dominated by the totalitarian states?" On June 14 Paris fell. Conant described the phenomenon which contemporary man was witnessing as "comparable to the sweep of Mohammed and his followers in their first success against the Byzantine empire." "If that be so," he argued, "our peril is real and force alone can provide the answer. For the moment can we escape the bitter truth that only through fighting has liberty been gained in the past; and that only by willingness and capacity to fight can freedom in the present be preserved? The free way of life is the hard way of life."

Following the bombing of Birmingham, Conant addressed the nation by radio on November 21, 1940, to warn that America's free way of life could be maintained only by the defeat of the aggressor. The opinion among experts, he said, was that the defeat of the Axis was possible only if, without reservation, the American people pledged the nation's resources to that end. On December 27, 1940, he joined with a hundred national leaders in a telegram to President Roosevelt expressing alarm at the "too prevalent indifference and apathy toward what is happening in the world and the threat to our vital national interests." He was alarmed by the public ignorance about the issue, about American lethargy, and about an apparent popular disbelief in what was actually taking place. "There may be only a little time left," he warned.

In a fireside chat near the end of the year President Roosevelt made his historic speech describing America as the "arsenal of democracy." Three months before this, Germany, Japan, and the Soviet Union had signed their compact establishing a united front. Conant now urged that practical steps be taken toward immediate action. On February 11, 1941, he testified before the Senate Foreign Relations Committee in behalf of the Lend-Lease bill. "Freedom," he told the senators, "lives because men believe in freedom and are willing to face the responsibility which liberty entails, because they are willing to make sacrifices that it may continue, because they are prepared to be courageous to choose between what is right and what is wrong, because having chosen, they are ready to fight if need be for their convictions."

Back from England as the chief of President Roosevelt's scientific liaison mission, Conant advocated immediate and unequivocal aid to the democracies overseas, "even if it leads to war." "I am arguing for immediate action. In my opinion strategy demands we fight tomorrow, honor and self-interest that we fight before the British Isles are lost. But whether we fight tomorrow or on a later day, we shall before long close our ranks and fight to win." On May 5, 1941, Conant declared on a nation-wide hookup: "I believe we should fight now. . . . Considering only the best interests of a free United States, the hour for action is at hand. . . ." Over the *Crimson* radio network he told the men of Harvard: "There can be no escape from the conclusion that only a decisive military victory can *terminate* this war. . . . The first task before us is by necessity a military one." To the National Education Association in Boston he observed, on June 30, 1941, "At the moment we in the United States dwell in an ambiguous halfway house." Immediately after Pearl Harbor, Conant cabled the *London Sunday Times* that "the date of December 7, 1941, marks the end of a period of difficult ambiguity in the United States."

Almost eleven years then went by before Conant felt again compelled to undertake activities of the type that had been carried on by the Committee to Defend America by Aiding the Allies. As in 1940 he had been concerned with the militant totalitarian imperialism of the National Socialists of Germany, so in 1951 he was to become alarmed by the spreading power of the Moscow Soviets. The necessity to soften and direct American public opinion to support all-out defense effort existed again. Senator Everett M. Dirksen said he recognized many of the same faces of persons in the new movement who had been active in the same kind of public-relations program a decade before. Among the most familiar of these old faces he recognized that of James B. Conant of Harvard.

The new movement first appeared on January 8, 1951, as a nonpartisan citizens' committee alarmed by the "peril facing the American people." The citizens' group operated under the name of the Committee on the Present Danger. The committee's first proclamation called for the people of the nation to give "full support" to General Dwight D. Eisenhower in his new mission to Europe as he endeavored to create and then to command the armed forces of the world on the European terrain. The Committee on the Present Danger held the position that the way to win the global struggle against the Soviets was by making aggression "unprofitable," by creating among the democracies a superior military might and a readiness to fight. "Build up balanced armed forces of great strength with utmost possible speed," said Conant. "Make it clear that the United States is prepared to dispatch adequate forces to Europe." To Conant this meant that the United States must be ready to engage if challenged in all-out-war to defeat the Soviet system in decisive military encounter. To him the American tradition made inevitable the contribution of all the human, material, and spiritual resources of the nation to the support of the free world. All-out war could be a possibility; by courageous and prompt action there was a chance it might be avoided.

As a matter of fact Conant had predicted before the seventy-fifth anniversary session of the American Chemical Society that war would be avoided. In speaking on the subject "A Skeptical Chemist Looks into the Crystal Ball," he prophesied that the world crisis would be averted "only by a narrow margin," that the turning point had come in 1950 with the first year of collective security, that atom bombs would not be used in the struggle that rocked the divided world because time and again, when one side or the other might be about to take the plunge during the period of extensive armament which preceded the great settlement, expert military advisers could not guarantee ultimate success. From the moment when the free world made up its mind to meet each type of military threat of the Soviet Union with a defense against that threat and no longer relied on the atom bomb as a major weapon, hopes of disarmament revived. The ball showed that in the 1960's constructive steps away from war were taken. Within twenty years after the first atom bomb was fired, leaders made debits and credits involved in the exploitation of atomic fission and decided the game was not worth the candle. A self-denying ordinance on all sides restored common sense. Once the illusion of prosperity for all achieved by means of splitting the atom had vanished from people's minds, the air began to clear. By the year 1976 solar energy was practicable, and by the year 2000, when the era of liquid fuel had ended, solar energy had become the dominant factor in the production of industrial power; atomic power had not proved to be as adequate. By the year 2050 the problem of overpopulation was in hand. Some time between 1960 and 1980 the climate of opinion altered. In the year 1984, Marx-Lenin dogmas were still honored in vast areas, but "worried humanity" by trying one political device after another had found its way out of the atomic age and by the end of the twentieth century had surmounted the peril of annihilation of the human species without the triumph of totalitarian society and without the advent of world government. This achievement of the Western world, according to Conant, resulted from the arming of the democracies and their readiness to fight.

Speaking to Harvard men in Memorial Church on the subject of "My Optimism and My Faith," Conant two years after the end of World War II said that "no one but a congenital Pollyanna can look the facts of the present in the face and not realize that we are living in both a somber and an uncertain period of history. But to realize that one is up against a tough job in which one may fail with catastrophic consequences and being afraid of the assignment are two different things."

Conant went on to say that a reason for his optimism was that there seemed to be just as good a chance that "we shall see the beginning of an effective world government in the next ten years as that we shall witness the total obliteration of the heavily industrialized nations. We ought to keep both possibilities equally before our minds." He concluded his chapel talk with these words: "It has been given to some people at certain times to open a mighty sluiceway. The waters they have liberated soon lose their identity but the sudden swirl of the new currents has become legendary with the course of time. So it was with the Greeks more than twenty centuries ago; so I believe it is with the democratic nations of the world today and above all with the republic of free men. Our unique contribution is not in abstract thought nor in art or poetry but rather in a demonstration that a certain type of society long dreamed of by idealists can be closely approached in reality — a free society in which the hopes and aspirations of a large part of the members find enduring satisfaction through outlets once reserved for only a small minority of mankind." "Why are ye fearful, O ye of little faith?" asked Conant.

As seen in his "crystal ball," the power of military might which stemmed the Soviet tide and turned the course of history resulted from the willingness of the American people to support the participation of the United States in the defense of the free world completely and without reservation. In that commitment Conant included a program of universal military service. He took the position that every American youth without exception should be called to service for two years immediately after graduation from high school. He wanted no exemptions and no deferments for college students. Any deferment on the basis of intelligence to his mind was undemocratic and violated the principle of equality of sacrifice.

Thus, as the 1940 decade substituted the Soviets for the Nazis as the foe of the Western world, Conant was convinced that the new threat required an all-out effort of the kind that had overcome the previous one. In supporting the bill to enact universal military service as an American policy and on behalf of the Committee on the Present Danger, Conant appeared once again on a nationwide hook-up on February 7, 1951, to warn: "The United States is in danger. The danger is clearly of a military nature."

In June 1940 President Roosevelt had appointed James B. Conant a chemical member of the National Defense Research Committee headed by Vannevar Bush. To this committee Roosevelt had assigned responsibility, on a very secret basis, for exploring the possibilities of the utilization of atomic energy for military purposes. In the summer of 1941 Conant had become chairman of the committee, and when the National Defense Research Committee became a part of the office of Scientific Research and Development headed by Bush, Conant became deputy director. At this time reports from the British as well as the American experts closest to the atomic energy project seemed to agree that the chances for success were sufficiently high for an "all-out effort." A highly secret review was made by an outside committee. Bush assigned to Conant the responsibility for watching the atomic energy development. Conant reported to Bush and Bush reported to President Roosevelt. Just before Pearl Harbor, Roosevelt made the decision to proceed vigorously with the first development stage of the project. Conant became chairman of the committee which guided vast expenditures of money for the construction program placed in the hands of the Manhattan District headed by General Groves. Conant served as the special adviser to General Groves and was constantly with him. At the same time Conant served as Bush's deputy on a four-man committee which was directly responsible for the whole atomic energy project to the Secretary of War and to the President. Because of this dual relationship Conant often remarked to General Groves that he was not sure whether he was the general's adviser or deputy to his boss. Whatever his line of authority may have been, Conant worked side by side with Groves, recruiting scientific personnel and keeping in touch with scientific groups.

From the very moment of his appointment he stepped behind a political veil. Because his performance for the next five years was carried out under utmost conditions of secrecy, it is sufficient to note that Conant was a part of every top policy, scientific, political, and military group dealing with pure and applied science. A revolution in weapons was taking place. Scientists were at work on radar, especially microwave radar for use in land, air, and naval warfare. Chemists were developing the new explosive "RDX" from formaldehyde. New ways were being devised to meet the submarine menace. Laboratories were at work on the development of proximity fuses and rockets. In the first year of the effort the National Defense Research Committee spent ten million dollars, awarded two hundred and seventy contracts to forty-seven different institutions and thirty-nine individual firms, and had two thousand scientists at work. Conant was a scientific partner in secret weapon development.

In the summer of 1945 Conant stood on a New Mexico desert to observe the explosion of the first atom bomb. When the mushroom rose into the air, a top government official grasped his hand and exclaimed, "Congratulations. It worked." Conant drew back. "I'm not so sure congratulations are in order," he commented. "It remains for history to decide."

At the end of 1945 Conant, accompanied by Secretary of State James F. Byrnes, arrived in Moscow as a special adviser on atomic energy. How closely his name had been associated in the world's mind with the atom bomb was illustrated by an incident which occurred when Conant went with Byrnes to the Kremlin for Christmas dinner in 1945. At the end of a banquet which included lavish quantities of vodka, champagne, rare wines and brandy, caviar, smoked sturgeon, guinea hen breasts, beef, lamb, and other delicacies, Molotov led the drinking of toasts to the various guests around the table. When he came to Conant, he paused to center attention on the guest and said: "Now we've had enough to drink so that we can speak of secret matters. Here's to this man Conant, who probably has an atom bomb in his pocket with which he could blow us to tiny pieces." Before Molotov could finish, Stalin jumped up. "Conant and the atom bomb," he said, "are not joking matters. The American scientist has done a truly great job in helping to win the war. The atom bomb was developed to speed victory. Now," he continued, "we must develop atomic energy for the uses of peace. In this spirit," said Stalin, "I raise my glass. Here's to President Conant!"

At the close of World War II Conant became a member of the Acheson Committee to consider the problem of the international control of atomic energy. In January 1947 he was appointed to the general advisory committee to the Atomic Energy Commission. When the National Science Foundation was created by Congress in 1950 to promote research and education in the sciences, Conant became the first chairman of the board of twenty-four members. Then, in April of 1951, he was appointed a member of the advisory board of the Office of Defense Mobilization, to help co-ordinate scientific research and defense planning.

James B. Conant's experience in government scientific service had thus spanned more than three and a half decades, from the time that he first began as a young chemist to work on poison gas. No man is more qualified to describe the impact of modern science on modern man.

World War II, as Conant analyzed it, established a pattern of partnership among scientists, engineers, industrialists, and political leaders in a heavily industrialized society. This new pattern, he pointed out, was a historic milestone in social development. Conant liked to say that in World War I Thomas A. Edison had been appointed as the best national brain to apply science to naval problems. In building his group he had appointed one solitary physicist to his board with the comment that "we might have one mathematical fellow around in case we have to calculate something." And when the American Chemical Society offered the services of chemists to Secretary of War Newton D. Baker, in 1917, he responded the next day that the offer was unnecessary: he had looked into the matter, and found that the War Department already had *a* chemist!

To Conant the changed status of the scientist which came with World War II altered the relation of science to organized society. "To me," he explained, "the fact of prime importance is this: in the period 1940 to 1945 a whole army of specialists was engaged in advancing science in a spectacular fashion *and* at the same time were developing a new weapon of great military power. This combined activity was a new social phenomenon; we are still struggling with its consequences."

The development of the atom bomb, as Conant saw it, only demonstrated to the public the fact which was already known to many industrialists: *scientists had become inventors.* The scientist was no longer to be thought of as a man in an ivory tower, gradually unraveling the secrets of nature for his own spiritual satisfaction, but as "a miracle-worker who like Watt or Edison before him could bring about tremendous transformations of man's relation to his material surroundings." This situation in which the inventor and scientist merge has enormous implications for the future. It caused Conant to take issue with a good many of his fellow scientists both on the definition of what science is and on how it actually works. It is Conant's interpretation of science that gives significance to his views of the future.

As Conant reads the history of science, he finds that the advances which have been made since the time of Galileo have occurred because of a kind of pattern: "An age-old process of inquiry by which artisans and skillful workers improved the methods of handling inanimate nature became gradually associated with the type of thinking up to then characteristic of mathematics. Two streams of human activity, separated until the sixteenth century, gradually came together. These were abstract reasoning, as represented by Euclidian geometry, and experimentation, as represented by the work of the metallurgists who over the generations had improved the methods of winning metals from the ores." To Conant the history of science demonstrates that "the really revolutionary and significant advances

come not from empiricism [alone] but from new theories." Conant
came to look upon scientific theory as a "policy" highly useful as a
"guide to action." He defined science as "a series of interconnected
concepts and conceptual schemes arising from experiment and observation and fruitful of further experiment and observations." The
test of a scientific theory to Conant is its "fruitfulness." It is just this
combination of highly theoretical activities, "policies guiding action," and high utility that makes science so enormously important
to the future. National survival and human welfare to Conant depend upon planning for the life of science.

For a heavily industrialized American society in which science is
to play its full role, Conant sees four essential conditions necessary.
There must exist free discussion; a mobile and classless society; civil
courage; and spiritual awareness.

While the first condition seems easiest to explain, it is yet the most
difficult to achieve in a divided world. The development especially
of scientific theories in the past has depended upon a free discussion
of their nature and consequences. What happens then in a divided
world when public policy erects a wall of secrecy to prevent the
free circulation of ideas? "*Secrecy and science are fundamentally
antithetic propositions*," Conant answers. When science becomes a
national secret, says Conant from his experience, these consequences
are bound to follow: "Complete failure of communication between
the scientists involved in the secret undertaking and the general
public, complete failure of scientists and engineers to discuss new
proposals, and failure to have adequate appraisals of the significance
of each year's advance." Next, even in the forum of a democracy,
where policies ought to be debated from all angles in public discussion, a new and what Conant calls "an alarming situation" arises.
Political leaders must arrive at decisions on the basis of scientific
testimony which they may not fully understand. Scientists give their
testimony to political leaders in secret. While political leaders and
journalists make certain statements about the importance of certain "rumored" developments, "those who are competent to discuss
such matters cannot do so because of security regulations. Those
who have scientific ability and access to the technical facts must remain silent." Conant feels that it is essential for the public in free

countries to be aware constantly of the existence of this situation and to understand the special conditions now imposed on some phases of an activity that "industrialized societies can ill afford to damage."

Such a situation makes it even more imperative for academic communities to maintain a free atmosphere and respect for the importance of the communication of ideas. "To this end," Conant says, "absolute freedom of discussion and absolutely unmolested inquiry are essential. We must have a spirit of tolerance which allows the expression of all scholarly opinions however heretical they may appear. On this point there can be no compromise. We are either afraid of heresy within our universities or we are not. If we are afraid, then there will be no adequate discussion of the great questions of the day, no fearless exploration of the basic problems forced on us by the age in which we live."

Secondly, a heavily industrialized society makes necessary the achievement of a mobile and classless society because it demands a pathway by which gifted youths may reach the top. The discovery and training of young men of promise becomes for Conant the first task of a free society. If the outstanding men of each generation are to rise quickly, *all* American youth must have equal opportunity in public education to prepare for the life task best fitted to their aptitudes and interests. Such an equality of opportunity must exist because technological society demands a continuing flow of well-trained talented youths from the universities and technical schools into organizations where they can rapidly show their worth. Over and over again Conant has asserted that "there is only one thing that can outmatch young men with good ideas and that is still younger men with better ideas." Conant has an aversion to what he calls "noisy mediocrity." He sees as necessary to insure the welfare of American society provision for an aristocracy of leaders selected as an elite only by the rivalry of each man doing his best, through the provision by their society of an educational system which gives *every* boy and girl an even start in the competition. This spirit of competition, this rivalry of each man doing his best to surpass the best of other highly competent men, lies at the heart of our American system. Society and industry, as Conant sees the situation from his matured experience, must deliberately plan for and maintain this stimulating environment of competition. If society desires a maximum development of the natural sciences and a maximum application of their results to the production of those things which civilization can employ, then the development of the "broad base" of exceptional men who can compete for high-merit performance must occur through a truly universal system of education, enabling gifted boys or girls to study without regard to accidents of birth and geography. The emergence of an unending stream of exceptional citizens must be assured by the existence of public education. From the very beginning to the very end of the educational process, *equal opportunity and competition* must exist.

Continued progress results from leaving the road ahead open to these young persons of ability. Then no dead hand of the past dominates. Ideally, says Conant, one would like to see each research group dissolve itself at least every twenty years and a new outfit with a new frame of reference take its place. Tradition and continuity may have other values in society, and in other fields, but they have no place in the research development of new industries, new methods, and new machinery.

Because research, which is so fundamental an operation in contemporary society, becomes an expensive operation, the men of high promise must be adequately outfitted with the resources in equipment and staff which are necessary for their purposes. This fact means that more and more research development must be the task of the larger units of industry and of government. Yet science must never become a monopoly; indeed monopoly would sound the death knell of scientific endeavor. From his experience in government Conant says that the "vision of a scientific general staff floats before my eyes. God forbid!" Because the essence of research lies in its activities on the frontiers of an unknown world, a free society must keep open at the growing end. If the history of science shows anything it is its concern for the future, not the past. Even in the comparatively simple technical operations in time of war, Conant points out, few realize how great are the difficulties of planning and how unfocused and obscure are often the goals. Look back over the last hundred years, he suggests, and see how few technological developments could have been planned for on the basis of past experience.

To assure the technical undergirding of the mobile and classless American society, Conant thus sees the need for

1. An educational system which insures genuine equality of opportunity.
2. A program for identifying the exceptional man and giving him an opportunity to prove himself while in training.
3. The provision of every advantage and facility in the way of machines, materials, and helping hands to support such exceptional men.
4. The establishment of conditions of rivalry among individuals within units as well as among independent groups competing for scientific and technological achievement under policies so arranged that no group can long perpetuate itself.
5. The avoidance in times of peace of co-ordinating agencies with powers of scientific general staffs.

These conditions relate to the needs of science for maximum usefulness.

It is a most interesting fact to note that while Conant was under his greatest pressure in government service, while he was doing his most profound thinking about science and weapons, he was also giving brilliant chapel talks to Harvard men about values in a free society in which science was merely a useful instrumentality for the realization of a fuller life.

In Memorial Church he pointed out to the students: "Americans have suffered from undernourishment, from a lack of vitamins which their own unique heritage provides. Americans have suffered from an oversupply of imported social and intellectual ideas and standards. The only basis for a strong loyalty is first a realization of the vigor and uniqueness of America's own tradition and second a determination to make America's future a living embodiment of its past ideals. 'There is,' as President Eliot said in his inaugural four years after the close of the Civil War, 'an aristocracy' to which the sons of Harvard have belonged and let us hope will ever aspire to belong. The hallmarks by which such a group of aristocrats are known are two: 'integrity of character and excellence in performance.' If one breathes the essence of the American heritage, he becomes intensely democratic and yet proudly aristocratic. The democ-

racy lies in equality of opportunity; the aristocracy lies in achievement. The American tradition requires an elite of excellence and of
character, an elite chosen anew with each succeeding generation
with neither the accidents of birth nor of education sufficing to give
a man a high place among his fellowmen."

Thus Conant saw technological society rooted in spiritual values.
When he returned to Washington on the sleeper, he was engaged in
revolutionary scientific activity. When he returned to Cambridge,
which wears the tradition of American revolution, he expressed the
hope of witnessing the rebirth of what he called in the *Atlantic
Monthly* "an American radical."

As he tied American history together with the future of industrialized society, within the context of his experience in Washington,
James Bryant Conant came to see that the foreign policy of the
United States depends upon "*a solution of our internal problems.*"
He put the proposition this way: "Until we settle within the United
States our approach to such difficult questions as the relations of
management and labor, and the control and ownership of the tools
of production; until we square away on our course that will make
us both prosperous and free, we shall be irresolute in deciding upon
our foreign policy."

In his chapel talks Conant deplored the "benumbing influence of
certain events which have undermined the status of all reformers."
"To your college generations and succeeding classes," he said, "will
be given the privilege of making the reformer once again a highly
respected though bitterly controversial figure." Conant did not mind
in the least being himself such a controversial figure; he felt that
the whole changed tempo and quality of American life demanded
courageous adjustment of attitudes and institutions to the rigorous
necessities laid down by society.

He made his position doubly clear when he said that "a free
market of ideas assumes an educational system which believes in a
free market and impresses this belief in a free market on children —
let it be noted." A basic Conant premise becomes a free competitive
society. Granted private ownership and the profit motive, he says,
the question is how best to keep American society truly competitive
and moving toward a greater degree of equality of opportunity. "If

one abolishes competition the problem of rewards and incentives in a free society becomes increasingly difficult to solve. The American problem surely is to see how we can operate our private enterprises *and* our political institutions so that our society will in part be competitive and thereby increasingly productive of the goods and services. To this end we need men working willingly together toward known goals. We need workers who are informed, enjoy a sense of security, feel individual dignity, are properly and fairly paid, and are given nonfinancial incentives."

Conant became particularly concerned about incentives. "We must realize the importance of the rewards and incentives which actuate most Americans," he asserts. "These are a complex mixture of social ideals and personal aspirations including the desire to provide for one's family after death. We shall not want our tax laws to be so drastic as to block powerful human incentives from having desirable social and economic consequences. The American public must consider the conflict factors and strike a balance. High taxes on earned incomes have the reverse effect of high inheritance taxes on the fluidity of society. In so far as national expenditures permit, the case for keeping income taxes low is overwhelming both in terms of social ideals and human invention as well as balanced budgets. The welfare of our national economy must be considered in a formulation of our tax policy."

As points in an American creed Conant proposed a common set of goals which include equality of opportunity, minimum of class distinctions, fair play for all, maximum degree of individual freedom, and wide distribution of centers of initiative. In short, Conant's ideal for America is a free and classless — or casteless — society, a society made classless through a maximum social mobility.

He did not expect, he explained, to achieve such conditions all at once. "Ideals in an open society like ours," he pointed out, "represent goals toward which men and women may move by concerted action. They never can be reached in practice — almost by definition — but we can recognize whether we are moving toward them or retreating. Our American ideals in part correspond to the aims of all democracies, in part they represent a special contribution to the world. If we are to survive we must make these ideals explicit by our actions; words alone will not suffice. It is essential that we continually and critically reassess the rate of progress; complacent acceptance of the ideals will be of no avail; never-ending efforts must be made to move society forward."

To Conant one engine which pulls America in the direction of its ideals is the public school. His concern for the public schools came to take second place only to his concern for Harvard. To his mind it was the action of the public school that could shape America to the American ideal. During his administration he gave highest priority to the School of Education in his concern for the development of the professional schools.

Conant explained his interest in the public school in this way: "If large numbers of young people can develop their own capacities irrespective of the economic status of their parents, then the social mobility is high. If on the other hand the future of a young man or woman is determined almost entirely by inherited property or the lack of it, social mobility is nonexistent." Educators who possess the facts conservatively estimate, he said, that as many promising boys and girls fail to go to college for economic reasons as the number who now enter. To Conant the ultimate goal of America is an educational system in which at no level will a qualified individual in any part of the country encounter an insuperable barrier to the attainment of the kind of education suited to his aptitudes and interests. To achieve these ends at all levels Conant asked for Federal funds to aid states according to need, but only when such states themselves are doing their utmost to supply adequate education for all American youth.

As public education at all levels becomes a reality, Conant recognizes that the homogeneous nature of the student group breaks down. "It is," he says, "as though a country parson who was used to ministering to a small and homogeneous congregation should suddenly find himself assigned the task of being the spiritual leader of the crowd that fills the Grand Central Station the day of the Fourth."

Conant's thinking so completely joins the American tradition with the needs of the scientific-technological society of the future that one who reads him must distinguish between the two. American history provides the roots of a revolutionary tradition of a free and classless society of high mobility which is tolerant of dissent. America's future demands such a classless society of high mobility to maintain its competitive place in the technological world. Thus, America's past and future are a part of the same pattern: the obligation of men acting in the present is to be aware of this connection and to act upon it. Out of the past comes a moral principle; down from the future comes an inexorable requirement. It is up to American industrial leaders — of all persons — to join the moral principle with the inexorable requirement into a genuine American faith. This is so, as Conant explains the relationship, because modern industrialized and highly urbanized society can prosper only if the professions are full of capable, imaginative, and forward-looking men. If one does not dispute the validity of this statement, then one must be guided by its consequences when applied to American society — or be ready to forfeit both the American heritage and the American promise.

The realization of this American promise as a continuation of this American heritage, as Conant states it, let it be remembered, depends upon the coexistence of the previously described four conditions — free discussion, a mobile and classless society, civil courage, and spiritual awareness. High on the list of these priorities Conant places civil courage — the quality of mind which befittingly enables a citizen to encounter danger and difficulties with firmness and without fear. Lack of civil courage, Conant asserts, fosters mass psychosis; strength in it may in decades ahead determine the handling of America's domestic crisis and the issues of war or peace. To Conant the citizens of a free society must be educated to possess strong loyalties and high civil courage: their unifying faith must be not a matter of words or intellectual concepts but a direct relationship between men, because what democracy means is better illustrated for some people by action than by words, by what they do than by what they say. The ethical ideal may well be "individual integrity in dealing with other people, human sympathy, and moral courage."

Finally, Conant comes to the requirement of spiritual awareness. What he means by spiritual awareness is a concern for the "continuing triumphs of the creative spirit." To Conant, the Harvard educator, this means recognition of the power of the humanistic disciplines to give life spiritual strength and moral purpose. To him the "humanities form the secular portion of the total boundary enclosing the area of spiritual values." Thus human ties become central in a general education. Indeed, for Harvard, "welcoming the children of all religious faiths," Conant found that "it is only this secular boundary that can be used as a baseline for the development of moral as well as intellectual and artistic standards." The humanistic studies have a central function which Conant does not find in circles considering appreciation of arts and letters as a "combination of antiquarianism, a collector's instinct, and the old snob appeal of a 'gentleman's education.'" In the moral values of the Hebraic-Christian tradition Conant found a source of values which he believes to be woven into the fabric of civilization. Especially from the Book of Job, Conant found comfort in the fact that "the universe is not explicable in human terms. The universe is not constructed along the lines of an automatic machine distributing rewards and punishments."

What Conant said he wanted to find out was "the minimal commitments required by a modern man to construct his philosophy of life if he be neither a religious dogmatist nor a materialistic atheist." Conant wanted to put his finger on a common denominator on which Americans could agree in their common life. In his own thinking he found the common ground in the affirmation that man is something more than a social animal, that man lives in a close relationship with other people, that there is a sharp cleavage between animal behavior and human conduct, and that man's intentions and overt actions may have a relation to some larger pattern of events. Such, he thinks, would be the minimal commitment for a modern man in the Judaic-Christian tradition who seeks to develop a philosophy of life without "jumping the fence into the materialistic camp."

In the reach of science Conant saw the development of scientific theories which gradually became part of man's common-sense ideas about the material universe, but which have little or no bearing on the age-old problem of good and evil. If a man will look within himself and list the scientific ideas which he accepts just in the matter of diet, said Conant, he will see how science becomes fused with the working equipment of everyday living. Perhaps, he thinks, the failure to assimilate science into our Western culture is one reason why "so many feel spiritually lost in the modern world." He looked forward to the time when science will be fused into the age-old problem of understanding man and his works, in short, secular education. He says science, with its constant outreach to lower the degree of "empiricism," provides man with more dependable ways of living.

Conant was frank in pointing out that the adherents of a religious creed which sets forth in detail the origin, nature, and destiny of man "are almost sure to repudiate any views of the nature of the universe that is as provisional and fragmentary" as the one which he suggests. His position, however, colored and directed the approach which Harvard made to the problem of spiritual awareness. His position was quite out of the pattern of religious routine. With the denominational institutions of religion Conant was less concerned than with this kind of awareness, which he found essential to the philosophically minded individual who recognized the dimensions of his life in the technologically oriented society to which the scientist, the engineer, and the industrialist had given birth. Perhaps the best statement of Conant's faith is summed up in the words of Jeremy Taylor so often quoted by President Eliot and repeated by Conant, that he wishes for every man "a mind apt to noble choices and a heart capable of mighty love."

A series of situations led to criticism of Conant's position. While there were other reasons for the low ebb, the fact remained that during his entire administration at Harvard the Divinity School remained the weakest of the professional divisions and the last to receive Conant's attention. When in the closing years of his presidency he did take up the problem of the Divinity School, he attacked it with the same determination to develop a fundamental policy which had characterized his performance in other fields. Yet Professor Henry J. Cadbury, incumbent of the Hollis Chair of Divinity, spoke pretty much the mind of the Divinity School faculty when he said that the school's condition was due to the "University's apathetic attitude." "If they want to kill a department," he challenged, "why don't they come out and say so?" Nevertheless Conant was already embarked on his program of developing policies and raising funds which would "revitalize the school and give it more the character of an impartial, entirely undenominational center of religious learning."

In the spring of 1951, the Canterbury Club (Episcopalian), the Wesley Foundation (Methodist), the Congregational-Presbyterian Fellowship, the Sunday Evening Club (Baptist), and the University Lutheran Association of Greater Boston, representing the United Ministry of Protestant denominational groups serving the Harvard students, issued a joint statement. "We feel," said these organizations, "that the religious viewpoint has been neglected at Harvard and because we are Christian we are most aware that Christianity has been neglected." The statement urged "courses in religion taught from the religious point of view" and religious counseling under the leadership of a university chaplain.

While as a matter of policy Harvard men are encouraged to worship in the community in the churches of their own faith, divine services are held in the Yard under the direction of a Board of Preachers. During Conant's entire administration attendance in the Memorial Church averaged five hundred on Sundays and seventy at daily morning prayers. "Church habits," Dean Willard Sperry reported to Conant, "remain fairly constant. It is reckoned that hardly more than 15 per cent of our Protestant church members are regular church attendants. Religion, supposedly a unifying force in society, is becoming as in years past a divisive force. Many of the resources and much of the energy of organized religion is now being wasted in a sad civil warfare when its united strength should be addressed to the flagrant materialism of much of our life. We throw some oil on the troubled waters."

On one principle, however, Harvard took a fighting position. It ran vertically from Conant back to Eliot, it ran horizontally from Massachusetts Hall to Dean Sperry and to the *Crimson*. The position was that public education must be secular education, free from the divisiveness of religious sectarianism. The assertion of this principle has corollaries. The teaching of religion has no place in the public schools. The use of public funds for the support of private schools is unwise policy. Religious instruction remains the task of the church and the home. "Otherwise," Conant observed, "a public instrument will be torn asunder in the conflict between rival theologies. Continuous sniping by franc-tireurs who do not publicly proclaim their real reasons for dissatisfaction with public schools ought to be condemned by all fair-minded persons." Both as president of Harvard and as a citizen, therefore, Conant was on record in his insistence about the separation of education and religion.

In the spring of 1952 Conant opened up another controversial area relating to religion and education in a speech to the American Association of School Administrators meeting in Mechanics Hall in Boston. In the course of this address he said that "a dual system of schools with tax money flowing in some form to private schools seems to be a possibility in some people's minds. I think it is important that the hostile critics of the public schools of the United States be made to show their colors." He went on to say that the greater the number of youth who attend independent schools, the greater will be the threat to democratic unity. "Therefore," he argued, "to use taxpayers' money to assist such a move is for me to suggest that American society use its own hands to destroy itself." He went on to show that in the previous decade and a half the Protestant denominational elementary schools had expanded 61 per cent and the Roman Catholic schools 35 per cent. "In terms of numbers involved," he added, "the dual nature of our present system may seem slight — 92 per cent of our secondary school pupils are in the public schools. In terms of the stratification of society on economic and religious lines, the duality is marked indeed."

Although Conant himself had attended private school and in time sent his son James to Phillips Exeter and his son Theodore to Putney, he was convinced of the unifying power of the public school where children have the common experience of rubbing shoulders with their neighbor.

As was to be expected, Conant's idea drew fire. United States Secretary of Labor Maurice Tobin at Catholic University in Washington observed that "Conant is not the first American, nor will he be the last, to misunderstand the meaning of democracy in the field of elementary and secondary education." Archbishop Cushing, devoting his Easter sermon to the subject from the pulpit of the Cathedral of the Holy Cross in Boston, directed his remarks to Conant. "It may seem strange to devote my Easter message to a warning against the direction which the battle against the independent school is taking," he began in introducing his ideas on the "aggression of a strictly secular concept of society pressing the claim of a totalitarian state." "Conant objects to the parochial and the private school as such," the Archbishop said bluntly. "He wants to close them all. I do not believe Dr. Conant will turn Harvard University over to the Commonwealth of Massachusetts." The headmaster of the William Penn Charter School in Philadelphia warned that "it would be bad for our free society to have all education state-controlled."

While Conant was thus engaged in fundamental thinking about social policy he was also still very much the chief executive of a huge educational enterprise.

"Who in the world runs this university?" a visitor once asked him.

Conant replied that the question could not be answered. If one seeks an organizational chart showing the administrative structure of the university, there is no such plan. If one talks about who reports to whom, the vocabulary is out of place in Cambridge. If one suspects that Harvard operates a high-powered public-relations office in charge of a vice-president, one is sadly disappointed. There is only Bill Pinkerton at work in Weld Hall in the Harvard news office and he has only one theory of public relations: sound policies clearly stated make good news. An industrial engineer would be — and many are — horrified at the absence of streamlining. Yet few can deny that the Harvard system works. It works because Harvard has a culture of its own, a kind of historic, informal, and accepted way of doing things that Harvard people understand. It makes little difference in the Yard that what seems normal to Harvard men may confuse outsiders by its directness and simplicity.

Harvard is first of all private and independent — with emphasis on both words. Its name comes from the Reverend John Harvard who bequeathed to it a seed endowment and his library. Stoughton Hall and Holworthy were constructed with revenue derived from a state lottery. In the early days its income was augmented by funds earned by the Charlestown-to-Boston ferry and "some bad wampum" as Harvard records relate. Until 1860 when legislation finally separated the university from the Commonwealth of Massachusetts, it operated as a sort of state university with an aristocratic clientele and a spirit of independence quite uninhibited by the political connection.

As a legal entity Harvard exists as a corporation — with title "the President and Fellows of Harvard College" — by charter dating from 1650. It is thus the oldest corporation in continuous existence in the Americas. Often referred to as "the Corporation," this entity is self-perpetuating, its board being composed of the president and treasurer of the university *ex officio,* and five fellows — who have always represented substantial citizens in business, financial, and professional circles.

In 1865, the Commonwealth divorced the university completely and provided for the election of a "Reverend and Honorable Board of Overseers," of thirty members, elected by mail ballot of the alumni in classes of five for staggered terms of six years. With "the Corporation" and the "Board of Overseers" Harvard has a sort of bicameralism which perhaps anywhere else but at Harvard might occasionally run into rough weather. The corporation initiates matters; the overseers, as a kind of second house, exercise a power of review, concurrence, and veto. In the election of a president, the corporation nominates for the concurrence of the overseers.

From this point on Harvard operates as a highly and purposely decentralized activity through the ruthless application of two policies. The first of these can be described by saying that Harvard proposes to obtain the one man best fitted to perform the right job. The application of this principle creates an elite of excellence and capability. The principle serves equally well as a personnel policy for the selection of a president, the permanent appointment of a professor to the faculty, the selection of an officer to operate the Harvard University Press, or the admission of a freshman to the student body. Once the one best man has been located in the one right job, he has full rein. Everywhere in Harvard the spirit is competitive; men are in the race to win. Competition for highest excellence among the excellent is highly regarded in the Harvard system.

The second policy principle at Cambridge is that "every tub stands on its own bottom." This means that good men are given full freedom and full responsibility. While different people interpret the "tub-buttom" principle in different situations to fit the context, Conant made it mean, as far as he was concerned, that every dean in charge of a faculty balances his own budget, raises his own funds, and cultivates his own alumni. No dean is expected to end the fiscal year with a deficit. If he operates with a surplus the balance is carried forward as an earmarked asset of the school and for its own use; it does not become a general university fund. Louis M. Lyons, who worked closely with Conant, says that after "running Harvard as a commuter from Washington for several years, he set up a system by which the university ran itself."

While the university funds care for general administrative services and cover deficits such as that regularly and unfortunately incurred by the Divinity School, Conant placed great emphasis on the importance of uninstructed, free, and mobile funds in the general university account which can be deployed in the discretion of the administration to whatever spot within the university most needs its benefit. "The great strength of American universities during the period of expansion of the last fifty years," Conant felt, "has lain in the ability to experiment with new educational procedures and to explore new areas of thought." Without adequate mobile funds, he kept insisting, the progress of a university would become frozen and Harvard would enter a static period of educational history which might become a period of stagnation. It was to guard against such possibility that Conant gave the solicitation of mobile funds first priority in the Tercentenary Fund drive.

One day Conant was walking across the campus of another institution when the dean became concerned with a minor matter related to the lawn. "I couldn't get into housekeeping details even if I wanted to," Conant observed. "I just have time to look after the dollars and the professors." In his mind both were closely related. To take care of the dollars Conant immediately after his appointment selected John Wilbur Lowes, a man of wide financial and business experience, as vice-president with about the same duties given to a military logistics command. Since educational policy and financial considerations are so complementary, Conant located Lowes next to his own office so that educational and costs policies could be interwoven. Thus he delegated all problems which may broadly be classified as financial. Lowes handled the preparation and administration of the budget, housing, feeding, and maintenance of buildings and grounds. The treasurer of the corporation handled endowments, received all income, and paid all bills. The secretary of the corporation and the Board of Overseers cared for the corporate business while the secretary of the university handled protocol, ceremonies, received important persons and alumni, and served as a general liaison officer. An assistant to the president for development, far from being a high-powered fund raiser, advised deans in their decentralized fund-raising efforts and kept lines of solicitation straight so that deans would not twice solicit the same person or foundation.

On the academic side Conant groped for what he felt was the right pattern. He found it at the end of World War II. In the beginning of his administration many felt that Harvard should have a dean of deans, a sort of dean of the university who would serve as a kind of deputy president. This system was not suited for Harvard. The deans of the various professional schools wanted to see and talk with the president of the university who sat as a member of the corporation; they did not want to transact business on the dean's level with any second-string person. With the responsible deans Conant had, such a position was entirely understandable.

In the early years of his administration, too, Conant felt that he could simplify the operations of the college faculty by setting up an elected and representative council to act for the faculty as a whole with the understanding that actions of the council could be reviewed upon petition of fifteen members of the faculty. This system did not prove to be permanently satisfactory. After World War II adjustments were made. The dean of the university was superseded by a provost who was ex officio dean of the faculty of arts and sciences, director of museums, the college library, and of the independent institutions associated with Harvard. This combination of duties seemed to work well. The faculty recovered its old authority in 1939 and discontinued the council idea which Conant had fathered in 1934. Departments fell into the habit of designating certain members to attend faculty meetings and when a substantial issue was on the agenda adequate representations were detailed. In 1945 Conant relinquished general oversight over the college, as Lowell had exercised it, and thus relieved himself of month-to-month detail. Conant served as *ex officio* chairman of all faculty meetings in all divisions.

From the beginning of his administration Conant struggled to make Harvard a "uni-versity" rather than a "multi-versity." "The administration of a great university," he said, "must endeavor to find methods of counteracting the centrifugal forces which tend to separate faculties into an ever-increasing number of subdivisions. There must be no regimentation which lays down specifications. Wherever the opportunity arises we should nevertheless encourage co-operation between specialities and emphasize programs of teaching and research which cut across the conventional boundaries." As a step in the direction of unity, Conant appointed advisory research committees in the divisions of humanities, social sciences, biology, and the physical sciences. These committees included distinguished men chosen from different faculties. They had no administrative functions and included no administrative officers. Their sole purpose was to advise the president on future developments in broad fields and to consider from time to time the desirability of initiating programs of co-operative research.

Conant further tried to promote unity by establishing a few university professors with roving commissions. Such faculty members could teach and engage in creative work unhampered by departmental considerations. They were in fact professors without portfolio, brilliant and imaginative men whose task was to synthesize modern knowledge. Conant moreover proposed to have certain professors engage in the study of the history of university education as a means of showing the unity that lies at the heart of the diversity of specialities attached to a university faculty.

Another means of holding the broad overview of the university function while keeping operations alert to the current world was the visiting committee idea. Committees composed of members of the board and other friends of Harvard "visit" various departments. Through the reports of these visiting committees the Board of Overseers is able to keep in touch with the many special interests of Harvard. Not only do departments profit from the expert knowledge of specialists on the committees; the members of the committees themselves come to have a love and high regard for Harvard.

An example of how special committees strengthen the Harvard operations is the group appointed to study the activities conducted under the Nieman Foundation after ten years of its operation to see what policy should be followed in this unusual experiment for the development of journalists. To select a representative committee Harvard asked some forty publishers, editors, and wire service executives to make nominations. On the basis of such suggestions Harvard appointed to the committee the chief editorial writer of the *New York Herald-Tribune*, the publisher of the *Providence Journal*, the editor of the *Christian Science Monitor*, the publisher of the *Delta-Democrat Times*, a Washington columnist, the publisher of the *Louisville Courier-Journal*, the publisher of the *Washington Post*, the publisher of the *Denver Post*, the editor of the *Washington Star*, the publisher of the *Philadelphia Bulletin*, the diplomatic correspondent of the *New York Times*, and the editor of the *San Francisco Chronicle*. This distinguished group spent two days at Harvard discussing issues with deans, faculty members, and former Nieman fellows. The members conducted a mail survey among employers of former and present Nieman fellows, set up subcommittees, and after a year of hard and thoughtful professional work submitted a report to the corporation. Out of this report came a policy.

Under Conant each Harvard operation was based on a carefully worked out policy. The policy constituted the determining guide to action. Sound policies of course were not a Conant innovation. They belong to the Harvard tradition. The development of the Graduate School of Business Administration provides an excellent example of the importance of policy. Up to the time of its founding, education for business had not been considered a professional activity. When the school opened in 1908, however, its policy was clearly stated in a definition. "Business," said the school, "is making things to sell at a profit, decently." The definition further broke business activities down into two parts — manufacturing or the art of production, and merchandising or the art of distribution. No established curriculums or materials existed so that the business faculty had to develop materials from scratch. This was fortunate for it led to a co-operative pattern which joined vocation and education. Professors and business executives worked side by side in developing instructional materials. As a result, the school evolved a method of teaching which combined the case method of teaching law and the clinical method of teaching medicine. The Graduate School of Business Administration under this pattern flourished, commanded large financial support, and took leadership as industry became big in size, complex in operation, and was compelled to take a scientific interest in its human problems. In 1941 Conant installed Donald K. Davis as dean. Under the principle that every tub stands on its own bottom, Davis conducted a fund-raising operation in 1949–1950 which produced twelve million dollars.

Throughout his administrative career Conant kept his balance. He maintained the modesty which he expressed, soon after his election, in a telephone call to Vernon Munroe, Jr., '10. Conant was inquiring whether Munroe would be interested in becoming a secretary in the president's office. The conversation ran like this:

MUNROE: What is it, please?
CONANT: Is this Vernon Munroe?
MUNROE: Speaking, who is this?
CONANT: James Conant.
MUNROE: Who did you say?
CONANT: Conant.
MUNROE: Sorry, I'm afraid I don't know you.
CONANT: James Conant, the chap they just elected as president of Harvard.

Conant was not only modest; he was also firm. He could say "no" politely. When Conant was new at his job, President Emeritus Lowell used to drop into the office to see how things were going. "As president," he told Conant, "you will be surrounded on all sides by wolves trying to tear off bits of the university. It is the first business duty of the president to resist pressure." One method Conant devised to resist pressure was to decentralize decisions to the deans. "The president's job," he said, "is to run interference for the various deans and to make sure interference doesn't get in anybody's way." His other way of resisting pressure was more unique. Always given to the symbolism of the crystal ball, Conant installed one in his office. This was inevitably brought out when an appointment on the calendar indicated a request. When the request did come in the course of an interview, Conant would rise, draw the supplicant over to the crystal ball, and with his guest peer into the glass ball. There magnified stood an enormous NO! The system helped. The applicant knew that his refusal was not unique.

Through all his twenty years as president Conant coveted warm and understanding relationships with the faculty, but the demands upon his time seemed to rule out the kind of personal contacts which he so much enjoyed. To provide opportunity for association, he scheduled monthly "at homes." A familiar Harvard notice read: "President and Mrs. Conant will be at home and glad to see all members of the faculty and their wives on Sunday between two and six o'clock at 17 Quincy Street."

As he settled down to the strenuous life which his office demanded, Conant, so the Harvard legend runs, made an appointment with a physician to obtain advice on how a man could be president of Harvard and still live. The doctor advised him never to make an appointment before ten o'clock in the morning, to get off to a good start each morning with a hearty breakfast, to relax during the meal, and to give himself a chance to do some quiet thinking about the work of the day. Conant did not heed the counsel. Over a period of twenty years he kept up a ferocious pace without apparent nervous or physical strain. Mrs. Conant spoke of her husband as a "jet-propelled missile"; others referred to him as that "damned shad-bellied Yankee."

As a general routine Conant followed breakfast with an hour and a half of work at home on speeches, reports, and book manuscripts. At ten o'clock he went to his office and remained until one. His lunch hour was usually devoted to business affairs. Afternoons he reserved for paper work in his office and for occasional interviews and personal conferences. At four o'clock on scheduled days he attended faculty meetings. Dinners usually meant formal functions or public events. Occasionally he had free evenings on which he gave his own formal dinners. Out of the thirty days in a month, perhaps he would have five evenings for his own affairs. He met regularly with the *Crimson* editors, annually visited the dinners of the seven houses and the Union, and gave occasional chapel talks to the students in Memorial Church. To preserve some semblance of family life, he arranged to eat with his wife at least twice a week. As he was drawn more into national affairs, his family life became sporadic.

As a public speaker Conant became a national preference. His addresses were logical and incisive presentations, rich with facts and studded with historical references especially from educational, American, and scientific records. He spoke with unquestioned authority and discussed both scientific developments and public policy with equal cogency. His style in both oral and written language was clear, lucid, analytical, and conversational. He developed a skill in relating apt anecdotes. His sentences averaged twenty-one words, mostly short and Anglo-Saxon. About one in five words exceeded two syllables. Wherever he went he gained and held both academic and non-academic audiences by the vigor and liberality of his ideas.

Lowell had confined his activities closely to Harvard Yard. Conant ranged the nation. For at least half the years of his administration he commuted to Washington. Taking his whole twenty years together he spent more time outside Cambridge than on the campus.

In 1940 the Custom Tailors Guild chose Conant as "the fifth best-dressed man in the United States." In commenting on his sartorial elegance the *Crimson* printed a brief verse:

> Wear seemly gloves; not black, nor yet too light,
> And least of all the pair that once was white.
> Be the tailor's goat if so your fancy bids
> But be a president: don't forget the kids.

When he fractured his collar bone as his ski broke through the crust on a slope at Calais, Vermont, the *Crimson* expressed the hope that students might now see him on the campus.

For the most part Conant found his recreation and his relaxation in his work. He planned two short vacations a year with his wife and connected them as a rule with business. Until World War II and a wrenched back put an end to the sport, he climbed mountains — "real rope stuff" as he says. He went up the Sierra Nevadas one summer and for the next two summers climbed the Canadian Rockies. For this performance he was elected to the

American Alpine Club. He made a hobby, he said, of "walking uphill." Later he took up trout fishing as an outdoor recreation.

A good part of his time naturally was consumed in meetings, conferences, and group work, or the preparation of reports and documents for group discussion. In group sessions he presented his ideas with clarity and brevity, listened intently, and sought to get the facts on the table for review and policies clearly stated for action. When he was alone on planes and trains, he read with a deep and critical enjoyment, especially books on educational history, philosophy, and current affairs. He smokes moderately — mostly cigars, drinks occasionally a glass of beer or an Old-fashioned, and lets his appearances at chapel take care of his religious duties.

How conscientiously he performed his university duties is nowhere more clearly expressed than in Conant's interest in the Harvard alumni. Between the time of his installation in 1933 and his appointment as High Commissioner for Germany in 1953, Conant spoke to more Harvard clubs and talked to more Harvard gatherings than any other president in Harvard history. In the summer of 1947 he took his first real vacation since 1939. It covered a little more than three weeks. He prefaced his trip by completing the syllabus for his fall course on the growth of experimental science. Between August 30 and September 18 he made sixteen formal talks, was guest at five public dinners, attended ten luncheons or outings, went to two formal receptions, shook hands with the members of seven Harvard Clubs and some hundreds of unattached alumni, enjoyed the hospitality of eleven Chambers of Commerce, college faculties, city clubs, and discussion groups, and made a broadcast. Mrs. Conant shared many of his appearances and added some formal luncheons and a dinner on her own. Everywhere the newspapers gave substantial attention to Conant's visits and especially wrote up and discussed what he said.

But, while he thus recognized the alumni, Conant gave especial attention to the educational process in Harvard College. During his twenty years of leadership he always kept foremost in his thinking the importance of inoculating students with that "virus of on-going education" which had from the beginning seemed to him the goal. "Modern Harvard," he said, "prides itself on the vitality of its undergraduate curriculum and the favorable opportunity afforded for the development of undergraduate life." He watched statistical trends and took them to heart. He felt that the contact of student with student provided a most important phase of education. When he saw a steady decline of certain traditional disciplines, he was grieved that the informal interaction of students was impaired. When classics majors fell to one per cent of the student body, he regretted that Harvard college men would have only one chance in a hundred to bump into a fellow student who was a classicist. Because he placed a premium on benefits accruing from "indirect education," he felt that an imbalance in areas of concentration prevented that circulation of ideas among students which was so much a part of the idea of a liberal education.

Soon after he was installed as president, Conant wrote a long letter to the faculty concerning the importance of the "extracurricular" study of American history. Ten years later he wrote another memorandum. This time it was a matured statement of a position. His letter was enriched by his own "extracurricular" readings, his experience in Washington, his concern for the defense of the "free world," his enthusiasm for the idea of education for *all* American youth stemming from his service on the Educational Policies Commission, his desire to restudy the Harvard college pattern as a means of educating the leading citizens, and his thinking about how science might be taught history by the case-study approach. His letter set in motion an idea.

In January 1943 Conant appointed a university "Committee on the Objectives of a General Education in a Free Society" and equipped it with sixty thousand dollars to do its job. The committee was headed by Professor Paul H. Buck, Dean of the Faculty of Arts and Sciences and subsequently provost of the university. The report was published in the spring of 1945. Over a period of two years the committee met weekly, periodically secluded itself for sessions of several days, maintained a central office, sought the advice of specialists from all over the world, tapped all the experience of American education, and finally made a comprehensive educational proposal the purpose of which was "to cultivate in the largest possible number of our future citizens an appreciation of both the responsibilities and the benefits which come to them because they are Americans and are free."

The report was thus a searching inquiry into the role and method of education. In style the document was an extended homiletic on the importance of education for *all* American youth. As such it probably became the most important educational document in the middle twentieth-century period. It provided within the years of his administration some fundamental thinking which made Conant's period fully as important as that of Eliot with his free electives and of Lowell with his concentration and distribution pattern. One day in the garden of the Cosmos Club in Washington Conant commented that the expenditure of sixty thousand dollars was well worth while if the sum had encouraged a few professors to climb up the fence and take a peek at one another's garden patches.

While the report has widely influenced American education, the concern here is with its observations about education in Harvard College. The report concluded that "general education" had been "neglected in Harvard College." It found no one course required of all undergraduates at Harvard. It found on the other hand that the system of concentration at Harvard was "clear, definite, and full of content." The concentration area was supported by an "impressive battery of educational machinery: teaching departments, prescribed courses, the system of honors, the tutorial system, and the general examination." The concentration system offered the "able and enterprising student an opportunity for a remarkably penetrating experience in the field of his choice." In striking contrast the committee found "general education at Harvard dismissed with a vague exhortation on its desirability and the essentially negative prescription that beyond this area of concentration the student should take two or three courses of something – almost anything." It found Harvard "weak indeed in the opportunities it provides for the development of a common body of information and ideas which would be in some measure the possession of all students. . . . There has been in other words," said the report, "no very substantial intellectual experience common to all Harvard students." The committee became mystical, evangelical, and hortatory in its report. "Special education instructs in what things can be done and how to do them; general education in what needs to be done and to what ends. General education is the appreciation of the organic complex of relationships which gives meaning and point to the specialty. To some degree it should suffuse all special education."

Without going into detail, it can be pointed out that the area which Lowell had labeled "distribution" under Conant became a general education program fully effective with the class of 1955. The new system of general education required all freshmen to take a half course in English composition known as General Education A. During his first two years each student must take three general education courses, one in each of the three major areas of knowledge defined as the humanities, the sciences, and the social sciences. During his last two years the student is required to take three additional courses outside his field of concentration from more advanced offerings in general education chosen from the three areas. Because Harvard believes in fewer things done more thoroughly, the normal student load is four courses.

Conant frankly said that the value of the program would be demonstrated at the twentieth reunion of the class of 1955. What he personally hoped for was that the result in 1975 would show that the general education program had stimulated Harvard men to a life of substantial reading, continued intellectual activity, and active citizenship. This was the same result which Conant has cherished when he proposed his "extracurricular" course in American cultural history back in 1933. It was the same outcome which he had in mind when in 1946 he delivered the Dwight Harrington Terry Foundation lectures at Yale "On Understanding Science." It was the same idea he had in mind when in 1947 he offered a regular 9 A.M. Monday-Wednesday-Friday course on "The Growth of the Experimental Sciences."

The faculty report made it clear that the Lowell pattern had not been an unqualified success. In 1939, as is well known in Cambridge, the *Crimson* had led a campaign to abolish the private, commercial tutoring schools, one of which advertised: "Instruction by Wolfe; diploma by Harvard." As a result of the abolition of the tutoring factories, Harvard was forced to strengthen its advising system. The faculty report pointed out that the expensive tutorial system had been superimposed on an elaborate course system, that very few members of the faculty who attained professorial rank were willing to give more than a small fraction of their time to tutorial instruction, that the closeness of the tutorial relationship added to the unhappy plight of the student when he was assigned a tutor whose immaturity of judgment, emotional instability, limited learning, or devotion to his own graduate work made him unsatisfactory either as a guide, a counselor, or an instructor. It was obvious that the tutorial system had not reached a degree of perfection which was attributed to the concentration pattern, although it was most helpful on that level.

While the Harvard College faculty seemed to feel that the general education program was off to a good start, the *Crimson* after six years of observation was not so sure. "A large part of Harvard education," said the *Crimson*, "has become diseased. Over two thousand non-honors men in five large departments see no more of any faculty member than the semi-annual study-card signing. Many are not well enough acquainted with even one professor to ask for a character reference. There is probably less personal contact between faculty and students than ever before." This sad situation had come about, the *Crimson* explained, "because many of the faculty members worry about research, graduate school work, outside projects, and last about undergraduate tutorials. Many senior professors in economics spend their time outside of course either in government or research. Since a man's worth as a teacher is measured largely by his competence as a scholar, his tutoring ability counts for little." In 1952, as a result of a special report steps were taken to correct the situation.

The *Crimson* referred to the general education program adopted in 1946 after six years of experience as "only a modest success both in its effect on students and in their conception of its objectives. The basic aims of the general education courses are not clear to the students and such courses are not so obviously distinguishable from survey courses." From the point of view of many students the general education program was having serious trouble fulfilling its aims. One fault lay in instruction, the *Crimson* felt. Instructors were not holding clearly enough to the case method of presentation.

Conant put his shoulder to the wheel in syllabus-building and in classroom instruction to make the general education program work. Beginning in 1947 he offered in the fall term Natural Sciences II dealing with "The Growth of the Experimental Sciences." The enrollment was limited to two hundred. Back in the classroom for the first time since 1933, Conant had the same flair for lucid and dramatic presentation which he had in his earlier days when he used to dip a raw egg in a fluid, hurl it over the heads of the horrified students, and bounce the solidified albumen on the far wall.

To provide the case studies necessary for science instruction in general education Conant proceeded to edit the *Harvard Case Histories in Experimental Science*. Between 1948 and 1952 the Harvard University Press published six of these reports on subjects ranging from *Robert Boyle's Experiments in Pneumatics* (1948) to *Pasteur's Study of Fermentation* (1952). What Conant wanted to do was to equip Harvard men who were to become lawyers, teachers, writers, public officials, businessmen — citizens all — with "a feel for the tactics and strategy of science." By his case material Conant proposed to help his students to "recapture the experience of those who once participated in exciting events in scientific theory." Even in this course Conant held the high hope that it would contribute to the "on-going education" of Harvard men. "No college course," he said, "can be a substitute for experience; it can only lay a foundation. With an introduction to an understanding of experimental science, the inquiring citizen ought to be in a position to continue his scientific education throughout his life."

Harvard's program of general education for a free society was just the attempt of another faculty generation to work out the fundamentals of a liberal education to equip a man for life in society. In part it expressed alarm over the world crisis. It sounded a call to academic arms to preserve the heritage of the Western world. In part it was an attempt to meet conditions created by the revolution in a highly industrialized society which made education for *all* American youth imperative. In part it was recognition that with all its enormous resources Harvard University had not fully succeeded in "infecting" students with the educational "virus." In part it was another perennially optimistic attempt on the part of a faculty to attack and overcome the intellectual inertia which prevents many students from taking full advantage of their opportunities.

Behind the new program, however, lay the purpose of James Bryant Conant. Education, he felt, is what is left after all that has been learned has been forgotten. To him general education in the college was a method of learning pursued through the intensive study of certain topics or certain phases of a problem. In life he wanted the method to carry over as a habit, as a continuing individual attack on intellectual problems. His administration of Harvard University has given him the kind of Harvard education which he wished to share with others and extend to new generations of students.

Meanwhile Conant was approaching the retirement age of sixty. Remembering how faculty speculation ran riot as Lowell approached the emeritus age, Conant without notice, and quite without expectation, asked for emeritus status as of September 1, 1953. Simultaneously with his request President Eisenhower on January 12, 1953, named him High Commissioner for Germany.

In his last report as president of Harvard University to the Board of Overseers, James Bryant Conant observed — and no man was in a better position to know — that for the first time in the university's three hundred and seventeen years of history the prospect of "physical annihilation" of all that Harvard is and stands for is "a present possibility." Likewise the spiritual premises on which the whole Harvard tradition rested was in present danger of destruction. In another statement he said: "Today once again we live in a period of peril far greater to my mind than many of us appear to realize. This peril results from the combination of ideas and weapons — a phenomenon new to the modern world, the combination of a soul-destroying philosophy and a man-destroying army." He noted that the atom bomb still stood as a deterrent to Soviet imperialism.

In taking his leave of Harvard, Conant described his vision of the role of the university in a short valedictory. "Short of a global war," he said, "the universities of this nation will be even more significant in 1973 than they are today. As vital centers of sound learning, as strong points defending individual liberty, as communities of creative thinkers, no industrialized democracy can do without them; each year will demonstrate their indispensability to this society of free men."

This last report was dated the same day that his appointment as High Commissioner was announced. The scientist who had become administrator had now become diplomat. As he traveled to his new post at the edge of the chasm that divides the world, he observed that "The only working hypothesis for Americans is a belief that by the collective use of our intelligence and a mobilization of our good intentions we can mold the history of the next fifty years." Our unique contribution, he repeated, lies in a demonstration that a certain type of society long dreamed of by idealists can be closely approached in reality — a free society in which the hopes and aspiration of the many find enduring satisfaction through outlets once reserved for only a small minority of mankind. "The goal which we desire is a unified, coherent culture suitable for an American democracy in this new age of the machine and experts."

Toward an American Culture

for an Industrial Age

IN THE TWENTIETH CENTURY DECADES OF WAR, DEPRES-
sion, conflict of ideas, and withal marvelous development, we have
seen how six American boys grew to mature leadership. Their experience had extended from the age of the combustion engine and
fossil fuel through the era of fission and fusion to the threshold of
the age of solar energy. As their careers reached into the corners
of the globe, they were of one mind that the "tomorrow" into which
mankind is moving holds a rich promise for a satisfying life.

"Harry" Spellman, one-time horseshoe-pitching champion of a
Massachusetts village, had become the cardinal administering the
richest and most influential archdiocese in the Roman Catholic
Church. "Bill" Foster, born beside a New England stove factory
fifteen miles from the spacious Spellman home in Whitman, as a
boy had raced the streets of Philadelphia in the "Bulldog" gang.
Now, as Chairman of the National Committee of the Communist
Party, he was under indictment for conspiring to overthrow the
government of the United States by force and violence. "Jim"
Conant, President Emeritus of Harvard University, was in Bonn
as United States High Commissioner for Germany. "Al" Sloan, who
had been, as he says, a grind at Massachusetts Institute of Technology, was chairman of the board of the largest corporation in
the world and administering his many philanthropies. As an MIT
man, he had courted Irene Jackson in Roxbury, where Conant had
attended Latin School and where Spellman as a young priest had
begun his duties as an assistant at the Church of All Saints. Paul
Hoffman, whose wife continued to own New England soil, was
enjoying life back again in his California home on El Mirador
Drive in Pasadena; an eventful quarter century had virtually ex-
iled him from the spot he loved so much. He had become Chair-

[411]

man of the Board of The Studebaker Corporation, and he was alarmed by what he saw happening within America: he described the danger as a "whittling away" of the civil rights of American citizens. He often traveled to Harvard. Walter Reuther, less than twenty years away from his youthful grand tour around the world, now was president of the largest trade-union in the world. In a crippled hand he bore the scars of fire from a would-be assassin's gun. He frequently visited Cambridge to talk on labor relations and to confer with Harvard professors who advised his union.

In the blood of all six men there flowed something of the spirit of independence and civil courage which belonged to the revolutionary tradition of New England. Yet while the relationships of these men were rooted in historic American soil, the ideas which dominated their lives also reflected patterns dividing the world on the fundamental question of *how* the social order can best be designed to promote the welfare of man. Considered in the context of world events, their respective positions make it gravely clear that America must possess a coherent policy for its guidance to achieve the promise which is almost within man's grasp.

Conant puts the proposition this way: "Until we settle within the United States our approach to such difficult questions as the relations of management to labor and the control of ownership of the tools of production; until we square away on our course that will make us both prosperous and free, we shall be irresolute in deciding upon our foreign policy." In one of his more academic moments, Walter Reuther referred to the area where policy must develop as the "field of economic sociology." In the next breath he caught himself and explained: "It is in this field where people are looking for answers as to how they can get the wrinkles out of their bellies, how they can get a decent roof over their heads, and some warm clothing on their kids. It is in this field in which the struggle is going on in the world, in which the fight of free men against the slave world will be won." In his Rockefeller Center office sixty-three floors above the pavements of Manhattan, Sloan observed that "American man stands on the threshold of a general upswing in technological progress. The direction is always up — more things for more people in more places — a better standard of living everywhere." Emphasizing his point with a stub pencil, with which he was writing a history of the Negro in the Americas, Foster predicted that socialism in the United States "will put an end forever to the dread insecurity about the morrow which now haunts the lives of the toiling masses in America." Hoffman was crusading for the maintenance of a society which provides an invigorating climate for the maintenance of men who want, as he says, "freedom, opportunity, and abundance; productive employment with rising standards of living in a peaceful world." Spellman felt that "Labor and Capital are destined under God's plan to achieve and maintain standards of living harmonious with God's will, and only thus shall posterity inherit its legacy of God's glory." At a solemn pontifical mass in St. Patrick's Cathedral commemorating the canonization of Frances Xavier Cabrini, the first citizen of the United States to become a Catholic saint, Spellman observed: "The chief call of the hour is not for statesmen, generals, scholars, diplomats, or economists. The essential need is for saints."

Behind the thinking of six American men, Foster and Hoffman, Reuther and Sloan, Spellman and Conant alike, stands a technological fact: the world of the late half of the twentieth century possesses a dynamic apparatus for the prolific production of good things for the use of man. The capabilities of a heavily industrialized society to supply more things to more people in more places opens up a promise of plenty and leisure which since the beginning of history has been the dream of sod-bound generations.

On this promise which the future holds for man there is general agreement. Hoffman predicts that within the next quarter-century America can abolish poverty and come close to creating conditions which give every man, woman, and child certainty of opportunity for growth and intellectual, social, and spiritual development. Foster for different reasons sees humanity standing on the threshold of an era of freedom, development, and happiness that man hardly dreams of. Sloan feels that the "opportunities for America are beyond the dream of any man now alive." Reuther has confidence that a social mechanism can be developed to provide all people with a full measure of both economic security and political freedom. Conant sees ahead as America's unique contribution a demonstration that a certain type of society long dreamed of by idealists can be closely approached in reality – a free society in which the hopes and aspirations of a large part of the members find enduring satisfactions through outlets once reserved for only a small minority of mankind.

For want of a fresh idiom to describe this outlook for — more things for more people in more places, together with the income, leisure, and spiritual poise necessary to acquire, use, and enjoy them — spokesmen for the new age conjure with the imagined world of Jules Verne. They refer to the rubbing of the new Aladdin's Lamp which summons technological jinni to perform the routine drudgery of existence. *Society holds in its hand the apparatus required to make man's timeless dreams come permanently true.*

This rich pattern of a productive society is threaded through the interrelationship of science and industry in an age of advanced technology. Conant describes this interrelationship as one of a partnership in living. He likes to picture it by referring to certain green algae which work together with fungi. The alga possesses the chlorophyll necessary to perform work for itself and the fungus. Reciprocally, the fungus protects and gives mechanical support to the alga. Neither of these two components can live alone, but in the partnership of symbiosis both can live well.

The web of relationships created by this productive partnership of science, engineering, and industry has given modern society a unique pattern. Conant sees the fabric of conceptual schemes which grow and fruitfully multiply as a result of observation and experimentation, comparable as a creation of the human spirit to the Parthenon of Greece or the cathedrals of the Middle Ages. The structure of the new age is as expressive of the quality of contemporary living as was the thirteenth-century Gothic architecture with its arches and vaults, its elasticity and equilibrium, its variety and audacity.

Perhaps the General Motors Technical Center, with its simple functional utility, stands as the symbol of this era of advanced technology quite as much as the Amiens Cathedral is representative of the ordered Continental Christian society of Roman Catholic Europe. Twelve miles from the Detroit city hall, and within easy distance from the assembly lines, the Center operates as a place where men, as Sloan says, have "space and time to think." It is the contemporary cloister. The grouping of the buildings themselves expresses the division of specialties in advanced technological society. There are buildings for the research laboratories, for the engineering staff, for styling, for process development — for science, engineering, system and organization, and design. In the blue-black metal stacks which stand before a utilitarian façade to exhaust engine gases from a laboratory, some visitors see a beauty which belonged to the stone pylons in the hypostyle halls of Egyptian colonnades of the thirteenth century B.C. To others the bold design of the Center buildings makes them look more like an "exalted industrial product."

The American social order of which this monumental Center stands as a symbol is presided over by a secular trinity — the scientist, the engineer, and the industrialist. Their fruitful teamwork makes inexorable demands upon the community which it serves. These requirements must be met if the promise of technological society is to be fulfilled; there can be no compromise or halfway measures. The most important of these requirements are nine: (1) a continuous inflow of quantities of high-quality young men; (2) a mobile and nonstratified society which keeps open a roadway to the top for talented and ambitious youth; (3) a climate of competition which stimulates good men to rivalry to surpass the best performance of other excellent men; (4) a free and unmolested forum for the discovery and discussion of ideas; (5) a steadily increasing current of consumer spending; (6) the recognition of the fact that the human being is not a commodity to be bought and sold according to supply and demand in the market place; (7) acceptance of the inevitability of corporate bigness in economic life; (8) a freely trading international community; and (9) a literate and active citizenry possessed of civil courage.

The first requirement of a heavily industrialized society is for that continuous inflow of quantities of high-quality young men. The laboratory, the drafting room, and the conference table — science, engineering, and administration — must have the fresh impact of many good minds. James B. Conant likes to say that the only thing which is better than a young man with good ideas is a younger man with better ideas. Competent youths must, therefore, be identified early in the educational process, and no economic obstacle must exist to prevent the maximum development of their abilities through education.

Paul Hoffman had made his way from salesman-on-the-hoof to corporation executive and citizen leader. Alfred P. Sloan, Jr., had risen from a draftsman — in a company which had difficulty in meeting its weekly payroll — to head a world-encircling industry moving always along new scientific and industrial frontiers to provide goods and services to mass markets through the miracle of mass production. From the chemistry laboratory, Conant had moved up to become president of the richest and most influential university in America and, emeritus, he had gone on to perform a difficult diplomatic assignment in the heart of the Continent. Spellman, reared as a grocer's son, became a cardinal with global influence. By sheer will power, family encouragement, and "programmatic alertness" to current problems, Reuther had risen to head the largest labor union in the world and to develop a new role for trade-unions in promoting what he believed to be the welfare of the whole community. With but three years of formal education, Foster had educated himself and maintained an almost pathetic reverence for the kind of advanced study which he so much wanted others to enjoy.

If a fluid technological society insistently demands excellence, it at once rules out selection on any basis other than merit. The laboratory, the drafting room, the conference table, and the assembly line are unconcerned about race, creed, color, sex, or age — and for reasons quite divorced from moral sentiment. They demand superior performance for their optimum production.

American society of today does not meet this requirement. As Conant says, pointedly, "Anyone familiar with education knows that for a very considerable portion of the population it is the family-financed status which places a ceiling on the educational ambitions of even the brilliant youth. The oft-repeated statement in certain smug circles that 'anybody who has what it takes can get all the education he wants in the U.S.A.' just is not so; it is contrary to the facts. . . . Measured in absolute, not relative terms the discrepancy between our ideal and the reality becomes so great as to be almost shocking. . . . A large number of talented youths in different parts of the country drop out of high school or fail to

enter college because of lack of funds. Educators who know the-
situation conservatively estimated that as many promising boys
and girls fail to go to college for economic reasons as the number
who now enter." Because of the economic circumstances of their
families, both Foster and Reuther were denied the privilege of
advanced formal education. Through his Foundation, Sloan had
made millions of dollars in grants to educational institutions and
had established scholarships to aid promising youth. As a project
close to his heart Conant had developed national scholarships at
Harvard to provide university education to young men of ability so that economic circumstances would not prevent the fullest
development of their capabilities. Shortly after his installation as
Archbishop of New York, Spellman undertook to raise a ten-million-dollar fund, a part of which was to be used to develop Catholic educational institutions in his archdiocese. Hoffman too felt a
tenderness toward youth which led him to encourage conditions
which would assist the growth of promising young men and women.

The second requirement is for a mobile and nonstratified society
which keeps open, as Conant says, a roadway to the top for the
talented and ambitious youth. Such a society implies an arrangement which provides, as President Eliot used to say at Harvard,
a democracy of opportunity and an aristocracy of achievement.
In such a society position is not determined by accident of birth.
A socially fluid society is essential to the proper functioning of the
industrial order in an age of advanced technology. Much of the
racial tension in Detroit in the 1940's stemmed from the fact that
before the machine, workers stood alike as efficient producers,
while in neighborhoods they lived with pre-industrial prejudices
and mind-sets. When Walter Reuther by unanimous action of the
UAW–CIO executive board wired the International Harvester Local 988 in Memphis, Tennessee, to end an unauthorized strike
protesting the promotion of a Negro worker, he was dealing with
an industrial fact: competitive industry must have the best of human performance. The fair-employment-practices clause in the
union contract affirmed a worker's right to be promoted, regardless of race, creed, or color.

*　　*　　*

The third requirement makes necessary a climate of competition which stimulates good men to rivalry to surpass the best performance or other excellent men. Under the invigorating but strenuous pressures of competition there is a constant upward push toward excellence in performance. A free society becomes a playing field on which performers who have enjoyed equal opportunity for preparation show what they can actually do.

Back in 1925 the Pope singled out Spellman for special attention because of the excellence of his translation of the Pope's informal remarks. Reuther's rise to trade-union leadership came about through the endless presentation of his ideas and programs to the union membership in fair combat with Communist theories and tactics. Hoffman sold Studebaker motor cars against competition by his persuasiveness and his untiring effort. The Harvard Corporation picked Conant for president of the university very strongly for the reason that members felt he gave the best promise of bringing the university through the depression years by introducing economies to produce a balanced budget.

Conant sees as essential conditions of free society the existence of competition, private ownership, and the profit motive. "The problem surely is," he says, "to see how we can operate our private enterprises *and* our political institutions so that our society will be in fact competitive and thereby increasingly productive of the goods and services required." Spellman finds in Pope Leo's encyclical letter *On the Condition of Labor* the Catholic position that the law should "induce as many people as possible to become owners," and that "men always work harder and more readily when they work on that which is their own." Under the drive toward excellence and personal advancement, the level of all life is lifted. It is a situation in which all can gain and none must necessarily lose.

The fourth requirement is for a free and unmolested forum for the discovery and discussion of ideas. Conant uses the words "a free market for ideas." A heavily industrialized society which relies on the scientist and the engineer looks forward. It is open-minded and unbound by traditions. It is experimentally objective. As a result, such a society has no place for thought-control and the enforcement of orthodoxy. Conant was particularly concerned with the conditions of freedom and unmolested inquiry within the university. "Leadership of a community of scholars," he said, "like the leadership of an individual, requires, first, capacity based on expert knowledge; second, broad vision; third, courage." In the absence of dogma, all segments of a heavily industrialized society tend to subscribe to the premises of old-fashioned tolerance of ideas. It is an "open society" because of necessity it must be "openminded" at the growing end.

Hoffman was proudest of a commencement address in which he stressed the bravery required to stand with honest reverence before the integrity of ideas. "If you don't get the facts," he once said, "the facts will get you." Sloan was strenuously objective. The famous "Reuther briefs," at any point from Congress to a union caucus, talked facts and dealt with ideas. In Foster's thinking, however, there was a Marx-Leninist finality with its lodestar of reference in a past when the technological conditions for abundance. the points mentioned as necessary for a scientifically oriented and heavily industrialized society, were as yet in a comparatively primitive stage.

The fifth requirement is for a steadily increasing current of consumer spending. The significant fact about contemporary industrial society with its broadly distributed base of ownership among shareholders is that the concept of personal ownership has been replaced by *a claim to dependable income*. It is *income* and not *ownership* which becomes important in an age of industrial bigness. The stability of free industrial society depends upon the steadily increasing flow of income to people who spend money. The achievement of such steady and dependable income has become a special objective of organized labor. To theories of monetary and fiscal policies, the pressures of organized labor — and especially the programmatic action of the UAW–CIO — have added a new "something" in the concept of consumer spending defined as the active flow of dependable *annual* income.

The annual progress factor, established at General Motors in a program to share with labor the increase in real income made possible by technological advance and organizational efficiency, is a recognition not alone of an emergent partnership in industrial advance, but also of the necessity of reliable consumer income to maintain full production and employment in free industrial society. The full significance of this fundamental shift to concern for consumer income as an economic principle is not yet fully appreciated.

The insistence upon a constantly increasing and dependable flow of spendable income strikes directly at corporate policy. In the controversy with General Motors when Reuther was demanding "a look at the books," it was clear that the boundaries of management's prerogative were at issue. In this encounter Reuther made it clear that UAW–CIO will intrude itself into policy making at any point where the dependable and increasing flow of spendable income is at issue. It will do this by professional economic memorandums, by waging publicity war, and by strikes. Perhaps no industrialist has been clearer about the importance of spendable income than Sloan. His whole concept of the General Motors Technical Center includes a desire to accelerate technological progress as a condition of consumer welfare. Spellman points out that Pope Leo XIII asserted "that the first duty of the rulers of the state should be to make sure that the laws and institutions, the general character and administration of the commonwealth shall be such as to produce of themselves public well-being and private prosperity."

The sixth requirement is recognition of the fact that the human being is not a commodity to be bought and sold according to supply and demand on the market. The labor struggles of Foster, beginning with the packing house and steel campaigns, the organizational battles of Reuther from the sit-down strikes to the construction of Solidarity House, raised the question of the status of the human being in industrial society. Spellman learned from the encyclical letter of Pope Leo XIII that "the first concern of all is to save the poor workers from the cruelty of grasping speculators as mere instruments for making money." "No man," he says, "should be slave nor master to another, but each should be servant to God and helpmate to his neighbor." Or as Pope Pius XI explained the dignity of the human person:

Man has a spiritual and immortal soul. He is a person, marvelously endowed by his Creator with gifts of body and mind. He is a true "microcosm," as the ancients said, a world in miniature, with a value far surpassing that of the vast inanimate cosmos. God alone is his last end, in this life and the next. By sanctifying grace he is raised to the dignity of a son of God, and incorporated into the Kingdom of God in the Mystical Body of Christ.

Thus the human being is a person with a human dignity whose social nature calls for an organic unity in society brought about through the exercise of the right of association. The moral exposition supports the practical movement to raise the dignity of the workingman. Looking back on the sit-down strikes in 1936 and 1937 from the perspective of the 1950's, Reuther says that most of the struggles were simply "for the right to sit down and talk about workers' problems" and "to establish the right of American citizenship in the great industries of America."

The seventh requirement is recognition of the inevitability of corporate bigness. A society presided over by the scientist, the engineer, and the industrialist demands large aggregations of capital, vast supplies of working and developmental money, command of outstanding talent, and equipment for mass production at decreasing costs. Sloan is outspoken in saying that traditional assumptions about bigness are outmoded, unrealistic. To him size and monopoly are two very different things. He sees the need for a public economic policy "consonant with the facts of life in our technological age." It is not alone General Motors and the great industries of America which are big. Trade-unions are also huge. Reuther's UAW–CIO is the largest union in history. Spellman's archdiocese is big. The Ford Foundation is the biggest of its kind. Bigness, as Sloan sees it, "is a natural expression of enterprise in the age of advanced technology." The industrial unions, first championed by Foster and now led by Reuther, represent labor's recognition of the fact that the workingman's interest in an age of big industry cannot be adequately represented by "medieval craft guilds."

The bigness of industry alters the morphology of the social order at the same time that it increases its fruitfulness. Both Reuther and

Sloan agree on this fact. They know that the words "big business" create semantic reactions against monopoly and call up nostalgic memories of the cracker-barrel small enterpriser. They know that large-scale enterprise intensifies rivalry in the market, as the corporate units become more steady, determined, and vigorous in their competition. The frank acknowledgment of bigness introduces something new into the economic, political, and social structure of America.

The eighth requirement is for a freely trading international community. Sloan makes his position on this clear by saying that he is "in favor of open competition everywhere." Against formidable obstacles he held world markets for General Motors products, even when doing so meant production outside the United States for markets dominated by Germany, England, and Australia. To intensify competition he even exported motor cars to national markets which were themselves being supplied by GM vehicles produced in these very countries. Walter Reuther firmly believes in the necessity for the freely trading international community. Spellman by the first premise of his calling thinks of the *whole* world, as a spiritual mission ground. In ten years he traveled the globe in mileage equivalent to six times around the equator. Hoffman has never ceased to preach the importance of a "two-way economic street," of the usefulness of the United Nations, and of the necessity of mass markets to consume the products of a heavily industrialized society. As ECA administrator he insisted that what Europe needed to encourage the economic climate of personal prosperity was economic bigness freed from the "chokeweeds" of political interference created by nationalistic policies. Quite naturally, Foster feels that "the insane greed of the Wall Street exploiters" prevents the world from achieving the miracle of international trade, which Senator Gore once defined as "the process by which two countries get what both want, parting with what neither needs so that both can profit by what neither loses."

The ninth requirement is for a literate and active citizenry possessed of civil courage. Economic illiteracy and political apathy are dangerous twins in a free society. In one form or another this means continuous adult education. It is no accident that all "Six upon the World" made a central factor in their careers a concern for "adult education." We have seen that Conant wanted desperately to develop a kind of Harvard education which would infect graduates with the "virus of an on-going education." Foster insisted on constant study for himself and for other Communists — especially in theoretical areas. Reuther made departmentalized education a fundamental operation in UAW–CIO. Sloan's whole concept was built on the discovery of men who were capable of "inner growth." From the time he began to deal with the public mind to stop "highway massacre" until he made huge grants from the Ford Foundation to stimulate adult study, Hoffman was an "educator." His first premise is that citizens cannot take the pattern of their social order for granted. As his world experience matured, Hoffman felt the need for an overpowering secular evangelism. In the words of Kipling, which he often quoted, he wanted to affirm a doctrine that would "walk up and down in the hearts of men." Sloan recognized that a great corporation "must become increasingly articulate" as to what is to be done or undone in national economic policies to make the system operate more effectively. "A great corporation," he said, "must think at the policy level with a maximum of intelligence and understanding."

In short, each of the "Six upon the World" recognizes the need for making *convictions* articulate. To a man, they recognize that society itself exists because of a *consensus of profoundly felt belief.* Hoffman likes to say with Emerson that "every great and commanding moment in the annals of the world is the triumph of some great enthusiasm." Reuther observes that in a former age of revolution Thomas Paine said that "an army of principles will penetrate where an army of soldiers cannot; it will succeed where diplomatic management would fail; it is neither the Rhine, the Channel, nor the Ocean that can avert its progress; it will march on the horizon of the world and it will conquer."

To make their convictions count, free men must act with what Conant calls "civil courage." They must be ready to encounter ideas face-to-face and at arm's length. The difference between the positive responsibility of the Reuther brothers in their caucuses to advance their candidates against trade-union Communists in order to place UAW–CIO leadership in the hands of officers who believe in free society, and the negative programs of political control such as that represented by the Massachusetts Teachers' Oath, which Conant so violently opposed, is one of kind rather than degree. Beginning his activities in the same year that the Massachusetts General Court enacted the statute, Reuther by his face-to-face caucus method achieved the complete elimination of Communist influence from leadership in UAW.

Perhaps the clearest current statement about the right of a citizen to make public utterance of whatever he pleases with immunity from censure or punishment was made by Granville Clark, senior member of the Harvard corporation at Conant's request. The occasion for the statement was the necessity to reply to a Harvard Law School graduate who declined to subscribe to an alumni fund on the grounds that certain Harvard professors were giving aid and comfort to Communism. To the Harvard alumnus Clark wrote:

> I cannot help wondering whether you have thought through the implication of what you propose.
>
> Since you wish to discipline professors for taking active part in meetings such as these at which Professors Ciardi and Shapley spoke, would it not be fair to pass in advance on the kind of meetings a professor could safely attend? Would this not call for a university licensing board? And would not such a board have an obnoxious and virtually impossible task?
>
> Moreover, I think you will agree that there would be little sense in censoring attendance at meetings and leaving free from censorship speeches on the radio or writings in the press, magazines, pamphlets, and books. Would not your proposals call for a censorship of all these?
>
> Beyond that, however, how could an effective "closer watch" on "extracurricular activities" be maintained unless the watch extended to conversations and correspondence? And how could that be done without a system of student and other informers — the classic and necessary method of watching for "subversive utterances"?
>
> What I have just said applies to the professors. But how about the students? Would it be sensible to have the teachers censored and watched while the students remain at liberty freely to speak and write and to attend such meetings as they

choose, subject only to the laws of the land? On your philosophy are you not driven on to restrict, censor, and discipline the students also?

What sort of place would Harvard be if it went down this road? It would, I think, not require six months to destroy the morale of both our teachers and students, and thereby our usefulness to the country. I think one need do no more than state the necessary implications of what you ask to demonstrate that nothing could be more alien to the principles of free expression that Harvard stands for.

Just as Conant insisted on an open road for the minds of citizens, Sloan was insisting on the open mind in industry. "Nothing impedes progress," Sloan said, "like too strict an adherence to precedent. The inertia of the human mind is great. We dislike to change our way of doing and our way of thinking but without changing our way of doing and thinking there can be no progress. Therefore we must have an open mind. Decisions are comparatively easy when one has the facts. The difficult task is to get all the facts on the table when it is time to make a decision."

Because in a free country the support of ideas by citizens must be won by their own decision based on information and the discussion of principles, active programs for the mobilization of opinion to direct society toward a course in a period of social change increasingly proceed through citizens' organizations formed and administered by those who themselves have "convictions" and "who really care."

These citizens' associations come into being to achieve a special goal. They represent a contemporary instrument to bring about social change or meet special problems in the "big society." Thus they may be referred to as *ad hoc* bodies. Paul Hoffman's Automotive Safety Foundation was such an *ad hoc* operation, to deal with the problem of highway massacre. His Committee on Economic Development was a research, educational, and action group designed to deal with the cyclical instability in free economic society. He felt so deeply about the importance of his Fund for the Republic that he made the devotion of part of his time to this project a condition of his return to Studebaker as board chairman. Sloan's National Highway Users Conference was also an *ad hoc* operation, designed to support the place of a motor car in a nation which was then pretty much dominated by railroad interests. Conant's Committee to Defend America by Aiding the Allies and his Committee on the Present Danger were contemporary expressions of the Minute Man philosophy. Within the Harvard community Conant's Committee on the Objective of a General Education in a Free Society provided the machinery to educate the faculty to work toward change. So too the Committee of Eight and the Student Committee to Save Harvard Education were operations created at the moment of need to deal with specific issues. Within the UAW–CIO the so-called Unity Caucus was the same kind of a freely organized informal association. Spellman's picket campaign to stop the exhibition of *The Miracle* at the Paris Theater by the combined activities of the Legion of Decency, the Catholic War Veterans, the Holy Name Society, the Knights of Columbus, and the Ancient Order of Hibernians, was another *ad hoc* operation designed to bring citizen influence to bear at a certain point to get action. Foster was a master of the *ad hoc* technique. Through his National Unemployed Council he promoted mass meetings, parades, petitions, hunger marches, picketing, and all forms of agitation and struggle. Block committees organized workers where they lived. Mass demonstrations brought pressure on industrialists and political officers. The American Cultural and Scientific Conference for World Peace, the Civil Rights Congress, the American Committee for the Protection of the Foreign Born, the Committee for a Democratic Far Eastern Policy, and the National Committee to Secure Justice for the Rosenbergs, to mention but a few of his interests, were *ad hoc* operations to deal with the mobilization of opinion.

What all these *ad hoc* associations mean is that in the bewildering maze of internal struggles, ideas and beliefs, information must be communicated with conviction. By the use of all the media of influencing, people must be alerted. The big society of advanced technology requires literacy, civil courage, and active and organized participation among citizens. The struggle of interests, good and bad alike, to direct the course of society means that agitation and propaganda are indispensable instrumentalities for the maintenance of a free society. They must be used by Hoffmans much more effectively than by Communists.

*   *   *

The promise which tomorrow holds out for modern man, however, stands in peril. The scientist, the engineer, and the industrialist who have pointed society in the direction of plenty and leisure have also produced lethal mechanisms capable of exterminating the human race. No person knows the horrible power of fission and fusion weapons better than the scientist who presided so closely over their secret development. In his last report as president of Harvard, Conant wrote that "we live in a period of peril, far greater peril to my mind than many of us appear to realize. The prospect of the physical annihilation of all of Harvard is for the first time in our history a possibility which we must admit. The destruction of the spiritual premises on which our whole tradition rests is likewise a possibility that no one can deny who recalls the fate of the University of Prague."

Yet the peril does not come from the possibility of physical annihilation alone. It also lurks in a suspicion that some dislocation in the American economic system may result in the reduction of income to vast masses of consumers, through unemployment. As a militant theoretical socialist, Foster confidently expects a general economic crisis to bring an end to capitalism. Reuther warns that unless continually increasing income is provided for the mass of men the sensitive free economic system will come to trouble. He describes the problem as "closing the gap between production and distribution which dries up purchasing power among the masses and makes the economy unstable." Sloan sees as a condition of progress the importance of generous spending and active savings. He too recognizes that labor must share generously, as a right, in the abundant production of American industry to insure full employment and that broad base of purchasing power necessary to consume the annual product. In his early days with the Committee on Economic Development Hoffman kept pointing out that unless the economic issue is solved, public opinion may demand structural changes in the American political and economic system. "We cannot live with a crash such as that which took place between '29 and '32," he said, "when the business volume dropped more than 50 per cent. The price of failure by American politics and business to solve this $64 question would be Socialism." In his "Creed," Spellman asserts that "Labor and Capital can reap the rewards of God's goodness only if Labor unstintingly produces with the skills with which God has so abundantly endowed it, and Capital unsparingly distributes the produce of Labor for all men's welfare."

Thus, the realization of the *promise* of plenty and leisure offered by a free and heavily industrialized society requires coherent policy to avoid the *peril* which pursues it. From his scientific experience Conant likes to define a policy as "a guide to a course of action." The examination of the life histories of *Six upon the World* raises a common question for discussion on a policy for American man. The question is this:

How shall society be organized around the means of production?

The putting of this question raises four collateral issues, namely:

> *What shall be the relation of man to God?*
> *What shall be the relation of man to man?*
> *What shall be the relation of man to the machine?*
> *What shall be the relation of man to the state?*

These questions confront American man with the necessity for defining his own personal policies for the guidance of his own life as a citizen. They are the most fundamental questions which a human being can ask.

To the question of *What shall be the relation of man to God?* Foster gives a quick answer: There is no God. Hoffman, Sloan, and Reuther, while concerned with humanistic values, have found little need or time for participation in organized religion. Their personal standards, however, would meet the rules in a Methodist discipline. Their association with others habitually encourages colleagues to outstanding performance and growth, much in the spirit of the psalmist who wrote that "counsel in the heart of man is like deep water; but a man of understanding will draw it out." Conant finds the Hebraic-Christian tradition a significant part of the culture of the West, which has led to the concept of the dignity of man. In the spirit of the encyclical letter of Pope Pius XI *On Atheistic Communism,* Spellman asserts: "Above all other reality there exists one supreme Being: God, the omnipotent Creator of all things, the all-wise, and just judge of all men." Man, who has been raised to the dignity of a son of God by sanctifying grace, is endowed by God with certain prerogatives. Among these are the right to life, to bodily integrity, to the necessary means of existence, to associate, to possess and use property. Atheistic Communism, as Spellman sees it in the words of the encyclical, "strips man of his liberty, on which the spiritual rules of conduct depend, robs human personality of all its dignity, and removes all the moral restraints that check his vicious inclinations." Spellman begins his thinking with the idea of God. At this point in history American man is forced to examine the personal policy of his life with reference to the Hebraic-Christian heritage and ask himself this question: "Do I believe in God?"

Contemporary man is then faced with the next question: *What shall be the relation of man to man?* In his study late one night, Spellman answered:

> We are free men — with the right to be free . . .
> We are free men because God gives us freedom.
> We are His image and likeness;
> We have rights because we are God-like,
> With the duty to strive manfully for God,
> Bringing God to man and man to God.

Being born of God, men are brothers. In the relations of man to man, Spellman, reaffirming that the human being is not a "vendible commodity," holds that the possession of money and private property makes man a trustee or steward rather than an absolute owner. Consequently, man in his exercise of his right of private property is accountable in conscience to meet the demands of both justice and charity in the use of his possessions. In other words, the right of private property does not admit *irresponsible* ownership. In speaking in support of Catholic Charities, the Cardinal put the idea this way:

> Did you ever day-dream and wonder what would be your feelings should you, one day, meet our Lord walking along the streets of our city of New York? While we who live today may never meet Christ Himself on our city streets, Our Blessed Lord truly walks among us this day and every day — in the person of our neighbors . . . and every man is our neighbor because Our Lord identifies Himself with the lowly, the sick

and the poor, the aged and the orphan, the helpless and hopeless, the disconsolate and despairing, yes – all the little peoples of this big city of New York. God desires that we love
Him and our neighbor and true love is best proved by charity
in action.

To Sloan his colleagues are competent persons to be entrusted
with responsibility as a condition of their growth. To Hoffman men
are partners in productive activity; society owes it to them to provide conditions which encourage their growth as persons. To Conant
man is a citizen who must live as a free man with vocational skill,
an open mind, a regard for tradition, and civil courage to share the
benefits of an industralized society. To Reuther men are brothers
and sisters in the lodge who deserve the fruits of their labor and
must live as active citizens to assure their rights. To Foster man is
a "comrade" in the vanguard of the proletarian movement, determined to dispossess the owners of the means of production.

In asking the question about the relationship of man to man, one
comes to the question of war. What of the human beings compelled
by law to kill other human beings? Among the *Six upon the World*
five are no appeasers. Spellman prays in the "Master's Benediction":

Greater love than this no man can have, that he lay down his
life that other men may live in peace.

Sloan would make no compromises with totalitarian aggressors
against the peace. Conant proposes to pursue peace from a position
of strength. Hoffman was himself an artillery lieutenant. Reuther
does not flinch from the use of force when necessary. Foster, while
supporting Communist peace crusades to soften American "con-
tainment" policies, makes bold statements that the United States
should think twice before it engages in war with the Soviet Union.

Beyond acceptance of the momentary military necessity, Hoffman likes to talk about "waging the peace." "If we must fight," he
says, "let us wage war not to win a war, but to win a peace. Let us
wage the peace with imagination, boldness, and a sense of dedication! To win the peace we must wage the peace. By peace with
freedom I mean a peace that is more than the absence of war and a
freedom that is more than the absence of slavery." Walter Reuther

wants to combine "a fully adequate military defense with a positive peace offensive." America as the strongest nation among the free peoples of the world has a moral obligation, he thinks, to mobilize a positive and material force in the world greater than the negative power of the H-Bomb. Spellman wrote a "Prayer for the United Nations" in which he said:

Here, within the council chamber of the nations,
We pray that Thy Spirit of Peace may dwell, . . .
Into man's hands, O God,
Thou hast placed power for his salvation or destruction.
Seek ye peace, life grows abundant;
Seek ye war, death dooms the world!

As the "atom-bomb chemist," Conant is surer that man's good sense will achieve control of the weapon than that the weapon will destroy man.

At this point in the twentieth century American man must examine the personal policy of his life with reference to his human relationship, and ask himself this question: *What shall be the relation of man to man?*

Again, America's man faces the question of the relationship of man to the machine in a heavily industrialized society. Foster's answer is definite: the worker who operates the machines should own them, and manage them in his own interests. To Reuther the fundamental question is not one of ownership at all — the issue is, to whom the benefits of the machine flow? Are they so managed that they provide security with freedom, plenty with leisure? To Sloan and Hoffman, the answer is that machines belong to shareholders and that they should be operated efficiently and profitably with fairness to all as a condition for the maintenance of free society.

The Catholic position, however, raises a question about the structure of the social order on a theoretical basis quite as provocative as that of the Marxists. In his encyclical letter known as *Quadragesimo Anno* Pope Pius XI called for a reorganization of the social economy, for the reform of morals, and for the development of self-governing occupational groups. His suggestion has caused Catholic social thinkers to give attention to a form of organization of the social order known generally as the "Industry Council Plan."

This plan would organize society through a nexus of government-recognized but functionally independent and democratic social and economic groups designed to recognize individual rights and promote the general welfare. This reorganization of the social economy would be based on the social nature of man and make economic society a real moral organism in place of the atomizing individualism now obtaining. For each industry and profession there would be "councils" on the local, regional, national, and international level, in which employers, workers and the consuming public would participate through their respective representatives. Such a pattern, it is held, would rectify two fundamental defects which the popes have recognized in the economic order. The first of these defects, structural in nature, stems from what Catholics believe to be a lack of organic unity in the machinery of industrial and agricultural life. This structural defect produces the functional disorder of "economic immorality leading to insecurity and inequality." The Church affirms as a purpose the obligation to "protect souls from an inhuman existence on earth" and to promote the good life "to make easier the acquisition of eternal life hereafter." Pope Pius XII has pointed out, as Spellman says, that the great misery of the social order is that "it is not deeply Christian nor really human" and that the reorganization of the social order "requires the efforts of all." What the Cardinal works for is a society in which "the gentle yet effective laws of Christian moderation," command man to seek first the Kingdom of God and His justice.

In Europe still another pattern for the organization of society takes form. It has come to be known as "co-determination." On the day that Paul Hoffman laid down his first and only public office, the Labor Information Service of the Economic Co-operation Administration issued a release to the labor press on this subject of "co-determination." It read:

> West German labor has attained with government approval a share in management of corporate enterprise far beyond anything achieved in the United States. Imagine a board of directors of a coal or steel corporation composed equally of management and labor representatives. In each of eight out of 23 steel companies at present operating under the co-determination plan, a trade-unionist is chairman of the board.

In the heartland of European recovery a new industrial morphology has been crystallizing. Clinton Golden, who, as a labor adviser of Hoffman's agency, was deeply interested in the development, had written in a book co-authored with Harold J. Ruttenberg on *The Dynamics of Industrial Democracy* (Harper and Brothers):

> The participation of organized workers in management provides an outlet for their creative desires, as it is essentially a creative and co-operative undertaking.

In his relationship to the machine, therefore, contemporary man has a choice of patterns for the organization of a heavily industrialized society. Hoffman stands squarely on what he calls "mutual capitalism" with the prerogatives of managerial leadership clearly defined and respected. Sloan and Conant agree with Hoffman. Reuther at the moment shares their position because a labor movement, unless it is moving toward "democratic socialism," must recognize management as its opposite number at the bargaining table. Foster believes wholeheartedly in socialism.

Pope Pius XI urged that men "must act in today's crisis." At this point in history American man must make clear his ideas of the relationship of human beings to apparatus. He must ask himself: *What shall be the relation of man to the machine?*

All of these questions converge in a final question: *What shall be the relation of man to the state?* How shall the economic order be arranged in relation to political power?

To Foster the answer is clear-cut: Workingmen must seize the state and establish a rule of the proletariat; in this political way the economic machine will be operated for the welfare of the toilers. As a consequence of the overthrow of capitalism, economic and social justice will be achieved. A world order of the International Soviet Republic will come about, governed by a world congress, with effective leadership exercised by the Communist executive committee.

Spellman's answer is likewise clear: All public authority must proceed from God. The function of the state is so to order the affairs of temporal life that the citizen will have opportunity to grow in physical, intellectual, and moral perfection. The state is always a means, never an end in itself, and it governs best when it fosters in the citizen the ability to govern himself. This fact, however, does not preclude the necessity for the state to take the initiative when the common good demands such a course of action. In failing to do so, the state would be remiss in its responsibilities and would fail in the purpose of its existence.

To Reuther the state is an instrument, to be used to curb greed and to encourage the distribution of the national product, to provide increasing dependable income to workers. To Hoffman and Sloan too the state exists to encourage economic stability and productive abundance; its policies must be designed to promote the general climate of personal prosperity.

Perhaps the concept which Paul Hoffman holds of the "public office of the private citizen" makes his idea of the relationship of man to the state clear. Man is a citizen. In his political capacity a man has the obligation to think and act with his neighbors, to promote their mutual welfare by providing the public conditions which give men equal opportunities for personal growth. The state is merely an association of men for the advancement of their common aspirations. One of its major functions is to encourage the climate of personal prosperity. If by default, apathy, or bad judgment men permit their political association to get out of hand, private citizens are at fault in the exercise of their public office. To Hoffman, economic freedom is the condition precedent to political freedom. He makes the responsibility of men especially clear when he says bluntly that "if we have a disastrous depression it will be because of the acts of men. All past depressions were caused by things men did, things which they could have refrained from doing, and things which they failed to do which they could have done." To Hoffman the state is nothing more nor less than the product of the common effort and interest of informed, responsible, conscientious citizens.

As America strengthens its belief in its way of life and pursues policies which lead progressively to a more unified and coherent culture, the citizen will have increasing quantities of three necessities for the good life. He will have more *leisure*, defined as the opportunity to enjoy time without compulsion. Freed from drudgery and strenuous physical labor, he will have abundance of *energy* and vitality for his recreation. He will be supplied with *money* to spend, above funds needed to pay for the minimum costs of existence.

Thus man will have free time, his own to command, abundant energy to use it as he pleases, and sufficient finances to undertake projects he chooses.

But leisure, energy, and money *for what?* This raises a moral problem placing new demands upon the inner resources of people. It places new responsibilities in the fields of adult education, recreation, and religion. Yet since the arrival of the shorter work week and the shorter work day, man has amply shown his capacity creatively to assimilate the privileges which were once narrowly contained by the upper classes.

American man possesses the wherewithal to achieve "a free society in which," as Conant says, "the hopes and aspirations of the many find enduring satisfactions through outlets once reserved for only a small minority of mankind." Guided by wise policy and courage to sustain it, a heavily industrialized society may in this generation provide the material support to assure all men of their inalienable rights, among which are "life, liberty, and the pursuit of happiness."

James Madison called America "the workshop of liberty" where the conditions were being forged to provide a secure life in a free society unafraid of change. Contemporary American man is a participant in the continuing activity of that workshop. Conant accepts the role when he says that "only by the best labor of each citizen can this vast instrument of democracy be made responsive to the needs of a free nation in a divided world. Who could ask for more than to be given an opportunity to live in a time when such possibilities of carrying forward ideals and aspirations lie ahead?"

Suggestions for Further Reading Listed
in Sequence for the Study of Ideas

FOR THE GUIDANCE OF READERS WHO WISH TO STUDY
the ideas of the men discussed in this book in greater detail the
following materials are recommended. By drawing upon the public
library and by purchasing a few dollars' worth of documents, a
reader can inform himself in a substantial way about the ideas in
motion in his contemporary world. Books recommended for purchase for personal use are marked with an "A." Books to be borrowed from the library bear the letter "B." Books which probably
must be purchased because of their general unavailability are indicated with a "C."

1. PAUL G. HOFFMAN
   Peace Can Be Won. Garden City: Doubleday & Company, 1951.
   Pages 188. $2.00 (B)
   This volume written by Hoffman at the time when he completed
   his assignment as chief of the Economic Co-operation Administra-
   tion describes the world struggle as he faced it. The book outlines
   Hoffman's convictions about action on the economic and psychologi-
   cal frontier.

2. WILLIAM Z. FOSTER
   The Twilight of World Capitalism. New York: International Pub-
   lishers, 1949. Pages 168. Paper-cover edition $.60 (C)
   This book, dedicated by Foster "To my great-grandson, Joseph
   Manley Kolko, who will live in a Communist United States" sum-
   marizes the position of the leading American Communist. *The Twi-
   light of World Capitalism* should be read together with:
   KARL MARX AND FREDERICK ENGELS
   Manifesto of the Communist Party (Authorized English Transla-
   tion) annotated by Frederick Engels. New York: International
   Publishers. Pages 47. $.15 (C)
   The *Manifesto* states the fundamental Communist creed as is-
   sued in 1848 and annotated at London by Engels in 1888.

[436]

Readers who wish to see the Communist line as it has been followed in recent American history should turn to William Z. Foster's *History of the Communist Party of the United States.* New York: International Publishers, 1952. Pages 600. $6.00 (C)

3. ALFRED P. SLOAN, JR.
   Adventures of a White-Collar Man. New York: Doubleday, Doran & Company, 1941. Pages 208. $2.00 (B)
   In this volume Sloan gives his autobiography written with Boyden Sparkes as a collaborator. The book tells the life story of the man who headed General Motors Corporation during its period of phenomenal growth. As a means of refreshing his knowledge about basic economics the reader at this point can turn to advantage to the following little volume:
   GEORGE SOULE
   Introduction to Economic Science: A Modern Guide for Laymen. New York: The New American Library [Mentor Book]. Pages 138. $.35 (A)

4. WALTER P. REUTHER
   Report to the Membership, comprising the entire issue of *The United Automobile Worker,* March 1953 (Volume 17, No. 3). Pages 20. (A)
   This monthly publication of the UAW–CIO contains Reuther's 1953 summary of the union's activities. Copies may be obtained by writing to Frank Winn, director of public relations, UAW–CIO, Solidarity House, 8000 East Jefferson Avenue, Detroit, Michigan.
   A Proposal for a Total Peace Offensive to Stop Communist Aggression by Taking the Initiative in the World Contest for Men's Minds, Hearts, and Loyalties. Detroit: International Union United Automobile, Aircraft, and Agricultural Workers, CIO, 1951. Pages 22. (A)
   This booklet gives a good example of Reuther's bold and programmatic thinking. Copies may be obtained from Frank Winn, director of public relations, UAW–CIO, Solidarity House, 8000 East Jefferson Avenue, Detroit, Michigan. As background for understanding the development of industrial trade unionism and the leaders of the UAW–CIO the reader may turn to:
   IRVING HOWE AND B. J. WIDICK
   The UAW and Walter Reuther. New York: Random House, Inc., 1949. Pages 309. $3.00 (B)
   This volume gives the social history background related to the rise of the industrial union. It pays special attention to the growth of the UAW–CIO and emphasizes on the role of the Reuther brothers.

A reader who wishes to understand how a union member works, feels, thinks, and acts should read the personal story:

CLAYTON W. FOUNTAIN

Union Guy. New York: The Viking Press, 1949. Pages 242. $3.00 (B)

This volume presents the autobiography of an automobile worker who came to Detroit, lured by the expectation of fat pay checks. He found himself in a city in an economic depression, joined a union, became a member of the Communist Party, left that party because its program and discipline violated his freedom, joined the "house-cleaning group" within the UAW–CIO, and began to work within the union to make democracy serve the welfare of workers and the nation.

5. FRANCIS CARDINAL SPELLMAN

What America Means to Me. New York: Charles Scribner's Sons, 1953. Pages 111. $2.50 (B)

Cardinal Spellman dedicates this book to "Our America — Beloved and Blest." He describes the kind of America which "I and millions of others stand ready to defend unto death." By its global range and contemporary idiom as well as by its spiritual earnestness this book can well serve as a starting point for thinking about the United States in its world relationships.

The Foundling. New York: Pocket Books, Inc., 1952. Pages 275. $.35 (A)

This moving novel tells the story of a child found by a wounded war veteran in St. Patrick's Cathedral at Christmas. It points to undiscovered goodness that resides in everyone but emphasizes dramatically the divisiveness which exists in society as a result of differences in religion.

The reader should study at first hand three papal encyclicals:

POPE LEO XIII

On the Condition of Labor. (New translation authorized by the Holy See.) Washington: National Catholic Welfare Council, 1942. Pages 54. $.15 (C)

POPE PIUS XI

On Reconstructing the Social Order. Quadragesimo Anno. (New translation authorized by the Holy See.) Washington: National Catholic Welfare Council, 1942. Pages 54. $.15 (C)

The letter *On Reconstructing the Social Order* was issued on the occasion of the fortieth anniversary of the encyclical letter of Pope Leo XIII *On the Condition of Labor.* It suggests the Catholic position on many economic issues and shows how society may be perfected in conformity with the law of the Gospel.

Pope Pius XI

On Atheistic Communism. (New translation authorized by the Holy See.) Washington: National Catholic Welfare Council, 1942. Pages 54. $.15 (C)

If the reader wishes to study these three encyclicals together with two others on "Education" and "Marriage," he should obtain: *Five Great Encyclicals,* with discussion outline by Gerald C. Treacy, New York: The Paulist Press, 1952. Pages 215. $.50

The two encyclicals most important to the theme of this book have been arranged with an outline syllabus for group discussion by

Francis Joseph Brown

On Reconstructing the Social Order. (Quadragesimo Anno.) Chicago 12: Outline Press, 2438 Flournoy Street, 1950. Pages 84. $.50 (C)

On Atheistic Communism. Chicago 12: Outline Press, 2438 Flournoy Street, 1949. Pages 71. $.50 (C)

An approach to the Protestant position in economics is suggested in:

HOWARD R. BOWEN

The Social Responsibility of the Business Man. New York: Harper & Brothers, 1953. Pages 276. $3.00 (B)

This volume is a part of the general study of "Christian Ethics and Economic Life" begun in 1949 under the auspices of the Federal Council of the Churches of Christ in America and continued by the National Council which succeeded it.

Because of the importance of the Catholic theory of social organization the reader should be familiar with:

MARY LOUS EBERDT AND GERALD J. SCHNEPP

Industrialism and the Popes. New York: P. J. Kennedy & Sons, 1953. $3.50 (B)

This book presents the papal texts with commentary on principles basic to the Industry Council Plan advanced chiefly by Roman Catholic social scientists. It has charts, bibliographies, and a comprehensive index.

6. JAMES BRYANT CONANT

Education in a Divided World. Cambridge: Harvard University Press, 1948. Pages 249. $2.50 (B)

This book summarizes the thinking of the President Emeritus of Harvard University on the role of education in free society.

Modern Science and Modern Man. New York: Columbia University Press, 1952. Pages 111. $2.25 (B)

This volume discusses the part which modern physics and chemistry are playing in the contemporary intellectual revolution. The author describes "modern" man as "deeply troubled" and shows the direction in which science is pointing.

On Understanding Science. New York: The New American Library [Mentor Book], 1952. Pages 144. $.35 (A)

In the Dwight Harrington Terry lectures given at Yale University the Harvard president suggested a case history method of teaching science to nonscientists. The book brings together much of Conant's matured thinking about science and pedagogy.

Our Fighting Faith. Cambridge: Harvard University Press, 1944. Pages 121. $2.00 (B)

In six talks to Harvard men during World War II Conant discussed with utter frankness the goals of a free and classless society built upon distinctly American traditions. He dreamed of an aristocracy of men recruited through competition who excel in performance and vie with one another, each man to surpass the best of others.

Wanted: American Radicals, in *Atlantic Monthly*, May 1943 (B)

In this essay Conant pleads for the appearance of a third dimension in current thinking which will be representative of the historic tradition of American reformers. This publication was one of the most provocative papers written by Conant.

Education and Liberty. Cambridge: Harvard University Press, 1952. Pages 168. $3.00 (A)

This volume, the last which Conant wrote as Harvard president, elaborates the general theme that the public high school is the most strategic institution for the continued vitality of democracy in America. It is the high school, he holds, which has shaped American society and extended faith in the democratic process.

To obtain something of the feeling which Conant has for spiritual values the reader should turn in his Bible to the *Book of Job*. Conant often takes this classic and timeless human biography as a starting point for thinking about the universe. He likes to point out that the universe is not constructed along the lines of an automatic machine distributing rewards and punishments.

To understand much of Conant's thinking on education the reader should study:

Education for All American Youth. Washington: Educational Policies Commission, 1944. Pages 44. $1.00 (B)

This is the report of the Educational Policies Commission of which Conant was a member. The Educational Policies Commission was jointly constituted by the National Education Association of the United States and the American Association of School Administrators. The volume deals with American education from the junior high school through the junior college. For those who wish to go still further into the policies and goals of the public schools the following report is recommended:

Education for All American Children. Washington: Educational Policies Commission, 1949. Pages 292. $1.00 (B)

This report focuses attention upon the elementary schools from the kindergarten through the sixth grade, although some of its recommendations apply to a wider range of ages.

No consideration of American education is adequate until attention has been given to the educational policies of the Roman Catholic Church. For this purpose the following volume is recommended:

Better Men for Better Times. Washington: Catholic University of America Press, 1943. Pages 125. $1.00 (C)

This book summarizes the purposes and ideals set for Catholic education by the Commission on American Citizenship.

Acknowledgments

The author is grateful to the six Americans whose biographies form the substance of this volume — for their objective co-operation, their patience, and their constructive interest in the theme.

These persons have been especially helpful in the preparation of the various chapters: (I) Harold Vance, president of The Studebaker Corporation; Wayne Chatfield Taylor, formerly associated with Mr. Hoffman in the Economic Co-operation Administration; President Donald Stone, of Springfield College, formerly personnel director of the ECA; and Maynard Stitt, of Hill & Knowlton. (II) Alexander Trachtenberg, editor of International Publishers, and Arthur M. Zipser, secretary to Mr. Foster. (III) Paul Garrett, vice-president; Dudley Britton; and Mildred K. Braeznell, librarian, Public Relations Department — all of General Motors Corporation; also Miss B. R. Kucher, secretary to Mr. Sloan; Arthur C. Butler, director, National Highway Users Conference, and Robert Taisey, Esq. (IV) Frank Winn, director of public relations, UAW–CIO; Clayton Fountain, UAW–CIO; and William G. Phillips, UAW–CIO Washington office. (V) Monsignor John M. M. Fearns, president of Saint Joseph's Seminary and censor of books, Archdiocese of New York; Miss Gertrude Algase, Catholic Charities, Association of Catholic Trade Unionists; and Sister Mary Lois Eberdt, Marycrest College. (VI) William N. Pinkerton, Harvard News Bureau; Robert H. Haynes, Harvard College Library; and staff members of the *Harvard Crimson*. (Concluding section) Professor Peter Viereck and Professor Ruth Douglass, Mount Holyoke College, and Sister Mary Lois Eberdt, Marycrest College.

Appreciation is also expressed to the Library of Congress, the New York Public Library, the Harvard College Library, the Detroit Public Library, and the Mount Holyoke College Library; and to Genevieve Simha, librarian, and J. Wesley Hughes, who have worked with the author on this and many other projects.

Date Due

MAY 8 '68			
May 6			
	PRINTED	IN U. S. A.	